CRITICAL READING FOR SUCCESS IN LAW SCHOOL AND BEYOND

■ ■ ■

Jane Bloom Grisé

Director of Academic Enhancement and
Assistant Professor of Legal Research and Writing
University of Kentucky College of Law

WEST
ACADEMIC
PUBLISHING

© 2017 LEG, Inc. d/b/a West Academic
    444 Cedar Street, Suite 700
    St. Paul, MN 55101
    1-877-888-1330

West, West Academic Publishing, and West Academic are trademarks of West Publishing Corporation, used under license.

Printed in the United States of America

ISBN: 978-1-63460-936-4

PREFACE

_____

Critical Reading for Success in Law School and Beyond presents the critical reading strategies and techniques used by expert legal readers. Law involves more than reading the words on a page. Attorneys read critically so they can understand legal concepts, apply legal principles to new situations, analyze and evaluate cases, and use cases to solve clients' problems.

The genesis of this book arose from my work with first year legal writing students who often struggle to understand the cases assigned for class and writing assignments. Given the fact that experts read differently than novice legal readers, it seemed that students and new practicing attorneys could become more effective and efficient readers if they used the reading strategies of the experts.

After receiving a 2014 Scholarship Grant from the Legal Writing Institute, the Association of Legal Writing Directors, and LexisNexis, I conducted an empirical study that analyzed the impact of critical reading instruction on writing. In connection with this study, I constructed a curriculum to teach law students to read like the experts. The curriculum was based on research as well as input from student focus groups, the participants in the empirical study, and students in orientation, legal writing, and academic success classes from 2014 to 2016.

This book is organized as follows:

Phase One: Before Reading

Chapter 1: The Purpose for Reading Cases

Chapter 2: Read as an Advocate and Read with Focus

Chapter 3: Case Structure and Civil and Criminal Procedure

Chapter 4: Context and Overview

Phase Two: During Reading

Chapter 5: Facts

Chapter 6: Strategies to Understand Text

Chapter 7: Strategies to Understand Main Ideas (Issue, Holding, and Reasoning)

Chapter 8: Finding Rules

Phase Three: After Reading

Chapter 9: Case Evaluation

Chapter 10: Case Brief

Chapter 11: Case Synthesis

Chapter 12: Reading Statutes

Phase One, Chapters 1 through 4, provides background information about reading cases, the structure of cases, and procedure. Phase Two, Chapters 5 through 8, provides more detailed strategies for understanding text and analyzing cases. Phase Three, Chapters 9 through 11, explains the techniques used by lawyers to solve legal problems and represent clients. Chapter 12 applies all of these strategies to statutes.

This book is called *Critical Reading for Success in Law School and Beyond* because the reading strategies are applicable to the law school setting as well as the practice of law. If you read this book before starting law school, you may find it useful to re-read Chapters 5 through 12 after you begin reading cases and statutes for class. If you use this book for reference in law practice, you may begin by reviewing Chapters 1 through 5 to increase your reading efficiency and then focus your attention on the remaining chapters. By incorporating critical reading strategies, all students and attorneys can become expert legal readers and more effective practitioners.

ACKNOWLEDGMENTS

There are many people who deserve my thanks. First, I wish to thank LWI/ALWD/LexisNexis for their 2014 Scholarship Grant. In addition, the input from student focus groups and students who used these materials from 2014 to 2016 has been invaluable.

I appreciate the helpful suggestions provided by University of Kentucky College of Law Assistant Professor Diane Kraft, Electronic Services Librarian Tina Brooks, Professor Mike Healy who reviewed Chapter 12 on statutes, Anne and Kaitlin Graff who reviewed the Read with Focus section of Chapter 2, and Anne Graff who wrote Reflection Exercise 2.3. I thank my research assistants Chris Johnson, Jake Miller (who prepared Figures 3.5, 3.12, and 5.5) and Andrea Reed. I appreciate the thoughtful comments of students who reviewed the final version of the book: Jamila Carter, Keziah Colleton, Cody Conner, Cody King, Chris Lewis, and LaKeysha Singleton. I also thank two additional students, Julie Greenlee, for her extensive written comments, and Brian Lock, for his feedback on the practice exercises he completed during his summer break.

Thanks to my daughter Michelle Grisé for her insightful comments from the perspective of a new lawyer and Alex Prilutsky for his thoughtful questions from the viewpoint of an engineer. Thanks to my husband Bill Grisé for his support and excellent editorial assistance. His background as a physicist, rather than a lawyer, made this book more comprehensible to students coming to law school from a variety of backgrounds. Finally, I want to express my gratitude to Frances Gorman Bloom, my amazing 98-year-old mother (who is the author of *Recipe for Reading* and who noted in her junior high yearbook that she wanted to be a lawyer), for her countless perceptive comments and editorial suggestions. I am most appreciative to my editor Elizabeth Eisenhart and West Academic Publishing for giving me the opportunity to write this book. Thank you as well to Laura Holle and Rebecca Schneider for their assistance throughout the production process.

Copyright Acknowledgments

Permission to reproduce excerpts from the following is gratefully acknowledged:

Leah Christensen, "One L of a Year," © 2012 Carolina Academic Press.

Mary Lundeberg, *Metacognitive Aspects of Reading Comprehension: Studying Understanding in Legal Case Analysis*, 22 Reading Res. Q. 407 (1987).

Laurel Currie Oates, *Beating the Odds: Reading Strategies of Law Students Admitted Through Alternative Admissions Programs*, 83 Iowa L. Rev. 139 (1997); *Leveling the Playing Field: Helping Students Succeed by Helping Them Learn to Read as Expert Lawyers* 80 St. John's L. Rev. 227, 240 (2006).

Victor E. Schwartz, Kathryn Kelly, David F. Partlett, *Prosser, Wade, and Schwartz's Torts Cases and Materials*, 12th ed. 2010 © Foundation Press.

In addition, permission from Thomson Reuters to reproduce the cases in the Appendices is acknowledged.

SUMMARY OF CONTENTS

PHASE TWO: DURING READING

PHASE THREE: AFTER READING

TABLE OF CONTENTS

———————

PHASE ONE: BEFORE READING

PHASE TWO: DURING READING

TABLE OF CASES

CRITICAL READING FOR SUCCESS IN LAW SCHOOL AND BEYOND

PHASE ONE

BEFORE READING

INTRODUCTION

I. OVERVIEW

Welcome to the study of law. You are welcomed to the **study of law** rather than **law school** because lawyers study and learn throughout their careers. As a law student, you will develop the skills and knowledge that are needed to engage in a wide variety of activities. From representing individuals, to advising corporations and government agencies, to utilizing legal training in a variety of settings, law graduates can make a positive difference in our society.

However, the law school journey is not always easy. Fortunately, research suggests that law students who master simple reading techniques can improve their reading comprehension and do better in law school. In addition, given the fact that reading constitutes the prime activity of law school graduates, critical reading is also an important skill to master for the practice of law. In a study of attorneys in the workplace, it was noted that "**lawyering** for these junior associates was fundamentally about **reading**."[1] (emphasis added).

A good question you may be asking at this point is—what is critical reading and how is it different from regular reading? Critical reading combines basic comprehension skills with the skills of evaluation and problem solving. Attorneys use all of these strategies every day.

II. STRATEGIES TO USE *BEFORE, DURING,* AND *AFTER* READING

Research indicates that expert legal readers read differently than novice legal readers. This critical reading program presents techniques used by the experts. These strategies will enable you to read with an effective plan of action and troubleshoot when your comprehension is challenged. While it is possible to read easy materials without using any strategies, it is necessary to read in a systematic way when confronting difficult texts such as legal cases.

This program breaks the reading process into three phases: information and strategies to use **before** you read, techniques to use **during** reading, and things to think about **after** you read. While these are not completely separate stages, it is helpful to think about activities that promote high levels of comprehension at different times in the reading process. Each chapter deals with a specific step in this process. Figure 1.1

---

[1] Ann Sinsheimer & David J. Herring, *Lawyers at Work: A Study of the Reading, Writing, and Communication Practices of Legal Professionals,* 21 Legal Writing J. 63, 72 (2016).

summarizes the chapters as well as the reading strategies of experts and novices.

Figure 1.1
Strategies of Expert/Novice Legal Readers

Chapter	Topic	Expert Readers	Novice Readers
Before Reading			
1	Purpose for Reading	**Read to resolve new problems.**	Read to memorize facts.
2	Read as an Advocate and Read with Focus	**Read as an advocate or judge.**	Read as neutral observers to avoid embarrassment in class.
3	Case Structure and Procedure	**Recognize that cases have a predictable structure and pay attention to procedural terms.**	Ignore case structure and skip over procedural terms.
4	Context and Overview	**Understand general subject matter of cases before reading.**	Read with no knowledge of case subjects.
During Reading			
5	Facts	**Create mental images of facts.**	Skip or skim facts.
6	Strategies to Understand Text	**Use a variety of techniques to understand text.**	Skip over unclear text.
7	Strategies to Understand Main Ideas: Issue, Holding, and Reasoning	**Identify main ideas.**	Look at individual sentences rather than general ideas.

Chapter	Topic	Expert Readers	Novice Readers
8	Finding Rules	**Find and formulate rules.**	Focus on holdings and do not construct rules.
		After Reading	
9	Case Evaluation	**Think about how cases can be interpreted.**	Assume cases have one correct interpretation.
10	Case Brief	**Prepare own case briefs.**	Use briefs prepared by others.
11	Case Synthesis	**Understand how to examine multiple cases.**	Look at cases in isolation from other cases.
12	Statutes	**Apply critical readings skills to statutes.**	Read statutes without any reading strategies.

Each chapter contains:

- a summary of the specific skills you will learn,

- a reading checklist,

- reading strategies with concrete examples of effective and less effective techniques,

- cases that illustrate concepts, and

- reflection and practice exercises as well as self-assessment tools.

**All legal readers can become excellent critical readers
by using the suggested strategies.**

Let's get started.

CHAPTER 1

BEFORE READING: THE PURPOSE FOR READING CASES

I. SUMMARY

Expert legal readers recognize:

- the purpose for reading cases, and

- the role of critical reading in law.

At the conclusion of this chapter, you will understand that:

- experts read cases to solve problems,

- critical reading involves skills such as analysis and evaluation rather than memorization, and

- while some of your current reading strategies may be suitable for reading cases, additional techniques will also be useful.

II. CHECKLIST

Each chapter starts with a reading checklist that summarizes all of the reading skills in this book. The technique that is the focus of the chapter is highlighted in bold. Use the checklist as a guide and create your own checklist with the techniques that work best for you. (A template to use to construct your checklist is located in Appendix A.)

CASE READING CHECKLIST

Warning: Do not just highlight and underline.

Phase 1: Before Reading

1. **Read for a purpose** and assume the role of advocate or judge.

2. Read with energy and focus.

3. Notice case structure.

4. Understand the general subject matter by examining:

   a. course syllabus, casebook table of contents, or research assignment, and

   b. parties, citation, court, and date.

---

5. Read for an overview by skimming and noticing organization, headings, who won, and what case is generally about.

Phase 2: Reading More Carefully

1. Understand the facts.

2. Reread, look up unfamiliar words, analyze confusing language, and vary reading speed.

3. Understand the main ideas set forth in the issue, holding, and reasoning.

4. Identify the rule.

5. Take notes with your reactions and brief the case.

Phase 3: After Reading

1. Evaluate the decision, ask questions, and talk with professors.

2. Determine how cases fit together with other cases and synthesize.

III. BEFORE READING STRATEGIES

Expert legal readers take specific actions **before** they read a case. They do not just dive into reading. As seen in Figure 1.2, the first four chapters focus on reading strategies that are used **before reading** a case more carefully. These four chapters examine reading goals. They also provide valuable information about the structure of cases and procedure as well as techniques for skimming cases for an overview. The **before reading** strategies will make your reading more efficient and effective.

Figure 1.2
Before Reading Topics

Chapter	Topic
1	Reading for a purpose
2	Reading as an advocate and reading with focus
3	Understanding case structure and procedure
4	Understanding case context and skimming for an overview

IV. THE PURPOSE FOR READING CASES

A. PURPOSE CHANGES THE WAY WE READ

This chapter examines the purpose for reading cases because we read differently depending on our **purpose** and the task at hand. For example, if you needed to fix the brakes in your car, you would read the owner's manual differently than if you were taking an exam that tested your knowledge of the manual. To fix your brakes, you would look for information in the manual related to brakes, find diagrams, and then try to solve the problem. To prepare for an exam, you would memorize terms and facts so that you could answer specific questions. **The purpose for reading affects what we pay attention to as we read and how we read.**

B. LAWYERS READ TO SOLVE PROBLEMS

The purpose for reading cases also affects how we read cases. **The purpose for reading cases is to solve legal problems.** People come to lawyers to get assistance when they have been evicted, arrested, or fired from a job. Lawyers read cases to understand legal principles and key rules and then apply those principles to the issues faced by their clients. One law school professor gave entering first year students the following advice: "[w]hat you will learn in law school . . . is not information in the usual sense, not a set of repeatable propositions, but how to *do* something. Our primary aim is not to transmit information to you, but to help you learn how to do what it is that lawyers do with the problems that come to them."[1]

The purpose for reading in law school is different than the purpose for reading in most undergraduate courses. As undergraduates, students often read to memorize facts. Students are required to demonstrate that they have learned facts and concepts when they write papers and take exams.

---

[1] James B. White, *Talk to Entering Students*, 13 Occasional Papers L. Sch. U. Chi. 1, 4 (1977).

When reading cases, it may not be important to memorize the specific date of a decision or the location of a crime or the name of the person who entered into a contract. However, it is necessary to understand and analyze rules and the rationale for the rules. Attorneys use this information to assist clients in resolving problems. Expert legal readers understand the purpose for reading law while novices read cases to memorize facts.

Figure 1.3 summarizes the differences in the purpose for reading judicial opinions and undergraduate texts.

Figure 1.3
Reading Purposes: Pre-Law/Law School

Pre-Law	Law School
Remembering dates, places, names	Finding and understanding rules
Mapping the sequence of events	Applying rules to factual situations
Understanding cause and effect	Understanding policy
Remembering scientific principles	Analyzing multiple cases

Although the purpose for reading is different in law school, some of the reading strategies you used in other courses may still be effective. If you looked up the meaning of words, skimmed for an overview before reading more carefully, reread material, and took notes, these techniques will work well in law school. Continue to use the strategies that were useful but be open to adopting new methods that may be more effective in meeting the demands of law school. In Reflection Exercise 1.1, think about reading strategies that have been helpful for you in the past. Practice Exercise 1.2 provides the opportunity to consider how the purpose for reading a case can affect the types of things you look for as you read.

Note: There are Reflection and Practice Exercises at the end of each chapter. For the Reflection Exercises, think about how techniques you have used may be helpful in law school. The Practice Exercises are opportunities to try out the strategies explained in the chapter. Answers for the Practice Exercises are in Appendix P.

C. PURPOSE FOR READING CASES: EXPERT LEGAL READERS

Experts read differently than novices, in part, because they recognize that the purpose for reading cases is to solve problems and not simply to memorize facts. In one study (Oates), the reading strategies of a law school professor and four law students were examined. All four students had undergraduate GPAs and LSAT scores that predicted they would be "in the bottom 10% of their entering class."[2] However, Figure 1.4 shows that Maria

---

[2] Laurel Currie Oates, *Leveling the Playing Field: Helping Students Succeed by Helping Them Learn to Read as Expert Lawyers*, 80 St. John's L. Rev. 227, 230 (2006).

ended up "in the top 15% of her class,"[3] in part, because she recognized that the purpose for reading in law school was different than the purpose for reading as an undergraduate. On the other hand, Jackie "was in the bottom 20 percent of her class"[4] at the end of the first year, in part, because she did not understand the significant differences between the demands of college and law school.

Figure 1.4
Reading Purpose: Oates Study

Student	Reading Purpose
Maria (Top 15%)	"understood that, while for most of her undergraduate exams her professors had wanted her to demonstrate that she knew a particular set of facts or that she knew how to do a particular act, for example, to solve a particular type of problem, **her law school professors wanted her to identify the issue, set out the rules that governed that issue, and to present and evaluate each side's arguments.**"[5] (emphasis added).
Jackie (Bottom 20%)	"She had gotten her undergraduate degree in history from a college that emphasized the memorization of facts. For her classes, Jackie would memorize events, names, and dates of historical events, and she would then recite these on exams." "Although at some level Jackie knew that her law school classes were different from her college classes, she did not understand the significance of those differences. Thus, **she read the cases for information.**"[6] (emphasis added).

V. CRITICAL READING

A. WHAT IS CRITICAL READING?

In order to solve clients' problems, attorneys must engage in **critical reading**. Critical readers understand a court's decision as well as the underlying rationale for the decision. In addition, they take the next step and evaluate the usefulness of the case to solve a problem. Critical reading

---

[3]   *Id.* at 239.

[4]   *Id.* at 230.

[5]   *Id.* at 240.

[6]   *Id.* at 240–41.

involves more than just memorization. Lawyers use the following types of critical thinking skills to read and analyze cases:[7]

Remembering: Lawyers must first have basic knowledge of the facts of a problem, the vocabulary used in a case, and the sequence of legal procedures.

Understanding: Lawyers need to understand the main ideas in a case.

Applying: Lawyers apply the principles in a case to solve new problems.

Analyzing: Lawyers analyze a case to understand the rules and the court's decision.

Evaluating: Lawyers evaluate multiple cases, analyze the interrelationships among the cases, and make judgments regarding whether the cases are appropriate to use to advance a legal position.

Creating: Lawyers use cases to create a solution to a problem by synthesizing multiple authorities and then writing a memorandum or making an argument on behalf of a client.

These skills build on each other. Therefore, if the reader does not **understand** the vocabulary in a decision, he will not be able to accomplish the higher level tasks of **analyzing** a case to understand the rules or **evaluating** several cases for clients. As illustrated in Figure 1.5, expert legal readers master these critical thinking skills differently from novice legal readers.

Figure 1.5
Critical Thinking Skills: Expert/Novice Legal Readers

Skill	Expert Readers	Novice Readers
Remembering	**Remember vocabulary and procedural terms**	Skip over unfamiliar words and procedures.
Understanding	**Create diagrams of facts.**	Skip over the facts.
Applying	**Think about problem to be solved.**	Read case in isolation from any actual problem.
Analyzing	**Brief cases (summarize key elements of cases).**	Use commercial briefs or other students' briefs.

---

[7] Bloom's Taxonomy is a framework for classifying educational objectives. David R. Krathwohl, *A Revision of Bloom's Taxonomy: An Overview*, 41 Theory into Practice 212, 215 (2002).

| Evaluating | Ask questions. | Assume cases have a fixed meaning |
| Creating | Synthesize cases to solve problems | Examine cases in isolation from each other. |

Each chapter identifies the thinking skills that will be used to master the reading strategies introduced in the chapter. This is done to emphasize that reading cases involves many critical thinking skills in addition to remembering and understanding concepts.

B. THE ROLE OF METACOGNITION

Another component of critical reading is the reader's awareness of his or her understanding. The fancy term for this is **metacognition**, which means knowing about knowing. It is essential to develop an awareness of when you understand something and when you do not. This is so important that major law firms have stated that a key skill new lawyers need to master is to "know when they don't know."[8] Studies have shown that we often overestimate our comprehension. Therefore, if you think you **might not** understand something, assume that you need to go back over the material.

Because metacognition is so important to your success, each chapter ends with a Practice Exercise titled Self-Assessment so that you can assess your own progress. Each self-assessment exercise contains a problem to solve using the concepts introduced in the chapter. The self-assessment exercises conclude with a rubric which is a scoring tool you can use to determine if you understand the topics in the chapter and if you can perform at a proficient level.

C. DOES EVERYONE FIND IT DIFFICULT
TO READ CASES?

The discussion of critical thinking skills would not be complete without mentioning that reading cases is difficult for **everyone**. Many law students believe that everyone else gets it and they are the only ones who find it difficult to understand cases. Students have reported the following feelings about reading cases:

- "I feel like an idiot. Why is this so hard for me to figure out?"[9]

---

[8] Michael Hunter Schwartz, *Teaching Law Students to be Self-Regulated Learners*, 2003 Mich. St. DCL L. Rev. 447, 472 (2003).

[9] Mary A. Lundeberg, *Metacognitive Aspects of Reading Comprehension: Studying Understanding in Legal Case Analysis*, 22 Reading Res. Q. 407, 416 (1987).

- "It's easy to get lost in cases, which can seem like just one following another."[10]

- It was like "looking for a purple dinosaur without knowing what a dinosaur was or what the color purple looked like."[11]

No one is born with the innate ability to understand complicated legal jargon and decipher the structure of judicial opinions. Law students must learn a new language and new ways to solve problems. Most law students, law professors, and practicing lawyers find some cases challenging to read. The good news is that you can learn how to read cases, and reading becomes easier as you become familiar with critical reading techniques. Practice Exercise 1.3 is an opportunity to examine a short excerpt from a case and identify some of the reasons why cases are difficult to read. Practice Exercise 1.4 is the self-assessment exercise for this chapter.

One reason that cases are difficult to read is that they contain many terms that are unfamiliar to novice legal readers. A glossary of common legal terms is provided in Appendix Q for reference.

D. A WORD ABOUT TIME

You may be concerned that you do not have time to complete all of the steps in the checklist. You may feel that it would be easier to use a highlighter and underline key points so that you can get reading done quickly for class. Actually, critical reading techniques take little additional time. The strategies suggested in the first four chapters, the before reading phase, probably take about 30 seconds. It takes no additional time to read for the purpose of solving a problem. It also takes no additional time to read as an advocate. (Chapter 2). Understanding case structure and procedure will add no time to your reading. (Chapter 3). Reading for an overview may add about 30 seconds. (Chapter 4).

These techniques will make you a more efficient and effective reader. One student who used this checklist said that he liked it because it was "nice to have a system in place for efficiency" when faced with the high reading demands of law school.[12] Remember that this is your checklist. Try out the suggested techniques and modify them to suit your needs.

E. A WORD ABOUT CASE BRIEFS

You may have heard about case briefs, which are summaries of the key elements of a case. Once you understand the components of a case and master the basic reading strategies addressed in Chapters 2 through 9, it

---

[10] William M. Sullivan et al., *Educating Lawyers: Preparation for the Profession of Law* 41 (2007).

[11] Jane Bloom Grisé, *Critical Reading Instruction: The Road to Successful Legal Writing Skills*, 18 W. Mich. Univ. Cooley J. of Prac. & Clinical L. (forthcoming 2017).

[12] *Id.*

is recommended that you prepare summaries of cases. Case briefing is fully addressed in Chapter 10.

VI. CASE EXAMPLE: PURPOSE FOR READING CASES

At the end of each chapter, *Fisher v. Carrousel Motor Hotel, Inc.*, 424 S.W.2d 627 (Tex. 1967) is used to illustrate the concepts addressed in the chapter. The reported case (with annotations) is found in Appendix B-1.

As discussed in this chapter, the purpose for reading the *Fisher* case determines how the case will be read. Assume that you have received a call from Joe Parker, who wants to make an appointment to discuss an incident that occurred at Smith Cars. Mr. Parker was injured when he fell after a mechanic at Smith Cars grabbed his cell phone.[13] After discussing this call with a senior partner, you have preliminarily concluded that Mr. Parker may have a claim for the intentional tort of battery.[14] **The purpose for reading the *Fisher* case is to get guidance regarding the law of battery before you meet with Mr. Parker to get additional information.**

Given that the purpose for reading is to begin to understand the law that applies to Mr. Parker's problem, an attorney reading the *Fisher* case would look for rules relating to battery to better understand how courts deal with these claims. The attorney would not read to memorize names and dates mentioned in the *Fisher* decision. The attorney would also think about the facts provided by Mr. Parker and compare those facts with the facts in *Fisher*. The purpose for reading the case affects what we look for as we read.

VII. PRACTICE

Reflection Exercise 1.1
Successful Reading Strategies

Goal: The goal of this exercise is to provide you with the opportunity to reflect on effective reading strategies you have used in the past and think about whether these techniques will be useful when you read cases to solve problems.

---

[13] This fictitious scenario is based upon an actual case, *Picard v. Barry Pontiac-Buick, Inc.*, 654 A.2d 690 (R.I. 1995).

[14] Torts are civil wrongs. This means that someone has caused physical, emotional, or economic injury to someone through their action or inaction. Intentional torts are civil wrongs where a person intends to do an act. The intentional tort of battery occurs when someone intentionally engages in the harmful or offensive touching of a person or something associated with a person.

1.1–1   Think about successful reading strategies you have used in the past and list them.

Effective Reading Strategies Used Before Law School

1.1–2   In addition to the strategies listed above, have you ever used the following techniques? Were they helpful?

Reading Strategy	Used Strategy?	Was Strategy Helpful?
Skim for overview		
Read headings		
Look for main ideas		
Look up words		
Take notes		
Use graphic organizers		
Reread		
Read aloud		
Talk with other students		
Talk with professor		

1.1–3   Given of the purpose for reading in law school, list strategies you plan to continue to use.

Reading Strategies to Continue in Law School

Practice Exercise 1.2
Reading Purpose Affects How We Read

Goal: This exercise is an opportunity to notice how your reading purpose affects what you look for as you read.

In this exercise, answer the questions below regarding *Fisher v. Carrousel Motor Hotel, Inc.*, 424 S.W.2d 627 (Tex. 1967) (Appendix B-1). Notice if the purpose for reading affects how you read.

Purpose #1: Historical Analysis

Assume that you are reading *Fisher* to write an article about the development of the law of battery in the United States.

1.2–1   Would the dates of other decisions referenced in the *Fisher* case be important to remember?

1.2–2   Would you pay attention to the law review article from 1939 referred to in the *Fisher* opinion on page 270 of Appendix B-1?

1.2–3   Would you analyze each stage in the development of the law?

1.2–4   Would you look for current rules regarding the law of battery?

Purpose #2: Representation of Client

Assume that you are reading *Fisher* to understand the law of battery before you meet with a client who wants to bring a battery lawsuit.

1.2–5   Would the dates of other decisions referenced in the *Fisher* case be important to remember?

1.2–6   Would you pay attention to the law review article from 1939 referred to in the *Fisher* opinion on page 270 of Appendix B-1?

1.2–7   Would you analyze each stage in the development of the law?

1.2–8   Would you look for current rules regarding the law of battery?

Practice Exercise 1.3
Why Is This Case Difficult to Read?

Goal: The goal of this exercise is to think about why cases are difficult to read.

Reading cases is difficult for everyone. Read the following short passage from *Fisher v. Carrousel Motor Hotel, Inc.*, 424 S.W.2d 627, 628 (Tex. 1967) and think about why the passage is difficult to read.

> "This is a suit for actual and exemplary damages growing out of an alleged assault and battery. The plaintiff Fisher was a mathematician with the Data Processing Division of the Manned Spacecraft Center, an agency of the National Aeronautics and Space Agency, commonly called NASA, near Houston. The defendants were the Carrousel Motor Hotel, Inc., located in Houston, the Brass Ring Club, which is located in the Carrousel, and Robert W. Flynn, who as an employee of the Carrousel was the manager of the Brass Ring Club. Flynn died before the trial, and the suit proceeded as to the Carrousel and the Brass Ring. Trial was to a jury which found for the plaintiff Fisher. The trial court rendered judgment for the defendants notwithstanding the verdict. The Court of Civil Appeals affirmed. 414 S.W.2d 774. The questions before this Court are whether there was evidence that an actionable battery was committed, and, if so, whether the two corporate defendants must respond in exemplary as well as actual damages for the malicious conduct of Flynn."

1.3–1   Circle any words you do not understand.

1.3–2   Underline any sentence you do not understand after reading the sentence once.

1.3–3   Why is the passage difficult to read?

Practice Exercise 1.4
Self-Assessment

Goal: Lawyers need to develop metacognition, which is an awareness of what they know and do not know. Each chapter ends with a self-assessment exercise so that you can determine if you understand the concepts presented. After completing the exercise, use the rubric at the end of the exercise to evaluate your proficiency.

In this exercise, think about how the purpose for reading affects how you read.

Assume that you are working in a law firm and have been contacted by Evelyn Michel, who is a nurse at Central Baptist Hospital in New York City. Evelyn has recently been terminated from her employment at Central Baptist because she failed the National Council Licensure Examination

(NCLEX). She wants guidance regarding whether or not she may be eligible for unemployment insurance benefits. A senior partner has given you a case to examine on this topic, *De Grego v. Levine*, 347 N.E. 2d 611 (N.Y. 1976),[15] which is in Appendix C.

As you answer the following questions, think about the types of information you will look for in the case to solve your client's problem.

1.4–1   Is it necessary to memorize the name of the first case mentioned, *In re James*?

1.4–2   Is it necessary to memorize the date that De Grego was discharged from his employment?

1.4–2   Is it useful to understand the rules relating to whether or not De Grego was eligible for unemployment benefits when he was terminated from his job?

Evaluate your understanding of the skills in this chapter by completing the following rubric. For each skill, circle whether you are at the proficient or developing level. Everyone can get to the proficient level over time.

Skill	Competency Level	
	Proficient	**Developing**
Understands purpose for reading cases.	• Reads case to solve new legal problem.	• Reads case to memorize dates, places, and names.
Understands that reading cases is difficult for everyone.	• Understands that reading cases is a new skill that must be learned. • Believes it is possible to learn effective case reading techniques. • Understands that reading cases is time consuming at the beginning of law school and allocates sufficient time to read.	• Feels inadequate because reading cases is difficult. • Believes good case reading is an innate skill that cannot be learned. • Believes reading cases should not take so much time.

---

[15] This case was selected because I represented Dominic De Grego when I worked at Mid-Hudson Legal Services in Poughkeepsie, New York. The fictitious scenario involving Ms. Michel is based upon an actual case, *Michael v. Long Island College Hospital*, 401 N.Y.S.2d 591 (N.Y. App. Div. 1978), where the court relied on the *De Grego* decision.

CHAPTER 2

BEFORE READING: READ AS AN ADVOCATE AND READ WITH FOCUS

I. SUMMARY

This chapter examines two reading strategies that are used by expert legal readers. Experts read:

- as advocates with the goal of representing clients, and
- with focus.

As discussed in Chapter 1, expert legal readers use a variety of skills beyond memorization. To read as an advocate, it is necessary to **analyze** cases by looking for arguments made by the parties and rules set forth by the court.

At the conclusion of this chapter, you will be able to:

- view a case from the perspective of an advocate,
- read with greater focus , and
- identify the timing of your peak energy levels.

II. CHECKLIST

CASE READING CHECKLIST

Warning: Do not just highlight and underline.

Phase 1: Before Reading

1. Read for a purpose and **assume the role of advocate or judge**.

2. **Read with energy and focus**.

3. Notice case structure.

4. Understand the general subject matter by examining:

   a. course syllabus, casebook table of contents, or research assignment, and

   b. parties, citation, court, and date.

---

5. Read for an overview by skimming and noticing organization, headings, who won, and what case is generally about.

Phase 2: Reading More Carefully

1. Understand the facts.

2. Reread, look up unfamiliar words, analyze confusing language, and vary reading speed.

3. Understand the main ideas set forth in the issue, holding, and reasoning.

4. Identify the rule.

5. Take notes with your reactions and brief the case.

Phase 3: After Reading

1. Evaluate the decision, ask questions, and talk with professors.

2. Determine how cases fit together with other cases and synthesize.

III. READ AS AN ADVOCATE

A. WHAT IS ADVOCACY?

An advocate is a spokesperson. The word advocate comes from the Latin word "advocatus," a person who assists someone. The root "voc" in advocate means voice. An advocate gives another person a voice. Advocates may speak out and help others solve problems. As we read cases, we see the work of advocates. Every case has at least two advocates, i.e., the attorneys representing the parties. Attorneys advocate or speak out on behalf of their clients.

B. READING AS AN ADVOCATE

One of the most useful techniques employed by expert legal readers is also one of the easiest to master. In research studies, students who took the role of an attorney for one of the parties (or a judge) consistently outperformed students who read cases to get through class. The students who took the role of an advocate picked one of the parties in the case and read the case as if they were that person's attorney. The students who took the role of a judge pretended to be the judge.

The results of four studies are summarized to demonstrate the effectiveness of this critical reading strategy. The first study (Oates) examined the reading strategies of a law professor and four law students. As explained in Chapter 1, based upon their undergraduate GPAs and LSAT scores, all four law students were expected to be "in the bottom 10%

of their entering class."[1] However, the study found that students with good reading skills performed better than expected. At the end of their first semester, the better readers, William and Maria, were in the top 10% and 15% of their class, respectively. The students with less effective reading skills, Jackie and James, were in the bottom 20% of the class.[2]

Figure 2.1 shows that the higher performing students, William and Maria, took the role of an advocate or judge as they read. The lower performing students read for information or out of fear of being called on.

Figure 2.1
Reading as an Advocate: Oates Study

Student	Reading Technique
William (Top 10%)	William "read to see how he would have decided the case and, in his interview, he stated that when he reads cases, **he puts himself in the role of the decision maker** and evaluates what the outcome of the case should be."[3] (emphasis added).
Maria (Top15%)	Maria "sometimes thought about how she might use the case in practice"[4]
Jackie (Bottom 20%)	Jackie "did not . . . assume a particular role."[5]
James (Bottom 20%)	"When I read cases, I usually read them not for briefing cases per se, but more out of **fear** of being called on in class. I don't want to look like a fool so I just want to know the basic principles."[6]

A second study (Stratman) confirmed these findings. Fifty-six law students in the second semester of their first year were divided into four groups to read a case and take one of the following roles:

- advocate on behalf of a client by planning an argument for an appeal, or

- advise a client regarding the resolution of a case, or

- make policy recommendations for a legislature considering changes to a statute, or

---

[1]   Laurel Currie Oates, *Leveling the Playing Field: Helping Students Succeed by Helping Them Learn to Read as Expert Lawyers*, 80 St. John's L. Rev. 227, 230 (2006).

[2]   *Id.*

[3]   *Id.* at 238–39.

[4]   Laurel Currie Oates, *Beating the Odds: Reading Strategies of Law Students Admitted Through Alternative Admissions Programs*, 83 Iowa L. Rev. 139, 155 (1997).

[5]   *Id.* at 153.

[6]   Oates, *supra* note 1, at 243.

- prepare for class recitation.

The students who read the case for the purpose of advocating on behalf of a client had higher reading comprehension scores.[7]

The third study (Christensen) also found that higher performing students read cases as advocates. The study examined the reading strategies of twenty-four law students who had completed their first semester of law school. Because their GPAs and LSAT scores were similar, it was expected that all students would perform about the same after the first semester. In fact, ten of the better readers were in the top 25% of the class and two were in the top 50%. Four of the weaker readers were in the bottom 50% of the class and eight were in the bottom 25%. As shown in Figure 2.2, the student with higher grades read the case as an advocate representing a client.

Figure 2.2
Reading as an Advocate: Christensen Study

Student	Purpose for Reading
Student (Top 3%)	"This student connected with purpose consistently throughout her reading, assuming the role of an attorney as she moved through the text."[8] **"All right. I am a practicing attorney and I'm reading the opinion to prepare for a meeting with a client and they have a case that is similar to the facts that I am reading."[9]**
Student (Bottom 10%)	This student "failed to connect with the given purpose during any part of his case reading. As a result, this student was more distracted as he read and he appeared to be overwhelmed by the details of the text."[10] "OK. Now I'm thinking what I'd like to purchase on ebay. I actually stopped drafting my briefs on the computer because I would become distracted by ebay."[11]

Finally, in a study (Grisé) that analyzed the impact of critical reading instruction on writing, students commented that they benefited from assuming the role of an advocate as they read.[12] Twelve students received

---

[7] James F. Stratman, *When Law Students Read Cases: Exploring Relations Between Professional Legal Reasoning Roles and Problem Detection*, 34 Discourse Processes 57, 77 (2002).

[8] Leah M. Christensen, *"One L of a Year": How to Maximize Your Success in Law School* 31 (2012).

[9] *Id.*

[10] *Id.*

[11] *Id.* at 32.

[12] Jane Bloom Grisé, *Critical Reading Instruction: The Road to Successful Legal Writing Skills*, 18 W. Mich. Univ. Cooley J. of Prac. & Clinical L. (forthcoming 2017).

critical reading instruction and twelve students (control group) did not. The writing performance of the two groups was compared and the students who received the critical reading instruction outperformed the control group with respect to their ability to explain cases in their legal writing memos. The critical reading instruction recommended that students read as an advocate. Students commented:

- this recommendation "changed the way I read."[13]

- "assuming the role of advocate or judge allows me to get a better idea of how the rule applies to facts and to the overall . . . class."[14]

Over half of the students in this study reported that reading as an advocate was the most useful strategy they learned in the critical reading course.[15]

Why do students who read as an advocate perform at a higher level? Perhaps they are more engaged because they are thinking about representing a real person. They may be reading more actively because they are formulating arguments to assist a client. Reflection Exercise 2.1 explores the general meaning of advocacy and asks you to think about how you have used advocacy skills in other contexts. It is useful to remember these experiences as you apply this concept to reading cases. Practice Exercise 2.2 is a simulation exercise where you will act as an advocate for a party in a dispute.

IV. READ WITH FOCUS

Critical reading requires energy and focus. As noted in Chapter 1, critical reading involves a variety of skills such as understanding text, applying rules to new problems, and analyzing cases. To perform these skills, the reader must be able to concentrate. This is not always easy. Rather than reading with focus, we are often distracted by thoughts, interruptions, and electronic devices. On the other hand, sometimes, we try to read for hours and find that it is difficult to concentrate for long periods of time.

Reading comprehension is highest when the reader can pay attention. To do this, it is important to get enough sleep, eat well, exercise, and manage stress. It is also useful to identify high energy times of the day. While these are challenges given the time demands of law school, there are simple steps that can be taken to increase reading efficiency and effectiveness.

---

[13] *Id.*

[14] *Id.*

[15] *Id.*

A. EXERCISE AND TAKE BREAKS

Exercise every day. Research shows that aerobic exercise improves academic performance. While the brain only weighs about three pounds, it uses 25% of the calories consumed during the day and 20% of the oxygen breathed. The brain needs lots of oxygen to function. Furthermore, the role of the hippocampus and amygdala are important to understand, as they play a central role in learning. The hippocampus is the center for learning and memory while the amygdala focuses on emotion and modulates the release of stress hormones. When people are stressed over extended periods, the hormones released from the amygdala (cortisol and adrenalin) can suppress the functioning of the hippocampus. The amygdala can actually make the hippocampus shrink in size, which decreases the ability to learn and remember.

Aerobic exercise improves academic performance because it:

- increases blood flow to the brain so that the brain can function more efficiently,

- encourages the growth of new brain cells (neurons) in the hippocampus, and

- decreases the release of stress hormones from the amygdala that can interfere with learning.

Even a short walk in the middle of the day can boost your mental functioning.

In addition to aerobic exercise, stretching exercises can improve brain functioning and focus. No one can sit for long periods of time and remain focused. Our brains and bodies are simply not designed to do this. Our shoulders, neck, and back muscles get tight, and blood flow to the brain decreases. Some exercises that can help counter these problems are described in Reflection Exercise 2.3.

To maximize your reading effectiveness, take exercise and stretching breaks on a regular basis. Divide reading assignments into manageable segments. Instead of trying to read 30 pages of contracts at a time, concentrate on one or two cases and then take a break. In the Grisé study, one student noted that it was useful to stop working periodically and "step away for a bit to regroup."[16]

B. TRY MEDITATION

Stress-relieving techniques such as mindful meditation can also assist with concentration. Reading requires the ability to pay attention to the present. This can be a challenge when you are interrupted with thoughts of the past and the future. In fact, you may find that most of the time you

---

[16] *Id.*

are probably not thinking about the present. Instead, you may be thinking about things you have done or your future plans. This is apparent to me when I walk my dog. While Darby is focused on the smells and animals she sees, I am often thinking about my plans for the rest of the day. I realize how little I have been paying attention when she jerks her leash to try to chase a rabbit or squirrel. Darby has taught me a great deal about paying attention.

Mindful meditation can assist in learning to pay attention to the present. Mindful meditation has been described as a way to pay "attention in a particular way: on purpose, in the present moment, and non-judgmentally."[17] It was first introduced into the legal profession in 1989 when Jon Kabat-Zinn, Director of the Center for Mindfulness in Medicine, Health Care and Society in Boston, conducted a program for judges. As judges must pay attention to everything going on in the courtroom, judges turned to meditation to reduce stress and learn concentration techniques. Judge Jeremy Fogel, Director of the Federal Judicial Center, has noted that mindfulness can assist judges in "slowing down one's mental processes enough to allow one to notice as much as possible about a given moment or situation, and then to act thoughtfully based on what one has noticed."[18] Many law firms and law schools provide mindfulness training.

So, how can mindful meditation help with critical reading? Meditation can increase the capacity for concentration and focus, skills that are essential for good critical reading. Meditation does this, in part, because it improves the functioning of the hippocampus.

- In one study, students who were given five days of meditation training for just 20 minutes a day performed better on tests that required attention than the students who did not receive this training.[19]

- In a study at the University of Massachusetts Medical School, participants in an eight-week meditation course had increased concentrations of gray matter in the hippocampus.[20]

Meditation also seems to "tone down the amygdala, helping us to perform better in high-stress situations."[21]

---

[17] Jon Kabat-Zinn, *Wherever You Go, There You Are* 4 (1994).

[18] Judge Jeremy D. Fogel, *Mindfulness and Judging, Federal Judicial Center* (2016) http://www.fjc.gov/public/pdf.nsf/lookup/Mindfulness-and-Judging-Fogel-FJC-2016.pdf/$file/ Mindfulness-and-Judging-Fogel-FJC-2016.pdf.

[19] Yi-Yuan Tang, et al, *Short-term Meditation Training Improves Attention and Self-Regulation*, 104 Proc. Nat'l Acad. Sci. 17152 (2007).

[20] Britta K. Holzel et al., *Mindfulness Practice Leads to Increases in Regional Brain Gray Matter Density*, 191 Psychiatry Research: Neuroimaging 36, 39 (2011).

[21] Shailini Jandial George, *The Cure for the Distracted Mind: Why Law Schools Should Teach Mindfulness*, 53 Duq. L. Rev. 215, 227 (2015).

Mindful meditation can be done in a variety of ways. While meditation is often done by focusing on breathing, it can be done by paying attention to everyday activities such as washing the dishes or walking to school. Think about your breathing or the walk you are taking rather than the past or future. It is not necessary to breathe or walk in any particular way. Just focus on the present and the activity.

Meditation can also be done by noticing your surroundings for a few moments. You can place your hand on a table and observe:

> "the sensations in your hand as it rests on this surface. Take a few moments to notice each of your fingers, your thumb, the back of your hand, and your palms. Notice the feel of the air on your skin and the points of contact with the surface."[22]

When your mind wanders, bring your attention back to your hand. Do not criticize yourself when your mind wanders. Just accept the fact that minds wander and focus attention on your hand.

By practicing mindfulness, you can learn what it feels like to focus attention on the present. Then you can apply this skill to reading. When students or attorneys read and pay attention to the text, reading efficiency increases. Meditation is not a big time commitment as focus can improve with just five or ten minutes a day of practice. There are YouTube videos that provide guidance for short meditations. Reflection Exercise 2.4 provides additional resources as well as a five-minute meditation.

C. IDENTIFY HIGH ENERGY TIMES OF DAY

Evaluate your own energy levels and try to read during high energy time periods. It can be helpful to record your energy levels throughout the day. Reflection Exercise 2.5 provides a log to chart these results. Try reading during your high and low energy periods and notice if there is a difference in comprehension. If you are a morning person and work best at 8 AM, read your challenging cases during this peak energy time.

Practice Exercise 2.6, the self-assessment exercise for this chapter, examines the skills of reading as an advocate and reading with focus.

V. CASE EXAMPLE: READ AS AN ADVOCATE AND READ WITH FOCUS

The skills in this chapter, reading as an advocate and reading with focus, are explained with *Fisher v. Carrousel Motor Hotel, Inc.*, 424 S.W.2d 627 (Tex. 1967) (Appendix B-1).

In Chapter 1, the *Fisher* case was examined to prepare for a meeting with Joe Parker, who had contacted our office to discuss an incident that

---

[22] Ruth Baer, *The Practicing Happiness Workbook* 105 (2014).

occurred at Smith Cars. Mr. Parker fell and was injured when a mechanic grabbed his cell phone. We reviewed the *Fisher* case because we needed to read a case that addressed the law of battery to prepare for this meeting. As noted in Chapter 1, the first step in critical reading is to identify the purpose for reading as that will affect what we look for as we read and how we read.

Now as we examine *Fisher,* we will read as an advocate which means to read from the perspective of an attorney representing Mr. Fisher. In addition to reading as an advocate, think about reading with focus. For fifteen minutes, just focus on the case. It can be helpful to take a short walk before reading, read during a high energy period of the day, or simply decide to turn off all electronic devices and focus on the decision. (When reading an electronic version of the case, avoid the urge to check email, chat, etc.). Try to avoid thinking about events from yesterday and all of the other things you must do today.

The following sections demonstrate what it means to read as an advocate from the perspective of Mr. Fisher's attorney.

A. LOOK FOR GENERAL INFORMATION

The *Fisher* case starts with **preliminary information** about the lawsuit and some facts. When reading from the viewpoint of Mr. Fisher's attorney, first try to get an **overview** of the case and think about the following:

- What type of lawsuit did Fisher bring? Looks like he brought a suit for assault and battery.

- Who was Fisher? A mathematician working at NASA.

- Who did he sue? A hotel as well as the manager of the hotel.

- What was it like to bring this type of lawsuit in 1967 given the social climate of the time?

In thinking about our client Joe Parker, could we bring a suit for battery? Who would we sue? Strategies for conducting a good case overview are addressed in Chapter 4.

B. NOTICE THE FACTS

The opinion sets forth the **facts** as follows:

"The plaintiff Fisher had been invited by Ampex Corporation and Defense Electronics to a one day's meeting regarding telemetry equipment at the Carrousel. The invitation included a luncheon. The guests were asked to reply by telephone whether they could attend the luncheon, and Fisher called in his acceptance. After the morning session, the group of 25 or 30 guests adjourned to the

Brass Ring Club for lunch. The luncheon was buffet style, and Fisher stood in line with others and just ahead of a graduate student of Rice University who testified at the trial. As Fisher was about to be served, he was approached by Flynn, who snatched the plate from Fisher's hand and shouted that he, a Negro, could not be served in the club. Fisher testified that he was not actually touched, and did not testify that he suffered fear or apprehension of physical injury; but he did testify that he was highly embarrassed and hurt by Flynn's conduct in the presence of his associates." *Id*. at 628–29.

In reading the **facts** from the perspective of Fisher, an advocate might notice that:

- Fisher went to a luncheon at the Carrousel Hotel.

- Fisher stood in line at a buffet and as he was about to be served, the manager Flynn took the plate from Fisher's hand and shouted that an African American person would not be served.

- While Flynn did not touch Fisher, Fisher was embarrassed.

In thinking about Joe Parker's case, an attorney might start comparing the facts in Parker's situation to the facts in Fisher's case. Were Mr. Parker's facts similar in anyway? Strategies for reading and understanding the facts are addressed in Chapter 5.

C. IDENTIFY ARGUMENTS

The opinion sets forth some information that provides clues about the **arguments** advanced by the parties.

"The jury found that Flynn 'forceably dispossessed plaintiff of his dinner plate' and 'shouted in a loud and offensive manner' that Fisher could not be served there, thus subjecting Fisher to humiliation and indignity." *Id*. at 629.

"The Court of Civil Appeals held that there was no assault because there was no physical contact and no evidence of fear or apprehension of physical contact." *Id*.

In reading these passages from the perspective of Fisher, an advocate would think about the arguments that Fisher might have made as well as the arguments that he had to respond to in the litigation. Fisher argued that there was a claim for battery because the dinner plate was grabbed. Carrousel Hotel argued that there was no battery because there was no physical contact.

When reading from the perspective of Fisher, these arguments start coming alive and you become a more active reader. Could we make similar arguments on behalf of Mr. Parker? Chapters 6 through 11 explore ways to understand and analyze arguments and then use rules from cases to solve a client's problem.

VI. PRACTICE

Reflection Exercise 2.1
What Is Advocacy?

Goal: This exercise is designed to explore the meaning of advocacy and your experiences in advocating on behalf of yourself or others.

2.1–1   What does it mean to be an advocate?

2.1–2   Can you recall situations where you had to advocate on behalf of yourself or someone else?

2.1–3   If you have advocated on behalf of yourself or someone else, explain what you tried to do and how you went about it.

2.1–4   Have you ever read an article and then used the article to advocate on behalf of someone? Would this influence how you read the article?

Practice Exercise 2.2
Thinking Like a Lawyer: Advocacy

Goal: This exercise gives you the experience of being an advocate for a client. Advocates analyze rules and think about arguments they can make to assist a client. This exercise also gives you the experience of being a judge.

Assume that the Baker family is faced with a problem regarding their July 4th celebration. Read the following scenario and complete the exercise.

Scenario:

On July 3rd, Joshua Baker was very excited about purchasing fireworks for July 4th. His father told Joshua that he had to complete the following chores by 6 PM if he wanted to go out to buy fireworks:

1.   clean his room by putting away his train set, picking up dirty clothes and taking them to the laundry room, and picking up his coin collection from the floor; and

2.   feed the dog; and

3.   brush the dog; and

4.   read for 30 minutes.

By 6 PM, Joshua had put away his train set, picked up his clothes, given the dog some water, brushed the dog, and read for 20 minutes. He did not take his dirty clothes to the laundry room. He never put away his coins.

Step 1:

The first step in advocacy is to understand the underlying rules and facts. Attorneys analyze a legal problem by breaking down rules into elements and sub-elements and matching facts to each element.

Identify the specific chores Joshua was supposed to do (the rules) and record those chores in 2.2–1, column A. Break the rules into elements and sub-elements.

Next, record the chores he completed (the facts) in 2.2–1, column B.

2.2–1 Rules and Facts

A. Chore Requirements (Rules)	B. Chores Completed (Facts)

Element 1:
    Sub Element 1:
    Sub Element 2:
    Sub Element 3:	

Element 2:	
Element 3:	
Element 4:	

Step 2:

The next step is to analyze the facts and determine the best arguments Joshua could make regarding why he should be allowed to buy fireworks.

For each chore Joshua was supposed to do, record in 2.2–2, column B, the best argument Joshua could make that he completed the chore. The chore requirements in column A are the same as those in 2.2-1 above.

2.2–2 Joshua's Arguments

A. Chore Requirements (Rules)	B. Joshua's Arguments

Element 1:
    Sub Element 1:
    Sub Element 2:
    Sub Element 3:	

Element 2:	
Element 3:	
Element 4:	

Then examine of all these arguments and record in 2.2–3 the best overall argument Joshua could make that he satisfied his parents' rules.

2.2–3 Best Overall Argument for Joshua

```
┌─────────────────────────────────────────────────────────┐
│                                                         │
│                                                         │
│                                                         │
│                                                         │
│                                                         │
└─────────────────────────────────────────────────────────┘
```

Step 3:

Record in 2.2–4, column B, the best arguments the parents could make that Joshua did not complete each chore. The chore requirements (rules) are the same as those in 2.2–1.

2.2–4 Parents' Arguments

A. Chore Requirements (Rules)	B. Parents' Arguments
Element 1: Sub Element 1: Sub Element 2: Sub Element 3:	
Element 2:	
Element 3:	
Element 4:	

Then examine of all the parents' arguments and record in 2.2–5 the best overall argument the parents could make that Joshua did not comply with the rules.

2.2–5 Best Overall Argument for Parents

```
┌─────────────────────────────────────────────────────────┐
│                                                         │
│                                                         │
│                                                         │
│                                                         │
└─────────────────────────────────────────────────────────┘
```

Step 4:

Finally, take the role of a judge, make a decision, and record your decision in 2.2–6.

2.2–6 Judge's Decision

```

```

Reflection Exercise 2.3
Brain Boosts[23]

Goal: The goal of this exercise is to provide ways that you can take breaks to maximize your reading productivity.

Activities That Help Focus the Brain

High Intensity Training (increases blood flow to the brain): Alternate between 20 seconds of exercise (push-ups, jump rope, fast walk, jog or sprint) and 10 seconds of rest. Do this for about 4 minutes. Energizing music makes the workout fun.

Cross Crawls (balancing): Right hand to left raised knee; left hand to right raised knee.

Crazy Jacks (energizing): Alternate jumping jacks with crossed arms and then crossed legs.

Stretching Exercises

Sitting for long periods creates tightness, especially in the muscles of the neck, shoulder, chest, back and hips. Some good exercises to relieve tightness follow.

1.   Neck and Shoulders

Neck Rotation: With chin parallel to the floor and shoulders relaxed, turn the head to one side and slowly nod while chin is over shoulder; repeat on other side. Next, drop the chin to the chest and roll from one shoulder to the other in a half-circle.

Shoulder Shrugs and Shoulder Rolls: Lift shoulders up to the ears and hold; press shoulders down. Roll shoulders back and down.

---

[23] This Reflection Exercise was written by Anne Graff, MS, OTRL/L Mind Body Fitness, PLLC.

Seated Cobra: Opens the chest, stretches the shoulders, and counters the standard forward seated posture.

A   B

1. As shown in A, place hands on thighs with shoulders stacked over hips and chest lifted.
2. As shown in B, rotate the thumbs towards the back of the room with palms facing upwards, gently squeezing the shoulder blades together.
3. Draw abdominals in towards spine.
4. Feel the chest open as the arms reach back.

2.   Chest, Back, Arms and Hands

Elbow Circles: Place hands on shoulders and circle the elbows; reverse direction. Bring elbows towards the center and spread apart.

"W": Press elbows down to the waist "w"; then raise both arms up to a "v" position; bring back to a "w" and press both arms down towards the floor.

Scissors: Start with both arms extended at shoulder level; separate arms with one arm reaching up towards the ceiling and the other pressing down towards the floor; reverse.

Hands: Make a fist and release, opening the fingers wide apart.

Seated Cat Cow: Promotes spinal mobility and relaxation.

A

B

1. As shown in A, sit straight in chair with feet hip distance apart.
2. While taking a deep breath, lift the chest and extend spine into a gentle backbend, lifting the chin slightly and sliding the shoulder blades down.
3. As shown in B, as the breath is exhaled, round the back, moving into a forward bend and drawing the chin to the chest.
4. Create a relaxing rhythm that matches the breath to the movements of spinal flexion and extension.

Seated Twist: Releases tension in the back due to sitting.

A

B

1. Sit tall and maintain length in the spine.
2. Take a deep breath. On the exhale, bring the right hand to the outer left thigh with the left hand anchored to the left side of the chair, as shown in A, or hold onto the back of the chair for a deeper stretch, as shown in B.
3. On the inhale, untwist slightly, drawing in breath. On the exhale move into the twist.
4. Initiate the rotational movement with the core and chest and then turn the head to look over the shoulder.
5. Repeat on the other side.

Wrist Stretch: Stretches muscles in the forearm and hands; beneficial as a break from typing or texting.

1. Extend the right arm with palms down and flex the wrist, bringing the fingers down towards the floor.
2. With the other hand, press the back of the hand to increase the stretch.
3. Turn the palm up and, with the assist of the other hand, draw the fingers towards the floor to bring the wrist into extension.
4. Make a fist and open and close fingers.
5. Repeat with left arm.

3.   Hips, Hamstrings and Legs

Piriformis Stretch (Seated Figure Four Stretch): Hip opener that helps relieve muscle tension from sitting at a desk.

1. Sit tall with the spine long and the crown of the head reaching up towards the ceiling.
2. Bend leg as shown.
3. Take a deep breath and inhale and during the exhale lean slightly forward from the hips while maintaining a lengthened spine.
4. Repeat on the other side.

Hamstring Stretch: Hamstring stretches help relieve tightness from sitting and may help the low back.

1. Sit with the spine lengthened and bend the right knee to 90 degrees.
2. Extend the left leg with the toe pointing up towards the ceiling.
3. Lean forward from the hips, keeping the back straight.
4. Feel the stretch in the hamstring muscle located behind the thigh.
5. Repeat on the other side.

Seated Lunge: Good stretch for tight hip flexors and quadriceps.

A

B

1. As shown in A, sit on the side of the chair with a lengthened spine and even weight on hips.
2. Position the left knee at 90 degrees with the foot flat on the floor.
3. Slide the right leg back into a lunge position with the knee reaching towards the floor and the heel lifted.
4. Contract the glute of the right leg to open up the hip flexor.
5. Repeat on the other side.

Variation: As shown in B, to intensify the stretch, lift the outside arm slowly as the hip presses forward.

Ankle Flex and Extend: Leg and ankle stretches that promote circulation.

A

B

1. Extend the legs with a slight bend at the knees.
2. As illustrated in A, flex ankles upward pointing the toes up towards the ceiling and hold for a count of 2.
3. As seen in B, extend toes down towards the floor and hold for a count of 2.

Variation: Circle the ankles in both directions or pedal with one foot pointing the toes up and the other foot extending the toes down.

Reflection Exercise 2.4
Mindful Meditation

Goal: The goal of this exercise is to try mindful meditation for five minutes.

In this meditation exercise, meditate for five minutes and focus on the present.

- Start by finding a comfortable place to sit that is quiet.

- Close your eyes if you like.

- Next, do a couple of shoulder shrugs and shoulder rolls. Lift the shoulders up to the ears and hold and then press the shoulders down. While doing this, think about how your shoulders feel.

- Think about your breathing and take a few deep breaths.

- For the next few minutes, pay attention to your breathing. While doing this, expect that your mind will wander. That is OK. When you notice your mind is wandering, direct your attention back to the present moment and your breathing.

- When you are ready, open your eyes.

Mindfulness Resources

Ruth Baer, *The Practicing Happiness Workbook* (2014).

Center for Mindfulness in Medicine, Health Care, and Society, University of Massachusetts Medical School http://www.umassmed.edu/cfm.

Scott L. Rogers, *Mindfulness for Law Students* (2009).

Scott L. Rogers, *The Six-Minute Solution: A Mindfulness Primer for Lawyers* (2009).

Reflection Exercise 2.5
Energy Levels and Focus

Goal: The goal of this exercise is to analyze your energy levels throughout the day.

For this exercise, select a day when you are working or attending school and record your energy levels throughout the day. Once you determine your high and low energy periods, you can adjust your reading times to correspond to higher energy periods so that you can read more effectively.

2.5–1   Record your energy levels and add a comment about how you felt. Rate your energy level on a scale of 0 to 10 with 0 representing no energy and feelings of distraction and 10 representing high energy and focus.

Time	Energy Level	Comment
6–8 AM		
9 AM		
10 AM		
11 AM		
12 PM		
1 PM		
2 PM		
3 PM		
4 PM		
5 PM		
6 PM		
7 PM		
8 PM		
9 PM		
10–12 PM		

2.5–2   What do you think contributes to your high/low energy levels at different times?

2.5–3   After you have identified your high/low energy times, read a case during a low energy time. Read another case during a high energy time. What differences do you notice?

Practice Exercise 2.6
Self-Assessment

Goal: In this exercise, you can determine if you understand the concepts of reading as an advocate and reading with focus.

For this exercise, assume that you are still representing Ms. Evelyn Michel, who has been terminated from her employment as a nurse because she failed the National Council Licensure Examination. Ms. Michel wants to know if she will qualify for unemployment insurance benefits. *De Grego v. Levine,* 347 N.E. 2d 611 (N.Y. 1976) (Appendix C) provides guidance on this subject.

Read the majority opinion in *De Grego* as if you were the advocate for Dominic De Grego. For 20 minutes, just focus on the case. It can be helpful to take a short walk before reading and read during your high energy time. Turn off all electronic devices and focus on reading.

2.6–1   As you read as an advocate for Dominic De Grego, did you notice why De Grego was fired?

2.6–2   Did you notice why he was initially denied unemployment benefits?

2.6–3   What argument did the employer make before the Unemployment Insurance Appeal Board?

2.6–4   Did you read during your high energy time of day?

2.6–5   Were you able to focus without interruption for 20 minutes?

Evaluate your understanding of the skills in this chapter by completing the following rubric. For each skill, circle whether you are at the proficient or developing level. Everyone can get to the proficient level over time.

Skill	Competency Level	
	Proficient	**Developing**
Reads as an advocate.	• Takes the role of the decision maker or the attorney for a party.	• Reads as a neutral observer. • Reads to avoid embarrassment in class.
Reads with focus.	• Reads complicated text during high energy times. • Focuses attention on text for short periods, i.e., 30 minutes, without interruption.	• Does not pay attention to high energy periods. • Does not focus attention for 30 minutes at a time. • Thinks about other things, texts, checks email, or tweets and is distracted.

CHAPTER 3

BEFORE READING: CASE STRUCTURE AND CIVIL AND CRIMINAL PROCEDURE

I. SUMMARY

This chapter introduces readers to:

- the structure of cases, and

- civil and criminal procedure.

While it is not necessary to memorize terms related to case structure and procedure, expert legal readers are more efficient readers because they understand the structure of cases and legal procedures.

At the conclusion of this chapter, you will be able to:

- identify the basic structure of cases, and

- understand the procedural terminology found in civil and criminal cases.

II. CHECKLIST

CASE READING CHECKLIST

Warning: Do not just highlight and underline.

<u>Phase 1: Before Reading</u>

1. Read for a purpose and assume the role of advocate or judge.

2. Read with energy and focus.

3. **Notice case structure.**

4. Understand the general subject matter by examining:

    a. course syllabus, casebook table of contents, or research assignment, and

    b. parties, citation, court, and date.

5. Read for an overview by skimming and noticing organization, headings, who won, and what case is generally about.

<u>Phase 2: Reading More Carefully</u>

1. Understand the facts.

---

2. Reread, look up unfamiliar words, analyze confusing language, and vary reading speed.

3. Understand the main ideas set forth in the issue, holding, and reasoning.

4. Identify the rule.

5. Take notes with your reactions and brief the case.

Phase 3: After Reading

1. Evaluate the decision, ask questions, and talk with professors.

2. Determine how cases fit together with other cases and synthesize.

III. BACKGROUND KNOWLEDGE IMPROVES COMPREHENSION

This chapter examines the structure of cases and terms related to civil and criminal procedure because reading comprehension improves when a reader is familiar with the organization of texts and vocabulary. When we read, we add to our existing knowledge. When a reader has some familiarity with a subject, it is easier to build on that foundation to learn new things. However, when a reader has little or no background in a field, it is more challenging to read. For example, it would be difficult to read about organic chemistry if a reader never took a basic chemistry class. Without an understanding of basic concepts and vocabulary, it would be hard to delve into the complexities of organic chemistry.

Reading cases is similar. One reason that reading cases is difficult is because law students are entering a new field with unfamiliar vocabulary and procedures. The information in this chapter about case structure and procedural terminology will make it easier for you to understand all cases. It will also make it possible for you to master more advanced critical reading skills. As noted in Chapter 1, understanding vocabulary is a prerequisite for moving to the higher level critical thinking skills of analyzing and evaluating cases.

IV. CASE STRUCTURE

A. HOW ARE CASES ORGANIZED?

The structure of cases is the first type of background information that will assist you in understanding cases. Knowing the structure of anything from books to college courses helps us locate information more efficiently. For example, when we read a mystery, we know that the book is divided into chapters and the solution is probably in the last chapter. If we want to find the resolution of a mystery, we skip to the end of the book. When we take a class, we expect that the professor will hand out a syllabus on the first day and provide an overview of the course. At the end of the semester, there is typically a final exam or paper due. This structure helps us plan.

Cases also have a structure. When readers understand the format of cases, they can read more efficiently because they have a reading plan and can look for information in specific places. This section outlines the configuration of most cases and notes the differences between cases in reported decisions that lawyers rely on in research and practice and the case excerpts that are found in legal textbooks. At the outset, it is good to remember that a court decision may be referred to as a case, opinion, or decision.

Before examining the organization of cases, it is useful to think in practical terms regarding the types of things that judges include in their decisions. Think about how you would structure an opinion if you were an appellate judge. What information would be important to include so that litigants would understand the basis for your decision and so that appellate courts could review the opinion? How would you order the opinion? Reflection Exercise 3.1 gives you the opportunity to be a judge and write your own opinion. Complete this exercise before moving on to Section B so that you can think about the organization of cases based upon logic and common sense. It is not necessary to memorize the structure of cases. Opinions are structured in a logical fashion and this structure will become apparent as you complete this exercise.

B. CASE STRUCTURE: REPORTED DECISIONS

This section sets forth the structure of most cases. You may notice that many of the items included in your opinion in Reflection Exercise 3.1 are a standard part of a case. Most reported decisions contain the following sections:

- an introductory statement that includes the legal claims,
- the facts underlying the dispute,
- facts relating to how the case progressed through the court system,
- key issues or questions raised by the parties,
- a discussion of cases that were previously decided on the same topic, and
- the court's decision and disposition or resolution of the case.

Judges are taught to include this information in their decisions. The Judicial Writing Manual published by the Federal Judicial Center recommends that judges include five basic elements in their opinions:

"1. an introductory statement of the nature, procedural posture, and result of the case;

2. a statement of the issues to be decided;

3. a statement of the material facts;

4. a discussion of the governing legal principles and resolution of the issues; and

5. the disposition and necessary instructions."[1]

This structure is important because the parties want to know the reasons for a decision. In addition, appellate courts need to know the facts and reasoning utilized by the lower court to determine if that court made a correct decision.

These case elements are arranged in a predictable order. The facts are usually found at the beginning of the opinion because they are the basis for the decision. The court typically discusses older cases dealing with similar subjects in the middle of the opinion. The court's decision is found towards the end of the case. However, **these are not ironclad rules.** Sometimes the facts are interspersed throughout an opinion. The decision may be found on the first page. However, opinions include all of the components listed above and, in most cases, follow a similar order.

Some text in reported decisions is written by editors at publishing companies rather than the judge. Editors write the **case summary** or **synopsis** (summary of case) and **headnotes** (summary of legal issues) to assist readers in understanding the case. The case summary and headnotes are located immediately before the court's decision. The Case Example section in this chapter contains a sample case summary (Figure 3.13) and headnote (Figure 3.14). The annotated *Fisher* case in Appendix B-1 points out the case summary and headnotes. Readers must distinguish between this text written by editors and text written by judges because the opinion written by the judge is the **only information that is actually the law**. For this reason, attorneys only reference the opinion written by the judge in legal memoranda and briefs. The text added by editors can be useful in researching and locating specific topics, but it cannot be quoted or cited.

---

[1] Federal Judicial Center, *Judicial Writing Manual: A Pocket Guide for Judges* 13 Federal Judicial Center (2th ed. 2013), http://www2.fjc.gov/sites/default/files/2014/Judicial-Writing-Manual-2D-FJC-2013.pdf.

Figure 3.1 outlines the structure of most cases.

Figure 3.1
Case Structure Outline

Citation	The volume, book, and first page of the opinion.
Caption	Names of the parties, court, and case number.
Date	Date of court decision.
Case Summary	Summaries explaining the nature of the lawsuit and the trial court and appellate decisions. **Written by editors.**
Headnotes	Summary identifying specific points of law addressed in the decision. **Written by editors.**
Attorneys	Attorneys representing the parties in the appeal.
Judge	Judge who wrote the opinion.
Introduction and Procedural Facts	Introduction to general legal issues and discussion of how the case started and progressed through the trial and appellate courts.
Facts	Summary of facts that formed the basis for the dispute.
Issue	Legal dispute or question, often summarized in a sentence.
Other Precedents	Older cases discussed in the opinion.
Holding and Rationale	Court's decision and reasoning.
Disposition	Who won or lost and next steps, if any, in the lawsuit.

Cases also include footnotes **that must be read**. Footnotes often include explanations of key legal principles.

Cases are published in books that are referred to as **reporters**. Each reporter contains opinions from different courts. For example, United States Supreme Court decisions are published in the United States Reporter (U.S.), as well as the Supreme Court Reporter (S. Ct.), and the United States Supreme Court Reports, Lawyers' Edition (L. Ed.). The United States Court of Appeals decisions are published in the Federal Reporter (F.) while the United States District Court decisions are published in the Federal Supplement (F. Supp.).

State decisions are sometimes published by the official reporter for the state. They may also be published in one of seven regional reporters, i.e., Atlantic (A.), North Eastern (N.E.), North Western (N.W.), Pacific (P.),

South Eastern (S.E.), Southern (S.), and South Western (S.W.). Most reporters have more than one series that are referred to as 2d, 3d, etc.

Practice Exercise 3.2 provides an opportunity to examine the structure of a reported decision.

C. CASE STRUCTURE: TEXTBOOKS

Cases in law textbooks, sometimes referred to as casebooks, are structured in a similar way. However, as shown in Figure 3.2, there are several differences between reported decisions and cases in casebooks.

Cases in casebooks often do not contain the complete decision. Cases are selected for casebooks to illustrate particular areas of the law. As most decisions deal with multiple topics, portions of a decision may be omitted that do not pertain to the topic addressed in the textbook. For example, the casebook version of *Fisher* (Appendix B-2) omits the section of the reported decision that addressed punitive damages and the liability of the corporation for the torts of its employees because the authors decided to use the case to illustrate only the issues of assault and battery and actual damages.

Figure 3.2
Differences Between Reported Cases and Textbook Cases

Case Components	Reported Cases	Textbook Cases
Complete Decision	Yes	Not always
Edited Text	No	Usually
Headnotes	Yes	No
Case Summary	Yes	Sometimes
Page Numbers	Numbers refer to pages in reporters	Numbers refer to pages in textbook

Cases in casebooks also contain edited versions of sections of the decision. Casebook authors often write summaries of the facts. For example, the first paragraph of the casebook version of *Fisher v. Carrousel Motor Hotel, Inc.*, 424 S.W.2d 627 (Tex. 1967) (Appendix B-2), contains an edited version of the facts. Furthermore, unlike reported decisions, cases in casebooks do not have headnotes.

Finally, page numbers in textbooks are different from page numbers in reporters. The page numbers for cases in textbooks follow the order of the pages in the book. Page numbers in reported decisions are different. As discussed earlier, decisions may be reported in the official reporter for a particular state or a regional reporter. When a case is viewed online, it may have three sets of page numbers: the page numbers from the official reporter, the page numbers from the regional reporter, and the page numbers from the online version of the case. For example, Figure 3.3 shows two sets of page numbers in an excerpt from *Garratt v. Dailey*, 46 Wash. 2d 197, 279 P.2d 1091 (Wash. 1955) (Appendix G). The number that follows the star, 200, is the page number from the official reporter, the Washington Reports, while the number that follows the double star, 1093, is the page number from the regional reporter, the Pacific Reporter. The online version of the opinion contains page numbers in the lower right corner of each page. When referring to a page number in a legal document, use the page number from the official reporter or the regional reporter. Do not use the page number in the lower right corner of the page. The Practice Exercises all reference the regional reporter page numbers.

Figure 3.3
Page Numbers

> It is conceded that Ruth Garratt's fall resulted in a fractured hip and other painful and serious injuries. To obviate ***200** the necessity of a retrial in the event this court determines that she was entitled to a judgment against Brian Dailey, the amount of ****1093** her damage was found to be $11,000. Plaintiff appeals from a judgment dismissing the action and asks for the entry of a judgment in that amount or a new trial.

Practice Exercise 3.3 provides an opportunity to examine the differences between a reported decision and the same case in a casebook. The reported decision for *Fisher v. Carrousel Motor Hotel, Inc.*, 424 S.W.2d 627 (Tex. 1967) (Appendix B-1) can be compared to the casebook version (Appendix B-2).

The reading strategies in the upcoming chapters apply to cases in reported decisions as well as cases in textbooks. However, because there are some differences, additional strategies will be recommended for reported decisions. Law students need to be prepared to read reported decisions because attorneys only read reported decisions.

V. CIVIL AND CRIMINAL PROCEDURE

The second type of background information that assists in understanding cases is the meaning of terms related to civil and criminal procedure. Every court decision contains references to civil or criminal procedure and this chapter demystifies the terminology. This chapter is not meant to provide a complete overview of civil and criminal procedure or focus on procedural terms that are not usually mentioned in court opinions. However, once the reader understands commonly used terms as well as the basic sequence of civil and criminal cases, decisions are easier to follow.

Before exploring procedure, it is important to recognize that there are a variety of rules that regulate civil and criminal procedures in state and federal courts. Federal courts are governed by the Federal Rules of Civil or

Criminal Procedure. Each state has its own procedural rules. In addition, many courts have local procedural rules. The rules of civil or criminal procedure control the progress of a civil case (a dispute between two parties) or a criminal case (a situation where someone is charged with a crime) from the beginning of the case to the resolution of the dispute.

The first set of terms that legal readers must understand are the words used in the rules of procedure to identify the parties. In a civil case, the **plaintiff** is the private person, government or corporation who initiates a lawsuit against another private person, government, or corporation. The **defendant** is the person, government or corporation who is sued. In a criminal case, the government initiates the case. The government may be referred to as a state, commonwealth, the people, or the United States. The **defendant** is the person accused of the crime. Some of the following words are used interchangeably:

> **Plaintiff** or **Petitioner**—party who starts a civil case
>
> **Defendant** or **Respondent**—party who is sued
>
> **Appellant** or **Petitioner**—party who appeals
>
> **Appellee** or **Respondent**—party who won in the trial court and must respond to appellant/petitioner's appeal

The terms **petitioner** and **respondent** are used to identify parties at the trial level as well as the parties to the appeal. Therefore, a petitioner may be the party who starts a civil case and/or the party who appeals.

VI. CIVIL PROCEDURE

The rules of civil procedure outline the steps that are taken during civil litigation. Civil procedure can be divided into five phases:

- **Phase One**—someone brings a lawsuit. Opinions sometimes refer to a lawsuit as an **action**.

- **Phase Two**—the party sued responds to the lawsuit.

- **Phase Three**—the parties get details about each other's case through discovery. Parties may obtain documents, interview witnesses (depositions), or obtain different types of information from the opposing side.

- **Phase Four**—the dispute is resolved.

- **Phase Five**—appeal.

At each stage of a case, parties prepare a variety of documents that are sent to the opposing party and filed with the court. These documents constitute the case record that is examined by an appellate court that reviews the lower court decision. Figure 3.4 outlines the key documents that are often mentioned in civil cases. The documents in the first and second phases are often referred to as **pleadings**, which are the documents that are filed to initiate a case as well as the documents filed by the defendant to respond to the lawsuit.

Figure 3.4
Terminology in Civil Cases

Phase One: Lawsuit Begins	**Summons:** Notice indicating that the plaintiff has filed a lawsuit and the defendant is required to answer the complaint.
	Complaint or Petition: Document filed by the plaintiff that initiates a lawsuit and sets forth facts and legal claims. The complaint must contain a "short and plain statement of the claim showing that the pleader is entitled to relief . . . and the relief sought."[2]
Phase Two: Response to Lawsuit	**Answer:** Response from the defendant to claims made in the complaint.
	Motion to Dismiss or Demurrer: Request to the judge from the defendant to end the case because the complaint does not state a legal claim.
Phase Three: Discovery	**Discovery:** Parties obtain facts and evidence from each other. Parties ask for documents and question witnesses.
Phase Four: Resolution of Dispute	**Motion for Summary Judgment:** Request to end the lawsuit without a trial because there are no factual disputes and one side is entitled to win based upon the law.
	Trial: The court or jury hears testimony from witnesses and reviews other evidence submitted by the parties.
	Motion for Directed Verdict or Judgment as a Matter of Law: Request to dismiss the lawsuit after the plaintiff has presented testimony because there is not sufficient evidence to award judgment.
	Jury Instructions and Verdict: Instructions provide the jury with the law that is the basis for their decision or verdict.
	Judgment Notwithstanding the Verdict. (JNOV): Request for the court to grant judgment to one side despite a contrary ruling by the jury.
	Opinion and Judgment: Decision of the court.

---

[2]   Fed. R. Civ. P. 8(a).

Phase Five: Appeals	**Appeal:** Party applies to higher court for different decision. **Court of Appeals or Supreme Court:** Depending upon the jurisdiction, there may be an intermediate and highest appellate court. **Briefs:** Documents filed by the parties setting forth the legal basis for the appeal. **Disposition:** The appellate court may reverse (decide lower court decision is incorrect) or affirm (uphold) the lower court decision or remand (send the case back to the trial court for further action).

The flowchart in Figure 3.5 outlines the basic elements of civil procedure. While there are many variations in the progress of a civil lawsuit, most civil cases follow these basic procedures.

Figure 3.5
Civil Procedure Flowchart

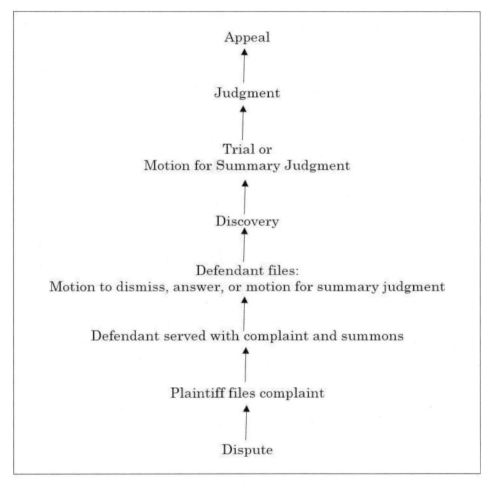

As it is easier to understand procedure and learn terms by looking at actual legal documents, samples of different documents are included in this section. Joe Parker's dispute with Smith Cars from Chapters 1 and 2 is used as the basis for these documents. After meeting with Mr. Parker and researching the law, you determine that Mr. Parker has a claim against Smith Cars and Karen Jones (the mechanic who grabbed his phone) for the intentional tort of battery. Mr. Parker provided the following information about the incident that was substantiated by investigators.

Joe Parker recently purchased a used car from Smith Cars. After having numerous problems with the car, Parker decided to try to document the problems he was having with Smith Cars. Mr. Parker brought his car in to have the brakes repaired. Smith Cars said it would be permissible for Parker to walk into the garage area while the repairs were being made. Once in the garage, Parker took out his phone and began to take pictures of the mechanic working on the brakes. The mechanic, Karen Jones, was not pleased, told him to stop photographing anything, and grabbed the phone. Parker fell backwards when the mechanic grabbed the phone, and he hurt his back. Parker stated that he was embarrassed and humiliated by the incident. Parker wants to sue the mechanic and the car dealer.

A. PHASE ONE: LAWSUIT BEGINS

Most civil cases begin with the filing of a document called a **complaint** or a **petition**. The complaint sets forth:

1. the **names** of the parties bringing the case and the parties being sued,

2. the **facts** underlying the dispute,

3. the **legal claims** that justify the lawsuit,

4. the **injury** suffered, and

5. the **relief requested**, i.e., what the parties bringing the lawsuit want.

The complaint alleges that the plaintiff has a legal claim, an enforceable legal right, against another party. Complaints may involve a contract dispute, a negligence case, a constitutional issue, or other types of claims.

Figure 3.6 is an example of a complaint[3] that could be filed in a civil case by Joe Parker against Karen Jones and Smith Cars.

---

[3] While complaints in federal court must contain a paragraph detailing the **jurisdiction** (or power of the court to hear the case), this is generally not required in state courts. However, the complaint must allege sufficient facts to show that the case can be brought in the particular state court. As the Circuit Court in Kentucky can only hear cases involving more than $5,000 in claimed damages, the complaint in this example had to claim damages in excess of this amount to be filed in Circuit Court.

Figure 3.6
Complaint

COMMONWEALTH OF KENTUCKY
FAYETTE CIRCUIT COURT
FIFTH DIVISION
ACTION NO. 16-AD-0001

JOE PARKER,   Plaintiff

   VS.   **COMPLAINT**

KAREN JONES and SMITH CARS,   Defendants

Plaintiff Joe Parker, by his attorneys, Jones and Jones, complaining of the defendants, alleges as follows:

   1.   Plaintiff Joe Parker resides at 251 Snaffle Avenue, Lexington, Kentucky.

   2.   Defendant Smith Cars is located at 55 South Drive, Lexington, Kentucky.

   3.   Karen Jones is employed by Smith Cars and resides at 2450 Main Street, Lexington, Kentucky.

   4.   On December 15, 2015, at 3 PM, the defendant Karen Jones intentionally grabbed the plaintiff's cell phone causing him humiliation. As a result, plaintiff was injured, suffered pain, and had medical expenses amounting to $6,000.

   WHEREFORE, plaintiff demands judgment against the defendant for damages, costs, and disbursements.

Date: Lexington, Kentucky
        August 1, 2016
                                        _____
                                        Sally Attorney
                                        300 Main Street
                                        Lexington, Kentucky

B.   PHASE TWO: RESPONSE TO LAWSUIT

1.   Motion to Dismiss

After the **complaint** is filed, the defendants (the parties sued), must respond to the complaint. They may file a **motion to dismiss**. A **motion** is a request that a court take specific action. A **motion to dismiss** is a request that the court end the litigation. One ground for filing a motion to dismiss is that the facts alleged in the complaint fail to set forth a legal claim.[4] The defendant claims that even assuming all of the facts in the complaint are true, there is no legal basis for the claims. In the Parker example, the defendants might claim that even if Jones grabbed Parker's phone, this type of interaction does not amount to battery. A motion to dismiss is shown in Figure 3.7.[5]

Figure 3.7
Motion to Dismiss

COMMONWEALTH OF KENTUCKY
FAYETTE CIRCUIT COURT
FIFTH DIVISION
ACTION NO. 16-AD-0001

JOE PARKER,	Plaintiff
VS.	**MOTION TO DISMISS**
KAREN JONES and SMITH CARS,	Defendants

Please take notice that upon the annexed memorandum of law, and upon all of the papers and proceedings herein, the undersigned will move this Court at a motion term thereof to be held at the Circuit Courthouse, Lexington, Kentucky, on the 20th day of September 2016 at 10 am, or as soon thereafter as counsel may be heard, for an order pursuant to Rule 12.02(f) of the Kentucky Rules of Civil Procedure dismissing the action because the complaint fails to state a claim against defendants upon which relief can be granted.

Date: Lexington, Kentucky
        September 1, 2016

                                        _____

                                        Mary Attorney
                                        200 Main Street
                                        Lexington, Kentucky

---

2. Answer

If the motion to dismiss is not successful or if the motion is not filed, the defendants file an answer to the complaint. In the **answer**, the defendants respond to each paragraph in the complaint and set forth defenses they have to the lawsuit. An answer is shown in Figure 3.8.

---

[4]   The federal rule is Fed. R. Civ. P. 12(b)(6). As seen in Figure 3.7, the Kentucky rule is different.

[5]   The motion to dismiss would be accompanied by a brief or memorandum setting forth the legal arguments in support of the motion.

Figure 3.8
Answer

COMMONWEALTH OF KENTUCKY
FAYETTE CIRCUIT COURT
FIFTH DIVISION
ACTION NO. 16-AD-0001

JOE PARKER,   Plaintiff

     VS.   **ANSWER**

KAREN JONES and SMITH CARS,   Defendants

Defendants, by their attorneys, answer the complaint as follows:

1. Deny knowledge or information sufficient to form a belief as to the truth of the allegations in paragraph 1 of the complaint.

2. Admit the allegations in paragraphs 2 and 3 of the complaint.

3. Deny the allegations in paragraph 4 of the complaint.

DEFENSE

4. The complaint fails to state a claim on which relief can be granted.

WHEREFORE, defendants demand judgment dismissing the complaint and granting such other and further relief as this Court deems proper, including costs and disbursements.

Date: Lexington, Kentucky
        November 1, 2016

                         _____

                         Mary Attorney
                         200 Main Street
                         Lexington, Kentucky

C. PHASE THREE: DISCOVERY

After the defendant files an answer, the parties engage in discovery which means that they try to get details about the facts in the case that are in the possession of the opposing party. In the course of discovery, the parties may serve each other with **interrogatories** (questions), take **depositions** (question parties or witnesses under oath), and request documents such as medical records. Terms related to discovery are usually not referenced in appellate decisions unless the dispute deals directly with discovery issues.

D. PHASE FOUR: RESOLUTION OF DISPUTE

Lawsuits are resolved in a variety of ways. Sometimes, parties try to win a case by submitting motions such as motions for summary judgment, judgment on the pleadings, or directed verdict. These motions are explained in this section. On other occasions, the case is tried by the court or a jury. Very often, a case is resolved when the parties decide to enter into a settlement agreement.

During the course of a case, courts may issue **Orders** to resolve motions and direct parties to take specific actions. Courts may also issue opinions that explain their decisions. At the end of the case, the court issues a **Judgment**, which is a document that outlines the rights of the parties. The difference between an Order and a **Judgment** is that an Order decides one specific aspect of a case while a Judgment resolves the entire case.

1. Motion for Summary Judgment

Before trial, one party will often file a **motion for summary judgment**[6] or a **motion for judgment on the pleadings**.[7] A motion for summary judgment is an application to the court for judgment where a party claims that there is no factual dispute and he/she is entitled to win based upon the law. Motions for summary judgment are usually supported by affidavits. A motion for judgment on the pleadings is similar to a motion for summary judgment. However, a motion for judgment on the pleadings only considers the pleadings in the case (usually the complaint and answer) and no other documents. Figure 3.9 is a motion for summary judgment.

---

[6]   The federal rule is Fed. R. Civ. P. 56.

[7]   The federal rule is Fed. R. Civ. P. 12(c). The motion for summary judgment or judgment on the pleadings would normally be accompanied by a brief or memorandum.

Figure 3.9
Motion for Summary Judgment

COMMONWEALTH OF KENTUCKY
FAYETTE CIRCUIT COURT
FIFTH DIVISION
ACTION NO. 16-AD-0001

JOE PARKER, Plaintiff

VS. **MOTION FOR SUMMARY JUDGMENT**

KAREN JONES and SMITH CARS, Defendants

Plaintiff, by his attorneys and pursuant to Rule 56 of the Kentucky Rules of Civil Procedure, moves this court to enter summary judgment for the plaintiff on the ground that there is no genuine issue as to any material fact, and the plaintiff is entitled to judgment as a matter of law.

In support of this motion, plaintiff refers to the record including the complaint, the answer, and plaintiff's annexed affidavit sworn to on the 15th day of November, 2016.

Date: Lexington, Kentucky
December 1, 2016

_____

Sally Attorney
300 Main Street
Lexington, Kentucky

2. Other Motions, Jury Instructions, and Judgment

If the case is not resolved by motion, the case will be set for **trial** before the court or a jury. After testimony is presented to the court or jury, the opposing party may make a motion for a **directed verdict** or for **judgment as a matter of law**.[8] In this motion, one party argues that the case should be dismissed because sufficient evidence was not presented to the jury or court to establish a legal claim.

At the end of the testimony, juries receive **instructions** so that they know what law to apply in deciding the case. Sometimes appellate decisions will reference these instructions if parties disagree regarding the underlying law.

After the jury issues its decision or verdict, the losing party can file a **Motion for Judgment Notwithstanding the Verdict (JNOV)** which is a request for the court to grant judgment to one side despite a contrary ruling by the jury. This happened in the *Fisher* case. The jury ruled in favor of Fisher, and the defendants filed a motion for judgment notwithstanding the verdict claiming that the judgment of the jury was based on incorrect

---

8   Fed. R. Civ. P. 50(a).

law. In *Fisher*, the trial court granted that motion as explained in its opinion.

The **Judgment** is the document that outlines the final resolution of the case. Figure 3.10 is a sample judgment.

Figure 3.10
Judgment

COMMONWEALTH OF KENTUCKY
FAYETTE CIRCUIT COURT
FIFTH DIVISION
ACTION NO. 16-AD-0001

JOE PARKER,   Plaintiff

    VS.   **JUDGMENT**

KAREN JONES and SMITH CARS,   Defendants

    This action having come on for trial before the Honorable June Smith, Circuit Court Judge, and the issues having been duly tried and the Court having duly rendered its decision on December 15, 2016, it is hereby

    ORDERED, ADJUDGED, AND DECREED, that the Plaintiff is awarded judgment against the Defendants and the Plaintiff shall have and recover the costs of the action from the Defendants.

Dated: Lexington, Kentucky
      December 20, 2016   _____

                               Circuit Judge

E. PHASE FIVE: APPEALS

Once the trial court issues its decision, a party may decide to appeal. The parties file briefs to set forth their arguments in the appeal. In the federal system, there are two levels of appeal, the United States Court of Appeals and the United States Supreme Court. In state court systems, there may be one, two, or three levels of appeal. The appellate opinion generally discusses all prior appeals in the case.

The appellate court can affirm the decision of the lower court, reverse, or remand. Remand means that the appellate court sends the case back to the lower court with specific instructions regarding the procedures or actions that need to be taken.

Practice Exercise 3.4 provides the opportunity to identify civil procedure terms in an actual case.

VII.　CRIMINAL PROCEDURE

Criminal law opinions often contain basic criminal procedure terms. Figure 3.11 contains a list of some key terms.

Figure 3.11
Terminology in Criminal Cases

Complaint, Warrant or Summons	Statement charging individual with criminal violation. "Counts" refers to the parts or charges in the complaint.
Preliminary Hearing	Hearing to determine if there is probable cause to try the defendant.
Indictment	Grand jury's written accusation charging a person or corporation with a crime.
Arraignment	Court appearance of party accused of a crime to hear charges and to enter plea of guilty or not guilty.
Motion to Suppress	Request that the court refuse to allow a particular piece of evidence to be admitted at trial.
Motion for Directed Verdict	Request for dismissal because there is no legally sufficient basis for a reasonable jury to reach a different conclusion. Directed verdict may be granted at any time, but usually occurs after one party has presented testimony.
Jury Instructions and Verdict	Instructions provided to the jury before deliberation that provide the law for the jury's decision. Verdict is the jury's decision.
Opinion and Judgment	Decision of the court.

A flowchart outlining basic criminal procedure is set forth in Figure 3.12. The order of criminal proceedings may be different in each state or jurisdiction.

Figure 3.12
Criminal Procedure Flowchart

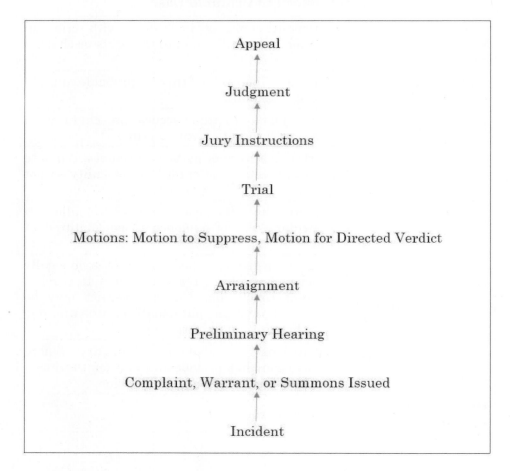

Practice Exercise 3.4 is an opportunity to identify criminal procedural terms in a criminal case. Practice Exercise 3.6 is the self-assessment exercise for this chapter that will allow you to apply your knowledge of case structure and procedure to a new problem.

VIII.   CASE EXAMPLE: CASE STRUCTURE AND CIVIL PROCEDURE

Case structure and civil procedure are explained using *Fisher v. Carrousel Motor Hotel, Inc.*, 424 S.W.2d 627 (Tex. 1967) (Appendix B-1).

Appendix B-1 contains annotations that point out the structure of the opinion.

A. CASE STRUCTURE

1. Citation

As seen in Figure 3.13, a shortened citation is provided on the first page of the decision. This citation provides the reader with the **volume number** of the reporter, the abbreviated name of the reporter, and the **first page** of the decision. *Fisher* was published in volume 424 of the South Western Reporter 2d (abbreviated S.W.2d) and the first page of the opinion is found on page 627.

When a case is referred to in a legal opinion or a memorandum or brief submitted to the court, the full citation is provided and includes the names of the parties as well as the volume number, reporter, first page of the decision, the court, and the year of the decision. The full citation of *Fisher* is ***Fisher v. Carrousel Motor Hotel, Inc.*, 424 S.W.2d 627 (Tex. 1967)**.

Figure 3.13
Citation, Caption, Date, Case Summary

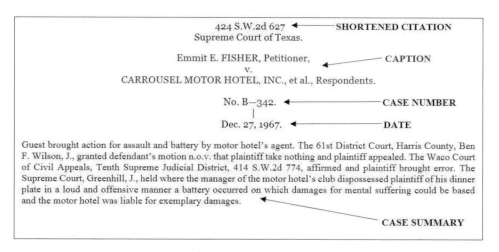

2. Caption

As seen in Figure 3.13, the caption contains the **names of the parties** to the appeal as well as the **court** and **case number**. In *Fisher,* the caption contains the name of the Petitioner (the party who brought the appeal), Emmit E. Fisher, as well the names of the Respondents (the parties who won in the lower court). The caption also includes the case number for the appeal, No. B-342, which is used to locate the case in the court files, as well as the name of the appellate court, the Supreme Court of Texas.

3.   Date

Figure 3.13 shows the decision date in the caption. *Fisher* was decided on December 27, 1967.

4.   Case Summary

The **case summary**, which is the first paragraph following the caption, is found in Figure 3.13. This summary of the case was written by editors, not the court, and may **never** be quoted or cited in a legal document.

5.   Headnotes

Figure 3.14 is a sample headnote from *Fisher*. Headnotes are summaries of particular areas of law found in an opinion. Each headnote contains a topic, number, and summary. Headnotes can be used to find additional cases relating to a topic. The **headnote, number, and summary may never be quoted** in any legal document as they are written by editors, not the court. There are ten headnotes in the *Fisher* case that reference topics such as assault and battery, damages, master and servant, and principal and agent. Figure 3.14 shows the first headnote in *Fisher* that relates to assault and battery.

Figure 3.14
Headnote

> "[1]   **Assault and Battery**
>   Nature and Elements of Assault and Battery
>
> Actual physical contact is not necessary to constitute a battery so long as there is contact with clothing or an object closely identified with the body. *Fisher*, 424 S.W.2d at 627.

6.   Attorneys and Judge

Figure 3.15 shows that the names of the attorneys and the judge who wrote the opinion can be found before the opinion starts. Sometimes the term **per curiam** is used instead of a judge's name. This means that the decision was a unanimous ruling by an entire panel of judges.

Figure 3.15
Attorneys and Judge

Attorneys and Law Firms

Ben G. Levy, Houston, for petitioner.

Vinson, Elkins, Weems & Searls, Raybourne Thompson, Jr. and B. Jeff Crane, Jr., Houston, for respondents.

Opinion

GREENHILL, Justice.

This is a suit for actual and exemplary damages growing out of an alleged assault and battery.

---

7. Introduction and Procedural Facts

Cases generally start with a reference to the subject of the case. *Fisher* starts with the following introduction:

> "This is a suit for actual and exemplary damages growing out of an alleged assault and battery." *Fisher*, 424 S.W.2d at 628.

This means that Fisher sued for money damages because he claimed that he was subjected to assault and battery. The court then summarizes the procedural facts, the facts related to the case's progression through the courts.

8. Facts

The facts underlying the case are in the first and second paragraphs of the opinion. Analyzing facts is examined more fully in Chapter 5.

9. Issue

The issue or dispute in *Fisher* is at the end of the first paragraph where the opinion states that the:

> "questions before this Court are whether there was evidence that an actionable battery was committed, and, if so, whether the two corporate defendants must respond in exemplary as well as actual damages for the malicious conduct of Flynn." *Fisher*, 424 S.W.2d at 628.

The court addresses three separate issues related to battery, actual damages, and exemplary or punitive damages. Techniques for finding issues are addressed in Chapter 7.

10. Other Precedents

Courts reference other cases because in the American common law system, judicial decisions are based upon precedent, i.e., older court decisions. Courts must follow decisions from higher level courts in the same jurisdiction. The concept of precedent is discussed more fully in Chapter 5. *Fisher* references other precedents such as *Morgan v. Loyacomo* and *S.H. Kress & Co. v. Brashier*.

11. Holding and Rationale

After discussing precedents, the court in *Fisher* issues its decision (the holding) as well as the rationale or reasoning for the decision. In *Fisher*, there are decisions on three different issues. The holding on battery is located at the top of page 630, the holding on actual damages is found on page 630, and the decision on exemplary or punitive damages is found on page 631.

Very often, courts explain their rationale or reasoning by discussing prior cases. Courts will sometimes examine policy considerations that support the decision. The *Fisher* court's rationale for battery is explained on page 629, the rationale for the damages decision is found on page 630, and the reasoning behind the exemplary damages decision is found on page 631. Holdings and reasoning are discussed more fully in Chapter 7.

12. Disposition

The outcome of the case is usually explained with the terms affirmance, reversal, or remand. In *Fisher*, the court reversed the judgment of the lower court and awarded judgment to the plaintiff. This means that the jury verdict of $900 was reinstated.

13. Page Numbers

As discussed in this chapter, in the online version of a case, the page numbers from the regional reporter are highlighted in bold and can be found following a star. Figure 3.16 shows the beginning of page 628. It is important to note these page numbers when citing or referring to a case in a legal document.

Figure 3.16
Page Numbers

Attorneys and Law Firms ⟵———— **PAGE NUMBER**

*628 Ben G. Levy, Houston, for petitioner.

Vinson, Elkins, Weems & Searls, Raybourne Thompson, Jr. and B. Jeff Crane, Jr., Houston, for respondents.

Opinion

GREENHILL, Justice.

This is a suit for actual and exemplary damages growing out of an alleged assault and battery.

B. CIVIL PROCEDURE

Fisher began with the filing of a complaint. The opinion does not indicate whether the defendants filed an answer or made a motion to dismiss. The opinion indicates that there was a jury trial that awarded judgment to Fisher. After this verdict, the trial court granted defendants' motion for judgment notwithstanding the verdict, which means that the trial court reversed the decision of the jury and the defendants won the case at the trial level. Fisher appealed to the intermediate appellate court in Texas where he lost and the Supreme Court of Texas where he won.

IX. PRACTICE

Reflection Exercise 3.1
Writing an Opinion

Goal: While cases have a consistent structure, it is not necessary to memorize this structure. The goal of this exercise is to think in practical terms and reflect on the types of information a judge might include in a decision so that litigants and appellate courts would understand the basis for the opinion.

We met Joe Parker in Chapters 1 and 2 because he consulted with us regarding a possible battery case against Smith Cars. In this exercise, you are now the appellate judge who is deciding Mr. Parker's case. For purposes of this exercise, assume the following information is now available to you regarding the case:

> Joe Parker recently purchased a used car from Smith Cars in Lexington, Kentucky. After having numerous problems with the car, Parker decided to try to document the problems he was having with the used car dealer. Parker brought his car in to have the brakes repaired. The dealer said it would be permissible for Parker to walk into the garage area while the repairs were being

completed. Once in the garage, Parker took out his phone and began to take pictures of the mechanic working on the brakes. The mechanic, Karen Jones, was not pleased, told him to stop photographing, and grabbed the phone. Parker fell backwards when Jones grabbed his phone. Parker stated that he was humiliated and embarrassed as a result of the incident and also injured his back. Mr. Parker filed a lawsuit against Smith Cars and the mechanic Karen Jones. The lawsuit claimed that Smith Cars and Karen Jones were liable for the tort of battery. The trial court decided that Parker had a claim for battery against defendants because Karen Jones intentionally made contact with Parker's phone that he was holding and the contact was offensive and humiliating to Parker. The trial court based its ruling on a decision of the Kentucky Supreme Court. The defendants have appealed claiming that battery did not occur because Karen Jones intended to touch the phone, not Parker.

Step 1: As the appellate judge, list the types of information you would incorporate in your decision. For example, it would probably be useful to reference the underlying facts related to the dispute. What else would you include?

Opinion

Step 2: How would you order the opinion?

Order
1.
2.
3.
4.
5.

Practice Exercise 3.2
Case Structure Exercise

Goal: The purpose of this exercise is to provide practice in determining how cases are structured. The goal is also to recognize which parts of decisions can be quoted in legal documents because they are written by judges and which parts cannot be quoted because they are written by editors.

Assume that you are doing some additional research into the law of battery for Mr. Parker's case and have found the case *Wishnatsky v. Huey*, 584 N.W.2d 859 (N.D. Ct. App. 1998). (The reported decision is found in Appendix D.) Review the case to see how it is structured. Then complete the following chart and indicate whether or not the particular case element can be quoted in a legal document.

Case Element	*Wishnatsky*	Can Element Be Quoted in Legal Document?
3.2–1 What is the **citation**?		
3.2–2 Who are the parties identified in the **caption**?		
3.2–3 What **court** decided the case?		
3.2–4 What is the decision **date**?		
3.2–5 Is there a **case summary**?		
3.2–6 How many **headnotes** are there?		
3.2–7 Who was the **Judge**?		
3.2–8 Are the dispute **facts** at the beginning of the decision?		
3.2–9 Does the court discuss other cases?		
3.2–10 Is the **disposition** at the end of the decision?		

Practice Exercise 3.3
Differences Between Reported Cases and Textbook Cases

Goal: This exercise provides the opportunity to understand the differences between reported decisions and cases in textbooks.

In this exercise, you will compare the reported decision and edited casebook decision of *Fisher v. Carrousel Motor Hotel, Inc.*, 424 S.W.2d 627 (Tex. 1967). The reported decision that would be used in doing legal research and would be relied upon by practicing attorneys is found in Appendix B-1. The edited version from a torts casebook is found in Appendix B-2. Compare the two versions of *Fisher* and complete the following chart:

Decision	Casebook	Reported Decision
3.3–1 How many paragraphs are in the decision?		
3.3–2 Does the decision contain a **summary** written by an editor?		
3.3–3 Does the decision contain **headnotes** written by an editor?		
3.3–4 Does the decision contain **facts** written by the judge?		
3.3–5 Which version of the case is easier to read?		

Practice Exercise 3.4
Civil Procedure

Goal: This goal of this exercise is to pick out procedural terms in a civil case. While it is tempting to avoid reading these unfamiliar terms, you will gain a greater understanding of the meaning of a case when you understand these words.

Assume that you are continuing to read *Wishnatsky v. Huey*, 584 N.W.2d 859 (N.D. Ct. App. 1998) (Appendix D) to understand battery and represent Mr. Parker. Circle all references to civil procedure terms in the first paragraph of page 860 of the opinion. Remember that the regional reporter page numbers are used to refer to pages in an opinion. Page 860 starts before the words "PER CURIAM." After circling the civil procedure terms, list and define the terms.

Civil Procedure Terms	Definitions
3.4–1	
3.4–2	
3.4–3	
3.4–4	

Practice Exercise 3.5
Criminal Procedure

Goal: This exercise focuses attention on procedural terms in a criminal case.

Haynes v. Commonwealth, 657 S.W.2d 948 (Ky. 1983) (Appendix E) is a criminal case that includes criminal procedure terms. Complete the following chart:

Case Element	*Haynes*
3.5–1 What is the **citation**?	
3.5–2 Who are the parties in the **caption**?	
3.5–3 What **court** decided the case?	
3.5–4 Can the summary that follows the date be cited in a legal document?	
3.5–5 There is a reference to "two counts" in the first sentence of the opinion. What document contains these two counts?	

Practice Exercise 3.6
Self-Assessment

Goal: In this exercise, you can determine if you understand the structure of cases and terminology related to civil procedure.

For this exercise, assume that you are still representing Ms. Evelyn Michel, who has been terminated from her employment as a nurse because she failed the National Council Licensure Examination. Ms. Michel wants to know if she will qualify for unemployment insurance benefits. *De Grego v. Levine,* 347 N.E.2d 611 (N.Y. 1976) (Appendix C) provides guidance on this subject.

As you read *De Grego,* notice the structure of the case and references to procedure. In analyzing the procedure in the opinion, be aware that this was an appeal from an administrative proceeding rather than a trial court. Rather than filing a complaint to start this lawsuit, De Grego applied for unemployment benefits. After he was denied benefits, he filed an appeal to a referee who functioned as the trial judge. The referee also denied De Grego's application for benefits and De Grego appealed to the Unemployment Insurance Appeal Board. The Unemployment Insurance Appeal Board denied benefits and De Grego appealed to the Appellate Division as appeals from decisions of the Unemployment Insurance Appeal Board go to the Appellate Division, the intermediate appellate court in New York.

3.6–1   Does the case start with any introductory statements that outline the general subject matter of the case?

3.6–2   Are the facts found towards the beginning of the case?

3.6–3   Does the court analyze previous opinions on the subject of provoked discharge in the middle of the opinion?

3.6–4   Which courts reviewed the decision of the Unemployment Insurance Appeal Board and what actions did they take?

Evaluate your understanding of the skills in this chapter by completing the following rubric. For each skill, circle whether you are at the proficient or developing level. Everyone can get to the proficient level over time.

Skill	Competency Level	
	Proficient	**Developing**
Understands that cases have a predictable structure.	• Can locate the caption at the beginning of the opinion. • Understands that the facts are usually at the beginning of the opinion. • Understands that the court's disposition is usually at the end of the opinion.	• Assumes that every case is structured differently. • Does not know where the names of the parties, facts, and disposition are usually located.
Understands civil and criminal procedure terms.	• Pays attention to procedural terms.	• Skips over procedural terms.

CHAPTER 4

BEFORE READING: CONTEXT AND OVERVIEW

I. SUMMARY

This chapter focuses on how legal readers:

- use their knowledge of the general subject of a case to place a case in context, and

- skim a case quickly for a general overview before reading more carefully.

At the conclusion of this chapter, you will be able to:

- understand the general subject of a case before reading more carefully, and

- skim a case for an overview.

II. CHECKLIST

CASE READING CHECKLIST

Warning: Do not just highlight and underline.

Phase 1: Before Reading

1. Read for a purpose and assume the role of advocate or judge.

2. Read with energy and focus.

3. Notice case structure.

4. **Understand the general subject matter by examining:**

   a. **course syllabus, casebook table of contents, or research assignment, and**

   b. **parties, citation, court, and date.**

5. **Read for an overview by skimming and noticing organization, headings, who won, and what case is generally about.**

Phase 2: Reading More Carefully

1. Understand the facts.

---

2. Reread, look up unfamiliar words, analyze confusing language, and vary reading speed.

3. Understand the main ideas set forth in the issue, holding, and reasoning.

4. Identify the rule.

5. Take notes with your reactions and brief the case.

Phase 3: After Reading

1. Evaluate the decision, ask questions, and talk with professors.

2. Determine how cases fit together with other cases and synthesize.

III. A NOTE ABOUT THE CHECKLIST WARNING

The reading checklist at the beginning of each chapter contains an important warning. *Do not just highlight and underline.* Every research study that has been conducted on critical reading in law school has concluded that students who **only** highlight and underline cases consistently perform at a lower level than students who

• understand the purpose for reading cases (Chapter 1),

• read as an advocate (Chapter 2),

• understand the structure of cases (Chapter 3), and

• utilize the reading strategies that will be discussed in this and upcoming chapters.

While some highlighting and underlining can be helpful, that strategy alone is not effective.

IV. CASE CONTEXT

A. THINKING ABOUT CONTEXT

The term context refers to the setting or facts that surround a situation or event. If we have general information or even just the name of an event, it is easier to understand what will be happening. For example, if we are told we are going to a basketball game, the term basketball triggers a host of associations. We know that there will be two teams, five players on a team, an orange ball, and lots of enthusiastic fans.

We use context to better understand a variety of situations, from understanding the meaning of words to picking out movies. When we use context to understand the meaning of words, we look at the words surrounding a term to figure out the definition of a word we do not know.

For example, if a reader was not familiar with the word "plaintiff," it would be possible to find the meaning of the term in the following sentence:

> The plaintiff, the person who initiated the lawsuit, is very interested in knowing when the trial will be scheduled.

The words surrounding the word plaintiff help explain its meaning. We can also use context to select a movie. If we want to watch a comedy rather than a horror film, the comedy category helps predict the subject of the movie and the types of events that will take place in the movie.

Context is also a powerful reading comprehension strategy. Readers can use context to understand text and make sense of new information. The simple step of looking at a title can improve comprehension because the reader becomes aware of the general topic of the book. Readers who read the table of contents have better comprehension because it helps them understand the organization of the book and the subjects in each section.

Research studies show that context has a positive impact on comprehension. In one study, a group of readers was presented with **only a paragraph** about a topic while another group was given the **paragraph and the title**. The group who read the paragraph with the title had higher comprehension scores.

Try this out for yourself. Read the paragraph in Figure 4.1 and try to answer the questions that follow.

Figure 4.1
Context Paragraph

The following procedure can eliminate confusion. Study the available space. Divide items by the appropriate season. Make sure that items are easily available. The characteristics of the items will determine where they are placed. The height of the user may also affect placement of the items.

- What procedure is being referred to?
- What does "available space" mean?
- Who is the user?

Now read the same paragraph with a title. Are the questions easier to answer?

Figure 4.2
Context Paragraph with Title

Organizing a Closet

The following procedure can eliminate confusion. Study the available space. Divide items by the appropriate season. Make sure that items are easily available. The characteristics of the items will determine where they are placed. The height of the user may also affect placement of the items.

- What procedure is being referred to?
- What does "available space" mean?
- Who is the user?

The second paragraph is easier to understand and the vague words now have a clearer meaning because the title provides a context for the entire paragraph. The title "surrounds" the text and helps us understand the general meaning of the paragraph before we even begin to read.

Before examining context strategies involving cases, think about context clues in crossword puzzles. Is the puzzle in Figure 4.3 easier to solve with or without the clues?

Figure 4.3
Context Clues

Puzzle with no context clues:	Puzzle with context clues:
Across	**Across**
1. type of fruit	1. type of fruit (color is orange)
2. type of transportation	2. type of transportation (goes in the air)

It is easier to solve the puzzle with the clues because the clues give us a framework and a way of focusing attention on a more limited range of choices. The clues also draw on our past experiences and knowledge of fruits and transportation so that we can make better predictions. Good legal readers use context to help focus attention on the precise topic of a case.

B. GENERAL CONTEXT STRATEGIES

We use context strategies in everyday reading. Most of the time, we use these techniques automatically. As set out in Figure 4.4, we read titles, tables of contents, and headings. We might look at summaries or abstracts and charts. It helps to notice dates and authors. Prefixes and suffixes can also assist in understanding the meaning of words.

Figure 4.4
Context Strategies

Titles, headings, or tables of contents
Abstracts or summaries of articles
Charts or photographs
Dates
Author
Word parts such as roots, prefixes, suffixes

All of these strategies are useful for reading cases. Reflection Exercise 4.1 gives you the opportunity to think about context strategies that have helped you understand text in the past.

C.   EXPERT LEGAL READERS USE CONTEXT

Expert legal readers use context to understand the type of case they are reading before they begin to read. One study (Lundeberg) compared the reading strategies of twelve law professors and lawyers with twelve non-lawyers who had master's degrees and were good readers. While all of the lawyers used context strategies so that they knew "before reading the case that it was a contracts case," only one non-lawyer used context to recognize that the case dealt with contracts.[1] As shown in Figure 4.5, the lawyers put the case in context by noticing case headings, the parties, the court, the date, and the name of the judge, while the non-lawyers generally did not. While most of the professors "noticed the parties involved in the cases," many of the non-lawyers did not.[2] Because the non-lawyers ignored the names of the parties, they were sometimes confused about who was suing whom.[3]

Figure 4.5
Context: Lundeberg Study

Context Strategy	Lawyers	Non-Lawyers
Headings	10	1
Parties	9	4
Type of court	9	1
Date	9	1
Judge's name	8	0

---

[1] Mary A. Lundeberg, *Metacognitive Aspects of Reading Comprehension: Studying Understanding in Legal Case Analysis*, 22 Reading Res. Q. 407, 412 (1987).

[2] *Id.*

[3] *Id.* at 413.

Another study (Oates) that compared the reading strategies of a law professor with beginning legal readers found that only the law professor put "the cases into their historical and legal context."[4] A third study (Christensen) also found that top performing students used context by noticing the court and type of case, while the lower performing students did not.[5] The Christensen study results are described in Figure 4.6.

Figure 4.6
Context: Christensen Study

Student	Context
Student (Top 10%)	"**All right this case is in Indiana and it comes from the northeastern quarter** *in the matter of Victor H.S. 02S009902 VI 151. The Supreme Court of Indiana.* **So this would be the highest court.**"[6]
Student (Top 10%)	"**OK. This case is from the Supreme Court of Indiana. August 22, 2000.** *It's in the matter of Richard J. Thonert. Disciplinary proceeding was brought against attorney in which disciplinary commission and attorney entered statement of circumstances and conditional agreement for discipline.* **It sounds a little juicy. Attorney on trial.**"[7]
Student (Bottom 10%)	"**The first thing is I would take out—I would take out my green marker, which means [holding] . . . and I would mark-the Supreme Court would get a thick line, and then I would try to break up the different phrases of that sentence so that it would be easier to pick up with the explanation, but it's all in one sentence and it's kind of confusingly written.**"[8]

V. CONTEXT STRATEGIES IN CASES

Context clues keep expert readers on track so they can focus on the precise topic in a case. When students read without understanding the subject of a case, it is easy to get sidetracked and start focusing on issues

---

[4]   Laurel Currie Oates, *Leveling the Playing Field: Helping Students Succeed by Helping Them Learn to Read as Expert Readers*, 80 St. John's L. Rev. 227, 233 (2006).

[5]   Leah M. Christensen, *"One L of a Year": How to Maximize Your Success in Law School* 32 (2012).

[6]   *Id.* at 33.

[7]   *Id.*

[8]   *Id.* at 33–34.

that are not significant. As seen in Figure 4.7, certain context strategies are useful for cases in casebooks, other techniques are appropriate for reported decisions, and some strategies can be used for all cases.

Figure 4.7
Case Context Strategies

Context Strategy	Case in Casebook	Reported Decision
Consult casebook table of contents	Yes	No
Read course syllabus	Yes	Yes
Review client assignment	Yes	Yes
Read case summary	No	Yes
Check headnotes	No	Yes
Consult secondary sources	Yes	Yes
Notice parties, court, judge, date	Yes	Yes

A.   CASES IN CASEBOOKS

For cases in casebooks, there are two ways to understand the general subject of a case and place it in context.

First, the **table of contents** sets forth the general topics for each chapter and the general subjects that the cases in each chapter illustrate. The table of contents contains information that "surrounds" the cases and can be used to help understand their meaning. For example, many tort casebooks include *Fisher*, and the table of contents indicates that the case is in the intentional torts section as an example of battery. Before a reader even begins reading the case, the reader who consults the table of contents would know that a key topic relates to battery.

Second, the **course syllabus** provides valuable clues regarding the subject of a case. In most tort syllabi, *Fisher* would be included as an example of the intentional tort of battery.

B.   REPORTED DECISIONS

For cases in reporters, different strategies must be used because reporters do not contain:

- ready-made tables of contents, or
- cases that are edited to focus on one topic.

In *Fisher*, as noted in Chapter 3, the full reported opinion dealt with battery, actual damages, and the liability of the corporation for punitive damages. In contrast, the casebook version of *Fisher* was edited and only contains excerpts relating to battery and actual damages. When reading reported decisions, the reader must create his or her own mental table of contents or outline to situate the case in a particular context. The reader must also "edit" the case to focus on the topic that is the subject of the assignment or client problem. This can be done in several ways.

First, if a case is assigned for a legal writing or work assignment, the **assignment** often provides explicit information regarding the reason for reading the case. As discussed in Chapter 1, the purpose for reading helps shape what we look for as we read. If an assignment is limited to the subject of battery, focus attention on the opinion's discussion of battery.

Second, the reader can learn something about the general subject of a decision by looking at the **case summary** and the **headnotes**. While the summary and headnotes are not written by the court and can never be quoted or cited in legal memoranda or briefs, they do provide information about the subject of the case. Read the summary and the headnote topics that pertain to the assignment.

Finally, **secondary sources** such as encyclopedias or digests can assist the reader in placing a case in context by providing background about a general topic. The reader is then in a better position to comprehend the subject addressed in the case. To start understanding cases in connection with Joe Parker's situation in Chapters 1, 2, and 3, it would be helpful to consult a legal encyclopedia or treatise to get a general overview of the subject of battery before reading specific cases.

C. ALL CASES

One simple comprehension strategy, that takes about thirty seconds, provides the reader with the context of reported decisions or cases in a textbook. Before reading more carefully, look at the caption at the beginning of the decision and notice the **names of the parties, the court, the judge, and the date of the decision**. These details provide valuable background or context clues. The Christensen study found that higher performing students noticed context clues almost five times as often as lower performing students.[9]

1. Parties

The names in the caption provide information about the parties involved in the dispute.

- Are the parties individuals, corporations, the state, or the United States?

---

[9]   *Id.* at 32.

- Who appealed (if the case is an appellate decision) or who initiated the case (if it is a trial court decision)?

- Who is involved in the dispute?

The caption contains preliminary information about the parties by indicating who appealed and who won in the lower court. The names in the caption give some facts about the theme of the case. As will be discussed more fully in Chapter 5, it is often necessary to review the entire decision to determine who initiated the case and who was sued.

2. Court

The type of court gives the reader additional valuable clues about a case.

- Does the case involve a state court or a federal court?

- If it is a state court, which state is involved?

- Is it a trial level, intermediate appellate court, or the highest appellate court?

These are important distinctions because some court decisions are more useful in addressing client problems than others. When researching Joe Parker's battery lawsuit, the researcher would look for recent cases in Mr. Parker's state, paying particular attention to cases from the highest appellate court.

3. Judge

Expert legal readers notice the name of the judge because judges have different points of view. As students and lawyers become more familiar with courts, they recognize the perspectives of individual judges.

4. Date

The date of a decision can be significant because attorneys often look for recent opinions. In addition, dates can reveal the historical context of a case.

VI. READ FOR AN OVERVIEW

After understanding the general context or subject matter of the case, read the entire decision quickly to get a general overview. Reading for an overview helps the reader get oriented before reading more carefully. We have been trained to read books from beginning to end (and not read the solution to the mystery until the end of the book). However, it is more efficient to read cases in a non-linear fashion and at different speeds.

As shown in Figure 4.8, Lundeberg's comparison of the reading strategies of lawyers and non-lawyers found that lawyers usually did a quick overview of a case to find out the length of the decision, the nature of the claim and the court's decision. They often started reading by going to the end of the decision to find the result.[10] Experts paid attention to the introduction at the beginning of the case, while the non-lawyers skipped over this crucial information.[11] After completing an overview, experts went back and read more carefully. Expert legal readers did not read cases just once at the same speed from beginning to end.

Figure 4.8
Overview: Lundeberg Study

Overview Strategy	Lawyers	Non-Lawyers
Check length	9	4
Notice result	8	0
Determine type of case	8	0

During a quick read for an overview, take the following steps:

- **Skim** to determine the length of the opinion. Are there majority opinions and dissents?

- **Find out what the case is generally about.** The first few sentences will generally direct the reader's attention to the subject of the case.

- Look for headings or paragraphs that separate issues. Remembering how **cases are structured** from Chapter 3, quickly skim to identify the facts and the main issues. The main ideas are often found in topic sentences at the beginning of paragraphs. As certain topics may be more pertinent to an assignment than others, it may be appropriate to ignore topics that are not relevant.

- Find out **who won.** It may help to read the conclusion or the last few paragraphs of the case.

Practice Exercises 4.2 and 4.3 provide the opportunity to use context and do a case overview. Practice Exercise 4.4 is the self-assessment exercise.

VII. CASE EXAMPLE: CONTEXT AND OVERVIEW

Using *Fisher v. Carrousel Motor Hotel, Inc.,* 424 S.W.2d 627 (Tex. 1967) (Appendix B-1), this section will demonstrate how to place *Fisher* in

---

[10] Lundeberg, *supra* note 1, at 413.

[11] *Id.* at 413–14.

context and do a quick case overview. These steps should not take more than a couple of minutes. However, they will make reading more efficient.

A. CONTEXT

1. Reading Purpose

Assume that we are still representing Joe Parker in his lawsuit against Karen Jones and Smith Cars and the purpose for reading *Fisher* is to understand the rules relating to battery.

2. Case Summary and Headnotes

Since we are examining the *Fisher* reported decision for a research assignment, there is no table of contents or syllabus to provide context. However, the **case summary** in Figure 4.9 provides a brief synopsis of the decision, which is helpful background information that places the case in context. *Fisher,* 424 S.W.2d at 627. Remember that this summary was written by editors, not the Judge, and that it can never be quoted or used in legal documents.

Figure 4.9
Case Summary

> Guest brought action for assault and battery by motor hotel's agent. The 61st District Court, Harris County, Ben F. Wilson, J., granted defendant's motion n.o.v. that plaintiff take nothing and plaintiff appealed. The Waco Court of Civil Appeals, Tenth Supreme Judicial District, 414 S.W.2d 774, affirmed and plaintiff brought error. The Supreme Court, Greenhill, J., held where the manager of the motor hotel's club dispossessed plaintiff of his dinner plate in a loud and offensive manner a battery occurred on which damages for mental suffering could be based and the motor hotel was liable for exemplary damages.
>
> Reversed.

The **headnotes** for *Fisher* further assist in identifying the key topics in the case and placing the case in context. If you turn to the *Fisher* decision in Appendix B-1, you will see that there are four separate headnote topics.

- Numbers 1–4 and 6–7 deal with the topic of assault and battery,

- number 5 deals with the topic of damages, and

- numbers 8–10 relate to the topics of labor and employment and principal and agent. *Fisher,* 424 S.W.2d at 627–28.

The headnotes can also be used to locate particular topics in the body of the opinion. As shown in Figure 4.10, the numbers that appear before the headnote indicate where a topic is located in the opinion. For example, the number [1] before assault and battery indicates that this topic is addressed in the section of the opinion that starts with [1]. This makes it possible to locate a particular topic in an opinion quickly.

Figure 4.10
Headnotes

Headnote: — HEADNOTE NUMBER
    [1] ◀ Assault and Battery
        ← Nature and Elements of Assault and
        Battery
        Actual physical contact is not necessary to
        constitute a battery so long as there is
        contact with clothing or an object closely
        identified with the body.
        Fisher, 424 S.W.2d at 627.

Reference in Opinion: _____ REFERENCE TO HEADNOTE TOPIC IN OPINION
        [1] The Court of Civil Appeals held that there was no assault because there was no physical
        contact and no evidence of fear or apprehension of physical contact.
        Fisher, 424 S.W.2d at 629.

3.   Parties, Court, Judge, and Date

The name of the case and the information about the parties in the first paragraph tells us that an individual, Emmit Fisher, has sued a hotel. The fact that the case was decided by the Supreme Court of Texas provides further context because the reader knows that the case must be followed by all courts in Texas. The date provides historical significance because of the racial climate in the United States in 1967.

B.   CASE OVERVIEW

1.   Skim for Length and Organization

Skimming tells us the case is five pages long and that there is an opinion with no dissents.

2.   General Topic

As indicated in Chapter 3, the introduction in the first sentence sets forth the general topic and explains that the case is a suit for "damages growing out of an alleged assault and battery." 424 S.W.2d at 628.

3.   Structure

The case is organized the way most cases are organized: introduction, procedural background and facts, analysis of prior decisions, rationale, holding, and judgment. While there are no headings, the paragraphs are organized by subject and the topic sentences give the reader information regarding the main ideas in each section.

4.   Who Won

The end of the opinion states that the Supreme Court of Texas reversed the lower courts' decisions and awarded judgment to Fisher.

VIII.   PRACTICE

Reflection Exercise 4.1
Using Context in Reading

Goal: This exercise provides an opportunity to reflect on your use of context in non-legal settings. We often use context clues without even realizing that we are using this valuable strategy.

Think about the steps you have taken to understand the general subject of a book before you started to read. Some of the more common techniques are listed below. Indicate if you have used the strategy and if it has been helpful. Then list other useful strategies you have tried. Some of these techniques may be useful in reading cases.

Context Strategy	Used Strategy?	Was Strategy Helpful?
Use context clues to understand the meaning of words.	✓	✗
Look at word parts such as roots, prefixes, and suffixes.	✓	✓
Use glossary in textbook.	✓	✓
Use images in books such as charts or photographs.	✗	✗
Read abstracts of articles.	✗	✗
Read titles, headings, or tables of contents.	✓	✓

Practice Exercise 4.2
Case Context and Overview: Civil Case

Goal: This exercise provides the opportunity to use context strategies to understand the general subject of a case and do a brief overview before reading the case more carefully.

For this exercise, assume that we are still representing Joe Parker in his lawsuit against Karen Jones and Smith Cars. You are continuing to research the law of battery and have decided to read *Morgan v. Loyacomo*, 1 So. 2d 510 (Miss. 1941) (Appendix F). Determine the general subject of *Morgan* and do a quick overview of the decision.

Step 1: Determine the general subject or context of *Morgan*.

Case Element	*Morgan*
4.2–1 What are the topics of the **headnotes**? Do any topics relate to battery?	
4.2–2 Who are the parties in the caption?	
4.2–3 What **court** decided the case?	
4.2–4 What is the decision **date**?	
4.2–5 Who was the Judge?	

Step 2: Skim the case quickly for an overview.

Case Element	*Morgan*
4.2–6 How long is the case?	
4.2–7 Where does the decision provide information about battery?	
4.2–8 Is the case divided into sections by topic?	
4.2–9 Looking at the end of the case, who won?	

Practice Exercise 4.3
Case Context and Overview: Criminal Case

Goal: This exercise provides another opportunity to use context strategies to understand the general subject of a case and to do a brief case overview.

For this exercise, assume that you have been asked to research whether a house should be considered a "dwelling" or a "building" for purposes of burglary law and consult *Haynes v. Commonwealth*, 657 S.W.2d 948 (Ky.1983) (Appendix E). Determine if the case addresses this subject and do a quick overview of the decision.

Step 1: What is the general subject or context of *Haynes*?

Case Element	*Haynes*
4.3–1 Does any information in the case summary relate to burglary?	
4.3–2 What are the topics of the **headnotes**? Do any topics relate to burglary?	
4.3–3 Who are the parties in the **caption**?	
4.3–4 What **court** decided the case?	
4.3–5 What is the decision **date**?	
4.3–6 Who was the Judge?	

Step 2: Skim the case quickly for an overview.

Case Element	*Haynes*
4.3–7 How long is the case?	
4.3–8 Does the first paragraph of the decision provide useful information about the general subject matter?	
4.3–9 Is the case divided into sections by topic?	
4.3–10 Looking at the end of the case, who won?	

Practice Exercise 4.4
Self-Assessment

Goal: In this exercise, assess whether you understand how to find the general subject of a case and skim for an overview before reading more carefully.

For this exercise, assume that you are representing Ms. Evelyn Michel, who was terminated from her employment as a nurse because she failed the National Council Licensure Examination. She wants to know if she will qualify for unemployment insurance benefits. *De Grego v. Levine,*

347 N.E. 2d 611 (N.Y. 1976) (Appendix C) provides guidance on this subject.

4.4–1   How can you determine the general subject of *De Grego* before reading the case more carefully?

4.4–2   How would you go about skimming for an overview before reading the case more carefully?

Evaluate your understanding of the skills in this chapter by completing the following rubric. For each skill, circle whether you are at the proficient or developing level. Everyone can get to the proficient level over time.

Skill	Competency Level	
	Proficient	**Developing**
Understands the general subject or context of a case before reading.	• Examines the case summary and headnotes to determine the general subject of the case. • Looks at the names of the parties, court, judge, and date of decision to understand the general subject before reading more carefully.	• Ignores the case summary and headnotes. • Begins reading before knowing anything about the subject of the case.
Skims for an overview.	• Skims through the case before reading more carefully. • Notices the parties and who won and lost.	• Reads the case once. • Ignores the parties.

Checklist Reminder: Remember to create your own checklist. A template is located in Appendix A. It may be helpful at the conclusion of each chapter to select the techniques you find helpful and add them to your checklist.

PHASE TWO

DURING READING

CHAPTER 5

DURING READING: FACTS

I. SUMMARY

This chapter focuses on how legal readers understand the:

- facts underlying a dispute (substantive facts), and
- facts related to the progression of a case through the legal system (procedural facts).

While it is generally not necessary to memorize the facts in cases, expert readers analyze facts to determine whether a case can be used to solve a legal problem.

At the conclusion of this chapter, you will be able to:

- use a variety of strategies to comprehend the substantive and procedural facts in a case, and
- grasp the significance of relevant facts.

II. CHECKLIST

CASE READING CHECKLIST

Warning: Do not just highlight and underline.

Phase 1: Before Reading

1. Read for a purpose and assume the role of advocate or judge.
2. Read with energy and focus.
3. Notice case structure.
4. Understand the general subject matter by examining:
    a. course syllabus, casebook table of contents, or research assignment, and
    b. parties, citation, court, and date.
5. Read for an overview by skimming and noticing organization, headings, who won, and what case is generally about.

Phase 2: Reading More Carefully

1. Understand the facts.

---

2. Reread, look up unfamiliar words, analyze confusing language, and vary reading speed.

3. Understand the main ideas set forth in the issue, holding, and reasoning.

4. Identify the rule.

5. Take notes with your reactions and brief the case.

Phase 3: After Reading

1. Evaluate the decision, ask questions, and talk with professors.

2. Determine how cases fit together with other cases and synthesize.

III. DURING READING STRATEGIES

Chapters 1 through 4 explored several **before reading** techniques such as reading:

- for the purpose of solving a legal problem (Chapter 1),

- from the perspective of one of the parties or the judge (Chapter 2),

- with an understanding of the structure of cases and procedural terms (Chapter 3), and

- by placing a case in context and skimming for an overview (Chapter 4).

These preliminary steps take only a few minutes and increase comprehension.

Expert legal readers also take specific actions **during reading**. As described in Figure 5.1, the next four chapters focus on reading strategies that are used while reading a case more carefully. The **during reading phase** starts with this chapter because facts are the basis for the entire decision. Chapter 6 addresses strategies for understanding language in cases. Chapter 7 introduces techniques for finding the main ideas by analyzing the issue, holding, and reasoning. Chapter 8 explores methods of finding rules that can be used to solve new legal problems.

Figure 5.1
During Reading Topics

Chapter	Topic
5	Reading facts
6	Understanding language

Chapter	Topic
7	Understanding the main ideas—issue, holding, and reasoning
8	Finding rules

IV. WHY ARE FACTS IMPORTANT?

Expert legal readers understand the underlying facts in a case while novice legal readers may skip the facts to concentrate on the law. One law professor observed that some law students believe,

> " 'I'm in law school, not fact school; I want to know what the law is, not just what happened in this one case.' But trust me: the facts are really important."[1]

The approach used by novices does not work.

On a practical level, it is necessary to make sense of the facts because cases start with facts. All cases involve real people and the facts may constitute the most important events that ever happened in their lives. These events are generally not positive and most people would prefer to avoid the legal system and never find their name in a caption! Cases usually start after something has gone wrong, and people cannot resolve a dispute. One student in the Grisé study noted that the critical reading instruction helped her "understand the facts thoroughly because everything arises from the factual situation."[2]

On a more theoretical level, facts are important because they are a basic element of our **common law system**. Courts rely on **precedent** (earlier cases decided on a subject) and stare decisis, which means "to stand by a decision." Using earlier decisions or precedent, courts analyze facts in a dispute and resolve new cases consistently with older court decisions. While courts may extend and change the law, facts form the basis for all cases.[3]

In our common law system, lawyers look for cases with similar facts so they can use the rule from another case to resolve a client's problem. This is called **analogical reasoning**, which is simply the process of comparing two sets of facts to determine if they are similar or different. The rule from a case can be used to solve a client's problem (problem facts) if the underlying facts in the reported decision (case facts) are similar to the

---

[1] Orin S. Kerr, *How to Read a Legal Opinion: A Guide for New Law Students*, 11 The Green Bag: An Entertaining J. of Law 51, 57 (2007).

[2] Jane Bloom Grisé, *Critical Reading Instruction: The Road to Successful Legal Writing Skills*, 18 W. Mich. Univ. Cooley J. of Prac. & Clinical L. (forthcoming 2017).

[3] This is different from the civil law system, used in European countries such as France and Germany, where court decisions have no precedential value for other disputes.

problem facts. If the facts are similar, an attorney can argue that the result in the new problem should be the same as the result in the court case.

This process of analogical reasoning could be used to solve Joe Parker's dispute from Chapters 1, 2, and 3. To determine whether a lawsuit is advisable, attorneys would compare the facts in Joe Parker's case with the facts in the *Fisher* case. If the facts in *Fisher* are similar to the facts in Mr. Parker's situation, Mr. Parker's attorney could argue that the result in *Fisher*, a finding of battery, should also be the result in Mr. Parker's case.

As this example demonstrates, the facts are key to determining the usefulness of a case. There is another practical reason to pay attention to the facts. **Law school exams consist of factual scenarios.** The exams are usually based upon the facts selected from a number of cases. Students who pay attention to the facts in cases are more likely to be successful in law school exams.

V. TYPES OF FACTS

There are two types of facts: substantive and procedural. Substantive facts are the facts underlying the dispute. Procedural facts are facts related to the progression of a lawsuit through the court system. (Chapter 3 examined terms relating to civil and criminal procedure so that references to procedure would be easier to follow.) For example, after a dispute occurs (substantive facts), a civil lawsuit begins with the filing of a complaint (procedural fact). In a criminal case, once an incident occurs (substantive fact), the case may begin with the issuance of an indictment (procedural fact). Expert readers pay attention to substantive and procedural facts.

VI. STRATEGIES FOR UNDERSTANDING FACTS

Readers organize facts in a variety of ways depending upon the subject. Sometimes it is useful to simply list facts chronologically. Other times it is more effective to create charts, diagrams, timelines, or graphic organizers. Before trying new strategies to organize facts, think about techniques you have used to organize information. Reflection Exercise 5.1 gives you the opportunity to reflect on these techniques.

In addition to the strategies you have used, the following techniques can assist in understanding the facts:

A. Identify the **parties**. Who initiated the litigation and who was sued? Does the plaintiff or defendant fit any particular category such as a landlord or an employee?

B. Create a mental image of the facts and write down a summary of the **substantive and procedural facts**.

C. Look for **relevant facts**.

D. Start asking **questions** and **take notes**. Think about how the facts in your client's problem are similar to or different from the facts in the decision under consideration.

E. Follow the recommendations of expert readers and **read facts slowly**, look up words, and reread when necessary.

Each of these techniques will be described in more detail with examples.

A. PARTIES

In a civil or criminal case, clarify and identify:

- Who initiated the case, and

- Who was sued?

To understand the facts, it is essential to first identify the parties. In Chapter 4, the names of the parties in the caption were examined to determine the general subject and context of the case. The caption provides the names of the parties, the court, and the case number. Normally in appellate decisions, the party or parties listed on the first line of the caption initiated the appeal and the party or parties on the second line (after the v.) won in the court below.

Now it is necessary to read more carefully to clarify who brought the suit and who was sued. In trial court decisions, the person who initiated the case is listed on the first line of the caption and the person who was sued is found on the second line after the v. However, in appellate decisions, the caption does not always indicate who initiated the suit and who was sued. For example, the caption in Figure 5.2 refers to Martin Wishnatsky as the Plaintiff and Appellant. It refers to David Huey as the Defendant and Appellee. These terms tell the reader that Martin Wishnatsky started the lawsuit as plaintiff, that the trial court ruled against him, and that he initiated the appeal as the appellant.[4]

---

[4] *Wishnatsky v. Huey*, 584 N.W.2d 859 (N.D. Ct. App. 1998).

Figure 5.2
Caption with Information About Parties

> 584 N.W.2d 859
>
> Court of Appeals of North Dakota.
>
> Martin WISHNATSKY, Plaintiff and Appellant,
>
> v.
>
> David W. HUEY, Defendant and Appellee.

On the other hand, the caption in Figure 5.3 provides no details regarding who initiated the case and who was sued. [5] It simply refers to Morgan et al. (and others) and Loyacomo. While it is appropriate to assume that Morgan is the appellant (because the name of the appellant is listed on the first line of the caption) and Loyacomo is the appellee, the caption does not indicate who filed the underlying case. (The reference to et al. means that there were additional appellants besides Morgan.)

Figure 5.3
Caption Without Information About Parties

> 190 Miss. 656
>
> Supreme Court of Mississippi.
>
> MORGAN et al.
>
> v.
>
> LOYACOMO

In this situation, it is necessary to examine the opinion more closely to identify the parties.

Sometimes there are multiple parties in a caption. Defendants may sue each other, which is referred to as a cross-claim. Defendants may sue additional parties so that there are three or more sets of litigants. All of this needs to be sorted out to understand the facts.

After identifying the parties, look for the general legal categories represented by the parties and the relationships between the parties. For example, is the plaintiff a tenant and is the defendant a landlord? Does the case involve an employer and employee? These categories help the reader grasp the general nature of the dispute.

---

[5] *Morgan v. Loyacomo*, 1 So.2d 510 (Miss. 1941).

B. OUTLINE THE SUBSTANTIVE AND PROCEDURAL FACTS

1. Substantive Facts

Expert legal readers create a mental image of the facts. In his "Talk to Entering Students," Professor White suggested that students try to

> "reconstruct from the opinion . . . the facts that occurred in the real world before any lawyer was brought into play . . . You should try to create a movie of life, a story of the experience of ordinary people in the ordinary world. Reflect in your story how each of the participants would characterize the events in his ordinary language."[6]

In addition to creating a mental image of the facts, it is helpful to create diagrams, chronologies, and flow charts to make sense of the facts. Expert legal readers have reported using the following techniques:

- a law professor "marked some of the facts, drew a diagram of the suit, or stopped to summarize the facts,"[7]

- a higher performing student drew a diagram "identifying the parties, their relationship(s) to each other."[8]

Certain strategies work better than others depending upon the subject of the case. For property cases, it can be helpful to draw a diagram. For contracts, a flow chart may be useful to show the relationships among the parties. In some criminal cases, a chronological list of events works well. It is important to use one of these methods. Just reading through the facts is not enough.

The following example demonstrates how a diagram can assist in understanding a tort (negligence) case. Complicated text can be reduced to a simple drawing. In *Commonwealth v. Henderson's Guardian*, 53 S.W.2d 695 (Ky. 1932) the guardian of a 15-year-old (Henderson) claimed that the state negligently left dynamite caps near a state garage. Henderson looked through garbage near the garage, found the dynamite caps, set them off, and the caps exploded, injuring his hand. Figure 5.4 sets forth the facts in the opinion.

---

[6]   James B. White, *Talk to Entering Students*, 13 Occasional Papers L. Sch. U. Chi. 1, 9 (1977).

[7]   Mary A. Lundeberg, *Metacognitive Aspects of Reading Comprehension: Studying Understanding in a Legal Case Analysis*, 22 Reading Res. Q. 407, 414 (1987).

[8]   Laurel Currie Oates, *Beating the Odds: Reading Strategies of Law Students Admitted Through Alternative Admissions Programs*, 83 Iowa L. Rev. 139, 155 (1997).

Figure 5.4
Substantive Facts: Text

"The commonwealth owns a lot on the south side of Greenup Avenue and between Twenty-Seventh and Twenty-Eighth Streets in the city of Ashland, improved by a building which is used by the state highway commission of Kentucky as a garage, and in which it stores and repairs its machinery. To the east and adjoining this lot is a lot and garage owned by Boyd County, there being a space between the buildings three or four feet in width. The buildings front toward but about 30 or 40 feet back from Greenup Avenue. The approach to the state garage from the avenue is paved with concrete, and in the intervening space there are two gasoline pumps. As we gather from the evidence, these pumps are near the building and between the side of the door and the corner of the building next to the county garage. It also appears that the state highway commission has for some years made use of the county garage under a lease or some arrangement whereby the county continues to use a portion of it for storage of county machinery and materials to which county employees have access.

On March 4, 1929, Claude Henderson, who was then 15 years of age, and a companion, Wade Adams, also an infant, but somewhat younger, were, as was their usual custom when not attending school, going about over the city with a pushcart which they had improvised, gathering such materials as are usually purchased by junk dealers. About 6:30 o'clock p. m. their quest led them to the premises of the state garage, where, in the absence of any state employee, and without invitation or permission so to do, they proceeded to gather and appropriate such materials found as suited their purpose. They testified that, in searching through a heap of refuse between the garage and the gasoline pumps, they found some rags, pieces of copper wire and automobile springs, and three dynamite caps. They then went back into an alley, where young Henderson, with two of the caps in the palm of his hand, used a match to remove some dirt from the other cap held between his thumb and fingers. The caps were thus caused to explode, and so lacerate his left hand as to necessitate its amputation at or near the wrist joint." *Commonwealth v. Henderson's Guardian*, 53 S.W.2d 695, 695 (Ky. 1932).

Figure 5.5 condenses all of those facts into a diagram that makes it easier to understand the incident and shows the relationships between different locations.

Figure 5.5
Substantive Facts: Diagram

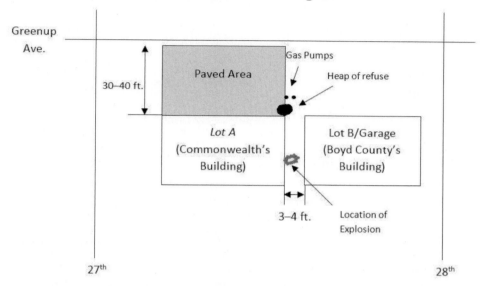

In summarizing the facts, use abbreviations to save time and space. The following symbols can be used to identify the parties:

π or P—plaintiff

Δ or D—defendant

Remember that while facts are often located at the beginning of the opinion, they may be found throughout the decision. Be sure to examine the entire opinion to find all of the facts.

2.   Procedural Facts

The procedural facts are the facts that show how the case started and worked its way through the court system. As explained in Chapter 3, a civil case starts with the filing of a complaint and a criminal case may begin with an indictment. The *De Grego* case, in the self-assessment exercises, started with the filing of an application for unemployment benefits. The explanations of civil and criminal procedure from Chapter 3 are useful in understanding the procedural facts. Sometimes the procedures in a case are important, and sometimes they are less significant. As you become familiar with the rules of civil and criminal procedure, it will be easier to make these distinctions.

Because the procedural posture of a case can affect a case's precedential value, it is important to outline or diagram the procedural facts. The chronology should include:

- the claims in a civil complaint or the charges in a criminal case,

- significant motions such as a motion to dismiss or motion for summary judgment in a civil case or a motion to suppress in a criminal case,

- the trial court or jury decisions, and

- intermediate appellate court decisions as well as the final appellate decision and disposition.

Figure 5.6 sets forth the procedural facts in *Commonwealth v. Henderson's Guardian*, 53 S.W.2d 695 (Ky. 1932) and Figure 5.7 shows how they can be condensed into four lines.

Figure 5.6
Procedural Facts: Text

The court opinion states as follows on the first page of the decision:

"Pursuant to an enabling act passed at the 1930 session of the General Assembly of Kentucky, George Roper, Jr., as guardian for Claude Henderson, an infant, instituted this action against the commonwealth seeking to recover damages for personal injuries to the ward, caused by the explosion of dynamite caps alleged to have been negligently left exposed by employees at the state garage in Ashland. Trial before a jury resulted in verdict and judgment for plaintiff in the sum of $6,000, and the commonwealth has appealed.

It is first argued as ground for reversal that the court erred in not sustaining appellant's motion for a peremptory instruction, and, while other grounds are argued, the conclusion we have reached renders it unnecessary to discuss the other grounds." *Id.* at 695.

On the last page of the decision, the court states as follows:

"In the light of the evidence and an overwhelming weight of authority favoring the contention of appellant, there is no escape from the conclusion that it was error to overrule the commonwealth's motion for a directed verdict.

Judgment reversed, and cause remanded for proceedings consistent with this opinion." *Id.* at 696.

Figure 5.7
Procedural Facts: Chronology

1.   P (Henderson) v. D (Commonwealth) for negligence.

2.   D motion DV (directed verdict) denied.

3.   Jury verdict for P, $6,000.

4.   Supreme Court reversed and remanded for trial court to grant motion for DV.

Figure 5.6 also shows that the procedural facts in *Henderson's Guardian* were located on the first and last pages of the decision. Procedural facts are not always located in one place. While the initial proceedings are usually found at the beginning of the opinion and the disposition is located at the end, references to motions and other procedures may be interspersed throughout the opinion. In constructing a procedural summary, look through the entire opinion. Practice Exercise 5.3 gives you the opportunity to use these techniques to organize the substantive and procedural facts in a case.

C.   IDENTIFY RELEVANT FACTS

Lawyers read cases to understand the relevant facts. What are relevant facts? **Relevant** facts are facts that would change a result. Sometimes relevant facts are referred to as **determinative** facts because they can determine the result. The relevance or legal significance of a fact is determined by the legal standard in the case. Sometimes one fact alone is not relevant but several facts viewed together are relevant. In practical terms, this means that the first time we read the facts, it is not possible to figure out which facts are relevant because we do not know the rules. It is necessary to read the facts, read the rest of the opinion to understand the law, and then go back to fully comprehend which facts are relevant. As noted earlier, reading cases is not a linear endeavor. A reader is not able to determine which facts are legally relevant until the reader understands the case as a whole.

The following examples illustrate how the relevance of facts is determined by the rules in a case. In these examples, the facts are the same and the rules are different. The rules determine whether or not the facts are relevant.

Example #1:

Rule #1: All moving vehicles in the state of Oz can travel no faster than 40 miles per hour.

Facts: James is stopped by a police officer for traveling 50 miles per hour in the State of Oz. James is driving a red Ford truck.

Relevant Fact: speed

Result: James violated the rule.

Example #2:

Rule #2: All blue moving vehicles in the State of Oz can travel no faster than 40 miles per hour.

Facts: James is stopped by a police officer for traveling 50 miles per hour in the State of Oz. James is driving a red Ford truck.

Relevant Facts: speed and color of truck

Result: James did not violate the rule.

In example #1, the color of the truck is not a relevant fact because color has nothing to do with the rule. The color of the vehicle would not change the result. However, in example #2, the color of the vehicle is part of the rule and is a relevant fact because the color of the truck would change the result.

When initially reading the facts, just focus on making sense of the big picture and what happened in the underlying dispute. After reading the entire case more carefully and identifying the rules, go back and look at the facts again to make a judgment regarding which facts are relevant and which facts are not.

D. ASK QUESTIONS AND TAKE NOTES

As you read the facts, start asking questions about anything that is confusing, problematic or just interesting. Asking questions helps readers figure out what they know and do not know.

While the relevant facts cannot be fully summarized until the reader understands the law, it is useful to begin taking notes with summaries, diagrams, or charts of the substantive and procedural facts. Start by writing the case name and identifying the parties. Then try to summarize the facts. The process of writing helps you sort out the facts. To be useful, summaries **must be written using your own words. Do not just cut and paste**. As will be discussed in more detail in Chapter 10, the summary of the facts is included in the case brief, which is a summary of the entire case.

E. READ FACTS CAREFULLY

Experts read facts carefully before going on to examine the rest of the opinion. As indicated in Figure 5.8, they read facts more slowly, look up unfamiliar words, and reread confusing sections.

Figure 5.8
Techniques for Reading Facts

Reading Techniques	Expert Legal Readers	Novice Legal Readers
Speed	Read slowly and vary pace.	Read everything at the same pace.
Vocabulary	Look up unfamiliar terms.	Skip over unfamiliar terms.
Rereading	Reread when confused.	Skip over confusing sections.

Experts vary their **reading speed** and often **read the facts more slowly**. While novice readers tend to read cases from beginning to end at the same pace, expert legal readers often read the beginning of a case and the facts more slowly and then speed up. Experts are like distance runners who vary their speed, sometimes starting slowly, and then increasing their pace. Novices who try to read everything at the same speed are like the "beginning distance runner who does not know how to set a pace that is sustainable through a long and difficult race."[9] In the Grisé study, one student commented that it was helpful to slow down "to better analyze" the cases.[10] Reading speed will increase as you accumulate a larger legal vocabulary and more familiarity with legal procedures and principles.

In addition to varying your reading speed, **look up unfamiliar words**. As will be discussed in more detail in Chapter 6, it is not advisable to skip over confusing words. In the Oates study, the two lower performing students skipped over words that were unfamiliar and misread some key facts. Jackie and James, who finished in the bottom 20% of their class, did not understand the word "palatial" that was used to describe a yacht. James also misread a key fact.[11] This affected their understanding of the entire case.

If the facts are confusing, **reread** the passage. As will be discussed more fully in the next chapter, rereading is essential. Do not just skip over difficult portions of opinions and keep reading. In the Oates study, the higher performing law student William reread facts that were confusing. When he was confused about the parties, he reread the facts.[12] While students sometimes assume it is more efficient to read everything once

---

[9] Peter Dewitz, *Reading Law Three Suggestions for Legal Education*, 27 Univ. Tol. L. Rev. 657, 663 (1995).

[10] Grisé, *supra* note 2.

[11] Laurel Currie Oates, *Leveling the Playing Field: Helping Students Succeed by Helping Them Learn to Read as Expert Lawyers*, 80 St. John's L. Rev. 227, 244 (2006).

[12] *Id.* at 236.

from beginning to end at the same pace and skip sections that are unclear, expert legal readers do not do this.

Practice Exercise 5.2 shows the disadvantages of trying to solve a legal problem without reading the facts in a case, and Practice Exercise 5.3 provides the opportunity to organize the facts. Practice Exercise 5.4 is the self-assessment exercise.

VII.   CASE EXAMPLE: FACTS

The skills in this chapter are explained with *Fisher v. Carrousel Motor Hotel, Inc.*, 424 S.W.2d 627 (Tex. 1967) (Appendix B-1).

A. IDENTIFY THE PARTIES

Any analysis of the facts starts by identifying the parties and determining who sued whom. The *Fisher* caption in Figure 5.9 does not provide any information regarding who initiated the lawsuit. It indicates that Fisher was the Petitioner in the appeal and Carrousel Motor Hotel, Inc., et al. were the Respondents.

Figure 5.9
Fisher **Caption**

Emmit E. FISHER, Petitioner,
v.
CARROUSEL MOTOR HOTEL, INC., et al., Respondents.

However, the first paragraph of the opinion identifies Fisher as the plaintiff, which means that Fisher filed the case. This paragraph also indicates that the defendants were the Carrousel Motor Hotel, Inc., the Brass Ring Club, and Robert W. Flynn. This information makes it possible to conclude that Fisher brought the case against Carrousel Motor Hotel, Inc., the Brass Ring Club and Robert Flynn, the manager at the Brass Ring Club.

B. SUBSTANTIVE FACTS

The facts in *Fisher* can be organized in chronological order. There are three types of facts in the opinion: the dispute facts, facts found by the jury, and agreed facts. The facts describing the incident are in the first paragraph of the decision. The important fact found by the jury was that Flynn " 'forceably dispossessed plaintiff of his dinner plate' and 'shouted in a loud and offensive manner' that Fisher could not be served there." *Fisher,* 424 S.W.2d at 629. The parties agreed that Flynn was the manager of the Club.

All of these facts can be summarized briefly. Remember to use abbreviations for the parties, i.e., π or P for plaintiff, and Δ or D for defendant, and make up other abbreviations. It is not necessary to use complete sentences. One way of summarizing the facts follows:

1. P attended professional meeting at D Carrousel Motor Hotel.

2. Lunch served at Brass Ring Club, Flynn manager.

3. As P stood in line at buffet, Flynn took plate from P's hand & shouted that P would not be served because he was African-American.

4. P was not touched by Flynn but was highly embarrassed (in presence of associates) & humiliated.

5. Jury found Flynn shouted in loud & offensive manner.

6. Parties stipulated Flynn was manager of the Club.

C. PROCEDURAL FACTS

The procedural facts are found in the opinion as follows:

"Trial was to a jury which found for the plaintiff Fisher. The trial court rendered judgment for the defendants notwithstanding the verdict. The Court of Civil Appeals affirmed. 414 S.W.2d 774." *Fisher,* 424 S.W.2d at 628.

"The Court of Civil Appeals held that there was no assault because there was no physical contact and no evidence of fear or apprehension of physical contact . . . The judgments of the courts below are reversed, and judgment is here rendered for the plaintiff for $900 with interest from the date of the trial court's judgment, and for costs of this suit." *Fisher,* 424 S.W.2d at 629.

These procedural facts can be summarized in chronological order as follows:

1. P sued D Carrousel Motor Hotel, Inc., the Brass Ring Club, and Flynn for assault & battery & for actual & exemplary damages.

2. Jury awarded P $400 actual damages & $500 exemplary damages.

3. Trial court granted JNOV to D.

4. Court of Civil Appeals affirmed.

5. Supreme Court of Texas reversed & awarded judgment to P for $900 w/interest & costs.

No additional details are provided about the procedures that took place in the trial court. If this information is important, sometimes it is possible to examine prior opinions in the trial or lower appellate courts. For example, in *Fisher*, the Court of Civil Appeals decision provides additional information about the proceedings at the trial level. That opinion states that Fisher "moved for judgment on the verdict; and defendant moved for judgment that plaintiff take nothing, asserting that as a matter of law the acts complained of by plaintiff, committed by Flynn, do not constitute an assault or other actionable cause." 414 S.W. 2d 774, 775 (Tex. Civ. App. 1967).

D. LOOK UP UNFAMILIAR WORDS

Some words in the *Fisher* opinion may be unfamiliar and should be looked up to fully understand the facts. This topic is explored more fully in Chapter 6.

E. RELEVANT FACTS

After reading just the facts, a reader may not know which facts are relevant. It is necessary to revisit this question after reading the rest of the opinion and understanding the law. The remainder of the opinion indicates that the key elements of battery consist of the "knocking or snatching anything from plaintiff's hand or touching anything connected with his person, when done in an offensive manner." *Fisher,* 424 S.W.2d at 629. Based upon this legal standard, it is clear that all of the facts listed in Section B above are relevant.

F. ASK QUESTIONS

Think about questions relating to the facts. Are the facts regarding the incident clear? Do you have any questions relating to how the case progressed through the Texas courts?

VIII.   PRACTICE

Reflection Exercise 5.1
Techniques for Organizing Facts

Goal: The goal of this exercise is to reflect on strategies you have used to organize facts in other situations so that you can use these techniques to organize facts in cases.

There are many ways to organize facts. Some strategies work better with some types of facts than others. Indicate whether or not you have used a specific technique and if you have found it helpful. Then add other strategies to this list that have been useful.

Organizational Strategy	Used Strategy?	Was Strategy Helpful?
Chronology		
Diagram		
Flow Chart		
Timeline		
Venn Diagram		
Graphic Organizer		
Cause/Effect Diagram		
Compare/Contrast Diagram		

Practice Exercise 5.2
Are the Facts Important?

Goal: The purpose of this exercise is to determine the usefulness of a case if the reader ignores the facts in the case and just reads the court's analysis of the law.

Assume that you have been contacted by Kaitlin Groves, who has a dispute with her employer, Fabulous Foods. Ms. Groves works for Fabulous Foods in Seattle, Washington. This company prepares food for the airline industry. Because of security requirements, employees of Fabulous Foods are not allowed to bring food to work. Fabulous Foods provides meals for its employees to eat during lunch and breaks. The company always provides a meat dish and a vegetarian option. Due to religious considerations, Ms. Groves does not eat pork. Fabulous Foods advised its employees that their meat dishes did not contain pork because several employees shared Ms. Groves' food requirements. Ms. Groves recently discovered that while Fabulous Foods served beef meatballs during 2015, starting in January of 2016 the company switched to pork meatballs without telling its employees. The company now refuses to change the employee meals.[13]

The senior partner in your law firm wants you to research a possible battery claim on behalf of Ms. Groves. The only case that you have located is *Garratt v. Dailey,* 279 P.2d 1091 (Wash. 1955) (Appendix G). You have

---

[13] This scenario is based upon the case *Kumar v. Gate Gourmet, Inc.*, 325 P.3d 193 (Wash. 2014).

decided to skip over the facts in the opinion because you are in a hurry and just read the following information about the law of battery.

> "We have in this case no question of consent or privilege. We therefore proceed to an immediate consideration of intent and its place in the law of battery. In the comment on clause (a), the Restatement says: '*Character of actor's intention.* In order that an act may be done with the intention of bringing about a harmful or offensive contact or an apprehension thereof to a particular person, either the other or a third person, the act must be done for the purpose of causing the contact or apprehension or with knowledge on the part of the actor that such contact or apprehension is substantially certain to be produced.' See, also, Prosser on Torts 41, § 8." *Id.* at 1093.

5.2–1   How useful is the *Garratt* case in solving Ms. Grove's legal problem if you skip over the facts in *Garratt* and just read this excerpt about the law of battery?

5.2–2   Is it possible to do analogical reasoning if you skip over the facts?

Practice Exercise 5.3
Organizing the Facts

Goal: The purpose of this exercise is to provide practice in selecting an organizational strategy for summarizing the substantive and procedural facts in a case and then summarizing the facts. This exercise will also serve as a review of concepts from Chapters 1 through 4.

Assume that you are still representing Kaitlin Groves and have decided to read *Garratt v. Dailey,* 279 P.2d 1091 (Wash. 1955) (Appendix G) more carefully. The purpose for reading the case is to represent Ms. Groves and learn more about the law of battery. Remember to read as an advocate. You might read the case from the perspective of Ruth Garratt.

Step 1: The first step is to determine the general subject matter or context of *Garratt.*

Case Element	*Garratt*
5.3–1 Does any information in the case summary relate to **battery**?	NO
5.3–2 What are the topics of the **headnotes**?	
5.3–3 Who are the parties in the **caption**?	
5.3–4 What **court** decided the case?	

Case Element	*Garratt*
5.3–5 What is the decision **date**?	
5.3–6 Who was the **Judge**?	

Step 2: The next step is to skim the case quickly for an overview.

Case Element	*Garratt*
5.3–7 How long is the case?	
5.3–8 Does the first paragraph of the decision provide useful information about the general subject matter?	
5.3–9 Are there any headings that divide the case into sections?	
5.3–10 Does the decision indicate who won on the last page?	

Step 3: Read the facts related to the underlying dispute, the substantive facts, and complete the chart.

Facts	*Garratt*
5.3–11 Who are the parties in the underlying dispute?	
5.3–12 Looking at page 1092[14] of the decision, what is the best way to organize the facts?	

5.3–13 Summarize the substantive facts:

Step 4: Review the procedural facts and complete the following chart:

Procedural Facts	*Garratt*
5.3–14 Looking at the end of page 1093, did the trial court dismiss the case?	

---

[14] Remember that page 1092 refers to the page number from the regional reporter which is found on pages 307 and 308 of the case in Appendix G.

5.3–15 Looking at page 1095, what was the decision of the Washington Supreme Court?	
5.3–16 What is the best way to organize the procedural facts?	

5.3–17 Summarize the procedural facts:

Practice Exercise 5.4
Self-Assessment

Goal: In this exercise, assess whether you understand how to organize the substantive and procedural facts in a case.

For this exercise, assume that you are representing Ms. Evelyn Michel, who was terminated from her employment as a nurse because she failed the National Council Licensure Examination. She wants to know if she will qualify for unemployment insurance benefits. *De Grego v. Levine*, 347 N.E. 2d 611 (N.Y. 1976)(Appendix C). Try to apply the concepts introduced in this chapter relating to understanding the substantive and procedural facts.

5.4–1   Does the caption indicate who brought the appeal? Is there anything unusual about how the caption is arranged?

5.4–2   Who initiated the case and who was sued?

5.4–3   What is the best way to organize the substantive facts?

5.4–4   Summarize the substantive facts.

5.4–5   Summarize the procedural facts.

Evaluate your understanding of the skills in this chapter by completing the following rubric. For each skill, circle whether you are at the proficient or developing level. Everyone can get to the proficient level over time.

Skill	Competency Level	
	Proficient	Developing
Understands that the substantive facts are important.	<ul><li>Identifies the parties and legal claims.</li><li>Creates a mental image of the facts and prepares charts, diagrams, or chronologies.</li><li>Asks questions about the facts.</li><li>Reads facts slowly and rereads when necessary.</li></ul>	<ul><li>Skips over the parties and legal claims.</li><li>Does not take notes.</li><li>Does not ask questions.</li><li>Skips over confusing sections.</li></ul>
Understands that the procedural facts are important.	<ul><li>Identifies how the case was resolved in the trial and appellate courts.</li><li>Summarizes the procedural chronology.</li></ul>	<ul><li>Does not examine the procedural sequence of events.</li><li>Does not take notes.</li></ul>

CHAPTER 6

DURING READING: STRATEGIES TO UNDERSTAND TEXT

I. SUMMARY

Expert legal readers:

- recognize that the language in some cases is complex, and

- use a variety of strategies to understand this language.

At the conclusion of this chapter, you will be able to employ a variety of techniques to analyze language such as:

- rereading,

- looking for topic sentences,

- looking up unfamiliar words,

- noticing conjunctions and repeated words, and

- reading passages aloud.

II. CHECKLIST

CASE READING CHECKLIST

Warning: Do not just highlight and underline.

Phase 1: Before Reading

1. Read for a purpose and assume the role of advocate or judge.

2. Read with energy and focus.

3. Notice case structure.

4. Understand the general subject matter by examining:

   a. course syllabus, casebook table of contents, or research assignment, and

   b. parties, citation, court, and date.

5. Read for an overview by skimming and noticing organization, headings, who won, and what case is generally about.

Phase 2: Reading More Carefully

1. Understand the facts.

2. **Reread, look up unfamiliar words, analyze confusing language, and vary reading speed.**

3. Understand the main ideas set forth in the issue, holding, and reasoning.

4. Identify the rule.

5. Take notes with your reactions and brief the case.

Phase 3: After Reading

1. Evaluate the decision, ask questions, and talk with professors.

2. Determine how cases fit together with other cases and synthesize.

III. UNDERSTANDING LANGUAGE

Sometimes it is easy to understand books, and sometimes they are difficult to follow. Whether they are easy or hard to comprehend, we often notice new things when we read a book for the second time. When books are confusing, we use strategies to make sense of them. We may look up words, reread, or talk with friends to get clarification. Practice Exercise 6.1 provides an opportunity to reflect on strategies you have used to analyze confusing text.

Reading cases is similar. Some cases are clear, and it is easy to pick out the issue, rule, holding, and rationale as the court explicitly sets forth these parts of the case. Even in these situations, the reader may notice new things after a second read. However, some cases are more difficult. Perhaps the language is unclear, or the topic is less familiar. In these situations, it is necessary to employ different strategies to figure out the meaning of the text.

As discussed in Chapter 1, expert readers recognize when text is confusing and are aware of what they know and do not know. They accept the fact that some sections of cases are complex, and they try to make sense of these sections **before** continuing to read. Instead of simply reading a case from beginning to end without stopping, expert readers go back and review passages and use a variety of techniques to better comprehend the text.

In contrast, novice readers are often unaware that they are confused. They may expect to be able to read everything just once. They may try to ignore confusing parts of cases, or just keep reading, and hope that they will be able to figure things out. They also do not employ strategies to resolve their confusion. One difference between expert and novice readers is that when novice readers "encounter a comprehension problem. they don't seem to have active ways to *fix up* the difficulty."[1]

If you think you do not understand something, assume that you do not. Studies have shown that law students tend to "overestimate their understanding" of text.[2] This chapter provides troubleshooting strategies so that the reader is equipped with specific steps that can be used to understand text. The techniques introduced in this chapter will be used throughout this book to assist in identifying main ideas (Chapter 7) and rules (Chapter 8). The strategies will also be used in connection with case evaluation (Chapter 9), case briefing (Chapter 10), case synthesis (Chapter 11), and statutory analysis (Chapter 12).

IV. STRATEGIES FOR UNDERSTANDING LANGUAGE IN CASES

When reading a case, it is necessary to look at the big picture and examine text in the context of the entire decision. It is also essential to look at specific words and phrases. This chapter presents both large-scale and small-scale techniques to assist the reader in understanding language in cases.

The large-scale or macro strategies are:

- use context clues,

- reread,

- look for topic sentences, and

- analyze the main ideas and supporting details in paragraphs.

The small-scale or micro techniques are:

- look up unfamiliar words,

- notice conjunctions such as and/or,

- notice repeated words,

- keep track of pronoun references,

- break complex sentences into shorter sections, and

- read passages aloud.

Each of these techniques can be useful in different reading situations. It is not necessary to use all of these strategies for every case. The goal is

---

[1]   Beth Davey, *Think Aloud: Modeling the Cognitive Processes of Reading Comprehension*, 27 J. of Reading, No. 1 44, 45 (1983).

[2]   Dorothy H. Evensen, James F. Stratman, Laurel C. Oates, and Sarah Zappe, *Developing an Assessment of First-Year Law Students' Critical Case Reading and Reasoning Ability: Phase 2* 3, LSAC Research Report Series (March 2008).

to equip readers with an arsenal of ways to resolve different types of language challenges.

Some of these techniques have been mentioned in previous chapters. Figure 6.1 indicates where the strategy has been discussed so that you can review the basic information that has been provided. This chapter provides more detail as well as specific examples.

Figure 6.1
Techniques for Understanding Text

Technique	Chapter	Information in Chapter
Think about context	4	Use context to understand cases.
Reread	4	Read for a general overview and then read more carefully.
	5	Reread facts.
Look for topic sentences	4	Notice topic sentences during case overview.
Analyze paragraphs		New
Look up words	5	Look up words when reading facts.
Notice conjunctions		New
Notice repeated words		New
Keep track of pronoun references		New
Break up sentences		New
Read aloud		New

A. LARGE-SCALE STRATEGIES

1. Think About Context

Context clues found in the case summary and headnotes can help the reader understand complex language in cases. These context clues essentially provide the reader with a title for a passage. Just as the title made it easier to understand the paragraph in Chapter 4 about organizing a closet, context clues also make it easier to understand language. *Garratt v. Dailey,* 279 P.2d 1091, 1093 (Wash. 1955) (Appendix G) provides an example of how context clues in the case summary and headnotes can clarify language. In *Garratt*, Brian Dailey, a five-year-old, was in the backyard and moved the lawn chair plaintiff Ruth Garratt was about to sit on. The plaintiff fell and claimed that Dailey was liable for battery because he intended to move the chair and cause her to fall. The court's discussion of battery in Figure 6.2 is not easy to understand.

Figure 6.2
Context: *Garratt*

> " '*Character of actor's intention.* In order that an act may be done with the intention of bringing about a harmful or offensive contact or an apprehension thereof to a particular person, either the other or a third person, the act must be done for the purpose of causing the contact or apprehension or with knowledge on the part of the actor that such contact or apprehension is substantially certain to be produced.' " *Garratt v. Dailey,* 279 P.2d 1091, 1093 (Wash. 1955).

Context clues in the case summary help clarify this passage. The case summary in *Garratt* states:

> "case would be remanded to obtain finding whether boy, when he moved chair, knew, with substantial certainty, that plaintiff would attempt to sit down where chair had been." *Id.* at 1091.

This summary (**that can never be quoted or cited in a memorandum or brief**) gives the reader some information to begin understanding the sentence in Figure 6.2. It is easier to comprehend the phrase

- whether a boy "knew, with substantial certainty, that plaintiff would attempt to sit down where chair had been,"

than the phrase

- "the act must be done for the purpose of causing the contact or apprehension or with knowledge on the part of the actor that such contact or apprehension is substantially certain to be produced."

Context clues can assist in understanding complex language.

2. Reread

Rereading is an essential step in understanding language in cases. While some decisions are clear after one reading, on the second read, the reader may see new information and interrelationships that were not apparent at first. Whether the meaning of a case is clear or confusing, a second read will always reveal additional details and nuances.

As discussed in Chapter 5, rereading assists in understanding the facts. During the first read, it is necessary to figure out a chronology or diagram the facts. During the second read, after the reader understands the legal concepts, it is possible to determine which facts relate to the legal concepts. Rereading facts places the facts in the context of the law. It is not possible to analyze facts in one reading.

Expert readers also expect to read a case more than once to locate the issue and holding and understand the court's reasoning, which will be discussed in Chapter 7. Sometimes the court sets forth complicated tests that need to be taken apart and analyzed. On other occasions, the court's reasoning is based on precedents that are not easy to understand. Furthermore, expert legal readers always reread rules or statutes (Chapter 12) that need to be broken down into elements. On many occasions, attorneys read a case multiple times to fully extract the key ideas.

Finally, rereading is necessary when language is complex or unclear. If the reader tries to ignore the confusion and hopes it will go away, it is very likely that the reader will just get more confused. Experts routinely reread when they do not understand a passage. Rereading clears up confusion and makes subsequent reading more efficient and effective.

Contrary to what you might think, rereading does not take more time. As demonstrated in the Christensen study in Figure 6.3, while the higher performing students reread portions of an opinion until they understood them, the lower performing students did not reread the case. While all of the students spent the same overall amount of time reading the case, the higher performing students had higher levels of comprehension.[3] This study demonstrates that while students may believe they will save time by reading cases just once, rereading may not add to the total reading time.

Figure 6.3
Rereading: Christensen Study

Student	Rereading
Student (Top 10%)	"Ok. So here, this is probably the third or fourth time that I read this sentence. And now, it's finally clear what's going on."[4]
Student (Bottom 2%)	Student made an "incorrect assumption about the subject matter of the case"[5] after reading the first paragraph. Instead of rereading the text, he stated, **"Okay, I'm going to read on."**[6]

There is an important caveat regarding rereading. While rereading is an excellent comprehension strategy, it is not a good study strategy. This means that it **is** necessary to reread cases to comprehend what they mean. However, when studying for law school exams, it **is not** helpful to simply

---

[3] Leah M. Christensen, *"One L of a Year": How to Maximize Your Success in Law School* 38 (2012).

[4] *Id.* at 37.

[5] *Id.* at 35.

[6] *Id.*

reread cases. It is more effective to do practice problems, explain information to other students, and create your own hypothetical problems to solve as is discussed in Chapter 9.

3. Notice Topic Sentences

Topic sentences summarize the main ideas in a paragraph and are often found in the first or last sentences of a paragraph. Topic sentences were useful to notice when doing a quick overview of a case in Chapter 4. They can also assist the reader in understanding language in cases. The topic sentence can be used as a title for the passage. If language in a paragraph is confusing, identify the topic sentence to clarify where the sentence is going. For example, the difficult sentence from *Garratt* in Figure 6.2 is introduced with the following topic sentence:

> **Topic sentence:** "We have in this case no question of consent or privilege. We therefore proceed to an immediate consideration of intent and its place in the law of battery." *Garratt v. Dailey,* 279 P.2d 1091, 1093 (Wash. 1955).

> **Complex *Garratt* Sentence:** " '*Character of actor's intention.* In order that an act may be done with the intention of bringing about a harmful or offensive contact or an apprehension thereof to a particular person, either the other or a third person, the act must be done for the purpose of causing the contact or apprehension or with knowledge on the part of the actor that such contact or apprehension is substantially certain to be produced.' " *Id.*

The topic sentence helps the reader understand that the general topic of the sentence relates to intent. This information makes the complex *Garratt* sentence easier to follow.

4. Analyze Paragraphs

When a sentence is not clear, it may be useful to analyze the sentence in light of the entire paragraph and identify the topic, main idea, and supporting details in the paragraph. The following steps can be taken:

1. Figure out the general topic or overall subject of the paragraph. Sometimes the general topic can be determined by the repetition of key words.

2. Next, find the main idea which is often found in the topic sentence of the paragraph.

3. Finally, look for supporting details such as cases that are explained in the decision.

For complicated paragraphs, it can be helpful to create outlines that set forth the topic, main idea and supporting details in this manner.

Once the main idea is identified, go on to the next paragraph and if it is confusing, do the same thing. Once the main idea in each paragraph is identified, create an outline to show the relationships between the paragraphs as it is always important to look at cases as a whole. While it is not necessary to do this for each paragraph in an opinion, this can be helpful for more troublesome sections.

B. SMALL-SCALE STRATEGIES

1. Look Up Words

Look up all words that are unclear. Lawyers and students must learn new vocabulary. It is not advisable to guess at the meaning of words. If you were learning a new language, you would expect to learn new words and would not skip over or make up meanings for unknown words. Law is a new language and the meanings of words need to be examined in four different situations:

- terms may have purely legal meanings that non-lawyers would not be expected to know,

- words may have everyday meanings that are different from legal meanings,

- terms may have multiple meanings, and

- words may be unfamiliar.

The *Garratt* case provides examples of all four situations. First, some words have **specialized legal meanings** such as the term "preponderance of evidence" found at the beginning of the opinion. The reader must understand the legal meaning of this term.

Second, some words have **everyday meanings that are different from their legal meanings**. If the reader uses an everyday meaning rather than the correct legal definition, the reader may interpret the passage incorrectly. For example, *Garratt* uses the term "intent" in the passage in Figure 6.2. This term has different everyday and legal meanings. The everyday meaning of the term "intention" is to have a goal or purpose. However, there are multiple legal definitions of intent depending upon whether the case is a civil case such as battery or a criminal case. There are also different types of intent in criminal cases. The reader must use the correct definition of the term.

Third, some words in *Garratt* have **multiple meanings**. The word "apprehension" can mean an arrest or fear. The word "deliberately" can mean to do something on purpose or to do something slowly. The word "concede" can mean to agree that something is true or to give up. These terms must be defined appropriately.

Finally, a reader may **not be familiar** with some everyday words. For example, "obviate," which means to avoid, is used in the first page of the *Garratt* opinion. The trial court "obviated" the need for a retrial by deciding that the plaintiff would be entitled to $11,000 if there was a judgment against Brian Dailey, even though the court did not find that Dailey was liable. The reader must understand this word to fully comprehend the decision.

2. Notice Conjunctions

To make sense of confusing passages or to understand any passage, the reader must pay attention to conjunctions such as "and" and "or." These terms are often used in connection with rules in cases. The conjunction "and" means that multiple elements of a rule must be met to establish a claim. The term "or" indicates that there are alternate requirements for a rule or test. Conjunctions are key words that assist the reader in properly identifying the requirements or elements of a rule.

The *Garratt* case demonstrates the importance of understanding conjunctions. Figure 6.4 sets forth a sentence from *Garratt* where the court states a rule for battery. It is important to carefully read the conjunctions, "and" and "or," to understand this passage. The conjunctions are highlighted in bold and underlined.

**Figure 6.4
Conjunctions: *Garratt***

"An act which, directly **or** indirectly, is the legal cause of a harmful contact with another's person makes the actor liable to the other, if

    (a)   the act is done with the intention of bringing about a harmful **or** offensive contact **or** an apprehension thereof to the other **or** a third person, **and**

    (b)   the contact is not consented to by the other **or** the other's consent thereto is procured by fraud **or** duress, **and**

    (c)   the contact is not otherwise privileged." *Id.* at 1093. (emphasis added).

This rule can be outlined by separating out the conjunctions as demonstrated in Figure 6.5.

**Figure 6.5
Conjunction Outline**

An act which, directly

      or

  indirectly,

is the legal cause of a harmful contact with another's person makes the actor liable to the other, if the

(a) act is done with the intention of bringing about a harmful

> **or**

offensive contact

> **or**

an apprehension thereof

> > to the other

> > > **or**

> > > a third person,

> **and**

(b) the contact is not consented to by the other

> **or**

the other's consent thereto is procured

> > by fraud

> > > **or**

> > duress,

> **and**

(c) the contact is not otherwise privileged."

The reader can clarify language and rules by paying attention to conjunctions.

3. Notice Repeated Words

One effective way of understanding confusing sections of opinions is to look for recurring words or phrases. Courts will often repeat key terms, and this repetition can help explain the meaning of a passage. In *Garratt*, the passage set out in Figure 6.6 is not easy to comprehend. However, once the reader notices the repeated words, the meaning is clarified. The repeated terms are highlighted in bold and underlined:

Figure 6.6
Repeated Words: *Garratt*

"In this connection, we quote another portion of the comment on the 'Character of actor's **intention**,' relating to clause (a) of the rule from the Restatement heretofore set forth:

'It is not enough that the act itself is **intentionally** done and this, even though the actor **realizes** or should **realize** that it contains a very grave risk of bringing about the contact or apprehension. Such **realization** may make the actor's conduct negligent or even reckless but unless he **realizes that to a substantial certainty**, the contact or apprehension will result, the actor has not that **intention** which is necessary to make him liable under the rule stated in this section.'

A battery would be established if, in addition to plaintiff's fall, it was proved that, when Brian moved the chair, he **knew with substantial certainty** that the plaintiff would attempt to sit down where the chair had been. If Brian had any of the **intents** which the trial court found, in the italicized portions of the findings of fact quoted above, that he did not have, he would of course have had the **knowledge** to which we have referred. The mere absence of any **intent** to injure the plaintiff or to play a prank on her or to embarrass her, or to commit an assault and battery on her would not absolve him from liability if in fact he had such **knowledge**. Mercer v. Corbin, 1889, 117 Ind. 450, 20 N.E. 132, 3 L.R.A. 221. Without such **knowledge**, there would be nothing wrongful about Brian's act in moving the chair and, there being no wrongful act, there would be no liability." *Id.* at 1093–94.

The words **realize**, **intent** and **knowledge** are found three times. By noticing these words, the reader learns that knowledge and realization are important themes that are related to the idea of intent. The term **substantial certainty** is repeated twice. The terms realize and knowledge are also connected with the phrase substantial certainty in two sentences. By noticing these repeated terms, the reader can recognize that the passage means that someone has the requisite intent for battery if he **realizes or knows with substantial certainty** that a result will occur.

4. Keep Track of Pronoun References

When a sentence is not clear, keep track of pronoun references. Courts often use nouns and then refer to these nouns or names with pronouns. For example, in *Garratt*, the opinion introduces the plaintiff Ruth Garratt and then refers to her as "she." When reading the opinion, it is important to remember that "she" refers to the plaintiff. When there are multiple persons in an opinion, pronoun references can be confusing. These references can also be unclear if the noun and pronoun are not on the same page. If a party is mentioned on page one of an opinion and the pronoun reference is on the last page, it is easy for the reader to get confused regarding the identity of the person. Be careful in matching pronouns and nouns.

It is also important to pay attention to other types of pronouns such as this, that, and which. These words can refer back to an entire idea. For example in *Garratt*, the court notes that "plaintiff based her case on **that** theory, and the trial court held that she failed in her proof." *Id.* at 1093. (emphasis added). The word "**that**" refers back to the previous paragraph where the court explained plaintiff's theory of the case.

5.   Break Complex Sentences into Shorter Sections

Sometimes, sentences are unclear simply because they are very long. Breaking a sentence into shorter sentences or phrases is an easy way to clarify language. The sentence from *Garratt* in Figure 6.7 is an example of a long sentence.

Figure 6.7
Long Sentences: *Garratt*

"While a finding that Brian had no such knowledge can be inferred from the findings made, we believe that before the plaintiff's action in such a case should be dismissed there should be no question but that the trial court had passed upon that issue; hence, the case should be remanded for clarification of the findings to specifically cover the question of Brian's knowledge, because intent could be inferred therefrom." *Id.* at 1094.

This sentence would be easier to understand if it was divided into three parts:

1.   While a finding that Brian had no such knowledge can be inferred from the findings made.

2.   We believe that before the plaintiff's action in such a case should be dismissed there should be no question but that the trial court had passed upon that issue.

3.   Hence, the case should be remanded for clarification of the findings to specifically cover the question of Brian's knowledge, because intent could be inferred therefrom.

A fast and easy way to improve comprehension is to break long sentences into shorter sections by adding periods.

6.   Read Passage Aloud

Sometimes it helps to read passages aloud. This technique forces the reader to slow down and focus more carefully on the text. It can be helpful to read passages aloud by yourself or with other people. After you read aloud, try to put the passage in your own words and explain the text.

Practice Exercise 6.2 provides an opportunity to use some of the strategies outlined in this chapter to understand complex language in cases. Practice Exercise 6.3 is the self-assessment exercise.

V. CASE EXAMPLE: STRATEGIES TO UNDERSTAND TEXT

This section will review the strategies outlined in this chapter using *Fisher v. Carrousel Motor Hotel, Inc.*, 424 S.W.2d 627 (Tex. 1967) (Appendix B-1).

A. LARGE-SCALE STRATEGIES

1. Think About Context

Context clues from the case summary and headnotes can assist the reader in understanding difficult passages. The case summary in *Fisher*, which can serve as a type of title to the case, states that:

> "where the manager of the motor hotel's club dispossessed plaintiff of his dinner plate in a loud and offensive manner a battery occurred on which damages for mental suffering could be based and the motor hotel was liable for exemplary damages." *Id.* at 627.

This summary indicates that battery can occur when someone's plate is grabbed in an offensive manner. This "title" makes it easier to understand the complex language from the *Fisher* opinion that is set forth in Figure 6.8.

Figure 6.8
Context: Unclear Language

"Since the essence of the plaintiff's grievance consists in the offense to the dignity involved in the unpermitted and intentional invasion of the inviolability of his person and not in any physical harm done to his body, it is not necessary that the plaintiff's actual body be disturbed." *Id.* at 629.

2. Reread

As discussed in Chapter 5, rereading assists the reader in understanding the relevant facts. While the basic incident is clear after one read, it is only after understanding the legal concepts, i.e., that battery can occur when there is offensive touching to an object "closely associated" with someone's body, that the relevant facts can be identified. The fact that Fisher went to a conference on telemetry equipment is not relevant. The result would be the same whether he was an engineer or a botanist.

However, the fact that he was in a setting with his professional peers does relate to his feelings of humiliation and the offensiveness of the contact.

Rereading *Fisher* also helps the reader integrate facts in different parts of the opinion. While the basic incident at the Brass Ring Club is outlined at the beginning of the case, the reader discovers on the last page of the opinion that Flynn was "attempting to enforce the Club rules by depriving Fisher of service." *Id.* at 631. In the context of the entire decision, it is significant that Flynn was enforcing accepted rules rather than simply acting on his own.

Finally, rereading makes it easier to understand passages that are not clear such as the sentence in Figure 6.8 above.

3.   Notice Topic Sentences

The topic sentences in *Fisher* introduce the separate subjects in the case. The following topic sentences assist the reader in analyzing the case:

- The first sentence in the opinion sets forth the overall general topics of battery and damages. "This is a suit for actual and exemplary damages growing out of an alleged assault and battery." *Id.* at 628.

- The paragraph that addresses the procedural facts begins with a topic sentence that summarizes the jury verdict and the intermediate appellate court decision. "The jury found that Flynn 'forceably dispossessed plaintiff of his dinner plate' and 'shouted in a loud and offensive manner' that Fisher could not be served there, thus subjecting Fisher to humiliation and indignity." *Id.*

- The paragraph on battery is introduced by a topic sentence that states, "Under the facts of this case, we have no difficulty in holding that the intentional grabbing of plaintiff's plate constituted a battery." *Id.* at 629.

- The paragraph on exemplary damages starts with the topic sentence, "[w]e now turn to the question of the liability of the corporations for exemplary damages." *Id.* at 630.

These topic sentences help the reader understand the paragraphs that follow.

4.   Analyze Paragraphs

Most paragraphs are composed of a general topic, main ideas, and supporting details. If a reader finds a portion of an opinion confusing, it is helpful to examine the general topic, main ideas, and supporting details in several paragraphs. The paragraphs in Figure 6.9 from *Fisher* can be analyzed in this way to elucidate the text.

Figure 6.9
Paragraph Analysis

"Under the facts of this case, we have no difficulty in holding that the intentional grabbing of plaintiff's plate constituted a battery. The intentional snatching of an object from one's hand is as clearly an offensive invasion of his person as would be an actual contact with the body. 'To constitute an assault and battery, it is not necessary to touch the plaintiff's body or even his clothing; knocking or snatching anything from plaintiff's hand or touching anything connected with his person, when, done is an offensive manner, is sufficient.' Morgan v. Loyacomo, 190 Miss. 656, 1 So.2d 510 (1941).

Such holding is not unique to the jurisprudence of this State. In S.H. Kress & Co. v. Brashier, 50 S.W.2d 922 (Tex.Civ.App.1932, no writ), the defendant was held to have committed 'an assault or trespass upon the person' by snatching a book from the plaintiff's hand. The jury findings in that case were that the defendant 'dispossessed plaintiff of the book' and caused her to suffer 'humiliation and indignity.'

The rationale for holding an offensive contact with such an object to be a battery is explained in 1 Restatement of Torts 2d s 18 (Comment p. 31) as follows:

'Since the essence of the plaintiff's grievance consists in the offense to the dignity involved in the unpermitted and intentional invasion of the inviolability of his person and not in any physical harm done to his body, it is not necessary that the plaintiff's actual body be disturbed. Unpermitted and intentional contacts with anything so connected with the body as to be customarily regarded as part of the other's person and therefore as partaking of its inviolability is actionable as an offensive contact with his person. There are some things such as clothing or a cane or, indeed, anything directly grasped by the hand which are so intimately connected with one's body as to be universally regarded as part of the person.' " *Id.* at 629.

The first sentence in Figure 6.9 sets forth the general topic, battery. The main idea or topic sentence is found in the next sentence which states that the "intentional snatching of an object from one's hand is as clearly an offensive invasion of his person as would be an actual contact with the body."

The details are found in the examples from previous cases. *Morgan v. Loyacomo*, 1 So. 2d 510 (Miss. 1941) is an example of a case where the court ruled that a battery could occur where there was an offensive touching if something was knocked or snatched from a person's hand. Another example is provided by a Texas appellate court decision, *S.H. Kress & Co.*

v. Brashier, where someone took a book from another person. The final example is found in sections of the Restatement of Torts. By examining the topic sentence, main ideas, and examples, the reader can more easily comprehend the passage.

B. SMALL-SCALE STRATEGIES

1. Look Up Words

Some words in the *Fisher* opinion may need to be looked up for several reasons. First, some terms have purely legal meanings such as the word "stipulation." This legal term means an agreement among the parties and has significance because it means that the parties agreed that Flynn was an employee of Carrousel Hotel.

Second, some words have legal meanings that are different from their everyday meanings. For example, the word "exemplary" has several meanings. In ordinary conversation, exemplary can mean a model or example and is considered a positive trait. Someone who is an exemplary student is a great student. However, exemplary damages are punitive damages that are awarded when a defendant's conduct is particularly offensive. This meaning is quite different from the everyday meaning. If a reader used the incorrect meaning of the word exemplary, the sentence "We now turn to the question of the liability of the corporation for exemplary damages," *Fisher*, 424 S.W.2d at 630, could be interpreted incorrectly. The reader might interpret the sentence to mean that exemplary damages would make a corporation a positive model for other corporations. In fact, the sentence means the opposite. The corporation could be liable for additional damages to make them an example of poor behavior and to deter other corporations from behaving in a similar manner.

Third, some words have multiple meanings. For example, "offensive" can mean to attack or to make someone feel hurt. It is important to pick out the correct meaning.

Finally, some words may be unfamiliar because they are not used in everyday conversation. For example, in *Fisher*, the jury found that Flynn " 'forceably dispossessed plaintiff of his dinner plate.' " *Fisher*, 424 S.W.2d at 629. The word "dispossessed" means taken from someone. The *Fisher* opinion also uses the word "inviolability" that is not often used in conversation, which means not violated. Readers must be familiar with the meaning of these words to understand the decision.

2. Notice Conjunctions

The following sentence in *Fisher* contains conjunctions that must be read carefully:

"The protection extends to any part of the body, **or** to anything which is attached to it **and** practically identified with it." *Id.* at 629. (emphasis added).

This sentence can be outlined as follows:

The protection extends to:

- Any part of the body

  or

- To anything which is

  ○ Attached to it

    and

  ○ Practically identified with it.

This outline helps the reader understand that the protection extends to two different things, the body or anything attached to the body and identified with the body.

3.   Notice Repeated Words

Repeated words can give the reader clues about important themes and main ideas. In *Fisher,* a key word, "offensive," is found five times at the beginning of the opinion. The court refers to "offensive manner" twice, "offensive invasion," "offensive contact," and "offensive." The words "dignity," "indignity," and "humiliation" are also repeated.

There are many references to terms relating to touching and contact. The terms "not actually touched," "no physical contact," "not necessary to touch the plaintiff's body," "not necessary that the plaintiff's actual body be disturbed," and "not actual harm done to the plaintiff's body" are repeated. In addition, the term "invasion" is used on three occasions. These repeated terms indicate that the court focuses on the meaning of offensive contact when someone is not actually touched.

4.   Keep Track of Pronoun References

The *Fisher* case uses pronouns clearly so that it is easy to understand the references to "he." However, it is also important to keep track of pronoun references to concepts. For example, the court mentions the " 'new tort' of intentional interference with peace of mind." *Id.* at 630. The court later makes reference to "such a cause of action" which is a reference back to this new tort of intentional interference.

5.   Break Complex Sentences into Shorter Sections

The sentence from Figure 6.8 is reproduced below and is easier to understand if it is broken into shorter sections. As there are several ideas in this sentence, breaking the sentence into parts helps the reader analyze the concepts.

Entire sentence:

"Since the essence of the plaintiff's grievance consists in the offense to the dignity involved in the unpermitted and intentional invasion of the inviolability of his person and not in any physical harm done to his body, it is not necessary that the plaintiff's actual body be disturbed." *Id.* at 629.

Sentence divided into shorter sections:

1. the essence of the plaintiff's grievance.

2. consists in the offense to dignity involved in the unpermitted and intentional invasion of the inviolability of his person and not in any physical harm done to his body.

3. it is not necessary that the plaintiff's actual body be disturbed.

Breaking up long sentences by adding periods is an easy way to improve comprehension.

VI. PRACTICE

Reflection Exercise 6.1
How Can I Understand This?

Goal: The purpose of this exercise is to reflect on strategies you have used to understand difficult texts in the past and determine if these techniques might be useful for reading cases.

We have all come across passages in texts and novels that are difficult to understand. What strategies have helped you understand complex text?

Strategy	Was Strategy Helpful?

Practice Exercise 6.2
Strategies for Understanding Language in Cases

Goal: The purpose of this exercise is to practice using a variety of strategies to understand text in cases.

In researching the law of battery for Mr. Parker's case, you have found *Morgan v. Loyacomo*, 1 So. 2d 510 (Miss. 1941) (Appendix F). You decide to read the case to understand the law of battery. In Practice Exercise 4.2, you examined the general context of *Morgan v. Loyacomo* and skimmed the case quickly for an overview. Now you will read the case more carefully.

Step 1: Read the facts related to the underlying dispute (the substantive facts).

6.2–1   Who are the parties in the underlying dispute?

6.2–2   What is the best way to organize the facts?

Step 2: As you read the facts, you find the following sentence:

> "Without making any inquiry either of the clerk or of appellee before appellee left the store, which if done would have readily revealed that the manager's suspicions were without any ground, White permitted appellee to leave the store, but followed her; and when about a block away and in the presence of several persons, he called to appellee, stated that he was obliged to investigate whether she had taken two articles while paying for only one, forcibly seized the package from under her arm, opened it, examined and exhibited the contents in the presence of the third persons, and found that he was in error, which, as already mentioned, he could easily have ascertained by a proper inquiry conducted in a proper manner before appellee left the store." *Id.* at 511.

What strategies can you use to better understand this sentence?

Strategy	Was Strategy Helpful?
6.2–3 Reread.	
6.2–4 Look up words.	
6.2–5 Notice conjunctions.	
6.2–6 Pay attention to pronoun references.	
6.2–7 Break sentence into parts.	
6.2–8 Read aloud.	

Step 3: Review the substantive facts.

6.2–9   Summarize the substantive facts in your own words.

Step 4: As you continue reading, the following sentences are found in the second paragraph of the decision:

> "It is the first contention that there was no assault and battery, and that the words of White, with his attendant conduct, did not amount to a slander. Appellants are mistaken that White's actions did not constitute an assault and battery. The authorities are agreed that, to constitute an assault and battery, it is not necessary to touch the plaintiff's body or even his clothing; knocking or snatching anything from plaintiff's hand or touching anything connected with his person, when done in a rude or insolent manner, is sufficient." *Id.* at 511.

What strategies can you use to read the sentences in this paragraph?

Strategy	Was Strategy Helpful?
6.2–10 Reread.	
6.2–11 Look up words.	
6.2–12 Notice conjunctions.	
6.2–13 Pay attention to repeated words.	
6.2–14 Break up sentence into parts.	
6.2–15 Read aloud.	

Practice Exercise 6.3
Self-Assessment

Goal: The purpose of this exercise is to assess whether you can use a variety of strategies to understand language.

For this exercise, assume that you are representing Ms. Evelyn Michel, who was terminated from her employment as a nurse because she failed the National Council Licensure Examination. She wants to know if she will qualify for unemployment insurance benefits. *De Grego v. Levine,* 347 N.E. 2d 611 (N.Y. 1976) (Appendix C). Try to apply the concepts introduced in this chapter relating to understanding complex language as you read the following sentence from *De Grego*:

"Provoked discharge, a gloss over the statutory disqualification for voluntary separation without good cause (Labor Law, s 593, subd. 1) is a narrowly drawn legal fiction designed to apply where an employee voluntarily engages in conduct which transgresses a legitimate known obligation and leaves the employer no choice but to discharge him." *Id.* at 613.

What strategies can you use to understand this sentence?

Strategy	Was Strategy Helpful?
6.3–1 Reread	
6.3–2 Look up words.	
6.3–3 Notice conjunctions.	
6.3–4 Break up sentences.	
6.3–5 Read aloud.	

Evaluate your understanding of the skills in this chapter by completing the following rubric. For each skill, circle whether you are at the proficient or developing level. Everyone can get to the proficient level over time.

Skill	Competency Level	
	Proficient	Developing
Rereads.	• Expects to reread portions of cases.	• Expects to read cases once.
Notices topic sentences.	• Looks for topic sentences to clarify difficult language.	• Does not pay attention to topic sentences.
Looks up unfamiliar words.	• Looks up unfamiliar words.	• Skips over unfamiliar words.
Notices conjunctions and repeated words.	• Notices conjunctions and repeated words.	• Does not pay attention to conjunctions or repeated words.
Notices pronoun references.	• Understands how pronoun references affect meaning.	• Fails to pay attention to pronoun references.

Skill	Competency Level	
	Proficient	Developing
Breaks sentences into shorter sentences or phrases.	• Separates long sentences into shorter sections.	• Is confused by long sentences.

Checklist Reminder: Remember to create your own checklist. It might be helpful at the conclusion of each chapter to select the techniques you find helpful and add them to your checklist.

CHAPTER 7

DURING READING: STRATEGIES TO UNDERSTAND MAIN IDEAS (ISSUE, HOLDING, AND REASONING)

I. SUMMARY

This chapter focuses on reading to understand:

- the main ideas in a case, and

- the court's issue, holding, and reasoning.

While expert readers may remember significant aspects of a case, their focus is not on memorization. They read cases to identify and analyze the main ideas.

At the conclusion of this chapter, you will be able to:

- understand the main ideas in a case, and

- locate the issue, holding, and reasoning.

II. CHECKLIST

CASE READING CHECKLIST

Warning: Do not just highlight and underline.

Phase 1: Before Reading

1. Read for a purpose and assume the role of advocate or judge.

2. Read with energy and focus.

3. Notice case structure.

4. Understand the general subject matter by examining:

   a. course syllabus, casebook table of contents, or research assignment, and

   b. parties, citation, court, and date.

5. Read for an overview by skimming and noticing organization, headings, who won, and what case is generally about.

Phase 2: Reading More Carefully

1. Understand the facts.

2. Reread, look up unfamiliar words, analyze confusing language, and vary reading speed.

3. **Understand the main ideas set forth in the issue, holding, and reasoning.**

4. Identify the rule.

5. Take notes with your reactions and brief the case.

Phase 3: After Reading

1. Evaluate the decision, ask questions, and talk with professors.

2. Determine how cases fit together with other cases and synthesize.

III. IDENTIFICATION OF THE COURT'S ISSUE, HOLDING, AND REASONING IS ONE PART OF THE CRITICAL READING PROCESS

The identification of the issue, holding, and reasoning is an important part of the critical reading process. However, it is not the only part. Some students think that the first and last step in reading cases is to identify the issue, holding, and court's reasoning. These students often decide that their reading is done as soon as they highlight these parts of a case in different colors. However, this method alone is not effective.

Chapters 1 through 6 show that it is more efficient and productive to also read:

*   for the purpose of **solving a client's problem**,

*   from the **perspective of one of the parties** in the case,

*   with an understanding of the **structure of cases** and **basic procedural terms**,

*   by noticing the **case context** (textbook table of contents or the case summary and headnotes in a reported decision),

*   by skimming quickly for a **general overview**,

*   by understanding the **facts**, and

*   by utilizing strategies to understand complex language.

After these steps are completed, the reader is ready to read the opinion more carefully and understand the court's **main ideas**, which are set forth in the issue, holding, and reasoning.

The identification of the issue, holding, and reasoning is not the end of the reading process. Expert readers identify rules from cases (Chapter 8) and question and evaluate opinions (Chapter 9). Students who take all of these steps consistently outperform students who begin and end their analysis with the identification of the parts of a case.

IV. UNDERSTANDING THE MAIN IDEAS

The goal in reading a case is to understand the main ideas. We look for main ideas in a variety of contexts. When attending a speech, the audience tries to understand the main points of the presentation. While it is possible to extract a 30 second sound bite from a talk, this clip may or may not be representative of the meaning of the entire lecture. The sound bite can be taken out of context and may attribute a remark to a speaker that is ultimately rejected. It is important to pay attention to the big picture.

Reading cases is similar. Expert readers look for the main ideas in a case and recognize that one sentence may not be representative of the central point of the court's decision. It is easy to get lost in a case by focusing on individual sentences that may or may not reflect the main ideas. Opinions are composed of lots of parts because judges:

- analyze other decisions,

- reference opinions they agree with and cases they decide not to follow,

- summarize a lower court's decision they may reverse,

- examine opposing arguments of the parties, and

- discuss facts that are the basis for the opinion as well as facts that are not relied on.

If a reader tries to identify the main ideas by picking out random sentences, these sentences may not relate to the central ideas and may actually relate to an idea that the court ultimately rejected. Novice readers who find a "great quotation" from a case may later discover that the quote does not reflect the overall point of the case.

While novice legal readers may focus on identifying separate sections of an opinion, experts make connections between parts of the decision and understand that sentences and phrases must be read in the context of the entire case. They do not read a case to find an isolated phrase to quote. In the Lundeberg study that compared the reading strategies of lawyers and non-lawyers, the lawyers were twice as likely to view the case as a "cohesive whole," while the novices focused "more narrowly on one element of the case."[1]

V. STRATEGIES FOR FINDING MAIN IDEAS

A. GENERAL STRATEGIES

Before examining strategies for locating the issue, holding, and rationale in cases, think about techniques you have used to find the main ideas in other texts. Main ideas can be identified by looking for topic sentences or thesis statements. Sometimes, it is helpful to create outlines, concept maps, or summaries. In Reflection Exercise 7.1, think about strategies you have used in the past. In Practice Exercise 7.2, apply some of these techniques to find the main ideas in a law review article.

B. STRATEGIES FOR CASES

After examining strategies for finding main ideas that have worked for you in the past, it is useful to add some additional techniques to find the main ideas in cases and identify the issue, holding, and reasoning. The goal is to look at the individual parts of an opinion in the context of the entire case. Some general methods will be summarized and then specific ways to find the issue, holding, and reasoning will be explained.

First, start by thinking about the **purpose for reading** and **context**. As indicated in Chapter 1, the reading purpose determines what the reader looks for. As courts often write decisions on multiple topics, be selective in looking for the specific subjects that pertain to an assignment. It may be appropriate to read more quickly through issues that are not relevant to the problem and more carefully to understand areas that are pertinent. Headings and headnotes can help the reader place a case in context and find particular topics. When reading cases from casebooks for class, it is not necessary to read selectively as casebooks are edited and extraneous material is not included. However, it is helpful to use context and examine cases in light of the legal principles they are illustrating.

Second, remember that **cases are usually structured in a similar way**. As discussed in Chapter 3, after the court summarizes the facts, the opinion often identifies the issue, discusses other cases, explains the holding and rationale, and ends with the disposition. This structure helps the reader locate the issue, holding, and rationale.

Third, during the first reading of a case (after skimming for a brief overview), **focus on understanding the language in the opinion that is clear**. Good readers " 'listen' carefully to what a text says" just as good

---

[1] Mary A. Lundeberg, *Metacognitive Aspects of Reading Comprehension: Studying Understanding in Legal Case Analysis*, 22 Reading Res. Q. 407, 414 (1987).

listeners pay attention to conversation.[2] Furthermore, make sure that you are reading the words in the opinion rather than language you might expect to find. All readers form hypotheses as they read. For example, when reading a mystery, we tend to try to solve the mystery. Reading a case is similar. We try to figure out what happened during the dispute and predict how the court will decide the case. Readers need to be careful to read what the court actually wrote rather than what they expect the court to say.

Fourth, look for **topic sentences**. Just as topic sentences were useful to examine when doing a brief overview of a case in Chapter 4 and in understanding difficult language in Chapter 6, they are also helpful in identifying main ideas. While topic sentences can be anywhere in a paragraph, in court decisions they are most often in the first or last sentence. In *Garratt v. Dailey*, 279 P.2d 1091 (Wash. 1955) (Appendix G), a case that was explored in Chapter 6, topic sentences at the beginning of the paragraphs introduce the main ideas and sections of the case. The topic sentences in Figure 7.1 assist the reader in locating the facts and main ideas.

Figure 7.1
Topic Sentences: *Garratt*

Topic Sentence	Main Idea
"The liability of an infant for an alleged battery is presented to this court for the first time." *Id.* at 1092.	Introduces the facts.
"It is urged that Brian's action in moving the chair constituted a battery." *Id.* at 1093.	Begins the discussion of battery.
"It is clear to us that there was no change in theory so far as the plaintiff's case was concerned." *Id.* at 1094.	Explains the court's theory of the case.
"The plaintiff-appellant urges as another ground for a new trial that she was refused the right to cross-examine Brian." *Id.* at 1095.	Explains decision relating to right to cross-examine defendant.
"The plaintiff complains, and with some justice, that she was not permitted to take a pretrial deposition of the defendant Brian Dailey." *Id.*	Introduces discussion regarding right to take deposition.

---

[2]   John C. Bean et. al., *Reading Rhetorically* 46 (4th ed. 2014).

By separating the subjects, the topic sentences also permit the reader to focus on the main ideas that are significant for a particular assignment and pay less attention to topics that are not important.

Fifth, be aware that while **issues, holdings, and reasoning** are usually found in a case, these elements **may not be explicitly set forth**. Sometimes the court identifies the issue or holding. Sometimes these parts of a case are not specifically discussed or may be referred to with different terminology. Holdings may be blended with rules, the court's reasoning, or the disposition. While all of these sections are found in most cases, courts address them in a variety of ways.

Sixth, recognize that **there is more than one way to interpret a case**. As will be discussed more fully in Chapter 9, cases can be interpreted narrowly or broadly. The rationale of a case can be applied in different ways to solve new problems. While the purpose of this chapter is to provide techniques to identify the issue, holding, and rationale, keep in mind that there may not be one "correct" answer. Law is not black and white; it is filled with a great deal of gray. Therefore, if it sometimes seems difficult or confusing to identify parts of a case, you may be dealing with a grey area that is confusing. The strategies in this and upcoming chapters will help resolve the confusion.

Finally, take **notes** and write down your reactions as you read so that you can remember your good thoughts and questions. A method for preparing a case brief is outlined in Chapter 10.

C. ISSUE

1. What Is the Issue?

Issues set forth specific problems. We examine issues in many contexts. If a student does poorly on an exam, he may try to pinpoint the issue or the reason for the grade. Perhaps the student did not understand the text or studied the wrong material? If you wake up feeling sick, you try to determine why you feel bad. You first identify the part of your body that is affected. Is it your stomach or head? If you go to the doctor, the physician will try to narrow the diagnosis to determine the precise problem or issue.

Issues in cases are similar. They constitute the main questions addressed by the court. Attorneys read cases to find the problems examined by the court. Attorneys want to know the specific issue so that they know whether or not a case addresses a question that is similar to the problem faced by a client. For example, going back to Mr. Parker's dispute from Chapters 1, 2, and 3, the attorney representing Mr. Parker reads cases to determine if they address a situation similar to Mr. Parker's problem where someone grabbed an object held by someone else. If a case addresses torts in general, that case may not be helpful in solving Mr. Parker's problem. Just like the physician who wants to determine the exact diagnosis, Mr. Parker's attorney looks for cases that contain issues similar to Mr. Parker's problem.

Issues may be phrased generally or more specifically. A **general statement of the issue** in *Garratt v. Dailey,* 279 P.2d 1091 (Wash. 1955) would be:

 a.   Did Brian commit battery?

A more **complete statement of the issue** would be framed as follows:

 b.   Whether the defendant had the intent to commit battery and knew with substantial certainty that the plaintiff would attempt to sit down where the chair had been, when the defendant moved a chair while the plaintiff was in the process of sitting down.

The shorthand statement (a) refers to battery in general and only contains a reference to Brian without any additional facts. In contrast, the complete statement (b) mentions the more specific aspect of battery addressed in *Garratt,* i.e., intent. The more complete statement also includes more detailed facts relating to how Brian moved the chair while the plaintiff was sitting down.

2.   Finding the Issue

Sometimes courts phrase issues in a shorthand or general way and on occasion they provide a more complete statement. Courts may signal that they are setting forth the issue with the following types of wording:

The issue is . . .

The question we address here is whether . . .

The principal issue before us is whether . . .

If the court identifies the issue, check to see if the court has provided a brief statement or a more complete statement. If the court has only provided a brief statement of the issue or has not identified the issue at all, it is important to formulate a more complete statement. For class, writing assignments, and for actual legal work, it is important to be able to articulate a complete statement of the issue so that the precise problem in the case is identified.

The complete issue can be constructed by piecing together key or relevant facts with the specific legal problem. As discussed in Chapter 5, relevant or determinative facts are the facts that can change a legal result. Make sure that the issue contains facts as well as legal concepts. For example, in *Garratt,* where the court did not state the issue, the relevant facts (plaintiff fell when defendant moved chair while she was in the act of sitting down) can be combined with the key legal issue (intent in battery and substantial certainty that contact would result) to create a complete legal issue.

The following statement of the issue in *Garratt* would not be helpful because it has specific facts but no law:

Did the defendant know that plaintiff was attempting to sit down when he moved a chair?

This issue would not assist Mr. Parker's attorney in deciding whether the legal concepts in the case are similar to Parker's situation.

A purely legal statement of the issue also would not be useful for Mr. Parker's attorney. The following statement of the issue in *Garratt* is not helpful because it has law but no facts:

Did the defendant commit battery?

This statement does not help the reader understand the case because it does not contain any facts. In addition, the reference to the law is general and does not explain that the court is examining one specific aspect of battery that deals with intent. Good issues combine key facts with reference to specific legal concepts.

When courts do not explicitly state the issue, they sometimes narrow the issue by indicating that certain topics are not pertinent to the decision. For example, in *Garratt*, the court indicates that it does not need to address the question of whether a five-year-old could commit battery. The court makes it clear that a "five or fifty-five" year old can be responsible. *Id.* at 1093.

Issues are not easy to construct. It is often helpful to analyze the facts, locate the court's holding and reasoning, and then go back to formulate the issue.

D. HOLDING

1. What Is the Holding?

The holding is the court's decision. The holding may be a brief description of the result or a more complete statement. For class or writing assignments, it is important to be able to explain the court's decision.

2. Finding the Holding

Courts often use key words to signal they are making a decision. Some of these key words and phrases are:

We find . . .

We conclude . . .

We hold . . .

Occasionally, this terminology can be misleading because the court uses the term "holding" to reference its reasoning. Sometimes courts use a term such as "rule" to reference a holding.

However, holdings can be found, even in the absence of key words such as holding or rule, when the court sets forth its resolution of the problem. The following are two examples where courts did not use the term holding but did describe their decision:

> "The employees allege that Gate Gourmet deceived them into eating food in violation of their religious beliefs, knowing that this would cause an offensive contact. These allegations are sufficient to support a claim for battery at this stage." *Kumar v. Gate Gourmet, Inc.*, 325 P.3d 193, 205 (Wash. 2014).

> "[W]hen Furman intentionally blew cigar smoke in Leichtman's face, under Ohio common law, he committed a battery." *Leichtman v. WLW Jacor Communications, Inc.,* 634 N.E. 2d 697, 699 (Ohio Ct. App. 1994).

There may be several holdings in a case that contains multiple issues.

When the court does not use key words to signal the holding or describe the decision, the holding can be formulated by examining how the court resolved the issue. Holdings usually reference key facts and legal concepts. In *Garratt v. Dailey,* 279 P.2d 1091 (Wash. 1955), the court does not explicitly set forth the holding. By combining facts related to the case and the court's decision on intent, the holding can be summarized as follows:

> The court held that intent for purposes of battery could be found if the defendant knew with substantial certainty that when he pulled the chair away, the plaintiff would attempt to sit down and fall.

This holding indicates how the court resolved the case and contains facts relating to the incident as well as the specific legal principle addressed.

E. RATIONALE

1. What Is the Rationale?

The court's rationale is the reasoning behind the court's decision. It is the court's explanation as to how and why it reached a conclusion. The court's reasoning may affect how the opinion can be applied to new factual situations. Lawyers can argue that if there is a particular rationale for a decision, the case could be interpreted to promote that goal in resolving a new dispute.

2.   Finding the Rationale

Sometimes, the court explicitly sets forth the rationale. The court may use terms such as reason, policy, or rationale to signal that it is discussing the reasoning. The court may explain policy considerations.

However, even if the court does not explicitly set forth its reasoning, it is possible to understand the court's logic by examining cases referenced in the opinion. The court often starts its analysis by reviewing cases in its jurisdiction to see how other courts have interpreted an area of law. The court may adopt or reject the reasoning in these opinions. If there is no definitive precedent from its jurisdiction, the court may look at precedent from other jurisdictions and rely upon the reasoning in those decisions. This type of analysis may reveal the justification for the decision. In addition, courts may mention Restatements, which are treatises that address specific areas of the law, or law review articles. All of these types of references are useful in understanding the court's rationale.

For example, in *Garratt v. Dailey,* 279 P.2d 1091 (Wash. 1955), the decision does not specifically state its rationale. However, the opinion does analyze prior cases that dealt with the question of intent in battery cases as well as the Restatement of Torts. All of these references provide information about the logic of the opinion. *Id.* at 1093–99.

F.   DICTUM

Obitur dictum means words that are unnecessary to a decision or words that are said in passing. Sometimes, courts include observations or statements in an opinion that are not essential to the holding. These statements do not have precedential value and are considered dictum.

An example of dictum is found in *Morgan v. Loyacomo,* 1 So. 2d 510 (Miss. 1941) (Appendix F) that was the subject of Practice Exercises 4.2 and 6.2. In *Morgan*, after a customer left the store, the manager followed her and took a package from her because he suspected she had not paid for the merchandise. The court found that this action constituted the tort of battery. After setting forth its holding and rejecting the argument that the damages awarded were excessive, the court noted in dictum that in the past it had been "lenient rather than harsh" with managers who tried to deal with customers stealing merchandise. *Id.* at 511. The court's comment about leniency is dictum as it is a gratuitous comment.

G.   DISPOSITION

In the disposition, the court explains the procedures that will take place to implement the court's decision. it At the trial court level, a court can grant or deny a motion or enter a judgment in favor of the plaintiff or defendant. An appellate court can affirm, reverse, and/or remand the case. An affirmance means the court upholds the lower court's decision. Reversal means the appellate court reaches an opposite conclusion. When an appellate court remands, it sends the case back to the trial court with instructions to take certain action such as to conduct further hearings.

The court uses specific language to indicate the disposition. Some examples of disposition language are:

- The trial court's order dismissing this claim is therefore reversed.

- We affirm the trial court's judgment as to the first and third counts of the complaint and remand with respect to the second count.

The disposition of the case is normally found at the end of the opinion.

Garratt is an example of a case where the court remanded the case back to the trial court with specific instructions. The court noted that the trial court was:

> "to make definite findings on the issue of whether Brian Dailey knew with substantial certainty that the plaintiff would attempt to sit down where the chair which he moved had been, and to change the judgment if the findings warrant it." *Garratt*, 279 P.2d at 1095.

On remand, the trial court reviewed the evidence, listened to arguments from the parties, and made the decision that Brian did know with substantial certainty that when he removed the chair "the plaintiff would attempt to sit down where the chair had been, since she was in the act of seating herself when he removed the chair." 49 Wash. 2d 499, 500 (Wash. 1956).

H. DISSENTING/CONCURRING OPINIONS

Sometimes opinions have dissenting or concurring opinions. Dissenting opinions disagree with the factual or legal conclusions in the majority opinion. Concurring opinions agree with the ultimate decision of the majority opinion but may set forth different or additional reasoning for the decision.

While dissenting opinions are not "the law" and cannot be considered mandatory authority for future cases, they can provide the reader with an opportunity to better understand the majority opinion. Furthermore, today's dissenting opinion may become tomorrow's majority opinion if public policy considerations change.

Practice Exercise 7.3 provides an opportunity to identify the main ideas and individual parts of a case. Practice Exercise 7.4 gives you the opportunity to assess your mastery of the skills in this chapter.

VI. CASE EXAMPLE: STRATEGIES TO UNDERSTAND MAIN IDEAS

The strategies for understanding main ideas are explained using *Fisher v. Carrousel Motor Hotel, Inc.*, 424 S.W.2d 627 (Tex. 1967) (Appendix B-1).

A. PURPOSE

The purpose for reading *Fisher* determines which aspects of the opinion the reader should focus on. The case deals with three separate issues that relate to battery, damages, and the liability of corporations for punitive damages. If the assignment for Joe Parker's case only relates to battery, focus on that aspect of the opinion.

B. ISSUE

In *Fisher*, the court identifies all of the issues at the end of the first paragraph:

> "The questions before this Court are whether there was evidence that an actionable battery was committed, and, if so, whether the two corporate defendants must respond in exemplary as well as actual damages for the malicious conduct of Flynn." *Fisher*, 424 S.W.2d at 628.

This issue provides a general statement of all of the issues. A more complete statement of the battery issue would combine key facts with a more precise statement of the specific legal issue. A more complete issue regarding battery would include the following facts and law:

> Did battery occur when someone grabbed a plate held by Fisher, did not have any direct physical contact with him, and humiliated Fisher?

This more complete statement of the issue is helpful in determining whether or not the case would be useful in solving a client's problem.

C. HOLDING

There are three separate holdings in *Fisher* related to the three issues. Key words such as "we hold" or "plaintiff was entitled" or the "Hotel was liable" signal the holdings. The court uses the term "holding" to identify the first two holdings related to battery and actual damages. With respect to battery, the court states:

> "We hold, therefore, that the forceful dispossession of plaintiff Fisher's plate in an offensive manner was sufficient to constitute a battery . . . " *Fisher*, 424 S.W.2d at 630.

On the subject of damages, the court states:

> "We hold, therefore, that plaintiff was entitled to actual damages
> for mental suffering due to the willful battery, even in the absence
> of any physical injury." *Fisher*, 424 S.W.2d at 630.

While the court does not use the term "holding" for the third holding
relating to punitive damages, the court does use language that signals it
has made a decision. With respect to the liability of Carrousel Motor Hotel
for damages because of the actions of Flynn, the court states that Carrousel
Motor Hotel was liable for Flynn's actions because:

> "Flynn was acting in the scope of employment at the time of the
> incident; he was attempting to enforce the Club rules by depriving
> Fisher of service." *Id.* at 631.

D. RATIONALE

Fisher explains the reasoning for its decision by referencing the
Restatement of Torts. The court notes that the Restatement explains that
the:

> "essence of the plaintiff's grievance consists in the offense to the
> dignity involved . . . and not in any physical harm done." *Id.* at
> 629.

The court also explains its decision by referring to several earlier cases
that found battery when an object was snatched from someone's hand in
an offensive manner. *Id.* at 629.

E. DICTUM

There is an example of dictum in *Fisher* when the court makes an
incidental remark about whether damages for mental suffering are
permissible in the absence of physical injury. The court notes that a Texas
Supreme Court decision decided 14 years earlier did not permit recovery
for mental injury in the absence of physical injury. The court comments
that the recovery for mental injury in the absence of physical injury "has
long been advocated by respectable writers and legal scholars." *Id.* at 630.
This comment is an example of dictum because it is an observation that is
not necessary for the court's decision.

F. DISPOSITION

The Texas Supreme Court reversed the judgment of the lower court
and awarded judgment to the plaintiff.

VII.   PRACTICE

Reflection Exercise 7.1
Strategies for Finding Main Ideas

Goal: This exercise gives you the opportunity to reflect on strategies you have used to locate main ideas in novels, textbooks or articles and continue to use techniques that have been helpful.

Think about some of the strategies you have used to locate main ideas. Indicate if you have used the strategy and found it helpful. Add additional strategies you have used.

Strategy	Used Strategy?	Was Strategy Helpful?
Identify topic sentences.		
Locate central ideas and thesis statements.		
Use supporting details to explain main ideas that are not explicitly stated.		
Paraphrase text in your own words.		
Create outlines.		
Create concept maps.		
Create summaries.		

Practice Exercise 7.2
Strategies to Find Main Ideas in a Law Review Article

Goal: The purpose of this exercise is to use some of the strategies outlined in Reflection Exercise 7.1 to summarize a portion of a law review article.

The following is an excerpt from a law review article[3] on the subject of critical reading. Read the excerpt and answer the questions that follow.

In *Alice in Wonderland*, the Duchess tells Alice that everything has a moral. She states: "Never imagine yourself not to be otherwise than what it might appear to others that what you were or might have been was not otherwise than what you had

---

[3]   Jane Bloom Grisé, *Critical Reading Instruction: The Road to Successful Legal Writing Skills*, 18 W. Mich. Univ. Cooley J. of Prac. & Clinical L. (forthcoming 2017).

been would have appeared to them to be otherwise." "I think I should understand that better," Alice says very politely, "if I had it written down: but I can't quite follow it as you say it."[4]

For many law students, the cases assigned in the first year of law school are as comprehensible as the words of the Duchess. Students find that reading cases is like learning a foreign language. One student in the top quartile of the class noted that reading cases in the first semester was analogous to looking for a purple dinosaur without knowing what a dinosaur was or what the color purple looked like.[5]

To make matters more challenging, students are required to write about these cases early in the first semester. While it is clear that students must understand the meaning of cases before they can use them to write memos or answer exam questions, many students have not been exposed to critical reading skills that are needed for law school. Furthermore, the first year curriculum often does not provide sufficient instruction in critical reading[6] which has been defined as "learning to evaluate, draw inferences, and arrive at conclusions based on evidence."[7] The inadequate student skills combined with the lack of critical reading instruction may have a direct impact on students' ability to become successful writers. This Article provides the results from the first empirical study to examine the impact of critical reading instruction on legal writing performance. Any impact on writing is significant as writing is a key skill for law school as well as law practice. As one legal writing authority has observed, "[g]ood writing is strength. If you are a better writer than other lawyers, your clients will have an advantage."[8]

7.2–1 Are any of the strategies identified in Reflection Exercise 7.1 useful in summarizing the main ideas from the article?

7.2–2 What is the main idea of the article?

---

[4]   Lewis Carroll, *Alice's Adventures in Wonderland* 134 (William Morrow & Co., Inc. 1992) (1866).

[5]   Interview with first year law student, University of Kentucky College of Law, in Lexington, Ky. (May 17, 2014). In May 2014, all first year students were invited to join a Legal Analysis Advisory Panel to provide input into the instructional materials for this project. The comments from students were very helpful and are referenced throughout this article.

[6]   *See* Leah M. Christensen, *Legal Reading and Success in Law School: An Empirical Study*, 30 Seattle U.L.Rev. 603, 603 (2007).

[7]   Norma Decker Collins, *Teaching Critical Reading Through Literature*, 1993 ERIC Digest 2, *available at* ED 363869.

[8]   Richard K. Neumann, Jr. et al., *Legal Writing* 1 (3d ed. 2015). It is important to note that legal writing requires the ability to write analytically as well as the ability to use proper grammar.

Practice Exercise 7.3
Finding Main Ideas in *Lucy*

Goal: The purpose of this exercise is to review the strategies introduced in Chapters 1 through 7 and practice finding the main ideas in a case as set forth in the issue, holding, and reasoning.

Assume that you have been contacted by Janet Mason, who is a first year law student, about representation in a possible contract case. After interviewing Ms. Mason, you discover the following facts:[9]

> On March 20, 2016, Ms. Mason watched an interview on television between Oscar Jones and National News. In the interview, Oscar Jones discussed a murder case he was handling for a criminal defendant, Nelson Smith. Smith was accused of murder and in this interview Jones indicated that the prosecution's theory of the case was not plausible given the fact that his client had an alibi. Oscar Jones stated that his client was on a business trip, and there was video surveillance that Smith was at a hotel 150 miles away from the murder scene one hour before the murder. At the end of the interview, Mason stated that he challenged anyone listening to demonstrate how it would be possible for his client to commit the murder. Mason said that, "If anyone can do this I will pay them two million dollars."

> After Ms. Mason heard the interview, she decided to take the challenge. She retraced the route between the hotel and the murder scene and provided Jones with information to show that the murder could have been committed. She stated that she performed the challenge and asked for payment. Jones refused and stated that this was not a serious offer. In researching Ms. Mason's case, you have decided to read *Lucy v. Zehmer*, 84 S.E.2d 516 (Va.1954) (Appendix H) to gain a better understanding of contract law.

Step 1: Determine the general subject or case context of *Lucy*.

Strategy	Used Strategy?	Was Strategy Helpful?
7.3–1 Does any information in the **case summary** relate to contracts?		
7.3–2 Are there any **headnotes**?		
7.3–3 Who are the parties in the **caption**?		

---

[9] These facts are based upon *Kolodziej v. Mason*, 774 F.3d 736 (11th Cir. 2014).

Strategy	Used Strategy?	Was Strategy Helpful?
7.3–4 What **court** decided the case?		
7.3–5 What is the decision **date**?		
7.3–6 Who was the Judge?		

Step 2: Skim the case quickly for an overview.

Strategy	*Lucy*
7.3–7 How long is the case in the South Eastern Reporter?	
7.3–8 Does the first paragraph of the decision provide useful information about the general subject matter?	
7.3–9 Are there any headings that divide the case into sections?	
7.3–10 Does the last page of the case in Appendix H indicate who won?	

Step 3: Read the facts related to the underlying dispute (the substantive facts).

Facts	*Lucy*
7.3–11 Who were the parties in the underlying dispute?	
7.3–12 What is the best way to organize the facts?	

Step 4: Review the substantive facts.

7.3–13 Summarize the substantive facts.

Step 5: Review the procedural facts.

7.3–14 Summarize the procedural facts.

Step 6: Understand language

7.3–15 On page 522 of the decision, the court quotes from the Restatement of Contracts as follows:

> "If the words or other acts of one of the parties have but one reasonable meaning, his undisclosed intention is immaterial except when an unreasonable meaning which he attaches to his manifestations is known to the other party."

Would any of the strategies reviewed in Chapter 6 be helpful to use to understand this sentence?

Strategy	Was Strategy Helpful?
Reread	
Think about context	
Look for topic sentences	
Analyze paragraphs	
Look up words	
Notice conjunctions	
Notice repeated words	
Keep track of pronoun references	
Break up sentences	
Read aloud	

Step 7: Identify the issue, holding, and reasoning.

7.3–16 What is the issue?

7.3–17 What is the holding?

7.3–18 Does the court set forth any reasoning?

Practice Exercise 7.4
Self-Assessment

Goal: In this exercise, you can determine if you understand the concepts presented, i.e., finding main ideas and issues, holdings, and rationale.

Assume that you are still representing Ms. Evelyn Michel, who has been terminated from her employment as a nurse because she failed the National Council Licensure Examination. Ms. Michel wants to know if she will qualify for unemployment insurance benefits. *De Grego v. Levine,* 347 N.E. 2d 611 (N.Y. 1976) (Appendix C) provides guidance. Answer the following questions:

7.4–1   What is the issue?

7.4–2   What is the court's holding?

7.4–3   What is the main idea in the dissenting opinion?

Evaluate your understanding of the skills in this chapter by completing the following rubric. For each skill, circle whether you are at the proficient or developing level. Everyone can get to the proficient level over time.

Skill	Competency Level	
	Proficient	**Developing**
Understands the main ideas in a case.	• Looks for main ideas.	• Looks at each part of case in isolation.
Can identify the issue.	• Locates the precise problem addressed by the court.	• Looks at general problems discussed.
Can identify the holding.	• Identifies the court's decision.	• Does not distinguish between general legal statements and the court's decision.
Can identify the disposition.	• Understands how the court resolved the case.	• Does not pay attention to case resolution.
Can identify dictum.	• Identifies incidental remarks that have no precedential value.	• Assumes that all statements have precedential value.
Understands the role of dissenting opinions.	• Understands that dissenting opinions do not represent the holding of the court.	• Does not distinguish between majority and dissenting opinions.

Checklist Reminder: Remember to create your own checklist. It might be helpful at the conclusion of each chapter to select the techniques you find helpful and add them to your checklist.

CHAPTER 8

DURING READING: FINDING RULES

I. SUMMARY

This chapter examines how attorneys:

- find rules in cases, and

- use strategies to construct rules when opinions do not explicitly set forth rules.

While attorneys do not memorize rules, they find and formulate rules from cases to resolve client problems.

At the conclusion of this chapter, you will be able to:

- find rules in cases, and

- formulate rules.

II. CHECKLIST

CASE READING CHECKLIST

Warning: Do not just highlight and underline.

Phase 1: Before Reading

1. Read for a purpose and assume the role of advocate or judge.

2. Read with energy and focus.

3. Notice case structure.

4. Understand the general subject matter by examining:

    a. course syllabus, casebook table of contents, or research assignment, and

    b. parties, citation, court, and date.

5. Read for an overview by skimming and noticing organization, headings, who won, and what case is generally about.

Phase 2: Reading More Carefully

1. Understand the facts.

2. Reread, look up unfamiliar words, analyze confusing language, and vary reading speed.

---

3. Understand the main ideas set forth in the issue, holding, and reasoning.

4. Identify the rule.

5. Take notes with your reactions and brief the case.

Phase 3: After Reading

1. Evaluate the decision, ask questions, and talk with professors.

2. Determine how cases fit together with other cases and synthesize.

III. RULES

Attorneys read cases to find rules or general principles that can be applied to solve new legal problems. For example, the attorney representing Joe Parker from Chapters 1, 2, and 3 needs to understand the general rules for battery so that he/she can determine if Mr. Parker has a valid battery claim. While it is necessary for the attorney to identify the facts, issue, and holding, the attorney really wants to know the general rules from cases that can be used to solve Mr. Parker's problem.

Sometimes, opinions contain clear rules that are easy to find. More often, the decision does not explicitly state a rule and the reader must formulate one. If you try to locate the rule in a case and cannot find one, it may not be there. This chapter explores strategies to find and construct rules.

A. WHAT ARE RULES?

A rule is a general principle that guides our conduct. Every game has a series of rules that regulate the behavior of the participants. Anyone who plays chess knows that the pieces are white and black, that chess is played on a board with 64 squares, and each piece can move in a specific direction. Players can win by checkmating the king, and there are several ways this can be done. The rules for chess are applicable to all chess games.

Rules from cases also guide conduct because they are general principles that can be used to solve new legal problems. Rules are found in cases when courts articulate the requirements for legal claims. The difference between a rule and a court holding is that the holding, as discussed in Chapter 7, is the court's resolution of a specific dispute. The rule from a case is a more general statement of a legal doctrine. For example, in *Garratt v. Dailey,* 279 P.2d 1091 (Wash. 1955) (Appendix G), examined in Chapter 7, the court discusses the requirements for intent in battery claims and holds that:

Intent for purposes of battery can be found if the defendant knew with substantial certainty that when he pulled the chair away, the plaintiff would attempt to sit down where the chair had been.

The rule from *Garratt* is a more general legal principle:

> The intent requirement of battery may be satisfied if a party knows with substantial certainty that his actions will result in harmful or offensive contact.

A more recent battery case that relies on Garratt provides another example of the distinction between a holding and a rule. In *Kumar v. Gate Gourmet, Inc.*, 325 P.3d 193 (Wash. 2014), plaintiffs alleged a variety of claims, including battery, against Gate Gourmet, Inc., for requiring employees to eat only food supplied by the company and then providing food that the company knew some employees could not eat for religious reasons.[1] The holding in *Kumar* sets forth a decision regarding the facts in the case:

> "The employees allege that Gate Gourmet deceived them into eating food in violation of their religious beliefs, knowing that this would cause an offensive contact. These allegations are sufficient to support a claim for battery at this stage." *Id.* at 205.

The rule from *Kumar* is more general and can be framed as follows:

> There is intent for purposes of battery when the defendant knows with " 'substantial certainty' that his actions will result in harmful or offensive touching" and the defendant deceives the plaintiff into agreeing to the contact. *Id.*

While the holding relates to the facts in *Kumar*, the rule is more general and can be used to solve new legal problems.

B. FINDING RULES

Sometimes, courts clearly articulate rules. When courts do so, they may use specific terms to signal that the opinion contains a rule or a test such as:

Must be,

Must show,

Must establish,

It is presumed,

The general rule is,

---

[1]   *Kumar* may sound familiar because the case was used as the basis for the factual scenario in Practice Exercises 5.2 and 5.3 from Chapter 5.

The test to be applied is,

Accordingly,

The court in *Craft v. Rice*, 671 S.W.2d 247 (Ky. 1984) used explicit language to signal the rule in the case. The court stated that it adopted the following section of the Restatement of Torts relating to the intentional infliction of emotional distress (IIED):

> "One who by extreme and outrageous conduct intentionally or recklessly causes severe emotional distress to another is subject to liability for such emotional distress, and if bodily harm to the other results from it, for such bodily harm." *Id.* at 251.

(Restatements are treatises that contain legal principles in different subjects such as torts.) After *Craft* was decided, attorneys had clear guidance regarding the rule for IIED in Kentucky.

However, very often courts do not identify a rule. They set forth facts and a decision but omit any discussion of the general rule. When the rule of law is not stated, legal readers must construct the rule. Rule formulation is an important critical reading skill that involves several steps. Before examining these steps, the role of inferences will be examined as rules are formulated by making good inferences.

C. WHAT ARE INFERENCES?

An inference is an educated guess. When a situation is not clear, we resolve confusion by looking at details and drawing conclusions. If I arrive home and my dog is hiding in the corner of the room, I can infer that something is wrong. If you arrive at school and the building is locked, it is reasonable to assume that classes are canceled. We make inferences based upon the facts, our general knowledge of dogs and schools, as well as our knowledge of our dog's behavior or the practice of the school in the past. We reach conclusions after considering the facts in light of our experiences.

Readers also make inferences to understand and fill gaps in text. Inferences have been described as "things the writer didn't say but which we know are probably true."[2] Readers can fill gaps by getting information from other sentences or paragraphs that come before or after a passage in a text. Readers also fill gaps by making connections to information they already know. The ideas in a sentence may trigger broader associations that help the reader understand the sentence. For example, when we read, "Jane is going to get the leash," we start thinking about a dog. The sentence does not tell us that Jane has a dog. However, we can infer that she has a dog because people use leashes for dogs.

---

[2]   Thomas G. Devine, *Teaching Study Skills* 116 (2d ed. 1987).

In making inferences, it is necessary to consider the facts, look at all parts of a situation to understand the big picture, and then make inferences that are neither too broad nor too narrow. For example, if you arrive at school and the building is locked, it would be unreasonable to assume that the school has been permanently closed for the semester. That conclusion would be too broad. On the other hand, if the building is locked at 9 AM, it would be unreasonable to expect that it will open at 9:05 AM. That conclusion would be too narrow. The scope of the inferences must be reasonable based upon the facts.

All of these techniques are used in finding rules. Before exploring these strategies with cases, it is helpful to practice making inferences with a photograph, as we often make inferences when looking at art. Reflection Exercise 8.1 gives you the opportunity to try these techniques with a photograph.

IV. STRATEGIES FOR CONSTRUCTING RULES

Before readers use inferences to construct rules, they must make sure that it is appropriate to do so. Legal readers should only make inferences if the opinion does not set forth a rule. Sometimes opinions are silent on an issue or do not address a particular point. It is not appropriate to rewrite decisions and add reasoning that is not provided by the court.

Once it is determined that it is necessary to construct a rule, take the following steps:

- First, examine the words in the opinion and make sure that you understand the text.

- Second, review the entire decision, including cases relied upon. Make connections between the information and ideas contained in different parts of the opinion and try to explain the general meaning of the decision. It can also be useful to examine subsequent cases that have interpreted the opinion.

- Third, extrapolate a rule from the material provided in the text.

- Finally, make sure that the rule is neither too narrow nor too broad.

A. UNDERSTAND THE TEXT

The first step in finding a rule is to understand the facts, holding, and all vocabulary in the decision. The reader must pay attention to the words and facts as valid inferences must be based upon accurate facts. If incorrect facts are used, the entire basis for the inference falls apart and the conclusion may be inaccurate. As noted in Chapter 6, **vocabulary** is key. Novice legal readers sometimes have difficulty making inferences because they fail to grasp the meaning of legal terms. If inaccurate definitions are used, the resulting inferences will not be valid.

It is also important to pay attention to the **words in the case**. While we all read in light of our prior experiences, we must focus on the text and avoid the inclination to substitute our knowledge for the facts in the text. If the reader thinks he knows something about a topic, he may rely upon his experiences rather than the text. This can adversely affect comprehension. In one study, readers were given a passage to read on a familiar subject. Readers tended to use their knowledge about the topic rather than the explicit details that were provided in the textbook.[3] As a result, their comprehension declined. Expert readers use their general knowledge but focus on the information that is actually in the text.

B. REVIEW ENTIRE DECISION

The next step is to look at the opinion as an integrated whole and make connections between different parts of the decision. A statement in one part of the opinion can help elucidate meaning in another section. Sentences cannot be viewed in isolation. As discussed in Chapter 7, cases have main ideas and must be read in the context of the entire decision. Good readers look at the big picture and recognize that reading "is like completing a jigsaw puzzle: all of the information must be used, the information must fit into place without forcing, all of the important slots must contain information, and the completed interpretation must make sense."[4] Practice Exercise 8.2 provides the opportunity to use facts from one sentence to complete another sentence.

In examining the entire opinion, check to see if the court discusses earlier cases. Sometimes, a case just consists of facts and a decision and does not reference any other authorities. An example of a case that includes facts and a decision, but no other authority, is a negligence case from the early 1900s that dealt with a passenger at a railroad station who slipped and fell. The entire decision in *Goddard v. Boston & M. R. Co.*, 60 N.E.486 (Mass. 1901), is found in Figure 8.1.

---

[3]   Richard C. Anderson and P. David Pearson, *A Schema-Theoretic View of Basic Processes in Reading Comprehension*, P. David Pearson, *Handbook of Reading Research* 271 (2002)

[4]   *Id.* at 286.

Figure 8.1
Goddard v. Boston & M. R. Co., 60 N.E. 486 (Mass. 1901)

> "The banana skin upon which the plaintiff stepped and which caused him to slip may have been dropped within a minute by one of the persons who was leaving the train. It is unnecessary to go further to decide the case.
>
> Exceptions overruled."

Here, it is necessary to examine the relationship between the facts and the decision to construct a rule.

Most often, an opinion does rely on other cases. In this situation, pay particular attention to the court's discussion of **earlier decisions**. As noted in Chapter 3, cases are organized in a predictable fashion and many decisions start their legal analysis by examining earlier cases. For example, in *Kumar,* discussed at the beginning of this chapter, the court analyzes older battery decisions. The court then considers the definition of battery in the Restatement of Torts. The earlier decisions and rules from the Restatement can be used to construct a rule for *Kumar*.

When courts analyze earlier cases or treatises such as the Restatement, they often start their analysis by **examining general topics** that deal with large areas of law. Then they examine more specific areas. In *Kumar,* the court first addresses a general rule from the Restatement dealing with battery, i.e., that battery is composed of intent to cause harmful or offensive contact with another. The court then examines a more specific rule that applies when a defendant engages in fraud to get a plaintiff to consent to the contact.

After the court looks at prior decisions and rules, the court then formulates its own decision. The court might **expand, modify, or change** an earlier decision as it addresses a new factual situation. It might decide that the facts in the case at hand represent an exception or variation to older authority. There may be **policy** or other considerations for the change. Once the reader understands the holding and reasoning in a decision and the earlier cases referenced, it is possible to formulate a rule.

C. CONSTRUCT RULE

After examining and understanding the words in the text and looking at the entire opinion, it is possible to formulate a rule. If the opinion, such as *Goddard*, does not discuss any earlier authority, the goal is to figure out how the facts relate to the court's decision. The factual details sometimes suggest a conclusion that can be used to help construct a rule. Try to explain the information that is provided in the decision.

In *Goddard*, set out in Figure 8.1, the facts indicate that a banana skin may have been dropped by one of the persons leaving the train. The opinion states that this occurred within a minute of a person leaving the train. The court finds that the carrier had no liability. One possible explanation for the court's conclusion would be that time is a significant factor in determining liability. From the facts, the decision, and this explanation, it is possible to formulate a rule that a train has no liability when a slippery object is dropped immediately before a passenger falls. It is reasonable to conclude that liability depends upon how long the object has been on the ground. Figure 8.2 demonstrates this analysis:

Figure 8.2
Construction of Rule: *Goddard*

Facts	Court's Decision	Inferred Rule
Passenger slipped on banana skin which may have been dropped within a minute of someone leaving the train.	No liability.	No liability when slippery object is dropped immediately before passenger falls.

If the opinion, such as *Kumar*, does discuss other authority, the cases and rules referenced can be helpful in formulating a new rule. The court in *Kumar* combined cases and rules from several sources in reaching its decision. As seen in Figure 8.3, by examining the facts, holding and the rules relied upon, a new rule for *Kumar* can be constructed.

Figure 8.3
Construction of Rule: *Kumar*

Kumar **Facts:**

- Plaintiffs worked for Gate Gourmet preparing meals for trains and airplanes. For security reasons, they were not allowed to bring food to work, and Gate Gourmet provided meals for its employees.

- Plaintiffs alleged that after they advised Gate Gourmet that they were not allowed to eat pork because of their religious beliefs, Gate Gourmet temporarily provided turkey meatballs and then switched to beef-pork meatballs without notifying the employees.

Kumar **Holding:**

A claim for battery exists when "employees allege that Gate Gourmet deceived them into eating food in violation of their religious beliefs, knowing that this would cause an offensive contact." 325 P.3d at 205.

Authority Relied on in *Kumar*:

***Garratt* Holding and Rule:**

Battery can occur when "the plaintiff comes in harmful contact with the ground but never touches the defendant." *Id.*

Battery occurs only when a defendant knows to a "substantial certainty" that his actions will result in "harmful or offensive touching." *Id.*

Restatement Rule:

Battery can occur when consent to contact is "procured by fraud or duress." *Id.*

Figure 8.4 combines the rules from *Garratt* and the Restatement, in light of the facts and holding in *Kumar*, into a new rule.

Figure 8.4
Rule: *Kumar*

There is intent for purposes of battery when the defendant knows with "substantial certainty" that his actions will result in harmful or offensive touching and the defendant deceives the plaintiff into agreeing to the contact.

In constructing a rule, it can also be helpful to examine cases that have interpreted the opinion at a later time. These cases can provide valuable insights and guidance regarding the scope of a rule. In the *Goddard* example, where the court did not rely upon any other decisions, *Goddard* was interpreted by a subsequent decision that sheds light on the case. In *Lyons v. Boston Elevated Ry. Co.*, 90 N.E. 419, 419 (Mass. 1910), the court considered a situation where a passenger entered an elevated train car and fell over "a number of bundles in the doorway." There was no "evidence as to the length of time the packages had been in the doorway." *Id.* at 420. The court ruled for the defendant and noted that:

> "There must at least be some notice to the defendant of such conduct before it can be charged with responsibility. There is nothing in the present case to show that the obstruction had been in the doorway more than an instant or that the defendant's employees had any knowledge of its presence there. Goddard v. B. & M. R. R., 179 Mass. 52, 60 N. E. 486; Thomas v. Boston Elevated Ry. Co., 193 Mass. 438, 78 N. E. 749." *Id.*

The *Lyons* decision indicates that the length of time the packages were in the doorway was an important factor in deciding whether or not there was liability. The *Lyons* court reference to *Goddard* confirms that it is appropriate to extrapolate a rule from *Goddard* that connects liability with time. Liability seems to depend upon how long something has been on the ground because employees need to have the opportunity to notice and remove dangerous objects.

Finally, it can be helpful to compare multiple cases on a similar topic and look for patterns when extrapolating a rule. A rule can be created by examining several cases and synthesizing a rule. Rule synthesis will be examined in Chapter 11.

D. SCOPE OF RULE

When formulating rules, it is important to make sure that the scope of the rule is appropriate and the rule is neither too narrow nor too broad. Using the *Goddard* case, set out in Figure 8.1, there are several possible rules that can be created.

Rule 1: There is no liability when a passenger slips on objects in train stations.

Rule 2: There is no liability when a passenger slips on a banana peel in a train station that was dropped a minute before the passenger slipped.

Rule 3: There is no liability when a passenger slips on a slippery object in a train station that was dropped shortly before the passenger fell.

The first rule is too broad because it applies to all objects regardless of the amount of time that transpired between the passenger slipping and the object being dropped. The second rule is too narrow because it only applies to banana peels dropped within a minute of the passenger slipping. The third rule is more reasonable because it could apply to any slippery object. The third rule also focuses on the important time factor and does not restrict liability to one minute.

Practice Exercise 8.3 is an opportunity to find the rule in a short case. Practice Exercise 8.4 is another opportunity to find a rule and review the critical reading strategies introduced in Chapters 1 through 7. Practice Exercise 8.5 is the self-assessment exercise for this chapter.

E. THE ROLE OF PRIOR KNOWLEDGE

When making inferences, **be careful to be aware of your own preconceptions**. Everyone reads and interprets text in light of their prior experiences. As noted earlier, we make inferences when we associate information in a passage with facts we already know. When reading cases dealing with criminal law, you may think about crimes that have been in the news. When reading tort cases, you may remember situations where cars have been recalled or products have been found to be unsafe.

While it is sometimes helpful to use this knowledge to interpret cases, be aware that these experiences can influence how we fill in gaps and make inferences. Studies have found that prior experiences shape our explanations of unclear situations. One study examined how a student's major could influence the student's interpretation of an event. College students in a variety of majors were given scenarios to read and the stories could be viewed in more than one way.[5] One text could be read to involve a "prisoner planning his escape from a cell or a wrestler trying to get out of his opponent's hold."[6] When physical education majors read this text, they concluded that the story involved a wrestler. The second text could be interpreted to involve four people getting ready to play cards or a quartet preparing to practice music."[7] When music majors read this text, they inferred that the text dealt with a quartet. This study demonstrates that prior experiences can influence the way we make inferences. Use caution in making inferences.

V. CASE EXAMPLE: FINDING RULES

The skills in this chapter, finding rules, are explained with *Fisher v. Carrousel Motor Hotel, Inc.*, 424 S.W.2d 627 (Tex. 1967) (Appendix B-1).

While the *Fisher* court makes a decision on the subject of battery, it does not articulate a rule. It is possible to formulate a rule by examining the opinion, looking at cases mentioned in the opinion, and reading cases that have interpreted *Fisher*.

A. UNDERSTAND TEXT

The first step in formulating a rule is to sort out the facts carefully and understand vocabulary.

B. REVIEW ENTIRE DECISION

The *Fisher* court does rely on other authorities in its decision on battery. To formulate a rule from *Fisher*, it is helpful to examine these sources. The court relies on a treatise, the Restatement of Torts, and cases such as *Morgan v. Loyacomo*, 1 So. 2d 510 (Miss. 1941) and *S.H. Kress & Co. v. Brashier*, 50 S.W.2d 922 (Tex. Civ. App. 1932). The *Fisher* court starts its analysis by examining the reasoning set forth in the Restatement of Torts relating to battery:

> "The interest in freedom from intentional and unpermitted contacts with the plaintiff's person is protected by an action for the tort commonly called battery. The protection extends to any

---

[5]   Pearson, *supra* note 3, at 270.

[6]   *Id.*

[7]   *Id.*

part of the body, or to anything which is attached to it and practically identified with it." *Fisher*, 424 S.W.2d at 629.

The decision in *Morgan* builds on the rule from the Restatement and states that for battery to take place,

> "it is not necessary to touch the plaintiff's body or even his clothing; knocking or snatching anything from plaintiff's hand or touching anything connected with his person, when done in an offensive manner, is sufficient." *Id.*

The decision in *S.H. Kress & Co.* adds another dimension by specifically finding that battery occurred when someone took a book from the plaintiff's hand and the plaintiff suffered "humiliation and indignity." The opinion then goes back to the Restatement of Torts to examine the rationale for battery and notes that:

> "the essence of the plaintiff's grievance consists in the offense to the dignity involved . . . . Unpermitted and intentional contacts with anything so connected with the body as to be customarily regarded as part of the other's person and therefore as partaking of its inviolability is actionable as an offensive contact with his person." *Id.*

All of these authorities assist in formulating a rule.

C. CONSTRUCT RULE

A rule can be constructed for *Fisher* by combining the rules and authorities cited in the opinion with the facts and holding in *Fisher*. The rule from the Restatement of Torts is that the "interest in freedom from intentional and unpermitted contacts extends to any part of the body, or to anything which is attached to it." *Id. Morgan* adds the idea that:

> "knocking or snatching anything from plaintiff's hand or touching anything connected with his person, when, done in an offensive manner" is sufficient. *Id.*

S.H. Kress & Co. notes that humiliation can occur when someone takes an object from the plaintiff's hand. The *Fisher* court also indicates that cases have found that mental suffering can be compensated in the absence of physical injury. *Id.* at 630. The *Fisher* court concludes that liability exists for actions that are "offensive and insulting." *Id.*

By examining the facts and holding in *Fisher* as well as the decisions and rules from these earlier authorities, it is possible to formulate the following rule for *Fisher*:

Figure 8.5
Rule: *Fisher*

> Battery can occur when someone touches a person's body or anything connected with a person's body in an offensive manner whether or not physical harm occurs.

Cases that have interpreted *Fisher* provide additional guidance regarding the appropriate rule for the case. In *City of Watauga v. Gordon*, 434 S.W.3d 586 (Tex. 2014), the Texas Supreme Court considered a case where Gordon claimed injury from handcuffs that were too tight. The court examined *Fisher* and concluded that in *Fisher* the court "noted that it was the offensive nature of the contact, not its extent that made the contact actionable." *Id.* at 590. *Gordon* reaffirms that the offensive nature of the contact is a key aspect of the rule from *Fisher*.

D. SCOPE OF RULE

The final step in formulating a rule is to make sure that the rule is neither too broad nor too narrow. It would not make sense to construct a broad rule such as the following:

Battery can occur when someone touches another person's body.

It would be inappropriate to construct a narrow rule such as:

Battery can occur when someone grabs a plate from someone's hand and shouts insulting remarks.

The suggested rule set out in Figure 8.5 strikes an appropriate balance.

VI. PRACTICE

Reflection Exercise 8.1
Inferences from a Photo

Goal: The purpose of this exercise is to practice making inferences by examining a photograph and making connections between different parts of the photo. This process is similar to examining an opinion and making connections between different parts of the case.

Use some of the strategies discussed in this chapter to make inferences regarding the photograph below.

8.1–1   First, look at the details in the photo. What do you see?

8.1–2   Next, look at the photo as a whole and examine parts of the picture in relationship to other parts. Does the furniture provide any clues? Are there any clues that you can use to determine where the photo was taken?

8.1–3   Try to explain the photo and extrapolate from the facts to determine where the photo was taken and what is going on.

8.1–4   Do you have any knowledge that would assist you in understanding this scene? Does your knowledge interfere with your ability to examine the photograph so that you read information into the photo that is not there?

Practice Exercise 8.2
Inferences in Texts

Goal: The purpose of this exercise is to make the reader aware that it is helpful to use general knowledge as well as all available information in a text to understand a passage.

This exercise provides an opportunity to use clues in a text as well as your general knowledge to assist in making inferences and understanding text. To fill in the blanks in this exercise, use your general knowledge as well as information that is provided in the surrounding sentences. It is not necessary to consult any other sources.

8.2–1   Read the following sentence and use your general knowledge to provide an answer.

Research has found that good legal readers take the following steps before they read: _____.

8.2–2   Read the following sentences and use your general knowledge as well as clues or information in other parts of the passage to complete the sentence.

Research has found that good legal readers take the following step before they read: _____. Knowing the purpose for reading can change what the reader looks for while reading.

8.2–3   Read the following sentences and use information in the first sentence to complete the second sentence.

All readers use prior knowledge to interpret text. However, sometimes it is dangerous to use _____, when that knowledge is relied upon to the exclusion of information in the text.

8.2–4   In making inferences, it is sometimes necessary to rely on your general knowledge if there are no clues. Use your general knowledge to complete the following sentence:

If someone is in a buffet line at a restaurant and the manager of the restaurant grabs their plate, the person in line would be _____.

8.2–5   Make an inference using information from the second sentence to complete the first sentence.

In the *Fisher* case, the court analyzed cases from a variety of _____. The court looked at decisions from Texas as well as Mississippi.

8.2–6   Make an inference using information from the first sentence to complete the second sentence.

The Supreme Court of Texas found that battery can occur without physical contact if there is contact with "clothing or an object closely identified with the body." When the plate was grabbed by the manager, the manager committed _____.

Practice Exercise 8.3
Finding Rules: *Ranson*

Goal: The purpose of this exercise is to practice finding a rule in a case that includes facts, a decision, and no other authority.

Ranson v. Kitner, 31 Ill. App. 241 (1788) is an opinion found in many tort textbooks. While there are facts and a decision, no rule is articulated. Read the opinion and answer the questions that follow:

"This was an action brought by appellee against appellants to recover the value of a dog killed by appellants, and a judgment rendered for $50.

The defense was that appellants were hunting for wolves, that appellee's dog had a striking resemblance to a wolf, that they in good faith believed it to be one, and killed it as such.

Many points are made, and a lengthy argument filed to show that error in the trial below was committed, but we are inclined to think that no material error occurred to the prejudice of appellants.

The jury held them liable for the value of the dog, and we do not see how they could have done otherwise under the evidence. Appellants are clearly liable for the damages caused by their mistake, notwithstanding they were acting in good faith.

We see no reason for interfering with the conclusion reached by the jury, and the judgment will be affirmed.

Judgment affirmed."

8.3–1   Summarize the key facts.

8.3–2   What did the court decide?

8.3–3   Now explain the decision.

8.3–4   What rule can you extrapolate? Make sure the rule is neither too broad nor too narrow.

Facts	Court's Decision	Rule

Practice Exercise 8.4
Finding Rules: *Starnes*

Goal: The purpose of this exercise is to find the rule in a case that provides a very brief explanation of its decision.

You are working in the law office of Bloom & Bloom in Lexington, Kentucky. You have received a phone call from Jennifer Craft who wants to meet with you to discuss possible representation. After meeting, you discover the following facts:

Craft has been charged with second-degree burglary. Ky. Rev. Stat. Ann. § 511.030(1) (West 2017) states that a person:

"is guilty of burglary in the second degree when, with the intent to commit a crime, he knowingly enters or remains unlawfully in a dwelling."

"Dwelling" is defined as

"a building which is usually occupied by a person lodging therein." Ky. Rev. Stat. Ann. § 511.010(2) (West 2017).

Craft is accused of entering the home of Fred Caskey on June 1, 2016. Fred died on May 15, 2016 from a heart attack. No one resided in the house on June 1. However, during the week following Fred's death, friends and family periodically used the home to stay overnight and divide up Fred's possessions. All of the utilities were discontinued after family and friends left. Craft admits that she entered the home but claims that it should not be considered a "dwelling." She wants us to try to get the charges reduced to third-degree burglary. For third-degree burglary, a person "knowingly enters or remains unlawfully in a building." Ky. Rev. Stat. Ann. § 511.040(1) (West 2017). A building is defined as a place where a person "lives." Ky. Rev. Stat. Ann. § 511.010(1)(a) (West 2017).

You have been asked to review *Starnes v. Commonwealth*, 597 S.W.2d 614 (Ky. 1980) (Appendix I) to determine if the case will help resolve Craft's charges. However, the *Starnes* decision does not appear to set forth a clear rule. Use the techniques from this chapter to extrapolate a rule.

8.4–1   What preliminary steps would you take to understand the *Starnes* case before reading the case more carefully?

8.4–2   Did you complete the following steps?

Strategy	Completed
Read as advocate	
Read with focus	
Notice case structure	
Notice procedural facts	
Understand context	
Do a brief overview	
Examine facts carefully	
Identify issue, holding, reasoning	

8.4–3   In trying to construct a rule, first identify the key facts that triggered the court's decision.

8.4–4   Are there any words that you do not understand?

8.4–5   What did the court decide?

8.4–6   Did the court rely on any legal authority?

8.4–7   Try to explain the decision.

8.4–8   Formulate a rule that is neither too broad nor too narrow.

8.4–9   Could *Starnes* help you resolve Craft's case?

Practice Exercise 8.5
Self-Assessment

Goal: In this exercise, you will assess whether you understand the concepts related to finding rules in cases.

Assume that you are still representing Ms. Evelyn Michel in her unemployment insurance benefits case. Review *De Grego v. Levine*, 347 N.E. 2d 611 (N.Y. 1976) (Appendix C). You summarized the facts in Practice Exercise 5.4–3 and the holding in Practice Exercise 7.4–2.

8.5–1   As *De Grego* does not set forth a rule, it is necessary to construct a rule from the case. Start by summarizing the holdings from two decisions discussed in *De Grego*, *In re Malaspina* and *In re James* and complete the following chart:

Case	Holding
In re Malaspina	
In re James	

Note: In some administrative appeals such as *De Grego*, cases are sometimes referred to as *In re Malaspino* rather than *Malaspino v. Corsi*. Malaspino was the petitioner who sued Corsi, the Industrial Commissioner.

8.5–2   Construct a rule by analyzing the facts and holding in *De Grego* and the holdings from *In re Malaspina* and *In re James*.

Evaluate your understanding of the skills in this chapter by completing the following rubric. For each skill, circle whether you are at the proficient or developing level. Everyone can get to the proficient level over time.

Skill	Competency Level	
	Proficient	**Developing**
Understands when inferences need to be made.	• Understands that courts sometimes do not articulate rules and/or reasoning.	• Assumes that courts always set forth a rule.
Views the entire opinion.	• Understands that the entire opinion must be considered in making inferences.	• Makes inferences by only reading sections of the opinion.
Extrapolates a rule.	• Draws a reasonable connection between the facts and decision.	• Extrapolates a rule based upon prior knowledge rather than the facts in the case.
Extrapolates a rule that is appropriate in scope.	• Understands that a rule must not be too broad or too narrow.	• Creates an overly broad or narrow rule.

Phase Three

After Reading

CHAPTER 9

AFTER READING: CASE EVALUATION

I. SUMMARY

Expert legal readers:

- recognize that cases can be interpreted in different ways, and

- evaluate cases to determine if they can be used to solve new legal problems.

At the conclusion of this chapter, you will be able to:

- interpret and evaluate cases, and

- use evaluation techniques to prepare for law school exams.

II. CHECKLIST

CASE READING CHECKLIST

Warning: Do not just highlight and underline.

Phase 1: Before Reading

1. Read for a purpose and assume the role of advocate or judge.

2. Read with energy and focus.

3. Notice case structure.

4. Understand the general subject matter by examining:

   a. course syllabus, casebook table of contents, or research assignment, and

   b. parties, citation, court, and date.

5. Read for an overview by skimming and noticing organization, headings, who won, and what case is generally about.

Phase 2: Reading More Carefully

1. Understand the facts.

2. Reread, look up unfamiliar words, analyze confusing language, and vary reading speed.

3. Understand the main ideas set forth in the issue, holding, and reasoning.

> 4.   Identify the rule.
>
> 5.   Take notes with your reactions and brief the case.
>
> Phase 3: After Reading
>
> 1.   **Evaluate the decision, ask questions, and talk with professors.**
>
> 2.   Determine how cases fit together with other cases and synthesize.

III. AFTER READING STRATEGIES

Chapters 1 through 4 explored **before reading** strategies and Chapters 5 through 8 addressed techniques that are used **during reading** to examine cases more carefully. These during reading strategies included reading the facts (Chapter 5), analyzing complex language (Chapter 6), examining the main ideas (Chapter 7), and finding the rules in cases (Chapter 8).

Expert readers also take specific actions **after reading**. As described in Figure 9.1, the next three chapters focus on strategies that are used after reading. Experts interpret and evaluate cases, prepare summaries of decisions, and examine and synthesize multiple cases to solve a client's problem.

Figure 9.1
After Reading Topics

Chapter	Topic
9	Interpreting and evaluating cases
10	Preparing case briefs
11	Synthesizing cases

IV. INTERPRETING AND EVALUATING CASES

We engage in the process of interpretation and evaluation in many aspects of our lives. When we interpret something, we explain its meaning. A language interpreter is someone who explains what someone is saying in one language to someone who does not speak that language. We interpret a book when we read a passage and try to make sense of it, and people may have different interpretations of the same text. Evaluation means to judge and determine the value or significance of something. We evaluate when we rate movies, judge the quality of restaurants, and decide which law school to attend.

For example, when you looked at law schools, you engaged in the process of interpretation and evaluation. You first gathered facts by visiting and meeting with students and faculty. You might have researched the quality of the faculty, the location of the school, job placement rates, and financial aid. Former students may have tried to convince you to go to a particular school. You interpreted these facts and then evaluated the school to decide whether or not to accept an offer of admission.

The same principles apply to cases. Expert legal readers understand that it is appropriate to interpret and evaluate cases. Attorneys routinely interpret cases in different ways and then evaluate cases to determine if the cases can be used to advocate on behalf of their clients. Interpretation and evaluation are key critical reading skills. This chapter provides specific strategies to interpret and evaluate cases appropriately.

A. EXPERT LEGAL READERS INTERPRET CASES

Experienced legal readers recognize that cases can be interpreted in different ways. Cases do not have one fixed meaning. One reading expert notes that it is "never simply enough to know what a case 'says.' One must know what plausible interpretations and applications of law could be made from it."[1] Each day, lawyers in trial and appellate courts interpret cases when they argue that specific cases support their clients' positions. These are not frivolous arguments. They are taking positions in good faith that cases should be read in a particular way. It is appropriate to interpret a case to advocate on behalf of a client.

Cases can be interpreted narrowly to apply to a limited range of facts or more broadly. For example, assume that you have a new client, George Simpson, who slipped on a black, flat, banana peel as he got on a city bus. George wants to sue the bus company for negligence. To represent Mr. Simpson, you decide to read *Lyons v. Boston Elevated Ry. Co.*, 90 N.E. 419 (Mass. 1910), discussed in Chapter 8, where the court found that a train company had no liability to a passenger who stumbled over a package that had been left in the doorway of a train.

You may interpret the *Lyons* case differently than the attorney for the bus company. You could argue that *Lyons* should be interpreted narrowly and only apply to situations where passengers carry packages onto a bus. You might argue that there should be liability in other situations where passengers drop garbage on the ground. The attorney for the bus company might interpret *Lyons* more broadly and argue that the case stands for the proposition that carriers should have only limited liability to passengers in most situations. Each interpretation is reasonable.

---

[1] James F. Stratman, *When Law Students Read Cases: Exploring Relations Between Professional Legal Reasoning Roles and Problem Detection*, 34 Discourse Processes 57, 88 (2002).

Judges also interpret cases when they write majority, concurring, and dissenting opinions. The judge who writes a dissenting opinion has a different interpretation and view of the law than the judge who writes the majority opinion. In *DeShaney v. Winnebago County Department of Social Services*, 489 U.S. 189 (1989), where a 4-year-old child was beaten by his father and suffered permanent brain damage, the Court decided that the Social Services Department did not violate the due process clause of the Fourteenth Amendment to the United States Constitution when it failed to protect the child from "private violence." *Id.* at 197. In a dissenting opinion, Justice Blackmun reached the opposite conclusion and stated as follows:

> "Like the antebellum judges who denied relief to fugitive slaves . . . the Court today claims that its decision, however harsh, is compelled by existing legal doctrine. On the contrary, the question presented by this case is an open one, and **our Fourteenth Amendment precedents may be read more broadly or narrowly depending upon how one chooses to read them**. Faced with the choice, I would adopt a 'sympathetic' reading, one which comports with dictates of fundamental justice and recognizes that compassion need not be exiled from the province of judging." *Id.* at 212–13. (emphasis added).

This powerful language from Justice Blackmun makes it clear that lawyers and judges may read cases in different ways.

Sometimes law students are reluctant to interpret a case because they believe that the decision is "the law." They may wonder whether it is appropriate to question what a judge has stated. Actually, questioning and interpreting are key parts of being a lawyer because the legal system is not composed of fixed decisions that never change. Professor Ruth Ann McKinney notes that some "students make the mistake of thinking their primary task is to *understand* each case, like a consumer of information, as if each was brought down from the mountain on tablets. They weren't."[2] Professor McKinney quotes Professor and former Dean Broun who "used to say in class, 'Written opinions are one judge's advice to the next judge.' "[3]

Law is constantly changing and evolving. Tort law today is very different from tort law 50 years ago. New concepts and theories have developed, and sometimes the minority opinions of yesterday become the majority opinions of today. Expert legal readers recognize that cases can be viewed in different ways.[4] As described in Figure 9.2, the Oates study found that the professor and two higher performing students recognized

---

[2]   Ruth Ann McKinney, *Reading Like a Lawyer* 159 (2d ed. 2012).

[3]   *Id.*

[4]   Leah M. Christensen, *Legal Reading and Success in Law School: An Empirical Study*, 30 Seattle Univ. L. Rev. 603, 646 (2007).

that cases are subject to different interpretations while the lower performing students believed that there was one correct way to look at a case.

Figure 9.2
Case Interpretation: Oates Study

Professor/Student	Case Interpretation
Professor	" . . . the role of the attorney is to persuade the judge to see the case in a particular way . . . "[5]
William (Top 10%)	"during a trial 'each side presents its version of the facts' and . . . the court by 'looking at prior cases, decides how to interpret them.' "[6]
Maria (Top 15%)	" 'there can be so many different interpretations of what happened,' and that the 'court gets to decide, by looking to precedent, which interpretation to adopt.' "[7]
Jackie (Bottom 20%)	"While Jackie stated that there was probably more than one way of interpreting an opinion, she also stated that if the judge wrote a good opinion, 'everyone would probably read it in pretty much the same way.' "[8]
James (Bottom 20%)	"while there was probably more than one way to . . . read a case, he usually tried to check his reading against one of the study guides to make sure that he had read the case correctly."[9]

B. EXPERT LEGAL READERS EVALUATE CASES

After interpreting cases, expert legal readers evaluate decisions. While novice readers end their analysis after they find the court's holding, expert legal readers take their analysis to a higher critical reading level when they engage in the process of evaluation. As noted earlier, evaluation means to determine the value or significance of something. Attorneys ask questions and evaluate cases to determine whether a case can be used to solve a client's legal problem. In the law school setting, expert readers evaluate

---

[5] Laurel Currie Oates, *Leveling the Playing Field: Helping Students Succeed by Helping Them Learn to Read as Expert Lawyers*, 80 St. John's L. Rev. 227, 236 (2006).

[6] *Id.* at 246.

[7] *Id.* at 240.

[8] *Id.* at 246.

[9] *Id.*

cases to prepare for exams by examining the significance of the facts in relationship to the court's decision.

Lundeberg's study of lawyers and non-lawyers found that all of the lawyers "spontaneously" expressed their approval or disapproval of a court's decision while only one non-lawyer offered an opinion.[10] Furthermore, the lawyers understood that decisions were a "creative process" while the novices "assumed legal decisions were more or less cut-and-dried" and assumed that decisions should not be evaluated.[11]

In the Christensen study, higher performing law students were more likely to ask questions and evaluate decisions than lower performing students. The lower performing students were more likely to just summarize decisions.[12] In the Grisé study, students found that questioning and evaluating decisions improved their comprehension. Once students realized that it was permissible and advisable to evaluate decisions, their class participation increased and they started thinking about whether they agreed with the decision. They also had "more thoughtful questions," and they went to class with "questions & discrepancies" they had found.[13]

V. STRATEGIES FOR EVALUATING CASES

Expert legal readers use a variety of strategies to evaluate cases. However, they recognize that before evaluation can take place, they must first identify the relevant facts. Then it is necessary to find the court's holding which is the court's interpretation of the case. After completing these two steps, it is appropriate to move to the interpretation and evaluation stage. Figure 9.3 sets forth the levels of analysis that must take place **before** evaluation. Practice Exercise 9.1 provides an opportunity to practice this sequence of analysis.

Figure 9.3
Levels of Analysis

Level	Analysis
Literal Meaning	Understand key facts and definitions
Court's Interpretation	Understand court's holding and rationale
Reader's View	Interpret and evaluate

For example, in your representation of George Simpson in his negligence suit against the bus company, it would be useful to evaluate the

---

[10] Mary A. Lundeberg, *Metacognitive Aspects of Reading Comprehension: Studying Understanding in Legal Case Analysis*, 22 Reading Res. Q. 407, 415 (1987).

[11] *Id.*

[12] Leah M. Christensen, *"One L of a Year": How to Maximize Your Success in Law School* 39 (2012).

[13] Jane Bloom Grisé, *Critical Reading Instruction: The Road to Successful Legal Writing Skills*, 18 W. Mich. Univ. Cooley J. of Prac. & Clinical L. (forthcoming 2017).

court's decision in *Lyons v. Boston Elevated Ry. Co*, 90 N.E. 419 (Mass. 1910). It is first necessary to understand the relevant facts and vocabulary. In *Lyons*, a passenger entered a train car and fell over packages that were in the doorway. Words such as obstruction, onerous, and needless are used to describe the incident and must be understood.

Next, analyze the court's decision. In negligence cases such as *Lyons*, the plaintiff must prove that there was a duty of care that was breached and caused damage. If a business knows that a dangerous situation exists on their property, it has the duty to keep premises in a "reasonably safe condition."[14] The court in *Lyons* concluded that the train company did not have a duty of care to a passenger who stumbled over a package that had been left in the doorway of the train because the carrier would not be expected to know that a package would be left there. After completing these two levels of analysis, it is appropriate to evaluate the decision.

Expert legal readers use the following strategies to interpret and evaluate a decision:

- write down reactions and ask questions,
- evaluate law rather than facts,
- evaluate the impact of policy, and
- evaluate by using analogical reasoning to solve new problems.

In addition, expert readers evaluate decisions to prepare for law school exams.

A. WRITE REACTIONS AND ASK QUESTIONS

Whether a case is being read for class or a writing assignment, write down your reactions as you read. It is not possible to reconstruct your thoughts at the end of a study session or at the end of the semester. These initial thoughts may be useful when you are in class, outlining for exams, or working on a research assignment. Chapter 10 explains techniques for preparing case briefs, which are summaries of cases.

It is also important to ask questions as you read. Some researchers have stated that the ability to generate questions after reading a text is as important as the ability to identify the issue, holding, and reasoning of a case. Asking questions while reading "helps students distinguish portions of the text they do and do not understand."[15]

---

[14] *Oliveri v. Massachusetts Bay Transportation Authority*, 292 N.E.2d 863, 864 (Mass. 1973).

[15] Dorothy H. Evensen, James F. Stratman, Laurel C. Oates, & Sarah Zappe, *Developing an Assessment of First-Year Law Students' Critical Case Reading and Reasoning Ability: Phase 3*, LSAC Grants Report (March 2008).

If a decision is confusing, use the suggested techniques in Chapter 6 to resolve your confusion. If these techniques do not work, speak with your professor. In addition to asking questions, it can be helpful to ask and answer questions with other students. This process can help clarify concepts. Just remember that the answers provided by other students should be treated as suggestions. Be sure to ask your professors questions on a regular basis.

B. EVALUATE LAW, NOT FACTS

Expert readers evaluate the holding and reasoning in an opinion rather than the facts. The facts are evaluated by the court or jury at the trial level. The appellate court usually accepts the trial court's view of the facts. For this reason, legal readers should not engage in an independent analysis of the facts or use their knowledge of the subject of a case to influence their view of the facts. For example, in the Oates study, the professor properly evaluated a case to determine whether the plaintiff had proven all elements of false imprisonment. However, a student engaged in an inappropriate evaluation of the credibility of a witness. The student questioned whether the testimony of one of the witnesses was believable and stated "I don't think the plaintiff's story holds water."[16] If the court made factual findings regarding this plaintiff's story, these findings are binding and are generally not subject to further review.

In evaluating the legal concepts, think about the following types of questions:

- Do you agree or disagree with the court's decision?
- Do you agree or disagree with the court's rationale?
- Is the opinion logically consistent?
- Are there legal or policy assumptions underlying the decision?

Be sure to ask questions that are relevant to the legal issues addressed in the decision. For example, in representing George Simpson in his negligence suit against the bus company, it would be appropriate to ask the following types of questions about the *Lyons* case:

- Do you agree or disagree with the result?
- What authority was relied upon by the court and is that authority still valid?

It would be inappropriate to raise questions related to:

- facts not in the record (What type of packages were the passengers carrying? How exactly did the passenger fall?), or

___
[16] Oates, *supra* note 5, at 238.

- the credibility of witnesses (Did the passengers testify truthfully about their activities?)

It also would be inappropriate to raise questions about subjects that were not raised in the case. For example, as the case deals with a negligence claim, it would not be necessary to consider whether there was any breach of contract issue. Questions related to other subjects may get you off track. Practice Exercise 9.2 provides the opportunity to practice evaluating legal concepts rather than facts.

C. EVALUATE THE IMPACT OF POLICY

In addition to evaluating legal issues, the expert legal reader evaluates the policy considerations underlying an opinion. Policies are the reasons or assumptions behind a decision. If the policy underlying a case is still valid, that is a good argument that the decision can be used to solve a new legal problem. However, if policy considerations have changed, that is a powerful reason to urge a court to reconsider or limit the reach of a decision.

A good example of the impact of policy is found in *Lyons* where the court discussed the policy considerations behind the decision. In ruling against the passenger, the court found that there was a "prevailing custom" for passengers to take bags onto a train. The court noted it was expected that passengers would be careful "of the safety of others." 90 N.E. at 420. The court also explained that it was "too onerous a burden to require the defendant to act upon the theory that every one of its passengers is likely to be careless as to his fellows." *Id.*

In evaluating *Lyons*, it would be appropriate to consider whether these policies have changed over the past hundred years. Is there an assumption now that passengers will consider the safety of other passengers? Is it considered burdensome for train or bus companies to regulate passenger behavior or is this expected? Attorneys evaluate a case to determine if the policy behind a decision has changed.

D. EVALUATION: ANALOGICAL REASONING

Attorneys also evaluate cases to determine if they can be used to solve new legal problems. While they may first read a case to understand the text and summarize the decision, they quickly go beyond this basic level of analysis. They need to determine if the court's decision can be used to advocate on behalf of a client. They try to predict how a court would apply the holding in one case to their client's situation.

As discussed in Chapter 5, lawyers use analogical reasoning to evaluate whether a decision is factually similar enough to a new legal problem to provide guidance for the solution of the new problem. In analogical reasoning, attorneys first analyze the law to determine if the legal question in a reported decision is similar to the legal question faced by a client. After identifying the legal question or claim, the attorney compares the **case facts** (facts in the reported decision) with the **problem facts** (facts from a client's problem or school assignment) to determine if they are similar or different. The rule and result from a case can only be applied to solve a client's problem if the case facts are similar to the problem facts. If the facts are similar, an attorney can argue that the result in the new problem should be the same as the result in the court case. If the facts are different, the attorney may argue that the rule should not govern the solution of the new problem because the facts are distinguishable.

To evaluate a case to determine if it can assist in solving a new problem, the reader:

- focuses on a specific legal claim in the case,

- identifies the case facts that relate to the claim,

- identifies the problem facts that relate to the claim, and

- compares the two sets of facts to determine if they are similar or different.

It can be helpful to create a chart such as Figure 9.4 to connect the legal claim with the facts.

Figure 9.4
Case Evaluation: Analogical Reasoning Chart

Legal Claim	Case Facts	Problem Facts	Comparison Case/Problem Facts

For example, an attorney would use analogical reasoning to evaluate whether the *Lyons* case could be used to solve George Simpson's problem. As demonstrated in Figure 9.5, the reader would first identify the specific legal claim, which is the carrier's duty of care to passengers. The reader would next identify the case facts from *Lyons* that relate to the legal claim. In *Lyons*, a passenger entering the train fell over a package that was in the train doorway. The problem facts would then be summarized. For purposes of this example, assume that the problem facts are that George Simpson got on a city bus and slipped on a black, flat, banana peel.

Figure 9.5
Case Evaluation: Analogical Reasoning

Element of Claim	Case Facts *Lyons*	Problem Facts	Comparison Case/Problem Facts
Carrier has a duty of care if it should have known about danger to passengers.	Passenger entering train fell over a package in the train doorway.	Passenger slipped on black, dirty banana peel on bus.	Different: Black bananas and packages are different. Officials would be expected to notice a black, dirty banana peel.

After identifying the case facts and problem facts, these facts would be compared. Mr. Simpson's attorney could point out that the problem facts are different from the case facts because black banana peels are different from packages. His attorney could argue that while there was no liability in *Lyons*, there should be liability in Mr. Simpson's case because the carrier should have noticed the banana peel. While a carrier might not have known that a package would be dangerous to other passengers, officials should have noticed a black banana peel when they cleaned the bus. The attorney for the bus company might argue that banana peels and packages are similar because bus or train personnel could not be expected to know that passengers would drop bananas or carry packages onto a bus or train.

Practice Exercise 9.3 is an opportunity to use analogical reasoning to evaluate whether a case can be used to solve a client's problem. Practice Exercise 9.4 provides an opportunity to evaluate whether you agree with the majority or dissenting opinion in a case.

E.   EVALUATION: PREPARE FOR EXAMS

While lawyers evaluate cases to determine how the rules from a case apply to a client's problem, law students can evaluate cases to prepare for exams. When taking exams, which are simply hypothetical client problems or facts, students are expected to analyze a factual scenario, demonstrate that they know the pertinent rules, and then apply the rules to the facts.

To practice solving real client problems or taking law school exams, it is useful to make up your own exam questions. This can be done by evaluating cases and thinking about the significance of the legal principles in light of the facts and policy considerations. First, read a case and note the key legal principles. Then identify the relevant facts. As discussed in Chapter 5, some facts in an opinion are relevant facts, i.e., key facts that would change a decision's result. These facts are significant because they must be present to establish a legal claim.

Then create a hypothetical scenario by altering a fact or set of facts from the case and think about whether that change would result in a similar or different case result. By creating hypothetical scenarios and changing the facts, readers gain practice in understanding the components of a legal claim. In addition to analyzing facts, it is helpful to think about policy considerations. Examine the court's reasoning, then change the policy assumptions, and think about whether that change would impact the result.

Research indicates that this type of analysis can significantly improve student performance and comprehension. In one study, it was found that student performance improved even two weeks after the original testing when students created their own examples and analogies.[17]

The *Lyons* case could be evaluated to prepare for exams by analyzing whether the result would change if some facts changed. For example, the following hypotheticals could be created:

- If a passenger slipped on ice, would the court have reached a similar result?

- Would the result be different if the passenger slipped on water that had been spilled by a passenger an hour earlier?

- Is it significant that the incident occurred at a train station or would the decision be applicable to other public settings such as grocery stores?

As the Lyons decision relies on the policy assumption that passengers are careful of the safety of others, would the result change if evidence was introduced that passengers were not careful and routinely blocked the entrance with packages? Figure 9.6 sets forth the rule, facts from *Lyons* and a set of hypothetical facts. The reader can then evaluate how the court might rule with the new facts.

Figure 9.6
Evaluation: Analyze Hypothetical Facts

Element of Claim	Case Facts *Lyons*	Hypothetical Facts	Result?
Carrier has a duty of care if it should have known about danger to passengers.	Passenger entering train fell over a package in the doorway of the train.	Passenger slipped on ice that had been there overnight **or** on water spilled an hour earlier.	

[17] Sherrie L. Nist, Michele L. Simpson, *College Studying*, in Michael L. Kamil, et al., *Handbook of Reading Research* Volume III 656 (2000).

Practice Exercise 9.5 is an opportunity to evaluate a case to prepare for an exam. Practice Exercise 9.6 is the self-assessment exercise for this chapter.

VI. CASE EXAMPLE: CASE EVALUATION

This section will review the strategies outlined in this chapter using *Fisher v. Carrousel Motor Hotel, Inc.*, 424 S.W.2d 627 (Tex. 1967) (Appendix B-1).

A. WRITE REACTIONS AND ASK QUESTIONS

Write your reactions to *Fisher* as you read. These reactions may relate to confusing words, your thoughts about a legal concept, or your view of the ultimate decision in the case. At this stage, do not filter your thoughts. Any reaction is fine.

B. EVALUATE LAW, NOT FACTS

It is appropriate to evaluate legal concepts but not the credibility of witnesses or your view of the facts. Therefore, an expert reader would not question whether Fisher really felt embarrassed and hurt because those facts were established at the trial court level and are not reviewed by the appellate court. It is not appropriate to question whether Flynn acted accidentally because the decision states that the jury found that Flynn "acted maliciously." *Id.* at 629.

However, an expert reader would ask questions about legal concepts that were considered by the court. It would be useful to examine the types of actions that would be considered offensive because this relates to the proof needed to establish an element of battery. It would also be relevant to ask about the extent to which an object has to be connected with an individual's body or clothing to be considered "closely identified with the body" because this relates to battery as well. *Id.*

C. EVALUATE THE IMPACT OF POLICY

The *Fisher* court provides some discussion regarding the reasoning behind the decision. The court explains that battery involves the "interest in freedom from intentional and unpermitted contacts with the plaintiff's person." *Id.* at 629. An attorney analyzing *Fisher* might examine whether this interest still exists. It might be interesting to explore whether these interests are dependent upon the setting for the encounter.

D. INTERPRETATION AND EVALUATION: ANALOGICAL REASONING

Going back to Mr. Parker's situation discussed in Chapters 1, 2, and 3, the attorney for Mr. Parker might interpret *Fisher* differently than the attorney representing Smith Cars. Mr. Parker's attorney could argue that *Fisher* applies when contact is made that is offensive and that in our culture it is rude and offensive to grab a phone. The attorney for Smith Cars might argue that the situation in *Fisher* was qualitatively different because racial epithets are plainly offensive and are in a different category from mere rudeness.

An attorney representing Mr. Parker would also evaluate *Fisher* to determine if the case could be used to solve Mr. Parker's situation. As demonstrated in Figure 9.7, the attorney would first focus on the particular element of battery in *Fisher* that relates to whether contact is harmful or offensive and then identify the case facts from *Fisher* that relate to this issue.

The next step would be to identify the problem facts from Mr. Parker's case that pertain to this element and then make a comparison between the case facts and problem facts. If the facts are similar, it is likely that a court would reach the same result in *Fisher* and Mr. Parker's case. If the facts are different, it is unlikely that the same result would be reached.

Figure 9.7
Case Evaluation: Analogical Reasoning *Fisher*

Element of Claim	Case Facts *Fisher*	Problem Facts	Comparison Case/Problem Facts
Contact must be harmful or offensive	Manager grabbed plate and made offensive comment.	Mechanic grabbed camera from customer	Similar: Object grabbed. Different: *Fisher* also involved offensive statement while problem facts did not.

E. EVALUATION: PREPARE FOR EXAMS

To evaluate *Fisher* for exams, analyze the elements of battery and then create hypothetical fact patterns related to the elements. Assume that you are examining the element of battery related to whether or not contact is harmful or offensive. Follow the procedure in Figure 9.8 and list this element as well as the case facts from *Fisher*. Next create some hypothetical facts that relate to this element and compare these facts to the facts in *Fisher*.

Evaluate whether the hypothetical facts would change the court's decision. While Flynn grabbed a plate from Mr. Fisher's hand and shouted offensive language in *Fisher*, would the result be the same in the following situations:

- Flynn took food from Fisher's plate and shouted offensive language,
- Flynn grabbed the plate and asked Fisher to leave,
- Flynn grabbed the plate and never said anything to Fisher.

Figure 9.8
Case Evaluation: Analyze Hypothetical Facts

Element of Claim	Case Facts *Fisher*	Hypothetical Facts	Result?
Contact that is harmful or offensive.	Manager grabbed plate and made offensive comment.	Manager grabbed food from plate and made offensive comment.	
		Manager grabbed plate and asked Fisher to leave.	
		Manager grabbed plate and said nothing.	

This type of analysis is excellent practice for law school exams because it insures that you can connect facts (exam questions) to legal principles.

VII. PRACTICE

Practice Exercise 9.1
Interpretation and Evaluation

Goal: The purpose of this exercise is to practice understanding the literal meaning of a decision as well as the court's decision before evaluating the decision.

In this exercise, assume that you have been hired to work in a Legal Services office in New York City. You are beginning to learn about Social Security disability cases and have been given *Guzman v. Califano*, 480 F. Supp. 735 (S.D.N.Y. 1979) (Appendix J) to review.

Step 1: Before Reading Strategies

9.1–1   What preliminary steps would you take to understand *Guzman* before beginning to read more carefully?

Step 2: During Reading Strategies

9.1–2   After completing these preliminary steps, how would you summarize the substantive and procedural facts?

9.1–3   What did the court hold?

Step 3: After Reading Strategies

As discussed in this chapter, it is necessary to understand the literal meaning of a case and the court's decision before evaluating the case. Question 9.1–4 asks about the literal meaning of a section of the opinion. Question 9.1–5 relates to the court's interpretation of a concept. Question 9.1–6 requires evaluation of the decision.

Level	Question	Answer
9.1–4 Literal Meaning	What notice was the plaintiff provided regarding her right to counsel?	
9.1–5 Court's Decision	Did the court find that this notice was adequate?	
9.1–6 Evaluative Question	Do you agree that the notice was adequate?	

Practice Exercise 9.2
What Is Appropriate to Evaluate?

Goal: The goal of this exercise is to practice evaluating legal concepts in a case rather than facts.

Assume that you are still reviewing *Guzman v. Califano*, 480 F. Supp. 735 (S.D.N.Y. 1979) (Appendix J) from Practice Exercise 9.1. If Ms. Guzman came to your office after she received this decision and wanted you to assist her with an appeal to the Second Circuit Court of Appeals, you would need to evaluate the decision. Assume for purposes of this exercise that it is only appropriate to review legal questions. Are any of the following questions relevant to your evaluation of the case?

9.2–1   Is it possible that Ms. Guzman did not understand the Administrative Law Judge when he discussed her right to counsel at the administrative hearing?

9.2–2   Did Ms. Guzman proceed without a lawyer because she felt rushed?

9.2–3 Should an Administrative Law Judge be required to appoint counsel in all disability cases whether or not the claimant makes a request?

Practice Exercise 9.3
Evaluation: Using a Case to Solve a Client's Problem

Goal: The goal of this exercise is to evaluate a case and use analogical reasoning to determine if the case would be useful in solving a client's problem.

You are working in the law office of Bloom & Bloom in Poughkeepsie, New York and have received a phone call from Gregory Jones who has been arrested and charged with second-degree burglary in Dutchess County, New York. During your meeting with Gregory, you learn the following facts.

> On January 5, 2016, Gregory decided to go hiking with his cousin Ralph Smith at Bear Mountain. They began hiking around 2 PM. At 4 PM, they realized the weather was getting bad; the temperature dropped 20 degrees in one hour. They got worried and tried to return to their car. Unfortunately, Gregory slipped down a steep hill on the trail and grabbed Ralph as he fell. They both tumbled down to the bottom of the hill. By 7 PM, after they had walked a mile, they noticed a cabin, broke the lock on the front door, rummaged through drawers to look for matches and started a fire in the fireplace. They found a can of beans and after they ate the beans, they noticed that the cabin had an old antique clock. Since the cabin looked abandoned, they left and took the clock. In the meantime, a neighbor noticed smoke from the fireplace, called the police, and Gregory and Ralph were arrested. The indictment charges them with burglary in the second degree, N.Y. Penal Law § 140.25 (West 2017).

> The cabin was owned by Janice Newman who has lived in New York City for 15 years. She has stated that she used the cabin with her husband each summer for two weeks. The cabin had no running water or electricity during the winter. In the summer, the Newmans had the water turned on and the electricity connected. The cabin was furnished with a bed and a rustic couch and chairs. The Newmans kept no clothes or personal items in the cabin. The cabin had no heat. They used the fireplace occasionally for cooking in the summer.

Gregory wants us to try to get his charges reduced from second degree to third degree burglary. Gregory admits that he entered the cabin but claims that it should be considered a "building" rather than a "dwelling."

A person is guilty of second degree burglary when "he knowingly enters or remains unlawfully in a dwelling." N.Y. Penal Law § 140.25 (West 2017). "Dwelling" is defined as "a building which is usually occupied by a person lodging therein at night." N.Y. Penal Law § 140.00(3) (West 2017). A person is guilty of third degree burglary when "he knowingly enters or remains in a "building." N.Y. Penal Law § 140.20 (West 2017). A "building" is defined as "any structure"... "used for overnight lodging of persons." N.Y. Penal Law § 140.00(2). You have been told to read *People v. Barney*, 742 N.Y.S.2d 451 (N.Y. App. Div. 2002) (Appendix K) to understand the legal issues in Mr. Jones' case.

Step 1: Before Reading Strategies

9.3–1   What preliminary steps would you take to understand *Barney* before reading more carefully?

Step 2: During Reading Strategies

9.3–2   After completing these preliminary steps, how would you summarize the substantive and procedural facts?

9.3–3   What did the court hold?

Step 3: After Reading Strategies

Evaluate *People v. Barney* to determine if it can be used to help solve Gregory Jones' case. Assume that the only element of burglary you need to examine relates to whether Janice Newman's cabin was a building or a dwelling.

9.3–4   Complete the following chart:

Element of Claim	Case Facts *Barney*	Problem Facts	Comparison Case/Problem Facts

9.3–5   Are the facts in *Barney* different enough from your client's situation to distinguish the case and argue that Gregory Jones' charges should be reduced from second degree to third degree burglary?

9.3–6   How would you interpret *Barney* if you represented the State of New York?

Practice Exercise 9.4
What Do You Think?

Goal: The purpose of this exercise is to determine if you agree or disagree with the decision in a case.

As discussed in this chapter, cases are subject to interpretation. *People v. Barney*, 742 N.Y.S. 2d 451 (N.Y. App. Div. 2002) (Appendix K) contains a majority opinion and a dissenting opinion. Analyze the reasoning in the opinions. Then decide who you agree with.

Opinion	Reasoning	Do you agree? Why?
9.4–1 Majority		
9.4–2 Dissent		

Practice Exercise 9.5
Evaluation: Prepare for Exams

Goal: The purpose of this exercise is to practice evaluating a case to determine if the case result would change if the underlying facts or policy considerations changed.

You have read *People v. Barney*, 742 N.Y.S. 2d 451 (App Div. 2002) (Appendix K) for criminal law and are now preparing for the final exam. You have been told that there might be an exam question based on *Barney* that examines the distinctions between second and third degree burglary.

You have decided to create a hypothetical exam question. In Practice Exercise 9.3, you have already identified the rule and the facts from *Barney* that relate to this rule. Now think about how changes to some of the facts in *Barney* might change the result.

9.5–1   Create a hypothetical exam question so that the result would be the same as *Barney*.

9.5–2   Create a hypothetical exam question so the result would be different from *Barney*.

Element of Claim	Case Facts *Barney*	Hypothetical Facts	Result

Practice Exercise 9.6
Self-Assessment

Goal: In this exercise, you can determine if you understand the process of evaluating cases.

For this exercise, assume that you are still representing Ms. Evelyn Michel, who has been terminated from her employment as a nurse because she failed the National Council Licensure Examination. It is undisputed that Ms. Michel tried to pass the exam and simply did not have time to work and prepare for the exam. It is also agreed that Ms. Michel's employment was conditioned on passing the exam. Ms. Michel wants to know if she will qualify for unemployment insurance benefits. *De Grego v. Levine,* 347 N.E. 2d 611 (N.Y. 1976) (Appendix C) provides guidance.

9.6–1   Are the facts in *De Grego* similar enough to Ms. Michel's situation to use the case in support of the argument that she did not provoke her discharge?

9.6–2   In Practice Exercise 7.4, you summarized the *DeGrego* majority and dissenting opinions. Who do you agree with?

Evaluate your understanding of the skills in this chapter by completing the following rubric. For each skill, circle whether you are at the proficient or developing level. Everyone can get to the proficient level over time.

Skill	Competency Level	
	Proficient	Developing
Understands that cases can be interpreted and evaluated.	• Understands that there is more than one way to interpret a case. • Writes down reactions to cases while reading. • Asks questions about legal concepts.	• Believes that there is one correct way to interpret a case. • Takes no notes while reading. • Reads without questioning.
Evaluates cases to solve new legal problems.	• Compares the factual similarities/differences between case and problem facts and uses analogical reasoning. • Evaluates legal concepts. • Examines policy considerations when evaluating cases. • Creates hypothetical factual scenarios to prepare for exams.	• Looks at cases generally without factual analysis. • Evaluates witness credibility. • Ignores policy implications. • Does not evaluate cases to prepare for exams.

CHAPTER 10

DURING AND AFTER READING: CASE BRIEF

I. SUMMARY

This chapter examines strategies to prepare a case brief that contains:

- key parts of a case, and
- the reader's reactions and comments.

At the conclusion of this chapter, you will be able to prepare briefs that:

- accurately identify the key sections of a case,
- assist in preparing for final exams, and
- assist in solving new legal problems.

II. CHECKLIST

CASE READING CHECKLIST

Warning: Do not just highlight and underline.

Phase 1: Before Reading

1. Read for a purpose and assume the role of advocate or judge.

2. Read with energy and focus.

3. Notice case structure.

4. Understand the general subject matter by examining:

    a. course syllabus, casebook table of contents, or research assignment, and

    b. parties, citation, court, and date.

5. Read for an overview by skimming and noticing organization, headings, who won, and what case is generally about.

Phase 2: Reading More Carefully

1. Understand the facts.

2. Reread, look up unfamiliar words, analyze confusing language, and vary reading speed.

3. Understand the main ideas set forth in the issue, holding, and reasoning.

4. Identify the rule.

5. **Take notes with your reactions and brief the case.**

Phase 3: After Reading

1. Evaluate the decision, ask questions, and talk with professors.

2. Determine how cases fit together with other cases and synthesize.

III. CASE BRIEFS

A. SUMMARIES

Before examining the mechanics of preparing a case brief, this section will address the components of good summaries. Summaries are brief statements that contain the main points of articles or other texts. Summaries may contain facts as well as the reader's reactions and evaluations. We summarize books, articles, or things we need to buy at the grocery store. Reflection Exercise 11.1 is an opportunity to reflect on strategies you have used in the past to prepare summaries.

Even a summary such as a shopping list contains facts as well as product evaluations. For example, a shopper may go to the store with a shopping list to buy milk, eggs, bread, and ice cream. However, he buys a particular brand and type of milk. He may like whole wheat bread rather than rye. He probably has a favorite flavor of ice cream. While his list may appear to only include "facts" or individual items, he prepares the list based upon his food preferences and evaluations of different foods. He also may organize the list, particularly if it is long, in accordance with the layout of the store. If he walks into the store at the produce aisle, it may be easier to list the fruits and vegetables first.

Case briefs are **short** outlines and summaries of a court's opinion. They are similar to shopping lists because they include factual information as well as evaluations. A case brief includes a summary of the case as well as the reader's reactions. As discussed in Chapter 9, evaluation is an important step in critical reading and the reader's thoughts and questions are key components of a good brief. While a shopping list does not include the reason that vanilla ice cream is selected rather than chocolate, the case brief includes a notes section so that the reader can record reactions, questions, as well as opinions. Like shopping lists that are organized according to the layout of the store, case briefs are arranged in accordance with the usual structure of cases that was discussed in Chapter 3. This chapter will first explain why case briefs are valuable, then address how they are organized, and conclude with specific guidelines for the preparation of briefs.

B. WHY PREPARE CASE BRIEFS?

Law students and lawyers prepare case briefs for several reasons. First, **writing case summaries helps readers understand** cases. The act of writing makes the reader more aware of what he or she knows and what is still unclear. If you start preparing a case brief and find that some things are still puzzling, take the time to go back and resolve the confusion. Do not continue with the brief until you have clarified the point.

Second, case briefs are excellent **reference** materials for class as professors often ask questions about the facts, the holding, and the court's reasoning. Bring briefs to class and use them to respond to questions. You can also refer to your notes to ask questions. During class discussions, add to or correct briefs based upon your **professor's** comments.

Third, case briefs can be used to **study for exams**. It is not possible or necessary to reread all cases at the end of the semester. Case briefs provide excellent summaries of key concepts as students prepare outlines for courses. Finally, case briefs are used in research and writing projects to keep good **notes** that will ultimately be used to prepare legal documents.

C. ORGANIZATION OF BRIEF

In preparing briefs, remember that briefing involves more than simply filling out a form or color coding different parts of a case. While it is useful to identify sections of a case, that is not the primary objective. The goal of the analysis is to understand the case as a whole and record reactions and questions. Furthermore, case briefs are notes to use for your own purposes. Make them useful and do not stress about format. No one will ever grade your briefs.

The sections of a brief correspond to the way a case is generally structured that was outlined in Chapter 3:

- substantive facts
- procedural facts
- issue
- holding
- rationale
- disposition

A summary of information often included in a case brief is found in Figure 10.1. **These categories are not ironclad**. Professors may want to emphasize certain aspects of cases over others. If a professor always asks questions about the facts, make sure the case briefs for that class include detailed fact sections. A research assignment may require a different emphasis as well. It may be useful to confine a brief to specific issues that are the focus of the assignment. Figure 10.1 provides an outline of the parts of a brief as well as reference to the earlier chapters that have explored the topics in more detail.

Figure 10.1
Case Brief Sections

Section	Description and Chapter Reference
Citation and Parties	• Citation and names of parties. • Court, date. *Chapter 3*
Substantive Facts	• Relevant or determinative facts. *Chapter 5*
Procedural Facts	• How the case started and plaintiff's legal claim or state's criminal charge. • Significant motions and decisions. • Trial and appellate decisions. *Chapter 3*
Arguments	• Arguments made by each party.
Issue	• Main questions addressed by the court. *Chapter 7*
Holding and Rule	• Holding (the court's decision). • Rule (general legal principle). *Chapters 7 and 8*
Reasoning	• Court's rationale. • Policy considerations. *Chapter 7*
Judgment or Order	• Disposition such as affirm, reverse, or remand. *Chapter 7*
Concurring or dissenting opinions	• Reasoning from non-majority opinions. *Chapter 7*
Notes	• Reactions, questions, and thoughts. *Chapter 9*

Figure 10.2 is a template that can be used to prepare briefs.

Figure 10.2
Case Brief Template

Case Name & Citation:

Facts:
     1.
     2.

Procedural History:
     1.
     2.

Arguments:

Issue:

Holding:

Rule:

Reasoning:

Judgment/Order:

Concurring/Dissenting Opinions:

Notes:

D. WHEN SHOULD BRIEFS BE PREPARED?

This chapter is titled During and After Reading because briefs are prepared during the reading process as well as after reading. As noted in

Chapter 1, it is useful to take notes while reading a case so that the reader can record specific reactions and questions. These reactions and questions may be significant and useful. If you wait to write these ideas down until you finish analyzing a case completely, you may forget your ideas.

After you understand the context for reading the case and do a brief overview, start by writing down the **citation** and identifying the **parties**. Next, focus on the **facts** and prepare a summary, diagram, or chart of key substantive and procedural facts. Remember that it will be necessary to go back to the facts after understanding the holding to make sure that all relevant facts are included. As discussed in Chapter 5, it is not possible to identify the relevant facts without reading and understanding the entire opinion.

After outlining the facts, identify the arguments made by the parties as well as the **issue**, **holding** and **reasoning**. While key phrases and quotations can be useful to note, focus on the main ideas in the case. If the decision includes rules, include those as well or formulate a rule. In the **notes** section, add questions. Think about the questions that are left unanswered by the case. Think about other factual scenarios and how a court might apply a rule from the case to a new situation.

E. CASE BRIEF GUIDELINES

1. Do Your Own

It is essential to prepare your own case briefs. While briefs are available from a variety of sources, using someone else's case brief provides you with someone else's thoughts. It does not give you practice in learning how to analyze a case. It also does not give you the opportunity to explain the case to yourself so that you know whether or not you understand it.

The purpose of legal education is to give students practice in analyzing a case so that they can perform this essential task when they are practicing law. Using someone else's brief does not give you any practice. Furthermore, in law practice, lawyers need to be able to do this analysis on their own. **There are no brief banks for cases you need to understand in law practice.**

2. Keep Briefs Short

Case briefs are **short** summaries. The operative word is **short**. Case briefs that are longer than the original case are not useful. Use abbreviations for terms. Some standard abbreviations are:

π or P—plaintiff

Δ or D—defendant

C—complaint

MD—motion to dismiss

SJ—motion for summary judgment

K—contract

Create any other abbreviations that will save time. Practice Exercise 10.2 gives you the opportunity to practice writing short factual summaries.

3.   Paraphrase—Do Not Cut and Paste

Paraphrasing, or summarizing text in your own words, is an excellent technique to use in preparing case briefs. However, summaries are only effective comprehension strategies if the reader summarizes text in his or her own words. The act of paraphrasing helps the reader process new information. It forces the reader to analyze material and think. One legal reading authority has noted that the "struggle to create the paraphrase is a large part of what creates the memory trace."[1] While it is tempting to just cut and paste sections of the case into a brief, reading experts uniformly agree that summaries are only useful if they are created by the reader. While it may be helpful to include key quotations, terms, or rules from an opinion, the brief should primarily contain your own words.

4.   Include Examples and Questions

In the Notes section of a brief, it is helpful to think about examples of the concepts presented in the case. Think about hypothetical or new factual situations and how a court might decide the case with different facts. As noted in Chapter 9, research indicates that this type of analysis can significantly improve student performance. It is also useful to include questions.

Practice Exercise 10.3 provides practice in briefing a case. Practice Exercise 10.4 is the self-assessment exercise for this chapter.

IV.   CASE EXAMPLE: CASE BRIEF

The skills in this chapter, case briefing, are explained with *Fisher v. Carrousel Motor Hotel, Inc.*, 424 S.W.2d 627 (Tex. 1967) (Appendix B-1). The brief is being prepared to address whether battery occurred when Mr. Parker's phone was grabbed. Therefore, the brief is confined to battery and other issues do not need to be addressed.

---

[1]   Michael Hunter Schwartz, *Expert Learning for Law Students* 185 (2d ed. 2008).

Figure 10.3
Sample Case Brief

Fisher v. Carrousel Motor Hotel, Inc., 424 S.W. 2d 627 (Tex. 1967)

Parties: Fisher (P) sued Carrousel (C), the Brass Ring Club (B) and Flynn (F), manager at B.

Facts:

1. P attended business meeting at C, went to B for lunch buffet.
2. When P was to be served, F took plate from P's hand and shouted that P, an African American, could not be served.
3. P testified he "was not actually touched," but was "highly embarrassed & hurt" by F's "conduct in the presence of his associates."
4. F was attempting to enforce B rules.

Procedural History:

1. P sued C, B, & F for assault & battery & for actual & exemplary damages (d).
2. Jury: $400 actual & $500 exemplary d.
3. Trial Ct award JNOV to Ds.
4. Ct. of Civil Appeals aff'd.
5. Sup. Ct. of Texas reversed and J to P for $900.

Arguments: D: battery requires physical contact. P: unpermitted & intentional touching of anything connected with body offends dignity.

Issue: Whether battery was committed when someone grabbed a plate from Fisher, did not have physical contact with him, and humiliated him?

Holding: Intentional grabbing of P's plate in an offensive manner constituted battery even though there was no physical contact with P.

Rule: Battery can occur when someone touches a person's body or anything connected with a person's body in an offensive manner whether or not physical harm occurs.

Reasoning: Since the essence of battery is an offense to someone's dignity, it is not necessary that an individual's body be touched. It is enough if something is touched that is "intimately connected with one's body."

Judgment: Texas Sup. Ct. rev'd Trial Ct. & Ct. of Appeals decision.

Notes: Decision seems to rely on "offensive invasion" of the person. Lots of references to dignity & indignity, offensive & insulting behavior. Are there any limits to rule relating to items connected to the body? Would result be different if plate was grabbed with no racial epithets? Is "offensive" idea a requirement or is any item connected to the body considered offensive if touched?

V. PRACTICE

Reflection Exercise 10.1
Summaries

Goal: The goal of this exercise is to think about techniques you have used to summarize in the past.

We prepare summaries for a variety of purposes. List the types of summaries you have prepared, things you have found useful to include in these summaries, and how you have organized the summaries.

Type of Summary	Types of Things Included and Organization

Practice Exercise 10.2
Writing Summaries

Goal: The goal of this exercise is to practice writing short summaries.

Case briefs are only useful if they are brief summaries of a case. Long summaries are not useful. This exercise will assist in developing your ability to write short summaries.

In this exercise, you will prepare a short summary of some of the sentences and paragraphs in *Picard v. Barry Pontiac-Buick, Inc.* 654 A. 2d 690, 691–92 (R.I. 1995), which was used as the basis for Mr. Parker's dispute in Chapters 1, 2 and 3.

First, read the following facts. (Footnotes have been omitted.) Specific instructions for the summaries follow the facts.

FACTS AND PROCEDURAL HISTORY

"This case began eight years ago with a broken signal light. The plaintiff, Victorie A. Picard, brought her mother's car to Barry Pontiac-Buick, Inc. (Barry Pontiac) in Newport, Rhode Island, where the car had been purchased, to have the light repaired. While the car was being repaired, plaintiff decided to have its annual inspection performed as well. The car failed this inspection because, according to a Barry Pontiac representative, the brakes needed to be replaced. The plaintiff brought the car to Kent's Alignment Service (Kent's Alignment), also located in Newport, where the car passed inspection.

The plaintiff then contacted a local television news "troubleshooter" reporter, presumably to report her experience at the two inspection sites. Shortly after Kent's Alignment had inspected plaintiff's car, Barry Pontiac phoned Kent's Alignment to ask that the car be checked again and the sticker removed because the brakes "were bad." Accordingly Edward Kent (Kent), the owner of Kent's Alignment, set January 27, 1987, as the date that plaintiff, accompanied by her goddaughter Kristen Ann Seyster (Seyster), returned with the car to Kent's garage.

Kent's Alignment was divided into a garage area separated by a glass partition from an office area. At the time of the incident at issue in this case, Seyster was in the office, while plaintiff was in the garage. After Kent inspected the car, he told plaintiff that he had been asked to call Barry Pontiac which also wished to inspect the brakes. Ray Stevens (Stevens), the service manager at Barry Pontiac arrived at Kent's Alignment, accompanied by defendant, who was employed by Barry Pontiac.

The defendant began to inspect the brakes. He and plaintiff gave vastly different descriptions of what next happened. The plaintiff said she began to take a picture of defendant as he was facing away from her, presumably as evidence for the troubleshooter report. The plaintiff testified that she *did* intend to photograph defendant although the photograph was not intended to identify defendant. The photograph did, however, clearly show defendant fully facing the camera, standing upright while pointing his index finger at plaintiff. After the camera snapped, the events that gave rise to this case occurred.

The plaintiff testified that defendant "lunged" at her and "grabbed [her] around around [*sic*] the shoulders," although plaintiff did not experience any pain. The plaintiff then testified on cross-examination that after defendant grabbed her by both her shoulders, she and defendant "spun around wrestling." According to plaintiff, defendant released her after someone said, "let her go." The plaintiff then left the garage with her goddaughter."

10.2–1 Read the first paragraph and summarize the first two sentences in one sentence.

10.2–2 Read the first paragraph and then summarize all of the sentences in two sentences.

10.2–3 Read the second paragraph and summarize the first and second paragraphs in three sentences.

10.2–4 Read the third paragraph and summarize it in one sentence.

10.2–5 Read the fourth paragraph and summarize it in one sentence.

10.2–6 Summarize all five paragraphs in no more than six sentences.

Practice Exercise 10.3
Case Brief

You are continuing to work on Gregory Jones' case from Practice Exercise 9.3. Mr. Jones was charged with second-degree burglary in New York. You have been advised that *Shackelford v. Commonwealth*, 757 S.W.2d 193 (Ky. Ct. App. 1988) (Appendix L) might be helpful to read. Prepare a case brief.

Brief Element	*Shackelford*
10.3–1 Case Name, Citation	
10.3–2 Facts	
10.3–3 Procedural History	
10.3–4 Arguments	
10.3–5 Issue	
10.3–6 Holding	
10.3–7 Rule	
10.3–8 Reasoning	
10.3–9 Judgment	
10.3–10 Notes	

Practice Exercise 10.4
Self-Assessment

Goal: In this exercise, you will be able to determine if you understand the concepts related to briefing cases.

Assume that you are still representing Ms. Evelyn Michel in her unemployment insurance benefits case. Read *De Grego v. Levine*, 347 N.E. 2d 611 (N.Y. 1976) (Appendix C) and prepare a case brief.

Brief Element	*De Grego*
10.4–1 Case Name, Citation	
10.4–2 Facts	
10.4–3 Procedural History	
10.4–4 Arguments	
10.4–5 Issue	
10.4–6 Holding	
10.4–7 Rule	
10.4–8 Reasoning	
10.4–9 Judgment	
10.4–10 Notes	

Evaluate your understanding of the skills in this chapter by completing the following rubric. For each skill, circle whether you are at the proficient or developing level. Everyone can get to the proficient level over time.

Skill	Competency Level	
	Proficient	**Developing**
Understands that case briefs help the reader clarify information, prepare for class, and prepare for exams.	• Prepares briefs for class and writing assignments.	• Does not brief cases.
Understands that briefs should include the reader's questions and thoughts.	• Includes comments in case briefs.	• No comments are included.
Understands that readers should paraphrase concepts.	• Prepares briefs using reader's own words.	• Prepares briefs by cutting and pasting from electronic sources.
Understands that briefs should be short.	• Briefs consist of short summaries.	• Briefs may be longer than the original case.

CHAPTER 11

AFTER READING: CASE SYNTHESIS

I. SUMMARY

This chapter examines how legal readers:

- use multiple cases to solve legal problems, and

- synthesize cases to prepare legal documents.

As discussed in Chapters 1 through 10, critical reading involves more than memorization. To synthesize cases, attorneys use many of the critical thinking skills that were summarized in Chapter 1 such as understanding, analyzing, and evaluating cases.

At the conclusion of this chapter, you will be able to:

- explain the meaning of case synthesis,

- identify when case synthesis is required,

- understand the steps that are used to synthesize cases, and

- synthesize several cases.

II. CHECKLIST

CASE READING CHECKLIST

Warning: Do not just highlight and underline.

Phase 1: Before Reading

1. Read for a purpose and assume the role of advocate or judge.

2. Read with energy and focus.

3. Notice case structure.

4. Understand the general subject matter by examining:

    a. course syllabus, casebook table of contents, or research assignment, and

    b. parties, citation, court, and date.

5. Read for an overview by skimming and noticing organization, headings, who won, and what case is generally about.

Phase 2: Reading More Carefully

1.   Understand the facts.

2.   Reread, look up unfamiliar words, analyze confusing language, and vary reading speed.

3.   Understand the main ideas set forth in the issue, holding, and reasoning.

4.   Identify the rule.

5.   Take notes with your reactions and brief the case.

Phase 3: After Reading

1.   Evaluate the decision, ask questions, and talk with professors.

2.   **Determine how cases fit together with other cases and synthesize.**

III. USING MULTIPLE CASES TO SOLVE PROBLEMS

A. SYNTHESIS IN GENERAL

The term synthesis means to put facts or ideas together to create something new. We synthesize information when we get data from a variety of sources to construct our own version of an event. For example, when a major storm hits, we get news from reporters, individuals on the scene, government weather agencies, and friends or relatives. Some individuals know about the storm's effect on one part of a city and other people have information about its impact on other areas. Some facts may be similar and others may conflict. We synthesize when we examine all of the information, determine which facts are similar, reconcile conflicting details, and construct our own view of the event.

B. CASE SYNTHESIS

Case synthesis is similar. Just as it is rare to rely on one piece of information about a storm, it is also unusual for an attorney to use one case to solve a legal problem. More often, an attorney will research a topic and discover that there are several cases that deal with a subject. The attorney must figure out how these cases relate to each other and how to reconcile conflicting results. As Professor K.N. Llewellyn noted, "*no case can have a meaning by itself! . . . What counts . . . is the background of the other cases in relation to . . . the one.*"[1]

---

[1]   Karl N. Llwellyn, *The Bramble Bush: On Our Law and Its Study* 49 (1965).

Expert legal readers think about how different cases relate to each other. They do not read cases in isolation from one another. One student in the Grisé study noted that the instruction in case synthesis assisted him because "I've been reading better, especially in the sense that I try & put everything into perspective w[ith] other things we've read."[2] When students in that study were asked to rate the usefulness of different sections of the reading checklist, case synthesis was one of the most helpful strategies identified.

Case synthesis is important in all types of legal work. When reading casebooks, students need to synthesize cases to understand how they fit together with other cases in the casebook. The main cases in casebooks are often followed by short summaries of cases that appear to have been decided differently. It is the student's task to figure out how to reconcile seemingly opposing results. Moreover, after reading cases on a specific topic, students are advised to synthesize cases and create outlines that set forth the main rules or ideas that pertain to a subject. When reading reported decisions, attorneys examine multiple cases that often have conflicting results. To write a memorandum or brief, attorneys must reconcile and synthesize cases to reach a conclusion.

C. WHEN IS CASE SYNTHESIS NECESSARY?

Synthesis is required when multiple cases on a topic are found and the cases come to different results and/or examine different facets of a rule. If all of the cases that address a similar subject have the same result and state the same rule, synthesis may not be necessary. The cases can simply be used to predict how a court will resolve a client's problem. As seen in Figure 11.1, synthesis may be needed when:

- cases apply similar rules to different factual situations and arrive at different results, and/or

- cases address different aspects of a rule.

Figure 11.1
When Is Case Synthesis Helpful?

Case Comparison	Facts	Rule	Result
A & B	Different	Similar	Different
A & C	Similar or different	Different aspects of rule	Similar or different

---

[2] Jane Bloom Grisé, *Critical Reading Instruction: The Road to Successful Legal Writing Skills*, 18 W. Mich. Univ. Cooley J. of Prac. & Clinical L. (forthcoming 2017).

Case synthesis is required in both situations so that the attorney can piece together the decisions to form an integrated rule.

Sometimes both of these situations occur with the same group of cases. For example, cases A and B may use the same rules but come to different results. Cases B and C may have similar or different outcomes and use different aspects of a rule. After explaining these two situations in more detail, this chapter provides a procedure for case synthesis.

1.   Cases Apply Similar Rules to Different Factual Situations

Cases may reach contrary results when similar rules are applied to **different factual situations**. As discussed in Chapter 5, the relevant or determinative facts are the facts that are needed to establish a legal claim. If one of these relevant facts changes or is missing, the case result may change. Relevant facts are referred to as determinative facts because they can determine the result. When an expert legal reader examines multiple cases with similar rules and different facts, the reader analyzes how the facts impact the results. There may be a wide range of combinations of facts and results. The goal is to look for themes and patterns so that an attorney can predict how new fact patterns will be decided.

For example, some cases address the tort of intentional infliction of emotional distress (IIED), which is an intentional tort like battery. One element of IIED is outrage. As noted in Chapter 8, IIED is found when someone engages in extreme and outrageous conduct and intentionally or recklessly causes severe emotional distress to another person. Conduct is considered outrageous if it is extreme behavior that goes beyond general standards of decency. While most courts apply this same general rule to find outrage, the case results depend upon the facts.

In Figure 11.2, the courts in both *Benningfield*[3] and *Wilson*[4] used the same general rule and came to different conclusions based upon the facts. As seen in Figure 11.2, there is a spectrum of conduct that may or may not constitute outrageous behavior. At one end of the spectrum, the *Benningfield* court found no outrage when an employee was terminated from a job. At the other end of the spectrum, the *Wilson* court found outrage when an employee was subjected to daily racial insults for seven years.

---

[3]   *Benningfield v. Pettit Environmental, Inc.*, 183 S.W.3d 567 (Ky. Ct. App. 2005).
[4]   *Wilson v. Lowe's Home Center*, 75 S.W.3d 229 (Ky. Ct. App. 2001).

Figure 11.2
Factual Analysis

Termination from work	7 years of racial remarks
Benningfield	*Wilson*

$\longleftarrow$ ─────────────────────────────────── $\longrightarrow$

No outrage   **Outrage**

If an attorney's client wants to pursue a possible IIED claim when an employer made demeaning comments to the client over a period of two years and fired the client, it is necessary to predict where on the spectrum the new case would fall. Are the facts more similar to the case that dealt with pure termination or are the facts more like the case that dealt with racial remarks? The cases need to be synthesized so the attorney can predict how the new case would be decided.

2.   Cases Address Different Aspects of a Rule

Sometimes cases are decided differently because they **focus on different parts of a rule**. This occurs because in the common law system, judges make decisions based on cases that come before them. The judge's job is to decide the specific case. The judge does not write a treatise on a subject or insure that a topic is completely analyzed. For this reason, decisions tend to analyze narrow areas of the law and do not present a complete picture.

When cases address different aspects of a rule, attorneys may need to combine the rules from different cases. This technique is referred to as **rule synthesis**. Attorneys combine the rules from several cases and formulate a general rule to solve a client's problem. For example, using the outrage element from IIED again, different cases may address different aspects of outrage. While *Wilson* and *Benningfield* address the same general rule for outrage, a third case uses the same rule but adds another aspect to the rule. *Kroger v. Willgruber*[5] found outrage where an employer's conduct went beyond the bounds of decency **and** where the employer continued to act outrageously after being informed that the employee had a mental breakdown. The new aspect of the rule is that if a perpetrator knows a victim is susceptible and continues to act outrageously, that is further evidence of outrage.

If an employer made demeaning comments to a client over a period of two years and fired the client and knew the client was suffering from extreme depression, an attorney could synthesize the rules from *Wilson*,

---

[5]   *Kroger Co. v. Willgruber*, 920 S.W.2d 61 (Ky. 1996).

Benningfield, and *Willgruber* to create a rule that would be applicable to the client's problem.

D. WHEN IS CASE SYNTHESIS NOT HELPFUL?

Case synthesis is not required when cases conflict because:

- courts in different jurisdictions adopt different rules, or

- courts adopt different rules over time.

1. Jurisdictions Adopt Different Rules

Synthesis may not be useful if cases are decided differently because they arise from different court systems or different states. There are federal and state court systems. The power or jurisdiction of federal courts is established in the United States Constitution, while state courts have broader powers or jurisdiction. While all courts are required to follow the United States Constitution, courts in different states may adopt different common law rules. For example, the New York courts may adopt rules relating to IIED that are different from the rules in California. When jurisdictions have different rules, it is not appropriate to synthesize cases. The rules are just different.

2. Rules Change over Time

Some rules are different because they have changed over time. For example, in 2015, the United States Supreme Court decided *Obergefell v. Hodges*[6] and found that the Constitution does not permit states to bar same-sex couples from marriage. In 1972, the Court had dismissed an appeal in *Baker v. Nelson*, 409 U.S. 810 (1972) because the exclusion of same-sex couples from marriage did not present a substantial federal question. These two results cannot be reconciled or synthesized. They are different because the rules have changed.

IV. HOW TO SYNTHESIZE CASES

If case synthesis is required, it must be conducted in an orderly fashion. As explained in Figure 11.3, after identifying the topic and reading cases, an attorney must first understand the facts, holding, and rules from the individual cases. Then it is possible to examine cases in relationship to each other and synthesize.

---

[6]   135 S. Ct. 2584 (2015).

Figure 11.3
Synthesis Steps

Step	Analysis
1	Identify topic.
2	Locate and read cases.
3	Identify facts, holding, rule, and result for each case.
4	Determine if synthesis is necessary.
5	Compare case facts, holdings, rules, and results.
6	Synthesize.

A. STEP 1: IDENTIFY TOPIC

The first step is to identify the particular topic for the class or writing assignment. In casebooks, the case topic is identified in the table of contents or class syllabus. Cases in casebooks are edited so everything in the case pertains to the topic. Writing assignments also focus on a specific topic. For example, if a writing assignment focuses on the tort of IIED which has four different elements, identify the particular element that needs to be addressed in the assignment. As reported decisions often address multiple subjects, focus on the particular topic in the case that pertains to the assignment. Here, it will be assumed that we are still representing a client whose employer made demeaning comments to him over a period of two years, fired him, and knew he was suffering from extreme depression. The topic is outrage in an IIED case.

B. STEP 2: LOCATE AND READ CASES

Locate and read cases that address the topic and categorize the cases by the result. When reading from a casebook, read all of the cases that pertain to a topic before trying to synthesize and reconcile the conflicting cases. Sometimes, the main cases are followed by a notes section where opposing or conflicting cases are presented. Read the main case and then sort out the cases in the notes section and group the cases based upon the result.

For writing assignments, it can be helpful to group cases by result or the court's ultimate conclusion. For IIED cases, the result would be a finding of outrage or no outrage. After researching the element of outrage for IIED, put all of the cases that find outrage together and all cases that find no outrage in a separate pile. It can be helpful to start by focusing on cases from your particular jurisdiction because these cases are considered **mandatory authority**. This means that courts in a particular state or jurisdiction must follow the decisions of the highest court in the state or jurisdiction. While courts in one state can also consider cases from other states (**persuasive authority**), it is useful to begin synthesis with mandatory cases from a single jurisdiction.

Here, assume we have found the three cases referenced earlier: *Benningfield*, *Wilson*, and *Willgruber*. They were all decided by Kentucky courts.

C. STEP 3: IDENTIFY FACTS, HOLDING, RULE AND RESULT FOR EACH CASE

Next, examine the facts, holding, rule, and result for each case. Figure 11.4 provides a convenient way to record the results of this analysis. *Benningfield*, *Wilson*, and *Willgruber* are analyzed in Figure 11.4.

Figure 11.4
Case Analysis

Case	Facts	Holding	Rule	Result
Benningfield	Employee complained that he did not receive proper training and was terminated from job.	No outrage found when employee was terminated after he complained that he did not receive appropriate training.	Termination from job is not outrageous conduct because it is not beyond the bounds of decency.	No outrage
Wilson	Employee subjected to daily racial insults over 7 years.	Jury could find outrage when employee was subjected to daily racial insults for 7 years.	Racial insults over many years go beyond the bounds of decency and are outrageous.	Outrage
Willgruber	Employer tried to induce employee to resign and sent him to interview for job that did not exist.	Outrageous conduct occurred when Kroger sent employee to interview for job that did not exist, pressured him	Fraud and deceit went beyond the bounds of decency. In addition, outrage exists when perpetrator	Outrage

Case	Facts	Holding	Rule	Result
	When notified employee was suicidal, employer tried to delay disability benefits.	to sign release papers while knowing he had suffered a mental breakdown, and tried to deceive the disability carrier.	has knowledge of victim's susceptibility and takes advantage of him in an outrageous way.	

In formulating rules, remember from Chapter 8 that rules are general statements of the legal principles in a case. Some court decisions articulate rules and some do not. If the court does not set forth a rule, formulate a rule for each case.

D. STEP 4: DECIDE IF SYNTHESIS IS NECESSARY

If all cases apply the same rule and find the same result, then synthesis may not be required. If cases conflict with others or address different aspects of a rule, then it is necessary to synthesize the cases. In considering *Benningfield*, *Wilson*, and *Willgruber*, synthesis is required because the cases apply the same rule with different results and one case addresses a different aspect of the rule.

E. STEP 5: COMPARE FACTS, HOLDINGS, RULES, RESULTS, AND POLICY

After individual cases are analyzed and it is determined that synthesis is necessary, compare the cases. Note the jurisdiction, dates, facts, holdings, rules, results, and policy considerations as set forth in Figure 11.5.

Figure 11.5
Case Comparisons

General	• Are the cases from the same jurisdiction?
	• What are the dates of the decisions?
Facts	• Are facts similar or different?
	• Is there a relationship between facts and results?
Holding	• Are there general patterns or themes?
Rules	• Is the language in the rules the same or different?
	• Does one case deal with an aspect of a rule that is not addressed in another case?

	• If the court does not explicitly set forth a rule, are there rules that can be inferred? • Should some rules logically be addressed before others?
Result	• Did the court find liability or no liability?
Policy	• Is policy addressed? • Have policy concerns changed?

1.   Similar Rules and Different Facts

If the **rules are similar but the cases deal with different factual situations**, examine more closely how courts have dealt with the different fact patterns. Notice the similarities and differences in the facts. As noted earlier, it can be helpful to place cases on a spectrum depending upon the case result and the facts. This process can help the reader determine if certain facts have triggered particular results.

Figure 11.2 demonstrated how the facts in two IIED cases were examined on a spectrum where the rules were similar and the facts were different. Figure 11.6 adds *Willgruber* where the court found outrage when a company fired an employee, told him to travel out of state to get a new job that did not exist, and provided misinformation to a disability insurance official while knowing that the employee was suicidal.[7]

Figure 11.6
Expanded Factual Analysis

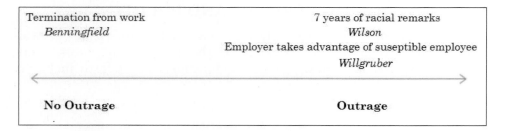

After cases are placed on a spectrum, analyze the spectrum more closely. When the facts are compared, it may be possible to find common themes or factors that influence whether courts have found outrage or no outrage. Make a list of these factors and categories on a chart such as Figure 11.7 and compare the cases. Sometimes courts explicitly mention that certain types of factors are important and sometimes it is necessary to infer that certain circumstances are significant.

---

⁷   *Kroger Co. v. Willgruber*, 920 S.W.2d 61 (Ky. 1996).

Figure 11.7 analyzes the themes in the IIED cases. Some of the factors that contribute to a finding of outrage are:

- the unusual nature of the action,
- the quality or extreme type of conduct, and
- the repetitive nature of the conduct.

Figure 11.7
Categories of Facts

Case	Unusual	Quality of Conduct	Conduct Repeated
Wilson		Racial insults are extreme and intolerable.	Conduct continued over seven years.
Benningfield	Termination of employment is not unusual.		Isolated incident.
Willgruber	Providing false information to disability carrier after victim had a mental breakdown is unusual.	Pressuring victim to sign release papers after mental breakdown is intolerable.	

One factor that seems to contribute to a finding of outrage is the unusual nature of an action. As terminations from jobs are not unusual, they are not considered outrageous. The quality of the conduct also seems to be a factor that determines whether conduct is considered outrageous. Racial insults are extreme and qualitatively different from insults. Courts may also examine whether an incident was isolated or repeated over time. By analyzing the facts and results more carefully, it is possible to start seeing patterns.

2.   Different Aspects of Rule

If the **cases address different aspects of a rule**, it is helpful to list the rules from each case to determine how the rules relate to each other. For example, using the outrage example, while *Benningfield*, *Wilson*, and *Willgruber* apply the same general rule, *Willgruber* also addresses another aspect of outrage where the employer continued to act outrageously after being informed that the employee had a mental breakdown. The new aspect of the rule is that if a perpetrator knows a victim is susceptible and continues to acts outrageously, that is further evidence of outrage. Figure 11.8 sets forth the rules for the cases.

Figure 11.8
Creating a Synthesized Rule: Part 1

Case	Rule
Wilson	Racial insults over many years go beyond all possible bounds of decency and are outrageous.
Benningfield	There is no outrage when someone is terminated from employment.
Willgruber	Outrage exists when employer takes advantage of employee's susceptibility in an outrageous way.

After the individual rules are identified, organize the rules as shown in Figure 11.9 to start with general rules and then add more specific aspects of the rule.

Figure 11.9
Creating a Synthesized Rule: Part 2

Type of Rule	Rule
General rules or rules that logically should go first	*Wilson*: Repeated racial insults over many years go beyond all possible bounds of decency and are outrageous. *Benningfield*: No outrage when someone is terminated from employment.
More specific aspects of rule	*Willgruber:* Outrage exists when employer takes advantage of employee's susceptibility in an outrageous way.

F. STEP 6: SYNTHESIZE CASES

Based upon the analysis in Steps 1 through 5, it is time to synthesize the cases to create a general rule that will be useful in solving a new problem. For cases with **similar rules and different facts**, reflect on the common themes and patterns in the cases as set forth in Figure 11.7. Perhaps cases fall at the no outrage end of the spectrum because they deal with situations that occur regularly in society such as job terminations. However, cases at the outrage end of the spectrum seem to deal with situations that are unusual. In addition, cases that find outrage seem to deal with qualitatively more serious situations. This type of analysis can assist in synthesizing the cases and determining where a new fact pattern fits on the spectrum. After examining the common themes in the three outrage cases, it is possible to synthesize as follows:

Figure 11.10
Case Synthesis: Similar Rules and Different Facts

> Outrage is only found when conduct is extreme and unusual. Situations that occur regularly such as job terminations are not considered to be outrageous. Outrageous conduct is found when the conduct is a serious deviation from decency.

For cases that contain **different aspects of a rule**, it may also be necessary to synthesize the rules in the cases. The synthesized rule should:

- provide information about the main rules as well as the more specific rules or variations, and

- follow in a logical order.

After identifying the individual rules (Figure 11.8), and organizing the rules in a logical order (Figure 11.9), combine the individual rules into a synthesized rule. As seen in Figure 11.11, *Willgruber* adds a more specific dimension to the rule as it addresses the situation where a defendant has knowledge of a plaintiff's susceptibilities and acts in an outrageous way to take advantage of those susceptibilities.

Figure 11.11
Case Synthesis: Synthesized Rule

> Outrage is only found when conduct is extreme and unusual. Situations that occur regularly such as job terminations are not considered to be outrageous. Outrageous conduct is found when the conduct is a serious deviation from decency. Outrage can also occur when the perpetrator knows the victim has particular susceptibilities and acts in an outrageous way to take advantage of these susceptibilities.

Figure 11.11 is a more complete synthesis of the three cases because it includes the rules from *Wilson* and *Bennington* as well as the additional rule found in *Willgruber* relating to susceptibility. Synthesis is not a listing of rules or cases. A list of cases or unrelated rules is not useful in solving a legal problem. Synthesis involves integrating the rules from cases into a cohesive rule that can be used to resolve a client's problem.

Practice Exercise 11.1 is an opportunity to practice synthesis with a series of factual scenarios. Practice Exercise 11.2 introduces case synthesis with three cases and Practice Exercise 11.3 is the self-assessment exercise for this chapter.

V.   CASE EXAMPLE: CASE SYNTHESIS

The skills in this chapter, case synthesis, are explained with *Fisher v. Carrousel Motor Hotel, Inc.*, 424 S.W.2d 627 (Tex. 1967) (Appendix B-1). This section will review case synthesis using *Fisher* as well as:

Wishnatsky v. Huey, 584 N.W. 2d 859 (N.D. Ct. App. 1998) (Appendix D) and

Leichtman v. WLW Jacor Communications, Inc. 634 N.E. 2d 697 (Ohio Ct. App. 1994)

A. STEP 1: IDENTIFY TOPIC

For purposes of this section, it will be assumed that the topic is battery and the specific element of battery that is the focus of the assignment is the intent to cause harmful or offensive contact.

B. STEP 2: LOCATE AND READ CASES

It will be assumed that the three cases listed above are the only cases that could be located on the topic.

C. STEP 3: IDENTIFY FACTS, RULE, HOLDING, AND RESULT FOR EACH CASE

Figure 11.12 is an analysis of the facts, holdings, rules, and results in the three cases.

Figure 11.12
Case Analysis

Case	Facts	Holding	Rule	Result
Fisher	Customer embarrassed when plate was taken from his hand, and he was told he could not be served because he was African American.	Offensive contact occurred when plate was grabbed from customer's hand, and he was told he would not be served because he was African American.	Intent to cause offensive contact occurs when defendant touches person or something "closely identified" with person in offensive manner.	Battery

Case	Facts	Holding	Rule	Result
Wishnatsky	W. opened door and entered office without knocking. When defendant closed door, W. was pushed into hallway.	No offensive contact occurred because plaintiff was unduly sensitive.	Contact is not offensive if someone is "unduly sensitive" and a reasonable person would not be offended.	No battery
Leichtman	When guest entered radio studio, host urged another host to blow cigar smoke in guest's face.	Offensive contact occurred when tobacco smoke was blown into person's face.	Battery is contact "which is offensive to a reasonable sense of personal dignity." 634 N.E. 2d at 699.	Battery

D. STEP 4: DECIDE IF SYNTHESIS IS NECESSARY

Even though the three cases are from different jurisdictions, it would be helpful to synthesize them because they have conflicting results. *Fisher* and *Leichtman* found that there was battery. *Wishnatsky* found no battery.

E. STEP 5: COMPARE FACTS, HOLDINGS, RULES, AND RESULTS

Case synthesis is required because the cases apply similar rules to different factual situations and arrive at different results. In addition, the cases address different aspects of the rules relating to battery.

All three cases use similar language regarding offensive contact and apply similar rules. The decisions in *Fisher* and *Leichtman* reach the same result (battery) while *Wishnatsky* reaches a different result (no battery). As all of the cases apply similar rules, it is helpful to examine the facts and determine where they fall on a spectrum as shown in Figure 11.13.

Figure 11.13
Factual Analysis

Pushed by closing door		Touch object & racial remarks
Wishnatsky		*Fisher*
		Blow smoke in face
		Leichtman
	←————————————————————————————→	
No Battery		**Battery**

If a more detailed factual analysis is done, it seems that courts look at the nature of the contact to determine whether or not battery has occurred. It is more offensive to grab a plate from someone and make racial insults than it is to close a door on someone. Smoke blown in someone's face is more offensive than the door closing which was characterized as rude and abrupt.

While all of the cases utilize the same rules, *Wishnatsky* addresses an additional aspect of the rule which is that the offensive behavior must be offensive to an ordinary person. If someone is "unduly sensitive," the behavior will not be considered offensive.

It is next helpful to list the rules from each case to determine how the rules relate to each other and determine the logical order of the rules. More general rules should come before more specific ones. Figure 11.14 lists the rules in logical order.

Figure 11.14
Creating a Synthesized Rule

Type of Rule	Rule
More general rules or rules that logically should go first	*Fisher:* Offensive contact can occur when the defendant contacts someone or touches an object closely identified with someone in an offensive manner. *Leichtman*: Offensive contact takes place when an act is offensive to personal dignity and may be disagreeable, embarrassing, or humiliating.
More specific aspects of rule	*Wishnatsky*: Contact is considered offensive only if it would be offensive to a reasonable person's dignity, not an overly sensitive person's dignity.

F. STEP 6: SYNTHESIZE CASES

Based upon the analysis in Steps 1 through 5, it is time to synthesize the cases to create a general rule. As the three cases utilize similar rules, the themes in the cases indicate that the cases can be synthesized as follows:

Figure 11.15
Case Synthesis: Similar Rules and Different Facts

> While battery does not occur any time a person touches another person and is rude, battery can occur when there is intentional touching in an offensive manner.

After analyzing the rules in *Fisher* and *Leichtman* and the additional rule in *Wishnatsky* and considering the appropriate order of the rules, it is time to create a **synthesized rule**:

Figure 11.16
Case Synthesis: Synthesized Rule

> Offensive contact can occur when the defendant contacts someone or touches an object closely identified with a person in an offensive manner that violates a person's personal dignity. Contact may be considered offensive if a reasonable person would consider the contact to be humiliating, embarrassing, or disagreeable.

VI. PRACTICE

Practice Exercise 11.1
Finding and Synthesizing Rules

Goal: The goal of this exercise is to formulate and synthesize rules.

This exercise is based upon the scenario from Chapter 2 that dealt with Joshua's July 4th fireworks purchases. For this exercise, assume that from 2012 to 2016, Joshua's parents decided that he would be permitted to buy fireworks if he read books, cleaned his room, and took care of his dog during the two weeks before July 4th. Joshua's activities and his parents' decisions are provided for each of these years. This exercise will use the six step procedure outlined in this chapter to analyze these "cases" and synthesize a rule from the five scenarios.

Step 1: Assume that the topic is limited to whether or not Joshua can buy fireworks.

Step 2: Read the following factual scenarios that contain the parents' decisions for each year as well as the steps Joshua took to comply with his parents' general rule that he read, clean his room, and take care of his dog during the two weeks before July 4th in order to buy fireworks.

July 3, 2012: Joshua never picked up the trains in his room, never took his dog for a walk, but he fed his dog for 2 days, and read 1 book. He was not allowed to buy fireworks.

July 3, 2013: Joshua's grandfather got sick, and Joshua helped his grandmother cook and clean for the two weeks before July 4. He did not clean his room, read any books or take care of his dog, and he was allowed to buy fireworks.

July 3, 2014: His parents decided that he was allowed to buy fireworks when he picked up his clothes each day and read 4 short books and half of a 200 page book. Most days he fed his dog and took her for a walk.

July 3, 2015: His parents did not allow him to buy fireworks when his friends came over to clean his room and he read 7 short books and a few pages from a 200 page book. His friends also fed and took his dog for walks during the two weeks.

July 3, 2016: Joshua decided to share his fireworks with a friend from school who could not afford fireworks. Joshua cleaned his room everyday, but he did not take care of his dog or read any books, and he was allowed to buy fireworks.

Step 3: 11.1–1 Is synthesis necessary because there are conflicting results?

Step 4: 11.1–2 Identify the facts, rules, and results for each year. Record this information on the Fact and Rule Analysis Chart. As there are no explicit rules, it will be necessary to make inferences and create rules based upon the facts for each year.

Fact and Rule Analysis Chart

Date	Facts	Rule	Result

Step 5: Compare the facts, rules, and results.

11.1–3 When the results are compared, are there common themes in the situations where Joshua was allowed to buy fireworks? Are there any common patterns that exist when he was not allowed to make the purchase? It might be helpful to create a spectrum and see where the activities for each year fit on the spectrum.

Allowed to buy fireworks   Not allowed to buy fireworks

11.1–4 After placing Joshua's conduct for each year on the spectrum, decide if there are any factors that were considered by the parents. Summarize those factors on the following chart:

More Detailed Factual Analysis

Date	Theme	Theme	Theme
2012			
2013			
2014			
2015			
2016			

11.1–5 Take the rules that you have created for each year, think about the common themes, and decide how to order the rules and case results.

Type of Rule	Rule
Most general rules or rules that logically should go first	
Rules that elaborate or address more specific aspects of rule	

Step 6: Synthesize.

11.1–6 Now synthesize the rules.

Practice Exercise 11.2
Synthesizing Cases

Goal: The purpose of this exercise is to synthesize the rules from three cases into a synthesized rule.

You are a summer associate at the Fayette County Prosecutor's office. Your first assignment deals with the law of burglary. John Jones was arrested and charged with second degree burglary, Ky. Rev. Stat. Ann. § 511.030(1) (West 2017).

The facts relating to Mr. Jones' case are as follows:

Sarah Smith bought a house on 44 Mantilla Drive, Lexington, Kentucky in January of 2005. She lived there for ten years but moved out in January of 2015 because the house had no heat. She keeps personal items in the bedroom. She checks on the house once a month and sleeps and eats at her daughter's house. The City claims that the house needs repairs and she has been arguing with building inspectors for several years. On June 1, 2014, the inspectors posted a sign that the house was condemned because there was no water. On July 1, 2016, John Jones broke into the house to steal some items. He stated that the house was a mess. There were clothes on the beds and some food in the freezer. The electricity was on.

Your supervisor wants you to analyze whether or not the charge should be reduced to third degree burglary. Your research indicates that the difference between second and third degree burglary relates to whether a building that has been entered is a "dwelling" or a "building." Second degree burglary requires that there be entry into a dwelling while third degree burglary only requires entry into a building. Dwelling is defined as "a building which is usually occupied by a person lodging therein." Ky. Rev. Stat. Ann. § 511.010(2) (West 2017).

Your supervisor has told you that three cases discuss whether or not a home should be considered to be a dwelling or building. She would like you to read these cases and synthesize the rules from these cases.

Starnes v. Commonwealth, 597 S.W. 2d 614 (Ky. 1980) (Appendix I)

Haynes v. Commonwealth, 657 S.W. 2d 948 (Ky. 1983) (Appendix E)

Shackelford v. Commonwealth, 757 S.W. 2d 193 (Ky. Ct. App. 1988) (Appendix L)

You have reviewed the context of *Haynes* in connection with Practice Exercise 4.3 and done a quick overview of the case. You have read *Starnes* carefully in connection with Practice Exercise 8.4. You have also read *Shackelford* carefully in connection with Practice Exercise 11.3 and briefed the case. Before beginning this exercise, it will be necessary to read *Haynes* more carefully.

Step 1: Topic

11.2–1 What is the topic of the assignment?

Step 2: Review the cases.

Step 3: Identify the facts, holding, rule and result for each case.

Case	Facts	Holding	Rule	Result
11.2–2 *Starnes*				
11.2–3 *Haynes*				
11.2–4 *Shackelford*				

Step 4: Decide if synthesis is necessary.

11.2–5 Is synthesis necessary because the rule is the same for all three cases but the facts and results are different?

11.2–6 Is synthesis necessary because the cases address different aspects of a rule?

Step 5: Compare the facts, rules, and results.

11.2–7 Are there common themes or patterns? See where the cases fit on a spectrum.

11.2–8 After placing the cases on the spectrum, decide if there are any factors that were considered in the cases and record the factors below for each case.

Case	Factor	Factor

11.2–9 Look at the rules listed in the chart in Step 3. If the cases address different aspects of a rule, how should the rule be ordered with more general rules going first followed by more specific rules?

Step 6: Synthesized rule

11.2–10 What is the synthesized rule?

Practice Exercise 11.3
Self-Assessment

Goal: In this exercise, you can determine if you understand the process of synthesizing cases.

For this exercise, assume that you are still representing Ms. Evelyn Michel, who has been terminated from her employment as a nurse because she failed the National Council Licensure Examination. Ms. Michel wants to know if she will qualify for unemployment insurance benefits. *De Grego v. Levine,* 347 N.E. 2d 611 (N.Y. 1976) (Appendix C) provides guidance.

You have discovered the following two cases that address the issue raised in *De Grego* relating to provoked discharge: *In re Bookhard*, 516 N.Y.S.2d 363 (N.Y. App. Div. 1987) (Appendix M) and *In re Ambrose*, 595 N.Y.S.2d 126 (N.Y. App. Div. 1993) (Appendix N).

Apply the concepts introduced in this chapter relating to case synthesis and create a synthesized rule for *De Grego*, *In re Bookhard*, and *In re Ambrose*.

Evaluate your understanding of the skills in this chapter by completing the following rubric. For each skill, circle whether you are at the proficient or developing level. Everyone can get to the proficient level over time.

Skill	Competency Level	
	Proficient	**Developing**
Identifies when case synthesis is necessary.	• Analyzes cases to determine if they have similar rules and results. • Determines if cases address different aspects of a rule.	• Looks at cases individually.

Skill	Competency Level	
	Proficient	Developing
Synthesizes cases in a step-by-step fashion.	• Follows synthesis steps. • Analyzes interrelationships among cases.	• Looks at cases without a plan. • Compares general legal concepts. • Does not attempt rule synthesis.

CHAPTER 12

READING STATUTES

I. SUMMARY

This chapter is an introduction to strategies for reading statutes. A new Reading Checklist is provided to guide the reader through the process of statutory analysis.

At the conclusion of this chapter, you will be able to:

- identify the structure of statutes,
- analyze the words in statutes, and
- understand major principles used to interpret statutes.

II. CHECKLIST

STATUTE READING CHECKLIST

Warning: Do not just highlight and underline.

Phase 1: Before Reading

1. Read for a purpose and assume the role of an advocate.
2. Read with energy and focus.
3. Understand the structure of statutes.
4. Understand the general subject of a statute by examining the table of contents.
4. Read for an overview by skimming the table of contents.

Phase 2: During Reading

1. Read the words of a statute, i.e., the plain language.
2. Pay attention to definitional sections.
3. Read individual statutes in the context of the entire law.
4. Examine legislative history when appropriate.

Phase 3: After Reading

1. Examine cases that have interpreted a statute.
2. Compile questions and talk with professors.

III. STATUTES

Statutes are laws that have been enacted by the legislative branch of government. Statutes affect every aspect of our lives. At the federal level, Congress has passed laws dealing with the environment (Clean Air Act), employment (Family and Medical Leave Act and the Americans with Disabilities Act), wildlife (Endangered Species Act), taxes (Internal Revenue Code), food (Food Safety Modernization Act), crime (Violence Against Women Act), and many other subjects. States and municipalities also enact laws and ordinances that regulate a wide variety of areas such as education, criminal justice, insurance, state personnel programs, highway safety, taxes, zoning, and health.

Many of the critical reading strategies discussed in Chapters 1 through 11 are also helpful in reading statutes. This chapter is not intended to be an exhaustive analysis of statutory construction as entire courses focus on this subject. However, there are basic concepts of statutory analysis that can make your reading more efficient and productive.

Before examining these critical reading techniques, it is helpful to step back and briefly examine how statutes fit into our legal system. According to the United States Constitution, there are three branches of government. Article I defines the legislative branch and its powers, Article II establishes the executive branch, and Article III creates the judiciary. Under this system, the legislature makes laws. Once Congress enacts laws, the executive branch implements them and the judiciary interprets the laws. As discussed in Chapter 5, in our common law system, the judiciary also creates law when it makes decisions that have a precedential effect on future cases.

The interplay of the three branches of government can be seen by examining the Social Security Act. After Congress created the Act in 1935, Congress delegated the responsibility for implementing the Act to the executive branch through an administrative agency that is now the Social Security Administration. The Social Security Administration administers the Act by creating regulations, which are rules authorized by the Act and issued by the agency. While the Act contains general laws, the regulations are more specific. For example, the Act provides that certain individuals are eligible to receive "old-age and survivors insurance" benefits. 42 U.S.C. § 401. However, the Social Security regulations indicate how many quarters of coverage are required for someone to be fully insured. 20 C.F.R. § 404.110.[1] When individuals disagree with a decision in their own social security case or challenge the interpretation of statutes or regulations, the judiciary resolves the dispute.

---

[1] Federal regulations are first published in the Federal Register and are then codified in the Code of Federal Regulations, C.F.R. Depending upon the jurisdiction, state regulations are found in administrative codes, codes of regulations, and administrative rules.

The example provided by the Social Security Act demonstrates that statutes and cases have different purposes. While the Social Security Act was passed by legislators to address general social problems, judges write opinions to resolve specific disputes under the Act. Statutes are written to address broad issues that affect many people, and cases are written with a more narrow focus.

Despite their differences, many of the strategies for reading cases are similar to the techniques used for reading statutes. The steps that should be taken before, during, and after reading statutes are summarized in the Statute Reading Checklist at the beginning of this chapter.

IV. BEFORE READING STRATEGIES

The reading strategies for cases and statutes in the **before reading phase** are similar. As noted in Figure 12.1, **before reading** statutes, the reader should:

- understand the purpose for reading,

- read as an advocate,

- understand the general structure of the statute,

- understand the context of the statute, and

- conduct a brief overview of the entire law.

Figure 12.1
Before Reading Statutes

Chapter	Topic	Cases	Statutes
1	Purpose	Solve problem.	Same
2	Read as an Advocate	Read from the perspective of client.	Same
3	Case Structure and Procedure	Understand the structure of cases.	Understand the structure of statutes.

Chapter	Topic	Cases	Statutes
4	Context and Overview	Understand the subject of the case before reading and skim for an overview.	Understand the subject of the statute and how it fits into the statutory scheme and skim for an overview.

A. PURPOSE FOR READING

The purpose for reading statutes is identical to the purpose for reading cases, i.e., to solve problems. The purpose is not to memorize information.

B. READ AS AN ADVOCATE

It is helpful to read as an advocate while reading statutes. This can be done by thinking about a client's problem while reading a statute.

C. STRUCTURE OF STATUTES

Statutes, like cases, have a basic structure. It is easier to locate information if the reader understands this organization. First, the two main statutory schemes in the United States are the federal and state systems.[2] According to the Supremacy Clause, U.S. Const. art. 6, cl. 2, federal law supersedes state law. This means that states are able to pass laws on a wide variety of subjects as long as state law does not conflict with federal law. State laws and constitutions are subordinate to federal law.

Second, most laws are arranged in a similar way. The legislature often enacts an entire act or code, which is a compilation of laws on a specific subject. For example, the social security laws are part of the Social Security Act which has over 450 individual sections. The entire act or code may be referred to in judicial decisions as the act, code, law or statute. Each act or code is composed of individual sections that are referred to as a statute, section, or law. Legislatures may also pass individual laws or statutes. All of these terms can be confusing because they are used interchangeably. For purposes of this chapter, the terms law or act mean an entire act and the term statute refers to an individual section of a law or act.

Figure 12.2 explains that laws or acts usually have a title or name, date of enactment, and definitional sections. Some laws have sections that describe their purpose. In addition, most laws are divided into parts that are referred to as titles, subtitles, chapters, and sections.

---

[2] Local governments such as cities and counties also enact laws which are commonly referred to as ordinances. Ordinances address subjects dealing with public safety, streets, zoning, and other local issues.

Figure 12.2
Structure of Laws

Type of Information	Description
Title or name	Name of the entire law.
Date	Date of enactment of the law or dates of amendments.
Definitions	Explanations of the meaning of specific words in the statutes.
Purpose, preamble, or findings	Details about the purpose of the law.
Titles, subtitles, chapters, sections	Organizational scheme for the law.

For example, federal law is codified in the United States Code which is organized by titles, subtitles, chapters, and sections. There are currently 54 titles on a variety of subjects such as Agriculture, Bankruptcy, Crime and Criminal Procedure, Education, Railroads, Telecommunications, and War and Defense. Title 18, which deals with Crime and Criminal Procedure, has five subtitles that address crime, criminal procedure, prisoners, youthful offenders, and witness immunity. Each chapter in the subtitle deals with still more specific topics.

State laws are structured in a similar way. Most states have laws that are organized by titles, chapters, and sections. Titles and chapters often have definitional sections similar to the federal system.

D. CONTEXT AND OVERVIEW

As discussed in Chapter 4, context is a powerful comprehension strategy because it gives readers information about cases or statutes before they even begin to read. For cases in casebooks, the table of contents provides readers with the subject of a case. For reported decisions, the case summary and headnotes can assist in identifying the general subject of a case.

For statutes, the table of contents provides readers with an outline of the entire statutory scheme and the topics in the titles, chapters, and sections. By looking at the table of contents, it is possible to do a quick overview of titles and chapters before looking at individual sections in more detail. This can provide valuable information about the relationship between a specific statute and the overall law. The table of contents also helps the reader locate definition and purpose sections.

The usefulness of the table of contents can be seen by examining the table of contents for Wis. Stat. § 125.035 (West 2017), which outlines the civil liability of persons who provide alcoholic beverages to underage individuals in Wisconsin. As seen in Figure 12.3, the excerpt from the table of contents shows that Section 125.035 is in the Trade Regulations title and is part of Chapter 125, which is titled *Alcohol Beverages*. Chapter 125, *Alcohol Beverages*, is divided into three subchapters and contains individual sections that address several topics. Section 125.01, titled Legislative Intent, outlines the purpose of Chapter 125. Section 125.02 provides the definitions for Chapter 125.

Figure 12.3
Table of Contents: Trade Regulations

Trade Regulations (Ch. 125–139)

Chapter 125, Alcohol Beverages

Subchapter I General Provisions

- 125.01. Legislative Intent
- 125.015. Severability
- 125.02. Definitions
- 125.03. Department Rule Making
- **125.035. Civil Liability Exemption: Furnishing Alcohol Beverages**
- 125.037. Civil Liability Exemption for Municipalities
- 125.039. Civil Liability Exemption for Retaining Proofs of Age
- 125.04. General Licensing Requirements
- 125.045. Booklet for Licensees and Permittees
- 125.06. License and Permit Exceptions
- 125.07. Underage and Intoxicated Persons; Presence on Licensed Premises; Possession; Penalties
- 125.075. Injury or Death by Providing Alcohol Beverages to a Minor
- 125.085. Proof of Age
- 125.09. General Restrictions
- 125.10. Municipal Regulation
- 125.105. Impersonating an Officer
- 125.11. Penalties

Subchapter II Fermented Malt Beverages

Subchapter III Intoxicating Liquor

Wis. Stat. § 125.035 should be read in the context of the definitional sections and the other sections in Chapter 125. By examining the table of contents, it is possible to understand the framework of Wis. Stat. § 125.035 before reading any of its provisions.

V. DURING READING STRATEGIES

There are similarities between reading cases and statutes in the **during reading phase** as noted in Figure 12.4. The reader utilizes many of the same techniques that were suggested in Chapter 6 for understanding language. The reader also looks for the main ideas (Chapter 7). While statutes do not contain issues and holdings, the main idea of a statute can be analyzed by examining the plain meaning of the statute in the context of the entire law and legislative history. Finally, while it is not necessary to find rules (Chapter 8) in statutes because statutes are rules, expert readers carefully analyze the elements or parts of a statute.

This introduction to statutory analysis examines techniques to understand a statute's plain meaning, purpose, and legislative history.

Figure 12.4
During Reading Statutes

Chapter	Topic	Cases	Statutes
5	Facts	Understand the facts.	No facts.
6	Language	Use strategies to understand language.	Same.
7	Main Ideas	Understand the issue, holding, and reasoning.	Understand the statute's plain meaning in the context of the entire law and legislative history.
8	Rules	Find and construct rules.	Analyze the elements of a statute.

A. PLAIN MEANING

The reader starts any analysis of cases by looking at the words in a decision. Likewise, laws are analyzed by examining the words in the statute. Interpreting a statute based only on the meaning of the statute's text involves the application of the plain meaning rule. The Supreme Court has referred to the plain meaning doctrine as the "cardinal canon" and has stated:

> "We have stated time and again that courts must presume that a legislature says in a statute what it means and means in a statute what it says there . . . When the words of a statute are unambiguous, then, this first canon is also the last: 'judicial inquiry is complete.'"

Connecticut National Bank v. Germain, 503 U.S. 249, 253–54 (1992). The Supreme Court has noted that if the statutory language is "plain and unambiguous . . . we must apply the statute according to its terms." *Carcieri v. Salazar*, 555 U.S. 379, 387 (2009). While the plain meaning rule has some intricacies[3] and qualifications, it is appropriate to start any analysis of a statute by examining the words in the statute.

To understand the plain meaning of statutes, attorneys utilize a variety of language canons of construction, which are rules that assist readers in interpreting statutes.[4] Some of the more common rules are:

- If a term is defined in a statute, use the statutory definition.

- If a term is not defined, use its ordinary meaning.

- If terms appear in several places in a statute, they are generally defined in the same way.

- The word "shall" is mandatory, while "may" is permissive.

- Singular words may include plural words.

- All words in a statute are important and none are considered superfluous.

These rules of statutory construction have been used for thousands of year in a variety of cultures. The *Mimamsa* of Jaimini contains rules for interpreting Hindu texts in 500 B.C. that are similar to statutory rules of construction used today. The *Mimamsa* principle that the "same words

---

[3] While the plain meaning rule seems straightforward, Justices may agree that language is "plain" and disagree regarding the meaning of the language. For example, in *Corley v. United States*, 556 U.S. 303, 324 (2009), the Supreme Court examined the meaning of 18 U.S.C. § 3501(a) which states that in "any criminal prosecution brought by the United States . . . , a confession . . . shall be admissible in evidence if it is voluntarily given." While the majority and dissenting opinions agreed that the language of the statute was unambiguous, they disagreed regarding the meaning of this "plain language."

[4] In addition to language rules, there are also substantive canons of construction such as the rule that statutes should be construed to avoid constitutional issues. *Ashwander v. Tennessee Valley Authority*, 297 U.S. 288, 347 (1936) (J. Brandeis, concurring) ("The Court will not pass upon a constitutional question . . . if there is also present some other ground upon which the case may be disposed of.") Other substantive rules relate to deference to administrative agency interpretations of statutes and regulations and the rule of lenity which requires that "before a man can be punished as a criminal . . . his case must be 'plainly and unmistakably' within the provisions of some statute." *United States v. Gradwell*, 243 U.S. 476, 485 (1917). These substantive canons will not be addressed in this chapter.

should have the same meaning" is almost identical to the rule applied in *Washington Metropolitan Transit Authority v. Johnson*, 467 U.S. 925, 935–36 (1984) where the Supreme Court followed the principle that the "same words used in the same statute should be taken to have the same meanings."[5] Judeo-Christian texts contain similar rules of interpretation.[6]

Today, every state, and the federal government, has rules of construction that are used in interpreting statutes.[7] For example, New Jersey's "General rules of construction," N.J.Stat. Ann. § 1:1–1, states that words shall "be given their generally accepted meaning, according to the approved usage of the language." Readers should start any analysis of statutes by locating the general rules of construction in the appropriate jurisdiction.

This section examines common techniques used to analyze the plain meaning of statutes such as examining the definitions of words, breaking statutes into parts, and paying attention to mandatory and permissive terms.

1. Examine the Meaning of Words in Context

An analysis of the plain meaning of a statute should start by examining the definitions of words. There may be definitional sections that apply to the entire law as well as definitions that apply to a particular title or chapter. For example, Wis. Stat. § 125.035, in Figure 12.5, addresses civil liability for giving alcoholic beverages to minors.

Figure 12.5
Text: Wis. Stat. § 125.035
Civil liability exemption: furnishing alcohol beverages

---

(1)   In this section, "person" has the meaning given in s. 990.01(26).

(2)   A person is immune from civil liability arising out of the act of procuring alcohol beverages for or selling, dispensing or giving away alcohol beverages to another person.

(3)   Subsection (2) does not apply if the person procuring, selling, dispensing, or giving away alcohol beverages causes their consumption by force or by representing that the beverages contain no alcohol.

(4)(a) In this subsection, "provider" means a person, including a licensee or permittee, who procures alcohol beverages for or sells, dispenses or gives away alcohol beverages to an underage person in violation of s. 125.07(1)(a).

---

[5]   Geoffrey P. Miller, *Pragmatics and the Maxims of Interpretation*, 1990 Wis. L. Rev. 1179, 1183 (1990).

[6]   *Id.* at 1184.

[7]   Jacob Scott, *Codified Canons and the Common Law of Interpretation*, 98 Geo. L.J. 341, 350 (2010).

(b)   Subsection (2) does not apply if the provider knew or should have known that the underage person was under the legal drinking age and if the alcohol beverages provided to the underage person were a substantial factor in causing injury to a 3rd party. In determining whether a provider knew or should have known that the underage person was under the legal drinking age, all relevant circumstances surrounding the procuring, selling, dispensing or giving away of the alcohol beverages may be considered, including any circumstance under subds. 1. to 4. In addition, sub. (2) does apply if all of the following occur:

1.   The underage person falsely represents that he or she has attained the legal drinking age.

2.   The underage person supports the representation with documentation that he or she has attained the legal drinking age.

3.   The alcohol beverages are provided in good faith reliance on the underage person's representation that he or she has attained the legal drinking age.

4.   The appearance of the underage person is such that an ordinary and prudent person would believe that he or she had attained the legal drinking age.

(5)   Subsection (2) does not apply to civil forfeiture actions for violation of any provision of this chapter or any local ordinance in conformity with any provision of this chapter.

There are two definitional sections that apply to Section 125.035. Subsection 125.035(1) refers to Section 990.01(26) that defines the term "person"[8] for all statutes in Wisconsin.[9] In addition, Section 125.02, the definition section for Chapter 125, contains definitions for many words in Section 125.035 such as "alcohol beverages" Wis. Stat. 125.02(1), "legal drinking age" Wis. Stat. § 125.02(8m), "person" Wis. Stat. § 125.02(14), "sell" Wis. Stat. § 125.02(20), and "underage person" Wis. Stat. § 125.02(20m). The plain language of the statute can only be understood by considering all of these definitions.

If words are not defined in a statute, it may be necessary to examine how a term is used in a particular area of the law. For example, in *Sullivan v. Stroop*, 496 U.S. 478, 483 (1990), the Supreme Court considered the meaning of the term "child support" in Title IV of the Social Security Act. The Court noted that because this phrase had a specialized meaning in domestic relations law, it had "become a term of art" and it was not appropriate to use a definition for the term from a regular dictionary. The

---

    [8]   There appear to be two definitions for "persons." The definition in Section 990.01(26) is more general and the definition in Section 125.02(8m) is more specific.

    [9]   Chapter 990, titled "Construction of Statutes," contains the rules for interpreting all statutes in Wisconsin.

best way to determine if there are terms of art in a statute is to consult cases that have interpreted the statute.

If words are not defined and are not terms of art, the reader may consult a dictionary to find the meaning of a word as courts often consult dictionaries. In *Kasten v. Saint-Gobain Performance Plastics Corp.*, 563 U.S. 1, 7 (2011), the Court analyzed the meaning of the phrase "filed any complaint" to determine if oral complaints were covered by the anti-retaliation provision of the Fair Labor Standards Act. The Court consulted several dictionaries to see if the word "filed" had been defined to include a writing.

In addition to examining the definitions of words, readers should pay attention to the way words have been used in different places in a law. If the same terms appear in different sections, they are generally defined in the same way. For example, in *Kasten*, the Court examined the entire Fair Labor Standards Act to see how the word "filed" had been used throughout the Act. 563 U.S. at 10. In *United Savings Ass'n of Texas v. Timbers of Inwood Forrest Associates*, 484 U.S. 365, 371 (1988), the Court analyzed provisions of the Bankruptcy Code and noted that

> "[s]tatutory construction, however, is a holistic endeavor. A provision that may seem ambiguous in isolation is often clarified by the remainder of the statutory scheme-because the same terminology is used elsewhere in a context that makes its meaning clear."

Terms are often defined consistently throughout a law.

Finally, the meaning of words must be considered in view of the entire law. Words should not be examined in isolation from the whole statutory scheme. Just as one phrase in a case may not be representative of the main idea in the decision, one word in a statute may not be indicative of the meaning of the statute when the entire law is considered. In examining provisions of the Affordable Care Act, the Supreme Court noted in *King v. Burwell*, 135 S. Ct. 2480, 2489 (2015) that "we must read the words 'in their context and with a view to their place in the overall statutory scheme.'" The Court specifically noted that "[o]ur duty, after all, is 'to construe statutes, not isolated provisions.'" Statutes should be read with an understanding of other sections in the statutory scheme.

2. Break Statute into Elements

In addition to understanding words in the statute, it is important to break down a statute into parts to understand how the statute operates. One way to analyze a statute is to pay attention to conjunctions such as "and" and "or" that often connect different parts of a statute to each other. As discussed in Chapter 6, it can be helpful to circle or underline these words or create an outline that highlights the conjunctions.

For example, Wis. Stat. § 125.035, contains several elements that can be understood by breaking the statute into parts and noticing the conjunctions. Figure 12.6 demonstrates how the statute can be outlined.

Figure 12.6
Outline: Wis. Stat. § 125.035
Civil liability exemption: furnishing alcohol beverages

(1)   In this section, "person" has the meaning given in s. 990.01(26).

(2)   <u>A person is immune from civil liability arising out of the act of</u>
- **procuring** alcohol beverages for
  <u>or</u>
- **selling, dispensing**
  <u>or</u>
- **giving away** alcohol beverages to another person.

(3)   <u>Subsection (2) **does not apply if**</u>
- the person procuring, selling, dispensing, or giving away alcohol beverages
- causes their consumption by force
  <u>or</u>
- by representing that the beverages contain no alcohol.

(4)(a)   In this subsection, "provider" means a
- person, including
  - ➤ a licensee
    <u>or</u>
  - ➤ permittee,
- who **procures** alcohol beverages for
  <u>or</u>
- sells,
  <u>or</u>
- dispenses
  <u>or</u>
- gives away alcohol beverages to an underage person in violation of s. 125.07(1)(a).

(4)(b)   <u>Subsection (2) **does not apply if the provider**</u>
- knew
  <u>or</u>
- should have known
  - ➤ that the underage person was under the legal drinking age
    <u>and</u>
  - ➤ if the alcohol beverages provided to the underage person were a substantial factor in causing injury to a 3rd party.

In determining whether a provider knew or should have known that the underage person was under the legal drinking age, all relevant circumstances surrounding the procuring, selling, dispensing or giving away of the alcohol beverages may be considered, including any circumstance under subds. 1. to 4.

In addition, sub. (2) does apply **if all of the following occur**:

1. The underage person falsely represents that he or she has attained the legal drinking age.
2. The underage person supports the representation with documentation that he or she has attained the legal drinking age.
3. The alcohol beverages are provided in good faith reliance on the underage person's representation that he or she has attained the legal drinking age.
4. The appearance of the underage person is such that an ordinary and prudent person would believe that he or she had attained the legal drinking age.

(5) Subsection (2) does not apply to civil forfeiture actions for violation of any provision of this chapter or any local ordinance in conformity with any provision of this chapter.

This outline shows that the statute consists of four main sections.

First: civil immunity is provided to persons who procure, sell, dispense, or give away alcohol.

Second: there is no civil immunity if a person forces someone else to consume alcohol or represents that the beverage does not contain alcohol.

Third: there is no civil immunity if the provider knew or should have known that the person drinking was underage and if drinking was a substantial factor in causing injury to a third person.

Fourth: there is civil immunity if the person who is drinking falsely represents his age, provides documentation, gets drinks in reliance on the representations, and looks over the legal age.

Each section contains specific elements that must be satisfied to meet certain conditions in the statute. For example, in the fourth section of the statute, there is civil immunity if all four conditions of the statute are met:

*   person falsely represents his age,
*   provides documentation,
*   gets drinks in reliance on the representations, **and**
*   appears to be over the legal age.

By outlining the statute, highlighting the conjunctions, and separating sentences into shorter phrases, the reader can better understand the organization and meaning of the statute.

In addition to noting conjunctions, pay attention to exceptions. Section 125.035 contains two sections that provide civil immunity and two sections that do not. Words such as **not**, **except**, **if**, and **unless** signal exceptions.

After creating an outline of the statute, it is useful to take notes to simplify the statute even more. Figure 12.7 shows how Wis. Stat. § 125.035 can be summarized.

Figure 12.7
Notes: Wis. Stat. § 125.035
Civil liability exemption: furnishing alcohol beverages

Person is immune from civil liability arising out of the act of
1.   procuring alcoholic beverages for, (or)
2.   selling, (or)
3.   dispensing, (or)
4.   giving away alcohol beverages to another person.

Person is not immune if he
1.   forces someone to consume alcohol, (or)
2.   represents that beverage does not contain alcohol.

Person is not immune if provider
1.   knew or should have known that person drinking was underage, (and)
2.   drinking was a substantial factor in causing an injury to a 3rd person.

Person is immune if person drinking
1.   falsely represents age, (and)
2.   provides documentation, (and)
3.   gets drinks in reliance on representations, (and)
4.   looks over the legal age.

There are many methods of taking notes and outlining statutes. It can be helpful to highlight certain words in different colors. The main point is to carefully break down the statute into its component parts.

3.   Pay Attention to Mandatory and Permissive Terms

In addition to paying attention to definitions and the elements in statutes, it is important to examine words such as "shall" and "may" because they indicate whether or not a statute is mandatory or permissive.

For example, Chapter 125 of the Wisconsin statutes contains a section that outlines the penalties for underage drinking, Wis. Stat. § 125.07. Some of the penalties are mandatory and some are discretionary. Section 125.07(1)(b)(2)(a) is discretionary and provides that a:

"person who commits a violation **may be**

    a. Required to forfeit not more than $500 if the person has not committed a previous violation within 30 months of the violation.

However, Section 125.07(1)(b)(3) is mandatory and provides that:

"A court **shall suspend** any license or permit issued under this chapter to a person for:

    a. Not more than 3 days, if the court finds that the person committed a violation within 12 months after committing one previous violation."

Words such as **shall** or **may** should be examined carefully.

B. CONSIDER THE PURPOSE OF THE LAW

Statutes should be read in light of the purpose of the entire law. When reading statutes, remember that the legislature enacted the law to address a social problem. Sometimes, the purpose is explicitly identified in the purpose or intent section, and the purpose can assist in interpreting the statutes.

For example, in *Kasten,* referenced earlier, the Court examined the purpose of the Fair Labor Standards Act to determine whether the term "filed" included oral complaints. The Court noted that the Act's objective was to prohibit "labor conditions detrimental to the maintenance of the minimum standard of living necessary for health, efficiency, and general well-being of workers." *Kasten*, 563 U.S. at 11. The Court observed that the enforcement of these standards was dependent upon employees coming forward and filing complaints. The Court reasoned that Congress would not limit the Act to written complaints because that would have made it difficult for poor or illiterate workers to submit their complaints. *Id.* The purpose of the Act assisted in interpreting the meaning of the term "filed."

In another case, the plain language of a statute was read in connection with the purpose of the statute. In *Bob Jones University v. United States*, 461 U.S. 574 (1983), the Court examined the meaning of Section 501(c)(3) of the Internal Revenue Code to determine if Bob Jones University was entitled to tax-exempt status given its policy of racial discrimination. While the University argued that there was nothing in Section 501 to prevent the school from being considered a charitable organization, the Court explained that Section 501 "must be analyzed and construed within the framework of the Internal Revenue Code and against the background of the Congressional purposes." *Id.* at 586. Once this analysis was completed, the Court found that there was "no doubt" that the IRS correctly denied tax-exempt status to Bob Jones. *Id.* at 598. Justice Burger noted that "a court should go beyond the literal language of a statute if reliance on that language would defeat the plain purpose of the statute." *Id.* at 586.

To understand Wis. Stat. § 125.035, discussed earlier, it is useful to examine the purpose for the statutory scheme as well as other sections in the chapter that deal with alcohol beverages. The purpose section for Chapter 125, Section 125.01, states in part that,

> "Face-to-face retail sales at licensed premises directly advance the state's interest in preventing alcohol sales to underage or intoxicated persons and the state's interest in efficient and effective collection of tax."

It is also useful to understand that the entire statutory scheme regulates civil liability as well as the issuance of licenses, penalties, and enforcement provisions. All of this information may be helpful in understanding individual sections of the law.

C. EXAMINE LEGISLATIVE HISTORY

If language in a statute is not clear, readers may examine legislative history, which is the history behind the law. As laws are proposed and enacted, a variety of documents and records are created such as committee reports, transcripts of hearings, and floor debates. In *United States v. Great Northern*, 287 U.S. 144, 154 (1932), Justice Cardozo stated the basic principle that courts will examine legislative history if the language of the statute is not clear and noted:

> "In aid of the process of construction we are at liberty, if the meaning be uncertain, to have recourse to the legislative history of the measure and the statements by those in charge of it during its consideration by the Congress."

In addition to reports and transcripts, legislative intent may be found in different versions of bills, changes in statutory language, and recommendations of commissions. Generally, there is more legislative history for federal statutes than state statutes.

VI. AFTER READING STRATEGIES

As noted in Figure 12.8, there are similarities between statutes and cases in the **after reading phase.**

Figure 12.8
After Reading Statutes

Chapter	Topic	Cases	Statutes
9	Evaluate	Use analogical reasoning to determine if case can be used to solve problem.	Determine if statute applies to problem.
10	Brief	Summarize case.	Summarize statute.
11	Synthesize	Examine multiple cases.	Examine statute as well as cases that have interpreted statute.

While attorneys use analogical reasoning to evaluate whether a case can be used to solve a client's problem (Chapter 9), attorneys examine statutes to determine if a statute applies to a client's situation. For example, Wis. Stat. § 125.035 only provides civil immunity in certain situations. As there is no civil immunity for persons who force underage persons to drink, the statute would not protect a client who did this. Attorneys examine statutes to decide if a client's situation is governed by a particular statute.

Furthermore, just as it is useful to prepare a case brief to summarize a case, the reader should summarize a statute by taking notes. Finally, case synthesis occurs in any situation where there are multiple cases that are pertinent. As there are usually several cases that interpret a statute, these cases may need to be synthesized to solve a client's problem.

VII. EXAMPLE: READING STATUTES

This section will analyze statutes using the steps suggested in this chapter. Assume for purposes of this example that Jack Phillips has contacted you because he was arrested for second degree burglary in Kentucky and wants to challenge his arrest. He claims that he should have been charged with third degree burglary, Ky. Rev. Stat. Ann. § 511.040 (West 2017), rather than second degree burglary, Ky. Rev. Stat. Ann. § 511.030 (West 2017), because he entered an abandoned building rather than a dwelling. Mr. Phillips entered a home that had been abandoned for six months.

A. PURPOSE/ADVOCATE

The purpose for reading the statute is to assist a client with his criminal case, not to memorize the statute. The statute should be read from the perspective of an attorney representing Mr. Phillips.

B. STRUCTURE OF STATUTES/CONTEXT

Kentucky statutes are structured like most other state statutes. There are 51 titles that deal with a variety of subjects from Title I, Sovereignty and Jurisdiction of the Commonwealth, to Title LI, the Uniform Juvenile Code. Each title contains chapters, and each chapter has sections.

It is useful to place the burglary statutes in the context of criminal laws in general in Kentucky. As set forth in Figure 12.9, the burglary statutes are part of Title L, the Kentucky Penal Code. The general provisions for the Penal Code are found in Chapter 500. Section 500.080 contains definitions for terms that apply to the entire Penal Code such as crime, deadly weapon, felony, and offense. Chapter 511, the burglary chapter, has its own set of definitions including definitions for building and dwelling.

Figure 12.9
Structure of Kentucky Penal Code

Title L. Kentucky Penal Code

    Chapter 500 General Provisions

        Section 500.030 Rules of Construction

        Section 500.070 Burden of Proof; Defenses

        Section 500.080 Definition for Kentucky Penal Code

    Chapter 501 General Principles of Liability

    Chapter 503 General Principles of Justification

    Chapter 504 Responsibility

    Chapter 511 Burglary and Related Offenses

        Section 511.010 Definitions

        Section 511.030 Burglary in the Second Degree

        Section 511.090 General Provisions

C. PLAIN MEANING

To determine whether Jack Phillips has a good argument that an abandoned building is a building rather than a dwelling, any analysis starts by examining the plain meaning of the statutes. As noted in Figure

12.10, the relevant statutes are the definitions for dwelling and building, Ky. Rev. Stat. Ann. § 511.010, second degree burglary, Ky. Rev. Stat. Ann. § 511.030, and third degree burglary, Ky. Rev. Stat. Ann. § 511.040.

Figure 12.10
Burglary Statutes

Ky. Rev. Stat. Ann. § 511.010 Definitions

The following definitions apply in this chapter unless the context otherwise requires:

(1) "Building," in addition to its ordinary meaning, means any structure, vehicle, watercraft or aircraft:

(a) Where any person lives; or

(b) Where people assemble for purposes of business, government, education, religion, entertainment or public transportation.

Each unit of a building consisting of two (2) or more units separately secured or occupied is a separate building.

(2) "Dwelling" means a building which is usually occupied by a person lodging therein.

Ky. Rev. Stat. Ann. § 511.030 Second degree burglary

(1) A person is guilty of burglary in the second degree when, with the intent to commit a crime, he knowingly enters or remains unlawfully in a dwelling.

(2) Burglary in the second degree is a Class C felony.

Ky. Rev. Stat. Ann. § 511.040 Third degree burglary

(1) A person is guilty of burglary in the third degree when, with the intent to commit a crime, he knowingly enters or remains unlawfully in a building.

(2) Burglary in the third degree is a Class D felony.

The definitions in Section 511.010 indicate that while a building is a place where "any person lives," a dwelling is a "building which is usually occupied by a person lodging therein." Ky. Rev. Stat. Ann. § 511.010(2). A dwelling is a special kind of building that is "usually occupied." To analyze the plain language in Section 511.010(1), it is helpful to break the statute into parts and pay attention to conjunctions. The definition section can be outlined as follows:

Figure 12.11
Ky. Rev. Stat. Ann. § 511.010(1)

> Building," in addition to its ordinary meaning, means any structure, vehicle, watercraft or aircraft:
>
> - Where any person lives;
>
>   **or**
>
> - Where people assemble for purposes of
>   - Business,
>   - government,
>   - education,
>   - religion,
>   - entertainment
>
>   **or**
>   - public transportation.

The definition of dwelling states that it is "a building which is usually occupied by a person lodging therein."

In addition to the definitions in Chapter 511, there are definitions and rules of construction that apply to the entire Penal Code. Section 500.030 states that "All provisions of this code shall be liberally construed according to the fair import of their terms, to promote justice, and to effect the objects of the law." Furthermore, there are general definitions and rules of statutory construction that apply to all statutes in Kentucky. Section 446.080 provides that:

> "(1) All statutes of this state shall be liberally construed with a view to promote their objects and carry out the intent of the legislature, and the rule that statutes in derogation of the common law are to be strictly construed shall not apply to the statutes of this state.
>
> (4) All words and phrases shall be construed according to the common and approved usage of language, but technical words and phrases, and such others as may have acquired a peculiar and appropriate meaning in the law, shall be construed according to such meaning."

The definitions in the burglary chapter, the Penal Code, and the general Kentucky rules of construction can all be used to interpret the meaning of the burglary statutes.

It is also necessary to break down the elements of second and third degree burglary. For example, Section 511.030(1), second degree burglary, provides that "A person is guilty of burglary in the second degree when, with the intent to commit a crime, he knowingly enters or remains unlawfully in a dwelling." This statute can be outlined as follows:

(1) A person is guilty of burglary in the second degree when,

- o   with the intent to commit a crime,

- o   he knowingly

    - o   enters

        or

    - o   remains

- o   unlawfully in a dwelling."

By breaking the language of the statute into sections, the reader can understand the components of the statute.

D. LEGISLATIVE HISTORY

In Kentucky, as in most states, there is limited legislative history. There is some commentary on Section 511.010 but it does not address the distinction between a building and dwelling.

E. AFTER READING STATUTES

To fully analyze the term "usually occupied" in Section 511.010, it is necessary to examine cases that have interpreted the statute. Several courts in Kentucky have interpreted this phrase. In *Starnes v. Commonwealth*, 597 S.W.2d 614 (Ky. 1980) (Appendix I), that you read in connection with Practice Exercise 8.4, the court consulted Webster's New International Dictionary to determine the meaning of the word "usually" and found that "usually" is defined as:

> "Such as in common use; such as occurs in ordinary practice, or the ordinary course of events; customary; ordinary; habitual." *Id.* at 615.

Using this definition of "usually," the court concluded that the home should be considered to be "usually occupied" when the owners were in the process of moving.

Other courts have also interpreted Section 511.010 to find that a house would be considered a dwelling. In *Haynes v. Commonwealth*, 657 S.W.2d 948 (Ky. 1983) (Appendix E), that you read in connection with Practice Exercises 3.5 and 11.2, the court found that a house was a dwelling when the owner had died and the heirs occasionally occupied the home. The court concluded that the home was "usually occupied" because "the house was used "as it had customarily been used, as a dwelling." *Id.* at 952. In *Cochran v. Commonwealth*, 114 S.W.3d 837 (Ky. 2003) the court decided that a home was "usually occupied" even though the owner had died and Cochran broke into the owner's trailer after his death. The court noted that there would be a good possibility of occupancy in a home immediately following a death as it might be used by friends and family members "as a place of temporary residence." *Id.* at 839. The court stated that "miscreants who would seek to take advantage of the misfortune of others" should not be protected and there was a need to "offer strong protection against the 'alarm and danger' inherent in unlawful entry into a dwelling." *Id.*

The final step in any analysis of a statute is to synthesize the cases that have interpreted Section 511.010 and decide whether or not Mr. Phillips has a valid argument that he entered a building rather than a dwelling. The steps outlined in Chapter 11 for case synthesis should be followed. Here, it appears that there may be an argument that the home was a building if no one ever entered the house for six months. However, it may be necessary to do further investigation to find out how the facts would compare to the situations in *Starnes*, *Haynes,* and *Cochran*.

VIII.   PRACTICE

Practice Exercise 12.1
Analyzing a Statute

Goal: The goal of this exercise is to practice analyzing a statute by paying attention to conjunctions.

Wis. Stat. § 125.075(1) provides criminal penalties for persons who give minors alcohol. The text of the statute is set forth below. Create an outline of the statute that focuses on conjunctions such as "and" and "or."

Wis. Stat. § 125.075(1)
Injury or death by providing alcohol beverages to a minor

(1)   Any person who procures alcohol beverages for or sells, dispenses or gives away alcohol beverages to a person under 18 years of age in violation of s. 125.07(1)(a)1. or 2. may be penalized as provided in sub. (2) if:

(a)   The person knew or should have known that the underage person was under the legal drinking age; and

(b)   The underage person dies or suffers great bodily harm, as defined in s. 939.22(14), as a result of consuming the alcohol beverages provided in violation of s. 125.07(1)(a)1. or 2.

Outline

Practice Exercise 12.2
Statutory Interpretation

Goal: The goal of this exercise is to examine how courts interpret statutes.

As noted in Practice Exercise 12.1, Wis. Stat. § 125.075 provides criminal penalties for persons who provide minors with alcohol. You have been contacted by Jeremy Jones, who has been charged with violation of Section 125.075 when he provided alcohol for a friend's 21st birthday celebration. While most of the people invited to the party were 21 years old, there were two individuals who were 17. One of the 17 year-olds drank at the party and got into an automobile accident when he drove home.

You have been asked to read a decision that interprets Section 125.075, *State v. Wille*, 728 N.W.2d 343 (Wis. Ct. App. 2007). Review the decision, only to the extent that it interprets Section 125.075 and examines the sufficiency of the evidence under Section 125.075. It is not necessary to examine the court's decision with respect to any other issues.

Step 1: Before Reading Strategies

12.2–1   What preliminary steps would you take to understand *Wille* before reading more carefully?

12.2–2   As the case is divided by headings, which heading relates to the assignment?

Step 2: During Reading Strategies

12.2–3   After completing these preliminary steps, how would you summarize the substantive and procedural facts?

12.2–4   What did the court hold?

12.2–5   What arguments does Wille make regarding the interpretation of Wis. Stat. § 125.075?

12.2–6   On page 349 of the regional reporter, what general rules of statutory construction does the court mention?

12.2–7   Does the court refer to any general rules of statutory construction in Wisconsin?

12.2–8   Why does the court examine other criminal statutes in Wisconsin?

12.2–9   How does the court view Wille's argument on page 352 regarding the purpose of the statute?

Practice Exercise 12.3
Self-Assessment

Goal: The goal of this exercise is to determine if you understand strategies for reading statutes.

For this exercise, assume that you are still representing Ms. Evelyn Michel, who was terminated from her employment as a nurse because she failed the National Council Licensure Examination. Ms. Michel wants to know if she will qualify for unemployment insurance benefits.

To prepare to represent Ms. Michel, you decide to review the unemployment insurance laws in New York. You start by reviewing N.Y. Labor Law § 590(1), Rights to Benefits. New York laws are organized by chapters and the labor laws are found in Chapter 31. The chapters are divided into articles, the articles are divided into titles, and the titles contain sections.

Section 590 is in Article 18 that has 11 titles. Title 2 contains the definitional sections. For this exercise you will need to read N.Y. Labor Law § 590(1) as well as an excerpt from Title 2 that lists terms that are defined. (The actual definitions are not provided.)

N.Y. Labor Law § 590(1)
Rights to Benefits

1.   Entitlement to benefits. A claimant shall be entitled to accumulate effective days for the purpose of benefit rights only if he has complied with the provisions of this article regarding the filing of his claim, including the filing of a valid original claim, registered as totally unemployed, reported his subsequent employment and unemployment, and reported for work or otherwise given notice of the continuance of his unemployment.

N.Y. Labor Law Chapter 31
Title 2: Definitions

§ 510. Application of Definitions	§ 522. Total Unemployment
§ 511. Employment	§ 523. Effective Day
§ 512. Employer	§ 524. Week of Employment
§ 513. Fund	§ 527. Valid Original Claim
§ 514. Benefit	§ 528. Transitional Provisions
§ 515. Claimant	§ 529. Average Annual Wage
§ 516. Paid	
§ 517 Remuneration	
§ 518. Wages	
§ 519. Week	
§ 520. Base Period	
§ 521. Benefit Year	

Answer the following questions:

12.3–1   Examine Section 590 and the list of words defined in Title 2. Circle the words in Section 590 that are defined in Title 2.

12.3–2   Prepare an outline of Section 590 that focuses on the conjunctions and exceptions in the statute.

Evaluate your understanding of the skills in this chapter by completing the following rubric. For each skill, circle whether you are at the proficient or developing level. Everyone can get to the proficient level over time.

Skill	Competency Level	
	Proficient	**Developing**
Reads the words in statutes.	• Understands that definitional sections must be examined. • Understands language rules of construction. • Pays attention to conjunctions such as "and" and "or."	• Ignores definitions. • Ignores rules of construction. • Skims over conjunctions.
Looks at individual statutes in relationship to the entire law.	• Understands that words are defined in similar ways throughout a law.	• Examines statutes in isolation from each other.

Skill	Competency Level	
	Proficient	Developing
Examines legislative history when appropriate.	• Examines legislative history after looking at the plain language of a statute	• Uses legislative history before examining the plain language of the statute.

INDEX TO APPENDICES

APPENDIX A

CASE READING CHECKLIST

Warning: Do not just highlight & underline.

Phase 1: Before Reading

1.

2.

3.

4.

5.

Phase 2: Read More Carefully

1.

2.

3.

4.

5.

6.

7.

8.

9.

10.

Phase 3: After Reading

1.

2.

3.

4.

5.

APPENDIX B-1

FISHER V. CARROUSEL MOTOR HOTEL, INC.

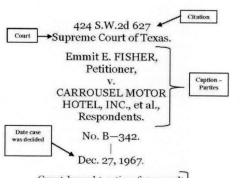

424 S.W.2d 627
Supreme Court of Texas.

Emmit E. FISHER,
Petitioner,
v.
CARROUSEL MOTOR
HOTEL, INC., et al.,
Respondents.

No. B—342.

Dec. 27, 1967.

Guest brought action for assault and battery by motor hotel's agent. The 61st District Court, Harris County, Ben F. Wilson, J., granted defendant's motion n.o.v. that plaintiff take nothing and plaintiff appealed. The Waco Court of Civil Appeals, Tenth Supreme Judicial District, 414 S.W.2d 774, affirmed and plaintiff brought error. The Supreme Court, Greenhill, J., held where the manager of the motor hotel's club dispossessed plaintiff of his dinner plate in a loud and offensive manner a battery occurred on which damages for mental suffering could be based and the motor hotel was liable for exemplary damages.

Reversed.

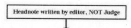

[1] **Assault and Battery**
⟜Nature and Elements of

Assault and Battery

Actual physical contact is not necessary to constitute a battery so long as there is contact with clothing or an object closely identified with the body.

[2] **Assault and Battery**
⟜Nature and Elements of Assault and Battery

An intentional snatching of patron's dinner plate from him by manager of motor hotel's club in a loud and offensive manner was sufficient to constitute a battery.

[3] **Assault and Battery**
⟜Nature and Elements of Assault and Battery

To constitute assault and battery, it is not necessary to touch the plaintiff's body or even his clothing; knocking or snatching anything from plaintiff's hand or touching anything connected with his person, when done in offensive manner, is sufficient.

[4] **Assault and Battery**
⟜Elements of Compensation

Where there was a forceful dispossession of patron's dinner plate in a loud and offensive manner which constituted a battery, patron was entitled to actual damages for mental suffering, even in absence of physical injury.

[5] **Damages**
↪Intentional or Reckless
Infliction of Emotional
Distress; Outrage

[6] **Assault and Battery**
↪Elements of Compensation

[7] **Assault and Battery**
↪Nature and Elements of
Assault and Battery

[8] **Labor and Employment**
↪Punitive or Exemplary
Damages
Principal and Agent
↪Rights and Liabilities of
Principal

[9] **Labor and Employment**
↪Intentional Acts

[10] **Principal and Agent**
↪Rights and Liabilities of
Principal

Attorneys and Law Firms

*628 Ben G. Levy, Houston, for
petitioner.

Vinson, Elkins, Weems & Searls,
Raybourne Thompson, Jr. and B.
Jeff Crane, Jr., Houston, for
respondents.

Opinion

| Judge |

→ GREENHILL, Justice.

This is a suit for actual and exemplary damages growing out of an alleged **assault and battery**. The plaintiff Fisher was a mathematician with the Data Processing Division of the Manned Spacecraft Center, an agency of the National Aeronautics and Space Agency, commonly called NASA, near Houston. The defendants were the Carrousel Motor Hotel, Inc., located in Houston, the Brass Ring Club, which is located in the Carrousel, and Robert W. Flynn, who as an employee of the Carrousel was the manager of the Brass Ring Club. Flynn died before the trial, and the suit proceeded as to the Carrousel and the Brass Ring. Trial was to a jury which found for the plaintiff Fisher. The trial court rendered judgment for the defendants notwithstanding the verdict. The Court of Civil Appeals affirmed. 414 S.W.2d 774. The questions before this Court are whether there was evidence that an actionable battery was committed, and, if so, whether the two corporate defendants must respond in exemplary as well as actual

| Procedural Facts |

| Attorneys |

| Issue |

damages for the malicious conduct of Flynn.

The plaintiff Fisher had been invited by Ampex Corporation and Defense Electronics to a one day's meeting regarding telemetry equipment at the Carrousel. The invitation included a luncheon. The guests were asked to reply by telephone whether they could attend the luncheon, and Fisher called in his acceptance. After the morning session, the group of 25 or 30 guests adjourned to the Brass Ring Club for lunch. The luncheon was buffet style, and Fisher stood in line with others and just ahead of a graduate student of Rice University who testified at the trial. As Fisher was about to be served, he was approached by Flynn, who snatched the plate from Fisher's hand and shouted that he, a Negro, could not be *629 served in the club. Fisher testified that he was not actually touched, and did not testify that he suffered fear or apprehension of physical injury; but he did testify that he was highly embarrassed and hurt by Flynn's conduct in the presence of his associates.

Facts related to Incident

The jury found that Flynn 'forceably dispossessed plaintiff of his dinner plate' and 'shouted in a loud and offensive manner' that Fisher could not be served there, thus subjecting Fisher to humiliation and indignity. It was stipulated that Flynn was an employee of the Carrousel Hotel and, as such, managed the Brass Ring Club. The jury also found that Flynn acted maliciously and awarded Fisher $400 actual damages for his humiliation and indignity and $500 exemplary damages for Flynn's malicious conduct.

[1] The Court of Civil Appeals held that there was no assault because there was no physical contact and no evidence of fear or apprehension of physical contact. However, it has long been settled that there can be a battery without an assault, and that actual physical contact is not necessary to constitute a battery, so long as there is contact with clothing or an object closely identified with the body. 1 Harper & James, The Law of Torts 216 (1956); Restatement of Torts 2d, ss 18 and 19. In Prosser, Law of Torts 32 (3d Ed. 1964), it is said:

Rules and Prior Cases

'The interest in freedom from intentional and unpermitted contacts with the plaintiff's person is protected by an action for the tort commonly called battery. The protection extends to any part of the body, or to anything which is attached to it and practically identified with it. Thus contact with the plaintiff's clothing, or with a cane, a paper, or any other object held in his hand will be sufficient; * * * The plaintiff's interest in the integrity of his person includes all those things which are in contact or connected with it.'

[2] [3] **Under the facts of this case, we have no difficulty in holding that the intentional grabbing of plaintiff's plate constituted a battery.** The intentional snatching of an object from one's hand is as clearly an offensive invasion of his person as would be an actual contact with the body. 'To constitute an assault and battery, it is not necessary to touch the plaintiff's body or even his clothing; knocking or snatching anything from plaintiff's hand or touching anything connected with his person, when, done is an offensive manner, is sufficient.' Morgan v. Loyacomo, 190 Miss. 656, 1

> Rules and Prior Cases

So.2d 510 (1941).

Such holding is not unique to the jurisprudence of this State. In S. H. Kress & Co. v. Brashier, 50 S.W.2d.922 (Tex.Civ.App.932, no writ), the defendant was held to have committed 'an assault or trespass upon the person' by snatching a book from the plaintiff's hand. The jury findings in that case were that the defendant 'dispossessed plaintiff of the book' and caused her to suffer 'humiliation and indignity.'

The rationale for holding an offensive contact with such an object to be a battery is explained in 1 Restatement of Torts 2d s 18 (Comment p. 31) as follows:

'Since the essence of the plaintiff's grievance consists in the offense to the dignity involved in the unpermitted and intentional invasion of the inviolability of his person and not in any physical harm done to his body, it is not necessary that the plaintiff's actual body be disturbed. Unpermitted and intentional contacts with anything so connected with the body as to be customarily regarded as part of the other's person and therefore as partaking of its inviolability is actionable as an offensive contact with his person. There are some things such as clothing or a cane or, indeed, anything directly grasped by the hand which are so intimately connected with one's body as to be universally regarded as part of the person.'

Rules and Prior Cases

*630 We hold, therefore, that the forceful dispossession of plaintiff Fisher's plate in an offensive manner was sufficient to constitute a battery, and the trial court erred in granting judgment notwithstanding the verdict on the issue of actual damages.

Holding on battery

[4] [5] [6] [7] In Harned v. E-Z Finance Co., 151 Tex. 641, 254 S.W.2d 81 (1953), this Court refused to adopt the 'new tort' of intentional interference with peace of mind which permits recovery for mental suffering in the absence of resulting physical injury or an assault and battery.

This cause of action has long been advocated by respectable writers and legal scholars. See, for example, Prosser, Insult and Outrage, 44 Cal.L.Rev. 40 (1956); Wade, Tort Liability for Abusive and Insulting Language, 4 Vand.L.Rev. 63 (1950); Prosser, Intentional Infliction of Mental Suffering: A New York, 37 Mich.L.Rev. 874 (1939); 1 Restatement of Torts 2d s 46(1). However, it is not necessary to adopt such a cause of action in order to sustain the verdict of the jury in this case. The Harned case recognized the well-established rule that mental suffering is compensable in suits for willful torts 'which are recognized as torts and actionable independently and separately from mental suffering or other injury.' 254 S.W.2d at 85. Damages for mental suffering are recoverable without the necessity for showing actual physical injury in a case of willful battery because the basis of that action is the unpermitted and intentional invasion of the plaintiff's person and not the actual harm done to the plaintiff's body. Restatement of Torts 2d s 18. Personal indignity is the essence of an action for battery; and consequently the defendant is liable not only for contacts which do actual physical harm, but also for those which are offensive and insulting. Prosser, supra; Wilson v. Orr, 210 Ala. 93, 97 So. 123

(1923). We hold, therefore, that plaintiff was entitled to actual damages for mental suffering due to the willful battery, even in the absence of any physical injury.

Holding on damages

[8] We now turn to the question of the liability of the corporations for exemplary damages. In this regard, the jury found that Flynn was acting within the course and scope of his employment on the occasion in question; that Flynn acted maliciously and with a wanton disregard of the rights and feelings of plaintiff on the occasion in question. There is no attack upon these jury findings. The jury further found that the defendant Carrousel did not authorize or approve the conduct of Flynn. It is argued that there is no evidence to support this finding. The jury verdict concluded with a finding that $500 would 'reasonably compensate plaintiff for the malicious act and wanton disregard of plaintiff's feelings and rights. * * *'

The rule in Texas is that a principal or master is liable for exemplary or punitive damages because of the acts of his agent, but only if:

(a) the principal authorized the doing and the manner of the act, or

(b) the agent was unfit and the principal was reckless in employing him, or

(c) the agent was employed in a managerial capacity and was acting in the scope of employment, or

(d) the employer or a manager of the employer ratified or approved the act.

[9] The above test is set out in the Restatement of Torts s 909 and was adopted in King v. McGuff, 149 Tex. 434, 234 S.W.2d 403 (1950). At the trial of this case, the following stipulation was made in open court:

'It is further stipulated and agreed to by all parties that as an employee of the Carrousel Motor Hotel the said Robert W. Flynn was manager of the Brass Ring Club.'

We think this stipulation brings the case squarely within part (c) of the rule announced *631 in the King case as to Flynn's managerial capacity.

It is undisputed that Flynn was acting in the scope of employment at the time of the incident; he was attempting to enforce the Club rules by depriving Fisher of service.

Holding on liability of corporation

[10] The rule of the Restatement of Torts adopted in the King case set out above has four separate and disjunctive categories as a basis of liability. They are separated by the word 'or.' As applicable here, there is liability if (a) the act is authorized, or (d) the act is ratified or approved, Or (c) the agent was employed in a managerial capacity and was acting in the scope of his employment. Since it was established that the agent was employed in a managerial capacity and was in the scope of his employment, the finding of the jury that the Carrousel did not authorize or approve Flynn's conduct became immaterial.

The King case also cited and relied upon Ft. Worth Elevator Co. v. Russell, 123 Tex. 128, 70 S.W.2d 397 (1934). In that case, it was held not to be material that the employer did not authorize or ratify the particular conduct of the employee; and the right to exemplary damages was supported under what is section (b) of the Restatement of King rule: The agent was unfit, and the principal was reckless in employing (or retaining) him.

After the jury verdict in this case, counsel for the plaintiff moved that the trial court disregard the answer to issue number eight (no authorization or approval of Flynn's conduct on the occasion in question) and for judgment upon the verdict. The trial court erred in overruling that motion and in entering judgment for the defendants notwithstanding the verdict; and the Court of Civil Appeals erred in affirming that judgment.

Disposition

The judgments of the courts below are reversed, and judgment is here rendered for the plaintiff for $900 with interest from the date of the trial court's judgment, and for costs of this suit.

All Citations

424 S.W.2d 627

APPENDIX B-2

FISHER V. CARROUSEL MOTOR HOTEL, INC. REPRINTED FROM *TORTS*, PROSSER, WADE AND SCHWARTZ (12TH ED. 2000)

Fisher v. Carrousel Motor Hotel, Inc.

Supreme Court of Texas, 1967.
424 S.W.2d 627.

[Action for assault and battery. Plaintiff, a mathematician employed by NASA, was attending a professional conference on telemetry equipment at defendant's hotel. The meeting included a buffet luncheon. As plaintiff was standing in line with others, he was approached by one of defendant's employees, who snatched the plate from his hand, and shouted that a "Negro could not be served in the club." Plaintiff was not actually touched, and was in no apprehension of physical injury; but he was highly embarrassed and hurt by the conduct in the presence of his associates. The jury returned a verdict for $400 actual damages for his humiliation and indignity, and $500 exemplary (punitive) damages in addition. The trial court set aside the verdict and gave judgment for the defendants notwithstanding the verdict. This was affirmed by the Court of Civil Appeals. Plaintiff appealed to the Supreme Court.]

GREENHILL, JUSTICE * * * Under the facts of this case, we have no difficulty in holding that the intentional grabbing of plaintiff's plate constituted a battery. The intentional snatching of an object from one's hand is as clearly an offensive invasion of his person as would be an actual contact with the body. "To constitute an assault and battery, it is not necessary to touch the plaintiff's body or even his clothing; knocking or snatching anything from plaintiff's hand or touching anything connected with his person, when done in an offensive manner, is sufficient." Morgan v. Loyacomo, 190 Miss. 656, 1 So.2d 510 (1941).

Such holding is not unique to the jurisprudence of this State. In S.H. Kress & Co. v. Brashier, 50 S.W.2d 922 (Tex.Civ.App.1932, no writ), the defendant was held to have committed "an assault or trespass upon the person" by snatching a book from the plaintiff's hand. The jury findings in that case were that the defendant "dispossessed plaintiff of the book" and caused her to suffer "humiliation and indignity."

The rationale for holding an offensive contact with such an object to be a battery is explained in 1 Restatement (Second) of Torts § 18 (Comment p. 31) as follows:

"Since the essence of the plaintiff's grievance consists in the offense to the dignity involved in the unpermitted and intentional invasion of the inviolability of his person and not in any physical harm done to his body, it is not necessary that the plaintiff's actual body be disturbed. Unpermitted and intentional contacts with anything so connected with the body as to be customarily regarded as part of the other's person and therefore as partaking of its inviolability is actionable as an offensive contact with his person. There are some things such as clothing or a cane or, indeed, anything directly grasped by the hand which are so intimately connected with one's body as to be universally regarded as part of the person."

We hold, therefore, that the forceful dispossession of plaintiff Fisher's plate in an offensive manner was sufficient to constitute a battery, and the trial court erred in granting judgment notwithstanding the verdict on the issue of actual damages. * * *

Damages for mental suffering are recoverable without the necessity for showing actual physical injury in a case of willful battery because the basis of that action is the unpermitted and intentional invasion of the plaintiff's person and not the actual harm done to the plaintiff's body. Restatement (Second) of Torts § 18. Personal indignity is the essence of an action for battery; and consequently the defendant is liable not only for contacts which do actual physical harm, but also for those which are offensive and insulting. [Cc]. We hold, therefore, that plaintiff was entitled to actual damages for mental suffering due to the willful battery, even in the absence of any physical injury. [The court then held that the defendant corporation was liable for the tort of its employee.]

The judgments of the courts below are reversed, and judgment is here rendered for the plaintiff for $900 with interest from the date of the trial court's judgment, and for costs of this suit.

NOTES AND QUESTIONS

1.   What if the plate had been snatched without a racial epithet? Or, suppose the waiter had not touched plaintiff's plate, but said in a loud voice, "Get out, we don't serve Negroes here!"? What if the doorman at the hotel shouted a racial epithet and kicked plaintiff's car when he was about to leave. Battery? Cf. Van Eaton v. Thon, 764 S.W.2d 674 (Mo.App.1988) (defendant struck horse plaintiff was riding).

2.   Does the utilization of the tort of battery confuse things? Why not characterize what happened as "intentional infliction of emotional harm"? Might the case be regarded as one of imaginative lawyering, assuming the state was not ready to recognize intentional infliction of emotional harm as a tort? What other remedies might have been available to plaintiff? Compare this with the *State Rubbish Collectors* case, page 51.

3.   Defendant, unreasonably suspecting the plaintiff of shoplifting, forcibly seized a package from under her arm and opened it. Morgan v. Loyacomo, 190 Miss. 656, 1 So.2d 510 (1941). Defendant deliberately blew pipe smoke in plaintiff's face, knowing she was allergic to it. Richardson v. Hennly, 209 Ga.App. 868, 434 S.E.2d 772 (1993), rev'd on other grounds, 264 Ga. 355, 444 S.E.2d 317 (1994).

4.   A is standing with his arm around B's shoulder and leaning on him. C, passing by, violently jerks B's arm, as a result of which A falls down. To whom is C liable for battery? Reynolds v. Pierson, 29 Ind.App. 273, 64 N.E. 484 (1902).

APPENDIX C

DE GREGO V. LEVINE

347 N.E. 2d 611
39 N.Y.2d 180
Court of Appeals of New York.

Claim of Dominic A. DE GREGO, Respondent,
v.
Louis L. LEVINE, as Industrial Commissioner, Appellant.

April 8, 1976.

Employee appealed from decision of Unemployment Insurance Appeal Board denying benefits. The Supreme Court, Appellate Division, 46 A.D.2d 253, 362 N.Y.S.2d 207, reversed and remitted, and Industrial Commissioner appealed. The Court of Appeals, Wachtler, J., held that evidence was insufficient to show that employee had provoked his own discharge by wearing 'Impeachment with Honor' button, since employer was not required to fire employee for such conduct.

Affirmed.

Jasen, J., dissented and filed opinion.

[1] **Unemployment Compensation**
⬥Provoking Discharge

Where employee voluntarily engages in conduct which transgresses legitimate known obligation and leaves employer no choice but to discharge him, Industrial Commissioner is entitled to conclude that employee voluntarily left job without good cause, thus disqualifying employee from unemployment insurance benefits. Labor Law § 593, subd. 1.

[2] **Unemployment Compensation**
⬥Good Cause in General

Evidence that employee's performance had been entirely satisfactory, that other employees occasionally wore emblems or buttons on their work uniforms, that no complaints had been received from customers regarding fact that employee wore "Impeachment with Honor" button on uniform, that employee was discharged for refusal to remove button, and that employer was not compelled to fire employee for such conduct, was insufficient to support finding that employee had provoked his discharge and was thus not entitled to unemployment benefits. Labor Law § 593, subd. 1.

277

Attorneys and Law Firms

*181 ***251 **612 Louis J. Lefkowitz, Atty. Gen. (Irving Jorrisch, Samuel A. Hirshowitz and Murray Sylvester, New York City, of counsel), for appellant.

*182 Jane E. Bloom, Poughkeepsie, for respondent.

Opinion

WACHTLER, Judge.

This appeal involves the concept of provoked discharge as a bar to eligibility for unemployment compensation benefits. In Matter of James (Levine), 34 N.Y.2d 491, 358 N.Y.S.2d 411, 315 N.E.2d 471, we circumscribed its application to cases where the employer lacked a choice in firing the claimant. In any other situation the Division of Unemployment Insurance may not deny benefits on the ground that the employee provoked his discharge.

At the time the instant controversy began, the claimant had been employed as a plumber's helper by Rhinebeck Plumbing & Heating, Inc., for over two years. Throughout this period his performance had been entirely satisfactory. Since most of his workday was spent away from Rhinebeck and on the premises of its customers, De Grego was provided with a uniform bearing his employer's name. The record is devoid of any company policy with respect to the uniform and it appears that other employees occasionally wore emblems or buttons on their work uniform.

For two successive days prior to his discharge on September 18, 1973, De Grego wore a button containing the statement *183 'Impeachment with Honor' in obvious reference to the crisis in Washington. On the second day claimant was approached by the president of the company who advised him that he could not wear the button if he wished to keep his job. Although no complaints or response had been received from customers, the employer felt that this button could affect Rhinebeck's relationship with its clientele. De Grego refused to remove the button claiming that he was entitled to express a strongly felt political statement. As a result of this refusal he was fired.

Two days later he applied for unemployment insurance benefits which were denied by the Labor Department on the ground that he had quit his job without good cause by refusing to comply with a reasonable directive from his employer. This determination was sustained by a referee and the Unemployment Insurance Appeal Board who found that De Grego had provoked his discharge which was the equivalent of voluntary leaving employment without good cause. In a proceeding to review this denial of benefits the Appellate Division reversed stating that unemployment benefits could not be denied where the discharged employee was exercising his freedom of speech as guaranteed by the Constitution (46 A.D.2d 253). We affirm but **613 deem it unnecessary to reach the constitutional issue in view of the agency's misapplication of the concept of provoked discharge and the lack of any other disqualifying condition.

[1] Provoked discharge, a gloss over the statutory disqualification for voluntary separation without good cause (Labor Law, s 593, subd. 1) is a narrowly drawn legal fiction designed to apply where an employee voluntarily engages in conduct which transgresses a legitimate known obligation and leaves the employer no choice but to discharge him. In such a case the agency is entitled to put substance over form and to conclude that the employee voluntarily left his job without good cause. This approach was first recognized by our court in Matter ***252 of Malaspina (Corsi), 309 N.Y. 413, 131 N.E.2d 709. There, provoked discharge was considered applicable where a collective bargaining agreement mandated the discharge of those who refused to join the union.

Since this concept was subject to arbitrary application and was inappropriately extended without statutory authority, our court in Matter of James (Levine), 34 N.Y.2d 491, 358 N.Y.S.2d 411, 315 N.E.2d 471, Supra, adopted a very strict view of it. We made it clear that a denial *184 of unemployment insurance benefits due to provoked discharge would be sustained only where the employer has no range of discretion but was compelled to terminate employment. In addition, James recognized that although provoked discharge might be inapplicable, the actions of the employee may amount to misconduct thereby disqualifying him from benefits. By the same token, where the employee has not provoked discharge or engaged in misconduct he will be entitled to benefits despite the fact that the employer may have fired the employee for valid reasons. As noted in Matter of Heitzenrater (Hooker Chem. Corp.— Catherwood), 19 N.Y.2d 1, 9—10, 277 N.Y.S.2d 633, 640, 224 N.E.2d 72, 77, this possibility was 'designedly incorporated into the legislative scheme.'

[2] Applying these principles to the case at bar, it is clear that De Grego did not provoke his discharge since the employer was not compelled to fire him. Nor is there any evidence to support the contention that claimant's conduct was detrimental to the employer's interest or in violation of a reasonable work condition so as to constitute misconduct.

In response to the erroneous contention pressed by the dissent that De Grego deliberately left his employment we need only look to the findings of fact which were made by the referee who conducted the hearing and which were adopted In toto by the appeal board. After a review of the testimony and evidence adduced at the hearing the referee explicitly found as a matter of fact that the claimant was Discharged as a result of his failure to remove the button. This clear and unequivocal finding is supported by the record which includes De Grego's testimony, the sole witness at the hearing, that he did not leave voluntarily but was discharged. Section 623 of the Labor Law provides that a decision by the referee which is adopted by the appeal board is final and conclusive on all questions of fact. The dissent's apparent reliance on the notice of ineligibility which was sent to De Grego prior to the hearing is misplaced.

Even if we were to accept all the factors articulated by the dissent it would only lead us to one conclusion—that the employer was entitled to fire De Grego. Both the dissent and the Unemployment Insurance Appeal Board, however, miss the point. An employee may be fired under these circumstances and yet still be entitled to unemployment compensation.

Aside from the extreme situation presented in *185 Malaspina, 309 N.Y. 413, 131 N.E.2d 709, Supra, the concept of provoked **614 discharge is without validity and may not be used to deny benefits.

Accordingly, the order of the Appellate Division should be affirmed.

JASEN, Judge (dissenting).

The officials charged with the responsibility for administering the State labor laws found that the claimant left his employment rather than report to work without wearing a potentially inflammatory political button. The record supports their conclusion that claimant abandoned his employment without cause or justification, thereby rendering him ineligible to receive unemployment insurance benefits without a period of subsequent employment. I would also hold that denial of unemployment insurance benefits, under the circumstances presented, is not precluded by the First and ***253 Fourteenth Amendments of the Federal Constitution.

The claimant was employed as a plumber's helper by a heating and plumbing concern in Rhinebeck, New York. His duties required him to work at the residences and business premises of his employer's customers. In September, 1973, at the height of the Watergate investigation, claimant began reporting to work with a button on his work uniform that impliedly advocated the impeachment of the President of the United States. On the second day, the president of the firm requested that claimant not wear the button to work on the ground that 'it was detrimental to his business.' Claimant refused and was fired. If the claimant had removed the button, he would not have been discharged. In a report of employment filed with the State Department of Labor, the employer reported that the claimant 'left because we would not allow him to wear a political button on our Rhinebeck Plbg. uniform. We felt the button could affect our relationship with the customers. We informed him that there was (sic) no personal feelings involved, but the manner in which he conducted himself during working hours could also reflect against Rhinebeck Plbg.'s name. This in turn could affect the outlook for the entire company.' Claimant's application for unemployment insurance benefits was denied by the industrial commissioner upon the ground that he 'quit (his) job without good cause.' This determination was sustained by a referee and the Unemployment Insurance Appeal Board affirmed. The Appellate Division, Third Department, reversed, finding that a denial of unemployment insurance benefits would be State action penalizing *186 the claimant for exercising his right to freedom of speech. (46

A.D.2d 253, 362 N.Y.S.2d 207.)

I would reverse. The Unemployment Insurance Law provides that an employee who voluntarily leaves his employment or who is discharged for misconduct in connection with his employment is ineligible to receive unemployment insurance benefits, at least until a subsequent requalifying period of employment is completed. (Labor Law, s 593.) In Matter of James (Levine), 34 N.Y.2d 491, 358 N.Y.S.2d 411, 315 N.E.2d 471, the court set forth the tests to be applied in assessing the applicability of the statute to a given set of facts. Voluntary separation is usually 'confined to the giving up of employment permanently or temporarily, without cause or justification' (at p. 498, 358 N.Y.S.2d p. 416, 315 N.E.2d p. 475). On the other hand, where an employee is discharged for valid cause, the cause must 'rise to the level of misconduct before an employee becomes ineligible to receive benefits' (at p. 496, 358 N.Y.S.2d p. 414, 315 N.E.2d p. 473). A voluntary separation from employment will only disqualify a claimant if the separation was 'without good cause'. (Labor Law, s 593, subd. 1.) Whether a particular separation from employment is voluntary and without good cause is usually a question of fact to be resolved at the administrative level. (Matter of Fisher (Levine), 36

N.Y.2d 146, 150, 365 N.Y.S.2d 828, 832, 325 N.E.2d 151, 153.) If there is substantial evidence to support the determination **615 made by the officials directly responsible for the administration of State labor laws, that determination may not be set aside by the courts. (Labor Law, s 623; Matter of Green (Republic Steel Corp.—Levine), 37 N.Y.2d 554, 559, 376 N.Y.S.2d 75, 79, 338 N.E.2d 594, 597.)

In this case, there is substantial evidence to support the conclusion that the claimant's separation was voluntary and without good cause. An employer, unless precluded by statute or collective bargaining agreement, is entitled to establish reasonable rules and regulations governing the conduct of his employees. (Matter of Gladstone (Catherwood), 36 A.D.2d 204, 205, 319 N.Y.S.2d 664, 666, affd. 30 N.Y.2d 576, 330 N.Y.S.2d 793, 281 N.E.2d 842.) Where the rules and conditions of employment promulgated by the employer are reasonable, an employee who refuses to abide by them, and leaves his employment, acts without good cause. ***254 (See, e.g., Matter of Blau (Catherwood), 29 A.D.2d 701, 285 N.Y.S.2d 919; Matter of Glassmith (Catherwood), 27 A.D.2d 584, 275 N.Y.S.2d 411; 62 N.Y.Jur., Unemployment Insurance, s 111, p. 98.)

Despite the majority's insistence upon a narrow reading of the referee's findings of fact, it is manifest that the administrative officials, at all levels of the adjudicatory process, found *187 that the claimant voluntarily left his employment, rather than comply with a reasonable rule established by his employer. The industrial commissioner specifically determined that the claimant 'quit' his job. The referee, after a hearing, concluded that '(t)he initial determination is sustained.' The referee's decision, in turn, was affirmed by the Unemployment Insurance Appeal Board.

In my view, the hearing record supports the finding that the claimant voluntarily left his employment. Although initially stating that he was discharged, claimant subsequently acknowledged that he had really been instructed that, if he desired to continue working with the employer, he would have to remove the button from his work uniform. He elected not to remove the button and left.

The majority places great reliance on the statement in the referee's descriptive findings of fact that claimant 'was discharged as a result of his failure' to remove the button. Ignored is the fact that the referee, in his decision, sustained the initial determination by the industrial commissioner that the claimant voluntarily quit his job. Indeed, in the course of the hearing, the referee stated: 'I am prepared to find that the claimant did quit his job because he was given an option, and he could have continued to work for the employer by complying with the employer's direct request, and he chose not to, and therefore he left the job.' When the claimant's attorney protested this proposed finding, the referee cut him off with the comment that 'the facts are clear here'. The referee went on to explain that the claimant 'was given an option to comply with the request or the directive or not, and he could have continued to work there, but he chose not to do so, and it was up to him, and he took action, and there is no way that can be interpreted any other way'. The sole conclusion to be drawn from this record is that the claimant was given the option of continuing his employment relationship under rules established by the employer. The granting of such an option is hardly consonant with the air of finality that attends ultimate discharge. A fair reading of the record belies the interpretation effected by the majority. The court obfuscates what was eminently clear to the labor officials who determined this case, that the claimant voluntarily left his job.

Moreover, the majority confuses voluntary separation without good cause with the doctrine of provoked discharge. Voluntary ***188** separation occurs when the employee, without valid cause or justification, declines to continue his employment. In this case, the claimant deliberately left his employment, rather than comply with a ****616** reasonable condition of employment. A provoked discharge, on the other hand, is a discharge by the employer necessitated by governmental regulation or union bargaining agreement. The classic example is a discharge mandated by the employee's refusal to abide by a union shop provision in a collective bargaining agreement. (Matter of Malaspina (Corsi), 309 N.Y. 413, 131 N.E.2d 709.) In both voluntary separation and provoked discharge, an act of the employee is the producing cause of the termination. The same might be said of employee misconduct, which even the majority concedes will result in ineligibility. The critical distinction between voluntary separation and provoked discharge is that the former is voluntary leaving of employment by the employee without good cause, whereas the latter is an involuntary discharge by the employer of the employee for good cause. The doctrine of provoked discharge must be carefully limited since it is but 'a legitimate and *****255** essential gloss on the statute to fill a gap.' (Matter of James (Levine), 34 N.Y.2d 491, 494—495, 358 N.Y.S.2d 411, 413, 315 N.E.2d 471, 472, Supra.) On the other hand, a voluntary separation without good cause must create ineligibility since the Legislature has specifically required that it should. It is for this reason that the crucial fact is not, as the majority views it, that the employer might not have chosen to fire the claimant. What is significant is that the claimant chose not to work for the employer rather than comply with work rules established by the employer and found to be reasonable by the State labor officials.

An employer whose employees come into contact with members of the public may reasonably require that the employees refrain from conduct that might trigger adverse public reaction. (See Eastern Greyhound Lines Div. of Greyhound Lines v. New York State Div. of Human Rights, 27 N.Y.2d 279, 317 N.Y.S.2d 322, 265 N.E.2d 745; Matter of Gladstone (Catherwood), 36 A.D.2d 204, 319 N.Y.S.2d 664, affd. 30 N.Y.2d 576, 330 N.Y.S.2d 793, 281 N.E.2d 842, Supra.) The need for such regulation is particularly acute where the employees perform their duties in homes or on the private property of the customers. Common experience reveals that the employer will be held responsible for employee actions that the client deems noxious or offensive. The average employer has no interest in acting as a self-appointed community censor. The real concern, and it is a valid one, is that the *189 employer will be financially damaged as a result of

consumer unhappiness with the actions of his employees.

It is a commonplace fact of the human experience that disputes or disagreements over controversial subjects may arouse anger or animosity in the participants to the discussion. Passions may be particularly inflamed by adverse comments directed at respected or venerated community leaders. In this case, the employer had every reason to be concerned that some of his customers might be offended by criticism of the President of the United States. The occupant of that office is generally widely admired and respected. The employer could reasonably fear that a button, sported by his employee, suggesting that the President should be impeached might offend the sensibilities of some of his customers. At the very least, it might touch off a rancorous political debate which could arouse a customer's ill will. An employer should be able to protect himself against that eventuality by requiring that his employees, during business hours, refrain from overt political activity. Moreover, the employer is not required to take a poll or otherwise measure the likelihood that his customers will react adversely to his employee's political views. The majority's insistence that the employer prove that the employee's conduct was detrimental to his business interest is both irrelevant and naive. It is sufficient if the employer believes that his business will be adversely affected by the employee's conduct.

**617 Denying an employee unemployment insurance benefits for failure to abide by a reasonable regulation of employee conduct does not involve State infringement of the employee's First Amendment rights. The freedom of speech is not an absolute right. It is subject to reasonable regulations under certain circumstances. (See, e.g., Tinker v. Des Moines School Dist., 393 U.S. 503, 513, 89 S.Ct. 733, 740, 21 L.Ed.2d 731, 741.) Expression may be 'basically incompatible with the normal activity of a particular place at a particular time.' (Grayned v. City of Rockford, 408 U.S. 104, 116, 92 S.Ct. 2294, 2303, 33 L.Ed.2d 222.) Entrance into an employment relationship necessarily entails some reduction in personal liberty. An employer may require, within reason, that an employee report to work at a given place, at a given time, dressed in a certain manner, that the work be done in accordance with established practices, that the employee heed the instructions of his supervisors and that fellow employees be permitted to work undisturbed. These restrictions are normally accepted by our society as ***256 necessary *190 for the orderly conduct of a business and as part of the process by which one earns a livelihood.

Persons who are unwilling to abide by reasonable regulations are, of course, free to decline employment. However, refusal to comply with reasonable work regulations should preclude receipt of unemployment insurance benefits.

Sherbert v. Verner, 374 U.S. 398, 83 S.Ct. 1790, 10 L.Ed.2d 965 is not to the contrary. In that case, an employee was denied unemployment insurance benefits because of her refusal to accept Saturday work for religious reasons. The court ruled that government could not permissibly require an employee to choose between abandoning the precepts of her religion in order to work and, on the other hand, following her religion and forfeiting unemployment insurance benefits. (374 U.S., at p. 404, 83 S.Ct., at p. 1794, 10 L.Ed.2d, at p. 970.) The effect of the State rule under consideration in Sherbert was to penalize the employee for holding a particular religious belief. Withholding unemployment insurance benefits where the employee insists on being able to make political statements to members of the public on company time, to the possible detriment of the business, does not penalize the employee from holding a particular belief. Nor does it require the employee to take an affirmative action in violation of his conscience. (Matter of Moran (Catherwood), 34

A.D.2d 694, 309 N.Y.S.2d 642, affd. 27 N.Y.2d 946, 318 N.Y.S.2d 318, 267 N.E.2d 104.) Rather, it is an affirmation of the general rule that an employer is not obligated to permit his employees to engage in overt political activity during business hours. The employee is not constrained to abandon his political opinions (see Sherbert v. Verner, 374 U.S., at p. 410, 83 S.Ct., at p. 1797, 10 L.Ed.2d, at p. 974, Supra), but may not insist on expressing them on his employer's time to his employer's customers.

For the reasons stated, I dissent and vote to reverse the order of the Appellate Division.

BREITEL, C.J., and GABRIELLI, JONES, FUCHSBERG and COOKE, JJ., concur with WACHTLER, J.

JASEN, J., dissents and votes to reverse in separate opinion.

Order affirmed, with costs.

All Citations

39 N.Y.2d 180, 347 N.E.2d 611, 383 N.Y.S.2d 250

APPENDIX D

WISHNATSKY V. HUEY

584 N.W.2d 859
Court of Appeals of North Dakota.

Martin WISHNATSKY, Plaintiff and Appellant,
v.
David W. HUEY, Defendant and Appellee.

Civil No. 980067CA.
|
Sept. 15, 1998.

Plaintiff brought action against defendant, seeking damages for offensive contact battery. Defendant moved for summary judgment of dismissal. The District Court, Cass County, East Central Judicial District, Georgia Dawson, J., entered judgment for defendant, and plaintiff appealed. The Court of Appeals held that defendant's actions in pushing shut door of office as plaintiff attempted to enter without knocking, so that plaintiff was pushed back into adjoining hallway, did not constitute offensive contact battery.

Affirmed.
See also, 1997 ND 35, 560 N.W.2d 878.

[1]   **Assault and Battery**
    ➤Overt Act in General

    Defendant's actions in pushing shut door of office as plaintiff attempted to enter without knocking, so that plaintiff was pushed back into adjoining hallway, did not constitute offensive contact battery, where defendant was engaged in private conversation with plaintiff's employer at time plaintiff attempted to enter employer's office, and defendant was unaware of plaintiff's identity or of plaintiff's reason for entering office.

[2]   **Appeal and Error**
    ➤Matters Not Necessary to Decision on Review

    Court of Appeals need not consider questions, the answers to which are unnecessary to the determination of the case.

Attorneys and Law Firms

*859 Martin Wishnatsky, Fargo, pro se.

Andrew Moraghan, Assistant Attorney General, Attorney General's Office, Bismarck, for defendant and appellee.

Opinion

*860 PER CURIAM.

[¶ 1] Martin Wishnatsky appealed a summary judgment dismissing his battery action against David W.

Huey, and an order denying his motion for an altered judgment. We conclude, as a matter of law, that no battery occurred, and we affirm the judgment and the order.

[¶ 2] On January 10, 1996, Huey, an assistant attorney general, was engaged in a conversation with attorney Peter B. Crary in Crary's office. Without knocking or announcing his entry, Wishnatsky, who performs paralegal work for Crary, attempted to enter the office. Huey pushed the door closed, thereby pushing Wishnatsky back into the hall. Wishnatsky reentered the office and Huey left.

[¶ 3] Wishnatsky brought an action against Huey, seeking damages for battery.[1] Huey moved for summary judgment of dismissal. The trial court granted Huey's motion and a judgment of dismissal was entered. Wishnatsky moved to alter the judgment. The trial court denied Wishnatsky's motion.

[1]   Wishnatsky also sought a disorderly conduct restraining order under N.D.C.C. Ch. 12.1-31.2 against Huey, based on the January 10, 1996, incident, and another on January 25, 1996. In affirming a judgment dismissing Wishnatsky's petition, our Supreme Court concluded "Huey's conduct did

not rise to the level of intrusive behavior which would warrant a reasonable person to conclude Huey committed the offense of disorderly conduct." *Wishnatsky v. Huey*, 1997 ND 35, ¶ 15, 560 N.W.2d 878.

[¶ 4] Wishnatsky appealed, contending the evidence he submitted in response to Huey's motion for summary judgment satisfies the elements of a battery claim and the trial court erred in granting Huey's motion. Wishnatsky also contends Huey is not entitled to prosecutorial or statutory immunity.

[¶ 5] Summary judgment is a procedural device for the prompt and expeditious disposition of a controversy without trial if either party is entitled to judgment as a matter of law, if no dispute exists as to either the material facts or the inferences to be drawn from undisputed facts, or if resolving factual disputes would not alter the result. *Perry Center, Inc. v. Heitkamp*, 1998 ND 78, ¶ 12, 576 N.W.2d 505. "In considering a motion for summary judgment, a court must view the evidence in the light most favorable to the party opposing the motion, who must be given the benefit of all favorable inferences which reasonably can be drawn from the evidence." *Mougey Farms v. Kaspari*, 1998 ND 118, ¶

12, 579 N.W.2d 583. "Disputes of fact become questions of law if reasonable persons can draw only one conclusion from the evidence." *Id.* In reviewing a summary judgment, an appellate court views the evidence in the light most favorable to the non-moving party to determine if the trial court properly granted summary judgment as a matter of law. *Tuhy v. Schlabsz*, 1998 ND 31, ¶ 5, 574 N.W.2d 823. On a defendant's motion for summary judgment, the question for the court is "whether a fair-minded jury could return a verdict for the plaintiff on the evidence presented. The mere existence of a scintilla of evidence in support of the plaintiff's position will be insufficient; there must be evidence on which the jury could reasonably find for the plaintiff." *Anderson v. Liberty Lobby, Inc.*, 477 U.S. 242, 252, 106 S.Ct. 2505, 91 L.Ed.2d 202 (1986).

[¶ 6] "In its original conception [battery] meant the infliction of physical injury." VIII Sir William Holdsworth, *A History of English Law* 422 (2d Impression 1973). By the Eighteenth Century, the requirement of an actual physical injury had been eliminated:

At Nisi Prius, upon evidence in trespass for assault and battery, Holt, C.J. declared,

1. That the least touching of another in anger is a battery. 2. If two or more meet in a narrow passage, and without any violence or design of harm, the one touches the other gently, it is no battery. 3. If any of them use violence against the other, to force his way in a rude inordinate manner, it is a battery; or any struggle about the passage, to that degree as may do hurt, is a battery. Vid.Bro.Tresp. 236. 7 E. 4, 26. 22 Ass. 60. 3 H. 4, 9.

Cole v. Turner, Pasch. 3 Ann., 6 Mod. 149, 90 Eng.Rep. 958 (1704). Blackstone explained:

The least touching of another's person willfully, or in anger, is a battery; for the law cannot draw the line between different degrees ***861** of violence, and therefore totally prohibits the first and lowest stage of it: every man's person being sacred, and no other having a right to meddle with it, in any the slightest manner.

3 William Blackstone, *Commentaries* *120. On the other hand, "in a crowded world, a certain amount of personal contact is inevitable, and must be accepted." W. Page Keeton et al., *Prosser and Keeton on the Law of Torts* § 9, at 42 (5th ed.1984).

[¶ 7] The American Law Institute has balanced the interest in unwanted contacts and the inevitable contacts in a crowded world in *Restatement (Second) of Torts* §§ 18, 19 (1965):

18. Battery: Offensive Contact

(1) An actor is subject to liability to another for battery if

(a) he acts intending to cause a harmful or offensive contact with the person of the other or a third person, or an imminent apprehension of such a contact, and

(b) an offensive contact with the person of the other directly or indirectly results.

(2) An act which is not done with the intention stated in Subsection (1,a) does not make the actor liable to the other for a mere offensive contact with the other's person although the act involves an unreasonable risk of inflicting it and, therefore, would be negligent or reckless if the risk threatened bodily harm.

....

19. What Constitutes Offensive Contact

A bodily contact is offensive if it offends a reasonable sense of personal dignity.

Comment c to § 18 notes that the contact need not be "directly caused by some act of the actor" and also notes that "the essence of the plaintiff's grievance consists in the offense to the dignity involved in the unpermitted and intentional invasion of the inviolability of his person and not in any physical harm done to his body." Comment a to § 19 explains what kind of conduct offends a reasonable sense of personal dignity:

In order that a contact be offensive to a reasonable sense of personal dignity, it must be one which would offend the ordinary person and as such one not unduly sensitive as to his personal dignity. It must, therefore, be a contact which is unwarranted by the social usages prevalent at the time and place at which it is inflicted.

[¶ 8] Huey moved for summary judgment of dismissal, because, among other things, "as a matter of law, a battery did not occur on January 10, 1996." Huey supported the motion with his affidavit stating in part:

8. That Attorney Crary and I had settled into a serious discussion about the case and had established a good rapport when the door to his office suddenly swung open without a knock. An unidentified individual carrying some papers then strode in unannounced. I had not been told that anyone would be entering Attorney Crary's office during the private meeting.... I subsequently learned that the individual's name is Martin Wishnatsky.

[¶ 9] Wishnatsky responded to Huey's motion for summary

judgment with an affidavit of Crary and with his own affidavit stating in part:

1. I am a born-again Christian and cultivate holiness in my life. [A]s a result I am very sensitive to evil spirits and am greatly disturbed by the demonic. However, in Christ there is victory.

2. On January 9, 1996, Mr. David Huey of the North Dakota Attorney General's office, visited the ministry where I was working at 16 Broadway in Fargo, North Dakota with an ex parte court order.

3. The following morning I entered the office of Peter Crary, an attorney for whom I do paralegal work, to give him certain papers that had been requested. Mr. Crary was speaking with Mr. David Huey at the time. As I began to enter the office Mr Huey threw his body weight against the door and forced me out into the hall. I had not said a word to him. At the same time, he snarled: "You get out of here." This was very shocking and frightening to me. In all the time I have been working as an aide to Mr. Crary, I have never been physically assaulted or spoken to in a harsh and brutal manner. My blood pressure began to rise, my heart beat accelerated and I felt waves of fear in the pit of my stomach. My hands began to shake and my body to tremble. Composing myself, I reentered the office, whereupon *862

Mr. Huey began a half-demented tirade against me and stormed out into the hall. I looked at Mr. Crary in wonder.

[1] [¶ 10] We certainly agree with the Supreme Court's determination that when Wishnatsky attempted to enter the room in which Huey was conversing with Crary, "Huey apparently reacted in a rude and abrupt manner in attempting to exclude Wishnatsky from that conversation." *Wishnatsky v. Huey,* 1997 ND 35, ¶ 15, 560 N.W.2d 878. As a matter of law, however, Huey's "rude and abrupt" conduct did not rise to the level of battery.

[¶ 11] The evidence presented to the trial court demonstrates Wishnatsky is "unduly sensitive as to his personal dignity." *Restatement (Second) of Torts* § 19 cmt. a (1965). Without knocking or otherwise announcing his intentions, Wishnatsky opened the door to the office in which Huey and Crary were having a private conversation and attempted to enter. Huey closed the door opened by Wishnatsky, thereby stopping Wishnatsky's forward progress and pushing him back into the hall. The bodily contact was momentary, indirect, and incidental. Viewing the evidence in the light most favorable to Wishnatsky, and giving him the benefit of all favorable inferences which can reasonably be drawn from the evidence, we conclude Huey's conduct in response to Wishnatsky's intrusion into his private conversation with Crary, while "rude and abrupt," would not "be offensive to a reasonable sense of personal dignity." In short, an "ordinary person ... not unduly sensitive as to his personal dignity" intruding upon a private conversation in Wishnatsky's manner would not have been offended by Huey's response to the intrusion. We conclude that Huey's conduct did not constitute an offensive-contact-battery, as a matter of law, and the trial court did not err in granting Huey's motion for summary judgment dismissing Wishnatsky's action.

[2] [¶ 12] Because we have concluded there was no battery as a matter of law, we need not address the immunity issues Wishnatsky has raised. We need not consider questions, the answers to which are unnecessary to the determination of the case. *See, e.g., Kaler v. Kraemer,* 1998 ND 56, ¶ 10, 574 N.W.2d 588; *Hospital Servs., Inc. v. Brooks,* 229 N.W.2d 69, 71 (N.D.1975).

[¶ 13] Affirmed.

[¶ 14] HOBERG, C.J., WILLIAM F. HODNY, Surrogate Judge, and DEBBIE G. KLEVEN, District Judge, concur.

All Citations

584 N.W.2d 859, 1998 ND APP 8

APPENDIX E

HAYNES V. COMMONWEALTH

657 S.W.2d 948
Supreme Court of Kentucky.

Terry Dean HAYNES,
Appellant,
v.
COMMONWEALTH of
Kentucky, Appellee.
and
COMMONWEALTH of
Kentucky, Cross-Appellant,
v.
Terry Dean HAYNES, Cross-
Appellee.

Oct. 12, 1983.

Defendant was convicted in the Circuit Court, Pike County, E.N. Venters, J., on two counts of third-degree burglary, one count of first-degree burglary, and three counts of second-degree arson, and defendant appealed. The Supreme Court, Aker, J., held that: (1) investigative report prepared by detective was clearly within purview of Rule of Criminal Procedure governing demand for statements and reports of witnesses; (2) trial court error in excluding report was not prejudicial; (3) statements made by defendant were not inadmissible on grounds they were made in context of plea bargaining; (4) defendant's rights to counsel were not violated by admitting his statements into evidence; (5) defendant was properly convicted under statute governing burglarizing a dwelling; and (6) any

comments by prosecutor which referred to accused's failure to testify were at most harmless error.

Judgment affirmed.

[1]   **Criminal Law**
    ⌐F. B. I., police and other investigative reports
    Criminal Law
    ⌐Statements of witnesses or prospective witnesses

Where investigative report made by detective was signed by him and clearly related to subject matter of his testimony, report was within purview of Rule of Criminal Procedure governing demands for written statements and reports of witnesses. Rules Crim.Proc., Rule 7.26.

[2]   **Criminal Law**
    ⌐F. B. I., police and other investigative reports

There is no generic work-product exception for investigative reports under Rule of Criminal Procedure governing demands for written reports and statements of witnesses. Rules Crim.Proc., Rule 7.26.

[3] **Criminal Law**
⟵Discovery and disclosure;
transcripts of prior
proceedings

Although trial court erred in
denying defendant access to
detective's police report, error
was not prejudicial, where
evidence in police report
added nothing to statements
made by police officer at trial
and would not have
established other facts which
might reasonably have altered
verdict. Rules Crim.Proc.,
Rule 7.26.

[4] **Criminal Law**
⟵Particular cases

Where after defendant asked
whether he could plea bargain,
officer told him that plea
negotiations were not his job,
that defendant had to get in
touch with Commonwealth
Attorney, and that defendant
could do that through his
attorney, and issue was not
raised again during trip from
West Virginia after
defendant's extradition,
defendant could not have been
misled into believing he was
actually negotiating deal with
officer when he made
incriminating statements;
thus, statements were not

inadmissible on ground they
were made in context of plea
bargaining.

[5] **Criminal Law**
⟵Particular cases or
questions

Where defendant was twice
read his *Miranda* rights after
he was put in custody, officer
did not initiate any
conversation with him while
in car, but rather, defendant
himself began talking about
plea bargaining and his past
crimes, defendant's comments
were voluntary, without
solicitation, and made
knowingly and intelligently;
thus, admission of statements
into evidence in defendant's
prosecution did not violate
defendant's right to counsel.
U.S.C.A. Const.Amend. 6.

[6] **Burglary**
⟵Occupancy of building

Although house was not
occupied as frequently as it
had been in past, where house
was used as it had customarily
been used, as dwelling, and at
no time was house abandoned
or totally emptied, defendant
was properly convicted on
charge of burglarizing a

"dwelling." KRS 511.020.

[7] **Criminal Law**
⬅Reference to failure to produce witness or evidence as comment on failure to testify

Prosecutor's arguments which did not directly refer to defendant's failure to testify, but only referred to fact that defense did not put on any witnesses at all, did not violate defendant's right against self-incrimination. U.S.C.A. Const.Amend. 5; Const. § 11; KRS 421.225.

[8] **Criminal Law**
⬅Comments on failure of accused to testify

Although prosecutor's comment during closing argument came close to being direct reference to accused's failure to testify, where trial court interrupted prosecutor after comment was made, and there was no further elaboration on that issue after discussion at bench, and in light of overwhelming evidence against defendant, comments by prosecutor were at most, harmless error. U.S.C.A. Const.Amend. 5;

Const. § 11; KRS 421.225.

Attorneys and Law Firms

*949 Steven L. Beshear, Atty. Gen., David K. Martin, Asst. Atty. Gen., Frankfort, for appellant and cross-appellee.

Jack Emory Farley, Public Advocate, Donna Boyce Proctor, Asst. Public Advocate, Frankfort, for appellee and cross-appellant.

Opinion

AKER, Justice.

This is a direct appeal of appellant's convictions in Pike Circuit Court on two counts of third-degree burglary, one count of first-degree burglary, and three counts of second-degree arson, for which the appellant received sentences totaling fifty years, twenty of which were ordered to run consecutively for a total sentence of thirty years. The Commonwealth also filed a cross-appeal claiming certain evidence was erroneously suppressed. On the basis of our review of the briefs and record in this case we affirm the judgment of the Pike Circuit Court and, as a consequence, will not reach the merits of the Commonwealth's cross-appeal.

On the night of March 14, and early morning hours of March 15, 1980, a number of buildings in Elkhorn City in Pike County were broken into and set on fire, including Peoples Grocery, the Elkhorn Medical Center, and a house belonging to the heirs of Lundy Elswick.

The appellant was arrested for public intoxication near the scene of the last break-in and fire when a deputy sheriff, who had been dispatched to assist with traffic problems resulting from the fire, noticed the appellant by the side of the road, holding a lunch pail from which money had spilled onto the roadway. In May of 1980, after being formally charged with burglary and arson, the appellant escaped from jail. He was eventually located and extradited from West Virginia in February of 1982.

On the trip back from West Virginia, the appellant told officers accompanying him that he was guilty and that he just wanted to plead guilty, get it over with and return to West Virginia where he was serving a sentence on unrelated charges.

As stated above, the appellant was, in due course, tried and convicted in Pike Circuit Court of three counts of burglary and the counts of arson. This appeal followed.

The appellant raises four assignments of error on appeal which will be discussed individually below.

The first issue raised concerns the trial court's denial of appellant's motion, pursuant to RCr 7.26, for a written report made by a witness. Prior to the testimony of Detective Phipps, the primary investigating officer in the case, appellant's counsel moved for production of any statement or written report made by the witness. The *950 trial court held that the detective's investigative report was his "work product," and therefore, the defense was not entitled to examine it.

RCr 7.26 provides:

(1) Before a witness called by the Commonwealth testifies on direct examination the attorney for the Commonwealth shall produce any statement of the witness in the form of a document or recording in its possession which relates to the subject matter of the witness's testimony and which (a) has been signed or initialed by him or (b) is or purports to be a substantially verbatim statement made by him. Such statement shall be made available for examination and use by the defendant.

[1] [2] The investigation report prepared by Detective Phipps was signed by him and clearly related to the subject matter of his testimony. Furthermore, case law makes clear that law enforcement officer's investigative reports are within the purview of RCr 7.26 and that there is

no generic work product exception for such investigative reports. *LeGrande v. Commonwealth*, Ky., 494 S.W.2d 726 (1973); *Maynard v. Commonwealth*, Ky., 497 S.W.2d 567 (1973); *Gaston v. Commonwealth*, Ky., 533 S.W.2d 533 (1976). Therefore, as the Commonwealth concedes in its brief, the trial court was clearly in error in denying the appellant's motion for production of the written report.

However, under Kentucky case law there remains the question of whether the trial court's erroneous failure to compel production entitles the appellant to any relief. In *Maynard v. Commonwealth, supra*, at 570, a case involving a similar error, this court stated:

RCr 9.24 provides however that errors which do not affect substantial rights shall be disregarded. We must therefore determine whether the error was prejudicial.

The appellant was prejudiced if as a result of the error, he was denied access to information which, had he possessed it, would have enabled him to contradict or impeach the witness or established some other fact which might reasonably have altered the verdict.

The appellant argues that only trial counsel can determine what use he might have made of this report had it been produced, and therefore we should presume prejudice from the error. This argument was specifically rejected in *Maynard*, p. 570.

Unlike the Maynard case, this court does have before it the police report in question and can reach a determination as to whether the failure to produce the report was prejudicial.

The appellant alleges that the report contains evidence that contradicts testimony given at trial by prosecution witnesses, but he does not specify what that contradictory evidence is or how it might have reasonably altered the verdict. This court is not able to find such evidence.

It is also contended that the report contains exculpatory evidence indicating that appellant was under the influence of drugs at the time the offenses were committed. This evidence, that appellant was in some way intoxicated, was referred to at trial on a number of different occasions. Melvin Salyers testified concerning his initial arrest of appellant for public intoxication (TE, p. 178 & 172). Both Barry McKenzie (TE, p. 23) and Detective Phipps (TE, p. 291) testified that the appellant told them that he committed the crimes while he was on drugs. The appellant had ample knowledge of and opportunity to develop this fact at trial. The evidence in the police report adds nothing to the statements made by the police officers at trial.

[3] Although it was error for the trial court to deny the appellant access to Detective Phipps' police report, this error was not prejudicial since the report would not have established some other fact which might reasonably have altered the verdict.

The second issue raised by appellant is the trial court's refusal to suppress appellant's *951 oral statements to Phipps and McKenzie on their trip back from West Virginia. Appellant contends that the statements should have been suppressed for two reasons. The statements were made by the appellant in the context of plea bargaining with the officers, and therefore not admissible at trial. Secondly, his Sixth Amendment right to the assistance of counsel was abridged because these statements were made in the absence of his appointed counsel.

Officers McKenzie and Phipps picked up Terry Dean Haynes at the Moundsville Penitentiary in West Virginia after his extradition hearing on February 22, 1982. Detective McKenzie advised him of his rights when he was turned over to them at the penitentiary and again when they got into the car for the trip back to Kentucky. McKenzie stated to Haynes that he was not going to interrogate him because they had enough evidence against him, and if the appellant did say something to incriminate himself, it would be used against him [TE, pp. 28–29]. A half-hour to an hour into the trip, the appellant initiated a conversation by asking if he could plea bargain to the charges. The appellant then proceeded to talk about the charges against him stating, "that the reason he done these things at Elkhorn City, the charges that were brought against him, was because he was under the influence of drugs and when he was not on drugs he was a pretty good fellow." [TE, p. 36]. At no time did the officers question him about the charges pending against him in Elkhorn City.

[4] The contention that the incriminating statements of the appellant were made as part of plea bargaining is not supported by the record. Officer McKenzie testified that after the appellant asked whether or not he could plea bargain, he told him that plea negotiations were not his job, that the appellant had to get in touch with the Commonwealth's Attorney, and that he could do that through his attorney (TE, pp. 31, 32). This seemed to be the total extent of the conversation about plea bargaining, and the issue was not raised again during the trip. The appellant could not have been misled into believing that he was actually negotiating a deal with the officers

when he made the incriminating statements.

The appellant relies on the cases of *Massiah v. United States*, 377 U.S. 201, 84 S.Ct. 1199, 12 L.Ed.2d 246 (1964), and *Brewer v. Williams*, 430 U.S. 387, 97 S.Ct. 1232, 51 L.Ed.2d 424 (1977) to support his position that his oral confession should have been suppressed because counsel was not present when it was made. Factually those cases are easily distinguishable from our own. In *Massiah* the police surreptitiously taped a conversation between co-defendants after both were indicted, and in *Brewer* the defendant confessed after a police officer had given him the now famous "Christian burial speech."

In the present case the trial court found that the statements "were made voluntarily after being advised of his rights without any solicitation" (TE, p. 78). The trial judge's ruling is supported by substantial evidence, which makes it conclusive as to the facts, RCr 9.78.

The facts in the present case are constitutionally indistinguishable from those presented in *Oregon v. Bradshaw*, 462 U.S. 1039, 103 S.Ct. 2830, 77 L.Ed.2d 405 (1983), in which the Supreme Court clarified their opinion in *Edwards v. Arizona*, 451 U.S. 477, 101 S.Ct. 1880, 68 L.Ed.2d 378 (1981). The court in *Oregon v. Bradshaw, supra*, quoting *Edwards* stated that the question to be asked after the accused himself initiates communication with the police is:

> ... whether a valid waiver of the right to counsel and the right to silence had occurred, that is, whether the purported waiver was knowing and intelligent and found to be so under the totality of the circumstances, including the necessary fact that the accused, not the police, reopened the dialogue with the authorities.

Edwards v. Arizona, 451 U.S. at 486, n. 9, 101 S.Ct. at 1885, n. 9.

*952 [5] The appellant was twice read his *Miranda* rights after he was put in the custody of Officers McKenzie and Phipps. They did not initiate any conversation with him while in the car, but it was he who began talking about plea bargaining and his past crimes. The trial court's finding that the statements of the appellant were voluntary and without solicitation supports the conclusion that the statements were made knowingly and intelligently by the appellant. The trial court did not violate the appellant's right to counsel by admitting into evidence his oral confession.

The third issue raised by the appellant concerns the meaning of the word "dwelling" as defined in

KRS 511.010 as it relates to KRS 511.020, Burglary in the first degree.

The house in question belonged to the heirs of Lundy Elswick, who had died in October of 1979. His wife lived in the house until her death in January of 1980. After that, the house was occupied for a day or two at a time by John Elswick when he visited Elkhorn City (TE, p. 158). The house was not occupied on March 15, 1980 when the break-in occurred.

This case was tried under the 1978 revision of KRS 511.020, which states in pertinent part:

A person is guilty of burglary in the first degree when with the intent to commit a crime, he knowingly enters or remains unlawfully:

(a) in a dwelling;

KRS 511.010(2) states that:

"Dwelling" means a building which is usually occupied by a person lodging therein.

The appellant contends that since the house was unoccupied on the night in question and was only occupied sporadically during the previous two months, no one "lodged therein" or "usually occupied" the house.

The most recent case to construe these statutes was *Starnes v.*

Commonwealth, Ky., 597 S.W.2d 614 (1980). In that case, the court affirmed a first-degree burglary conviction where the unlawful entry occurred while the former residents were in the process of moving out. They had stayed at another house on the night of the burglary. The court upheld the conviction and expressly declined to speculate at what point "in or after the moving process the house would cease to be 'usually occupied.' "

In that case the court quoted the definition of "usually" from *Webster's New International Dictionary,* second edition, "Such as in common use; such as occurs in ordinary practice, or the ordinary course of events; customary; ordinary; habitual...."

[6] From the facts in this case it is clear that although the house was not occupied by John Elswick as frequently as it had been in the past, the house was used by him as it had customarily been used, as a dwelling. We are not dealing in the present case with the issue upon which the court in *Starnes* declined to speculate. At no time was this house, after the death of Mrs. Elswick, abandoned or totally empty as contemplated in the Starnes case where a family has moved out. Therefore the appellant was properly convicted under KRS 511.020 for burglarizing a dwelling.

The last issue raised by the appellant concerns alleged improper comments by the prosecutor during closing argument.

The comments in question are as follows:

(1) Nobody gave him permission to go in there and set this house on fire. You tell me what evidence was put on here today by the defense to contradict Judge Elswick when he said that this man had no permission to be in there.

MR. BISHOP: Objection, Your Honor.

THE COURT: Overruled (TE 336).

(2) All this stuff, "you would have heard this from the witness stand if they had had it", and "you would have heard this *953 from the witness stand if they had had it". We have put on evidence here. What evidence did you hear from the defense that contradicts the evidence that we have put on?

MR. BISHOP: Object, Your Honor.

THE COURT: Overruled.

MR. SCOTT: They can pick all they want but the evidence that was testified to from right here, won't contradict it (TE 340).

That man right there, that man right there and myself spent a lot of time on this case. You all didn't put it together, we did. We selected what items to put in here. There were two other boxes over that at one time that I could have used. There was a lot of stuff that I could have used, but I put on my case and you all told me that you would decide this case from the witness stand. But, again and again, time and time again, it is the same argument; "why didn't they do this", and to suggest to you that we didn't, or that it would have been in their favor. Since they didn't testify to the points they have talked about and argued ...

THE COURT: Approach the bench, gentlemen (TE 340–341).

The appellant contends that these comments violate his right against self-incrimination as embodied in the Fifth Amendment of the United States Constitution, Section 11 of the Kentucky Constitution and also KRS 421.225 which states:

In any criminal or penal prosecution the defendant, on his own request, shall be allowed to testify in his own behalf, but his failure to do so shall not be commented upon or create any presumption against him.

The appellant argues that the above-listed comments by the prosecutor unnecessarily called the jury's attention to the fact that appellant failed to testify and, further, suggested that appellant had a need to testify to rebut the prosecution's evidence.

[7] The first two comments made by the prosecutor to which there was an objection did not directly refer to the appellant's failure to testify. They only refer to the fact that the defense did not put on any witnesses at all. Argument that a defendant has failed to contradict the prosecutor's evidence has been upheld as a proper form of argument. *Williams v. Commonwealth*, Ky., 464 S.W.2d 244 (1971), remanded in light of *Furman v. Georgia*, 408 U.S. 238, 92 S.Ct. 2726, 33 L.Ed.2d 346 (1972). See also *Anderson v. Commonwealth*, Ky., 353 S.W.2d 381 (1962), cert. den., 369 U.S. 829, 82 S.Ct. 847, 7 L.Ed.2d 795. The comments by the prosecutor did not refer to the appellant's failure to testify so they were a proper form of argument.

[8] The third comment by the prosecutor objected to by the appellant comes close to being a direct reference to an accused's failure to testify. It should be noted, though, that the trial court interrupted the prosecutor after the comment was made, and there was no further elaboration on that issue after a discussion at the bench. This court has found that even direct references to a defendant's failure to testify can be harmless error. *Caldwell v. Commonwealth*, Ky., 503 S.W.2d 485 (1972). The comments in the present case fall short of those in the cited case. This court is convinced, considering the overwhelming evidence against the appellant, the comments by the prosecutor were at the most, harmless error and did not contribute to the appellant's conviction. *Chapman v. California*, 386 U.S. 18, 87 S.Ct. 824, 17 L.Ed.2d 705 (1967).

The judgment of the trial court is affirmed.

All concur.

All Citations

657 S.W.2d 948

APPENDIX F

MORGAN V. LOYACOMO

1 So. 2d 510
190 Miss. 656
Supreme Court of Mississippi.

MORGAN et al.
v.
LOYACOMO.

No. 34520.

|

April 14, 1941.

In Banc.

Appeal from Chancery Court, Grenada County; L. A. Smith, Sr., Chancellor.

Action for assault and battery by Helen Loyacomo against Carl Morgan and others. From an adverse judgment, defendants appeal.

Affirmed.

[1]   **Assault and Battery**
        ☛Nature and Elements of
        Assault and Battery

Where store manager, without any substantial ground therefor, suspected that customer had taken two garments but paid for only one and without making any inquiry of clerk or of customer before customer had left store, manager followed customer and when about a block away and in presence of others stated that he was obliged to investigate and forcibly seized the package, the manager's action constituted an "assault and battery"

[2]   **Assault and Battery**
        ☛Nature and Elements of
        Assault and Battery

To constitute "assault and battery" it is not necessary to touch a plaintiff's body or even his clothing, but knocking or snatching anything from plaintiff's hand or touching anything connected with his person, when done in a rude or insolent manner, is sufficient.

[3]   **Labor and Employment**
        ☛Particular Cases

Where store manager suspecting, without any substantial ground, that customer had taken away two garments but had paid for only one, followed customer and when about a block away and in presence of others stated that he was obliged to investigate and forcibly seized package from under her arm, the acts were so closely embraced or connected in scope, in point of time, and in area with manager's evident duties, that the owners and operators of store could be held liable therefor.

Attorneys and Law Firms

*510 Cowles Horton, of Grenada, for appellants.

S. C. Mims, Jr., and W. B. Nicols, both of Grenada, and W. I. Stone, of Coffeeville, for appellee.

Opinion

GRIFFITH, Justice.

Appellants are the owners and operators of forty-eight retail stores, one of which is in Grenada. Appellee purchased in this store on the day in question an article of ladies' underwear and having paid for it departed from the store. One White was the manager of the store and witnessed the purchase. A trivial circumstance connected with the purchase caused White to suspect, but without any substantial grounds therefor, that appellee had taken away two garments but had paid *511 for only one. Without making any inquiry either of the clerk or of appellee before appellee left the store, which if done would have readily revealed that the manager's suspicions were without any ground, White permitted appellee to leave the store, but followed her; and when about a block away and in the presence of several persons, he called to appellee, stated that he was obliged to investigate whether she had taken two articles while paying for only one, forcibly seized the package from under her arm, opened it, examined and exhibited the contents in the presence of the third persons, and found that he was in error, which, as already mentioned, he could easily have ascertained by a proper inquiry conducted in a proper manner before appellee left the store.

[1] [2] It is the first contention that there was no assault and battery, and that the words of White, with his attendant conduct, did not amount to a slander. Appellants are mistaken that White's actions did not constitute an assault and battery. The authorities are agreed that, to constitute an assault and battery, it is not necessary to touch the plaintiff's body or even his clothing; knocking or snatching anything from plaintiff's hand or touching anything connected with his person, when done in a rude or insolent manner, is sufficient. 5 C.J. pp. 619, 620; 6 C.J.S., Assault and Battery, § 9, pp. 801, 802, and cases cited in the notes. See, also, 2 Bishop, New Criminal Law, Section 72.

[3] Appellants next contend that White's actions were not within the rules which would hold appellants to account therefor. The reply to this is by a quotation which we take from Scott-Burr Stores v. Edgar, Miss.,

165 So. 623: "The alleged acts done by the manager were so closely embraced or connected in scope, in point of time, and in the area thereof, with his evident managerial duties, that the said acts may be justly said to have been a part of the res gestae, using that language for want of a better term to briefly express it."

Appellants complain that the amount of the damages allowed is excessive. Pilfering in one form or another from large retail stores presents a serious problem for the management of such establishments. This is a matter of current knowledge and our attention has been drawn to it in several cases that have been in this Court. Our attitude towards management in this matter has, therefore, been lenient rather than harsh, as evidenced by what was done by us in Willis v. McCarty-Holman Co., 187 Miss. 381, 193 So. 337. But our courts must not tolerate conduct such as shown in this case; and upon the whole record we are not able to say with confidence that the amount of the damages allowed is excessive.

Affirmed.

All Citations

190 Miss. 656, 1 So.2d 510

APPENDIX G

GARRATT V. DAILEY

279 P.2d 1091
46 Wash.2d 197
Supreme Court of Washington,
Department 2.

Ruth GARRATT, Appellant,
v.
Brian DAILEY, a Minor, by
George S. Dalley, his Guardian
ad Litem, Respondent.

No. 32841.

|

Feb. 14, 1955.

|

Rehearing Denied May 3, 1955.

Action against five year old boy for injuries sustained when boy allegedly pulled chair from under plaintiff when she started to sit down. The Superior Court, Pierce County, Frank Hale, J., dismissed action, and plaintiff appealed. The Supreme Court, Hill, J., held that, where trial court had accepted boy's statement that he had moved chair and seated himself therein, but when he discovered that plaintiff was about to sit at place where chair had been, attempted to move chair toward plaintiff, and was unable to get it under plaintiff in time, case would be remanded to obtain finding whether boy, when he moved chair, knew, with substantial certainty, that plaintiff would attempt to sit down where chair had been.

Remanded for clarification.

[1] **Infants**
←Weight and sufficiency

In action against five year old boy for injuries sustained when boy allegedly pulled chair from under plaintiff when she started to sit down, evidence was sufficient to sustain trial court's finding that boy was a visitor and not a trespasser at time he moved chair.

[2] **Assault and Battery**
←Nature and Elements of Assault and Battery

Generally, a "battery" is the intentional infliction of a harmful bodily contact upon another.

[3] **Assault and Battery**
←Nature and Elements of Assault and Battery

Act which is legal cause of harmful contact with another's person makes actor liable if actor intended to bring about harmful or offensive contact or apprehension thereof, provided contact was not consented to or not otherwise privileged.

[4] **Appeal and Error**
←To determine issues, introduce evidence, or for new trial

Where, in action against five year old boy for injuries sustained when boy allegedly pulled chair from under plaintiff when she started to sit down, trial court accepted boy's statement that he had moved chair and seated himself therein, but, when he discovered that plaintiff was about to sit at place where chair had been, attempted to move chair toward plaintiff, and was unable to get it under plaintiff in time, case would be remanded to obtain finding whether boy, when he moved chair, knew, with substantial certainty, that plaintiff would attempt to sit down where chair had been.

[5] **Infants**
←Nature, scope, and extent of liability and defenses thereto

Law of battery, which is applicable to adults, would be applicable to child less than six years of age, and child's age would be of consequence only in determining what he knew as based upon his experience, capacity, and understanding.

[6] **Appeal and Error**
←Other testimony of same witness

In action against five year old boy for injuries sustained when boy allegedly pulled chair from under plaintiff when she started to sit down, fact that plaintiff was prevented, on cross-examination, from bringing out that boy had had chairs pulled out from under him at kindergarten was not prejudicial error, in view of fact that such information later came into record through boy's testimony.

[7] **Infants**
←Nature, scope, and extent of liability and defenses thereto
Infants
←Admissibility
Trial
←Reference to protection of party by insurance or other indemnity

Five year old boy's liability for tort would not depend upon size of his estate or even upon existence of an estate, and, therefore, trial court, in tort action against boy, properly refused to admit liability policy in evidence.

[8] **New Trial**
⬤Power and duty of court in general

Where case had been tried to court, denial of motion for new trial on ground of newly discovered evidence did not constitute an abuse of discretion.

[9] **Appeal and Error**
⬤Discovery and depositions

In tort action against five year old boy, even if refusal to allow taking of boy's deposition constituted an abuse of trial court's discretion, such refusal would not constitute reversible error in absence of showing of prejudice. Rules of Pleading, Practice and Procedure, rule 30(b).

Attorneys and Law Firms

*198 **1092 Kennett, McCutcheon & Soderland, Seattle, James P. Healy, Tacoma, for appellant.

Frederick J. Orth, Rode, Cook, Watkins & Orth, Seattle, for respondent.

Opinion

HILL, Justice.

The liability of an infant for an alleged battery is presented to this court for the first time. Brian *199 Dailey (age five years, nine months) was visiting with Naomi Garratt, an adult and a sister of the plaintiff, Ruth Garratt, likewise an adult, in the back yard of the plaintiff's home, on July 16, 1951. It is plaintiff's contention that she came out into the back yard to talk with Naomi and that, as she started to sit down in a wood and canvas lawn chair, Brian deliberately pulled it out from under her. The only one of the three persons present so testifying was Naomi Garratt. (Ruth Garratt, the plaintiff, did not testify as to how or why she fell.) The trial court, unwilling to accept this testimony, adopted instead Brian Dailey's version of what happened, and made the following findings:
'III. * * * that while Naomi Garratt and Brian Dailey were in the back yard the plaintiff, Ruth Garratt, came out of her house into the back yard. Some time subsequent thereto defendant, Brian Dailey, picked up a lightly built wood and canvas lawn chair which was then and there located in the back yard of the above described premises, moved it sideways a few feet and seated himself therein, at which time he discovered the plaintiff, Ruth Garratt, about to sit down at the place where the lawn chair had formerly been, at which time he hurriedly got up from the chair and attempted to move it toward Ruth Garratt to aid

her in sitting down in the chair; that due to the defendant's small size and lack of dexterity he was unable to get the lawn chair under the plaintiff in time to prevent her from falling to the ground. That plaintiff fell to the ground and sustained a fracture of her hip, and other injuries and damages as hereinafter set forth.

'IV. That the preponderance of the evidence in this case establishes that when the defendant, Brian Dailey, moved the chair in question *he did not have any wilful or unlawful purpose* in doing so; that *he did not have any intent to injure the plaintiff, or any intent to bring about any unauthorized or offensive contact with her person* or any objects appurtenant thereto; that the circumstances which immediately preceded the fall of the plaintiff established that the defendant, *Brian Dailey, did not have purpose, intent or design to perform a prank or to effect an assault and battery upon the person of the plaintiff.*' (Italics ours, for a purpose hereinafter indicated.)

It is conceded that Ruth Garratt's fall resulted in a fractured hip and other painful and serious injuries. To obviate *200 the necessity of a retrial in the event this court determines that she was entitled to a judgment against Brian Dailey, the amount of **1093 her damage was found to be $11,000. Plaintiff appeals from a judgment dismissing the action and asks for the entry of a judgment in that amount or a new trial.

The authorities generally, but with certain notable exceptions, see Bohlen, 'Liability in Tort of Infants and Insane Persons,' 23 Mich.L.Rev. 9, state that when a minor has committed a tort with force he is liable to be proceeded against as any other person would be. Paul v. Hummel, 1868, 43 Mo. 119, 97 Am.Dec. 381; Huchting v. Engel, 1863, 17 Wis. 230, 84 Am.Dec. 741; Briese v. Maechtle, 1911, 146 Wis. 89, 130 N.W. 893, 35 L.R.A.,N.S., 574; 1 Cooley on Torts (4th ed.) 194, § 66; Prosser on Torts 1085, § 108; 2 Kent's Commentaries 241; 27 Am.Jur. 812, Infants, § 90.

In our analysis of the applicable law, we start with the basis premise that Brian, whether five or fifty-five, must have committed some wrongful act before he could be liable for appellant's injuries. [1] The trial court's finding that Brian was a visitor in the Garratt back yard is supported by the evidence and negatives appellant's assertion that Brian was a trespasser and had no right to touch, move, or sit in any chair in that yard, and that contention will not receive further consideration.

[2] [3] It is urged that Brian's action in moving the chair constituted a battery. A definition (not all-inclusive but sufficient for out

purpose) of a battery is the intentional infliction of a harmful bodily contact upon another. The rule that determines liability for battery is given in 1 Restatement, Torts, 29, § 13, as:

'An act which, directly or indirectly, is the legal cause of a harmful contact with another's person makes the actor liable to the other, if

'(a) the act is done with the intention of bringing about a harmful or offensive contact or an apprehension thereof to the other or a third person, and

'(b) the contact is not consented to by the other or the *201 other's consent thereto is procured by fraud or duress, and

'(c) the contact is not otherwise privileged.'

We have in this case no question of consent or privilege. We therefore proceed to an immediate consideration of intent and its place in the law of battery. In the comment on clause (a), the Restatement says: *Character of actor's intention*. In order that an act may be done with the intention of bringing about a harmful or offensive contact or an apprehension thereof to a particular person, either the other or a third person, the act must be done for the purpose of causing the contact or apprehension or with knowledge on the part of the actor that such contact or apprehension is substantially certain to be produced.' See, also, Prosser on Torts 41, § 8.

We have here the conceded volitional act of Brian, *i. e.*, the moving of a chair. Had the plaintiff proved to the satisfaction of the trial court that Brian moved the chair while she was in the act of sitting down, Brian's action would patently have been for the purpose or with the intent of causing the plaintiff's bodily contact with the ground, and she would be entitled to a judgment against him for the resulting damages. Vosburg v. Putney, 1891, 80 Wis. 523, 50 N.W. 403, 14 L.R.A. 226; Briese v. Maechtle, supra.

The plaintiff based her case on that theory, and the trial court held that she failed in her proof and accepted Brian's version of the facts rather than that given by the eyewitness who testified for the plaintiff. After the trial court determined that the plaintiff had not established her theory of a battery (*i. e.*, that Brian had pulled the chair out from under the plaintiff while she was in the act of sitting down), it then became concerned with whether a battery was established under the facts as it found them to be.

In this connection, we quote another portion of the comment on the 'Character of actor's intention,' relating to clause (a) of the rule from the Restatement heretofore set forth: 'It is not enough that the act itself is intentionally done and this, even **1094 though the actor realizes or should realize *202 that it contains a very grave risk of bringing about the contact or apprehension. Such realization may make the actor's conduct negligent or even reckless but unless he realizes that to a substantial certainty, the contact or apprehension will result, the actor has not that intention which is necessary to make him liable under the rule stated in this section.'

A battery would be established if, in addition to plaintiff's fall, it was proved that, when Brian moved the chair, he knew with substantial certainty that the plaintiff would attempt to sit down where the chair had been. If Brian had any of the intents which the trial court found, in the italicized portions of the findings of fact quoted above, that he did not have, he would of course have had the knowledge to which we have referred. The mere absence of any intent to injure the plaintiff or to play a prank on her or to embarrass her, or to commit an assault and battery on her would not absolve him from liability if in fact he had such knowledge. Mercer v. Corbin, 1889, 117 Ind. 450, 20 N.E. 132, 3 L.R.A. 221. Without such knowledge, there would be nothing wrongful about Brian's act in moving the chair and, there being no wrongful act, there

would be no liability.

[4] While a finding that Brian had no such knowledge can be inferred from the findings made, we believe that before the plaintiff's action in such a case should be dismissed there should be no question but that the trial court had passed upon that issue; hence, the case should be remanded for clarification of the findings to specifically cover the question of Brian's knowledge, because intent could be inferred therefrom. If the court finds that he had such knowledge the necessary intent will be established and the plaintiff will be entitled to recover, even though there was no purpose to injure or embarrass the plaintiff. Vosburg v. Putney, supra. If Brian did not have such knowledge, there was no wrongful act by him and the basic premise of liability on the theory of a battery was not established.

[5] It will be noted that the law of battery as we have *203 discussed it is the law applicable to adults, and no significance has been attached to the fact that Brian was a child less than six years of age when the alleged battery occurred. The only circumstance where Brian's age is of any consequence is in determining what he knew, and there his experience, capacity, and understanding are of course material.

From what has been said, it is clear that we find no merit in plaintiff's contention that we can direct the entry of a judgment for $11,000 in her favor on the record now before us.

Nor do we find any error in the record that warrants a new trial.

What we have said concerning intent in relation to batteries caused by the physical contact of a plaintiff with the ground or floor as the result of the removal of a chair by a defendant furnishes the basis for the answer to the contention of the plaintiff that the trial court changed its theory of the applicable law after the trial, and that she was prejudiced thereby.

It is clear to us that there was no change in theory so far as the plaintiff's case was concerned. The trial court consistently from beginning to end recognized that if the plaintiff proved what she alleged and her eyewitness testified, namely, that Brian pulled the chair out from under the plaintiff while she was in the act of sitting down and she fell to the ground in consequence thereof, a battery was established. Had she proved that state of facts, then the trial court's comments about inability to find any intent (from the connotation of motivation) to injure or embarrass the plaintiff, and the italicized portions of his findings as above set forth could have indicated a change of theory. But what must be recognized is that the trial court was trying in those comments and in the italicized findings to express the law applicable, not to the facts as the plaintiff contended they were, but to the facts as the trial court found them to be. The remand for clarification gives the plaintiff an opportunity to secure a judgment even though the trial court did not accept her version of the facts, if from all **1095 the evidence, the trial court can find that Brian knew with substantial *204 certainty that the plaintiff intended to sit down where the chair had been before he moved it, and still without reference to motivation.

[6] The plaintiff-appellant urges as another ground for a new trial that she was refused the right to cross-examine Brian. Some twenty pages of cross-examination indicate that there was no refusal of the right of cross-examination. The only occasion that impressed us as being a restriction on the right of cross-examination occurred when plaintiff was attempting to develop the fact that Brian had had chairs pulled out from under him at kindergarten and had complained about it. Plaintiff's counsel sought to do this by asking questions concerning statements made at Brian's home and in a court reporter's office. When objections were sustained, counsel for plaintiff stated that he was asking about the conversations to refresh the recollection of the child, and made an offer of proof. The fact that plaintiff was seeking to develop came into the record by the very simple method of

asking Brian what had happened at kindergarten. Consequently what plaintiff offered to prove by the cross-examination is in the record, and the restriction imposed by the trial court was not prejudicial.

[7] It is argued that some courts predicate an infant's liability for tort upon the basis of the existence of an estate in the infant; hence it was error for the trial court to refuse to admit as an exhibit a policy of liability insurance as evidence that there was a source from which a judgment might be satisfied. In our opinion the liability of an infant for his tort does not depend upon the size of his estate or even upon the existence of one. That is a matter of concern only to the plaintiff who seeks to enforce a judgment against the infant.

[8] The motion for a new trial was also based on newly discovered evidence. The case having been tried to the court, the trial judge was certainly in a position to know whether that evidence would change the result on a new trial. It was not of a character that would make the denial of the motion an abuse of discretion.

*205 [9] The plaintiff complains, and with some justice, that she was not permitted to take a pretrial deposition of the defendant Brian Dailey. While Rule of Pleading, Practice, and Procedure 30(b), 34A Wash.2d 91, gives the trial court the right 'for good cause shown' to prevent the taking of a deposition, it seems to us that though it might well have been taken under the supervision of the court to protect the child from leading, misleading and confusing questions, the deposition should have been allowed, if the child was to be permitted to testify at the trial. If, however, the refusal to allow the taking of the deposition was an abuse of discretion, and that we are not prepared to hold, it has not been established that the refusal constituted prejudicial error. (Parenthetically we would add that the right to a review of the rulings on pretrial procedure or with respect to depositions or discovery or incidental procedural motions preceding the trial seems to be limited to an appeal from a final judgment, 2 Barron and Holtzoff, Federal Practice and Procedure (Rules Ed.) § 803; 3 Id. § 1552, and realistically such a review is illusory for the reasons given by Prof. David W. Louisell. See 36 Minn.L.Rev. 654.)

The cause is remanded for clarification, with instructions to make definite findings on the issue of whether Brian Dailey knew with substantial certainty that the plaintiff would attempt to sit down where the chair which he moved had been, and to change the judgment if the findings warrant it.

Costs on this appeal will abide the ultimate decision of the superior court. If a judgment is entered for the plaintiff, Ruth Garratt, appellant here, she shall be entitled to her costs on this appeal. If, however, the judgment of dismissal remains unchanged, the respondent will be entitled to recover his costs on this appeal.

Remanded for clarification.

SCHWELLENBACH, DONWORTH, and WEAVER, JJ., concur.

All Citations

46 Wash.2d 197, 279 P.2d 1091

APPENDIX H

LUCY V. ZEHMER

84 S.E.2d 516
196 Va. 493
Supreme Court of Appeals of
Virginia

W. O. LUCY AND J. C. LUCY
v.
A. H. ZEHMER AND IDA S.
ZEHMER.

Record No. 4272.
|
November 22, 1954.

*493 Present, **517 Eggleston, Buchanan, Miller, Smith and Whittle, JJ.

Suit to compel specific performance of land purchase contract claimed by defendant vendors to have been entered into as joke. The Circuit Court, Dinwiddie County, J. G. Jefferson, Jr., J., entered decree denying specific performance and dismissing suit and purchasers appealed. The Supreme Court of Appeals, Buchanan, J., held that evidence showed that contract represented serious business transaction and good faith sale and purchase of farm, that no unusual circumstances existed in its making, and that purchasers were entitled to specific performance.

Reversed and remanded.

[1]   **Specific Performance**
Making of contract in general

In suit to compel specific performance of land purchase contract admittedly prepared by one of vendors and signed by both vendors, clear evidence was required to sustain defense by vendors that writing sought to be enforced was prepared as bluff and that whole affair was joke.

[2]   **Contracts**
Physical or mental condition of party

Where maker of contract was not intoxicated to extent of being unable to comprehend nature and consequences of instrument executed, contract would not be invalidated on ground of intoxication.

[3]   **Specific Performance**
Making of contract in general

In suit to compel specific performance of land purchase agreement, evidence was sufficient to show execution of contract was serious business transaction and to rebut contention by defendant vendors that agreement had been entered into as joke.

[4]   **Contracts**
       ⟵Intent of parties
       Contracts
       ⟵Necessity of assent

Mental assent of parties is not requisite for formation of contract and if words or acts of one of parties have but one reasonable meaning, his undisclosed intention is immaterial except when an unreasonable meaning which he attaches to his manifestations is known to other party.

[5]   **Contracts**
       ⟵Intent of parties

Although agreement or mutual assent is essential to a valid contract the law imputes to person an intent corresponding to reasonable meaning of his words and acts and if words and acts would warrant reasonable person in believing he intended real agreement, person cannot set up as defense that he was joking.

[6]   **Vendor and Purchaser**
       ⟵Offer to purchase, and acceptance thereof

Where writing entered into called for sale and purchase of land upon title being satisfactory and circumstances surrounding transaction manifested no intent other than to enter into contract, binding contract of sale was entered into notwithstanding vendors secretly may not have been serious in acceptance of purchaser's offer.

[7]   **Specific Performance**
       ⟵Requisites and validity in general

Where circumstances surrounding making of land purchase contract showed some drinking by two parties involved but not to extent they were unable to understand fully what they were doing, and there was no fraud, misrepresentation, sharp practice or dealing between unequal parties, no grounds existed to preclude ordering specific performance notwithstanding vendors' claim that contract had been entered into as a joke and as result of drinking.

[8]   **Specific Performance**
       ⟵Discretion of court

Specific performance is not matter of right, but is

addressed to court's reasonable and sound discretion which is based on established doctrines and settled principles of equity.

VIRGINIA REPORTS SYNOPSIS

Appeal from a decree of the Circuit Court of Dinwiddie county. Hon J. G. Jefferson, Jr., judge presiding.

Reversed and remanded.

The opinion states the case.

VIRGINIA   REPORTS
HEADNOTES   AND
CLASSIFICATION

(1) Contracts — Drunkenness — Not a Defense Where Party Comprehends Nature of Instrument.
1. In suit by Lucy against Zehmer and his wife for specific performance of a contract requiring the latter to convey a farm to Lucy for a stated price, the evidence contradicted Zehmer's contention that he was too drunk to make a valid contract, since he clearly was able to comprehend the nature and consequence of the instrument he executed.
(2) Contracts — Claim Instrument Signed in Jest — Unsupported by Evidence.
2. There was no merit to defendants' position that the instrument sought to be enforced was signed in jest and was not intended by either party to be a binding contract. The appearance and terms of the contract and the circumstances of its execution indicated clearly that the transaction was one of serious business.
(3) Contracts — Assent of Party — May Be Established by Conduct.
3. Even if defendants entered into the contract in jest, they were bound by it since Lucy believed, and from the acts and statements of the Zehmers was warranted in believing, that the contract represented a serious and good faith sale and purchase. Mental assent is not essential for the formation of a contract; if the words and acts of a party, reasonably interpreted, manifest an intention to agree, his contrary but unexpressed state of mind is immaterial.
(4) Specific Performance — Should Be Decreed Where No Inequity Shown.
4. Specific performance is not a matter of absolute right, but rests in sound judicial discretion. Yet where, as in the instant case, there is no circumstance of fraud, misrepresentation, sharp dealing or other inequity, specific performance should be ordered.
END OF VIRGINIA REPORTS HEADNOTES AND CLASSIFICATION

Attorneys and Law Firms

*494 *A. S. Harrison, Jr.* and *Emerson D. Baugh,* for the appellants.

Morton G. Goode and *William Earle*

White, for the appellees.

Opinion

JUDGE: BUCHANAN

BUCHANAN, J., delivered the opinion of the court.

This suit was instituted by W. O. Lucy and J. C. Lucy, complainants, against A. H. Zehmer and Ida S. Zehmer, his wife, defendants, to have specific performance of a contract by which it was alleged the Zehmers had sold to W. O. Lucy a tract of land owned by A. H. Zehmer in Dinwiddie county containing 471.6 acres, more or less, known as the Ferguson farm, for $50,000. J. C. Lucy, the other complainant, is a brother of W. O. Lucy, to whom W. O. Lucy transferred a half interest in his alleged purchase.

The instrument sought to be enforced was written by A. H. Zehmer on December 20, 1952, in these words: 'We hereby agree to sell to W. O. Lucy the Ferguson Farm complete for $50,000.00, title satisfactory to buyer,' and signed by the defendants, A. H. Zehmer and Ida S. Zehmer.

The answer of A. H. Zehmer admitted that at the time mentioned W. O. Lucy offered him $50,000 cash for the farm, but that he, Zehmer, considered that the offer **518 was made in jest; that so thinking, and both he and Lucy

having had several drinks, he wrote out 'the memorandum' quoted above and induced his wife to sign it; that he did not deliver *495 the memorandum to Lucy, but that Lucy picked it up, read it, put it in his pocket, attempted to offer Zehmer $5 to bind the bargain, which Zehmer refused to accept, and realizing for the first time that Lucy was serious, Zehmer assured him that he had no intention of selling the farm and that the whole matter was a joke. Lucy left the premises insisting that he had purchased the farm.

Depositions were taken and the decree appealed from was entered holding that the complainants had failed to establish their right to specific performance, and dismissing their bill. The assignment of error is to this action of the court.

W. O. Lucy, a lumberman and farmer, thus testified in substance: He had known Zehmer for fifteen or twenty years and had been familiar with the Ferguson farm for ten years. Seven or eight years ago he had offered Zehmer $20,000 for the farm which Zehmer had accepted, but the agreement was verbal and Zehmer backed out. On the night of December 20, 1952, around eight o'clock, he took an employee to McKenney, where Zehmer lived and operated a restaurant, filling station and motor court. While there he decided to see Zehmer and again try to buy the Ferguson farm. He entered the restaurant and talked to Mrs. Zehmer until Zehmer came in. He asked Zehmer if he had sold the Ferguson farm. Zehmer replied that he had not. Lucy said, 'I bet you wouldn't take $50,000.00 for that place.' Zehmer replied, 'Yes, I would too; you wouldn't give fifty. ' Lucy said he would and told Zehmer to write up an agreement to that effect. Zehmer took a restaurant check and wrote on the back of it, 'I do hereby agree to sell to W. O. Lucy the Ferguson Farm for $50,000 complete.' Lucy told him he had better change it to 'We' because Mrs. Zehmer would have to sign it too. Zehmer then tore up what he had written, wrote the agreement quoted above and asked Mrs. Zehmer, who was at the other end of the counter ten or twelve feet away, to sign it. Mrs. Zehmer said she would for $50,000 and signed it. Zehmer brought it back and gave it to Lucy, who offered him $5 which Zehmer refused, *496 saying, 'You don't need to give me any money, you got the agreement there signed by both of us.'

The discussion leading to the signing of the agreement, said Lucy, lasted thirty or forty minutes, during which Zehmer seemed to doubt that Lucy could raise $50,000. Lucy suggested the provision for having the title examined and Zehmer made the suggestion that he would sell it 'complete, everything there,' and

stated that all he had on the farm was three heifers.

Lucy took a partly filled bottle of whiskey into the restaurant with him for the purpose of giving Zehmer a drink if he wanted it. Zehmer did, and he and Lucy had one or two drinks together. Lucy said that while he felt the drinks he took he was not intoxicated, and from the way Zehmer handled the transaction he did not think he was either.

December 20 was on Saturday. Next day Lucy telephoned to J. C. Lucy and arranged with the latter to take a half interest in the purchase and pay half of the consideration. On Monday he engaged an attorney to examine the title. The attorney reported favorably on December 31 and on January 2 Lucy wrote Zehmer stating that the title was satisfactory, that he was ready to pay the purchase price in cash and asking when Zehmer would be ready to close the deal. Zehmer replied by letter, mailed on January 13, asserting that he had never agreed or intended to sell.

Mr. and Mrs. Zehmer were called by the complainants as adverse witnesses. Zehmer testified in substance as follows:

He bought this farm more than ten years ago for $11,000. He had had twenty-five offers, more or less, to buy it, including several from Lucy, who had never offered any specific sum of money. He had given them all the same answer, that he was not interested in selling it. On this Saturday night before Christmas it looked like everybody **519 and his brother came by there to have a drink. He took a good many drinks during the afternoon and had a pint of his own. When he entered the restaurant around eight-thirty *497 Lucy was there and he could see that he was 'pretty high.' He said to Lucy, 'Boy, you got some good liquor, drinking, ain't you?' Lucy then offered him a drink. 'I was already high as a Georgia pine, and didn't have any more better sense than to pour another great big slug out and gulp it down, and he took one too.'

After they had talked a while Lucy asked whether he still had the Ferguson farm. He replied that he had not sold it and Lucy said, 'I bet you wouldn't take $50,000.00 for it.' Zehmer asked him if he would give $50,000 and Lucy said yes. Zehmer replied, 'You haven't got $50,000 in cash.' Lucy said he did and Zehmer replied that he did not believe it. They argued 'pro and con for a long time,' mainly about 'whether he had $50,000 in cash that he could put up right then and buy that farm.'

Finally, said Zehmer, Lucy told him if he didn't believe he had $50,000, 'you sign that piece of paper here and say you will take $50,000.00 for the farm.' He, Zehmer, 'just grabbed the back off of a guest check there' and wrote on the back of it. At that point in his testimony Zehmer asked to see what he had written to 'see if I recognize my own handwriting.' He examined the paper and exclaimed, 'Great balls of fire, I got 'Firgerson' for Ferguson. I have got satisfactory spelled wrong. I don't recognize that writing if I would see it, wouldn't know it was mine.'

After Zehmer had, as he described it, 'scribbled this thing off,' Lucy said, 'Get your wife to sign it.' Zehmer walked over to where she was and she at first refused to sign but did so after he told her that he 'was just needling him [Lucy], and didn't mean a thing in the world, that I was not selling the farm.' Zehmer then 'took it back over there * * * and I was still looking at the dern thing. I had the drink right there by my hand, and I reached over to get a drink, and he said, 'Let me see it.' He reached and picked it up, and when I looked back again he had it in his pocket and he dropped a five dollar bill over there, and he said, 'Here is five dollars payment on it.' * * * I said, 'Hell no, *498 that is beer and liquor talking. I am not going to sell you the farm. I have told you that too many times before.''

Mrs. Zehmer testified that when Lucy came into the restaurant he looked as if he had had a drink. When Zehmer came in he took a drink out of a bottle that Lucy handed him. She went back to help the waitress who was getting things ready for next day. Lucy and Zehmer were talking but she did not pay too much attention to what they were saying. She heard Lucy ask Zehmer if he had sold the Ferguson farm, and Zehmer replied that he had not and did not want to sell it. Lucy said, 'I bet you wouldn't take $50,000 cash for that farm,' and Zehmer replied, 'You haven't got $50,000 cash.' Lucy said, 'I can get it.' Zehmer said he might form a company and get it, 'but you haven't got $50,000.00 cash to pay me tonight.' Lucy asked him if he would put it in writing that he would sell him this farm. Zehmer then wrote on the back of a pad, 'I agree to sell the Ferguson Place to W. O. Lucy for $50,000.00 cash.' Lucy said, 'All right, get your wife to sign it.' Zehmer came back to where she was standing and said, 'You want to put your name to this?' She said 'No,' but he said in an undertone, 'It is nothing but a joke,' and she signed it.

She said that only one paper was written and it said: 'I hereby agree to sell,' but the 'I' had been changed to 'We'. However, she said she read what she signed and was then asked, 'When you read 'We hereby agree to sell to W. O. Lucy,' what did you interpret that to mean, that particular phrase?' She said she thought that was a cash sale that night; but she also said that when she read that part

about 'title satisfactory to buyer' she understood that if the title was good Lucy would pay $50,000 but if the title was bad he would have **520 a right to reject it, and that that was her understanding at the time she signed her name.

On examination by her own counsel she said that her husband laid this piece of paper down after it was signed; that Lucy said to let him see it, took it, folded it and put it *499 in his wallet, then said to Zehmer, 'Let me give you $5.00,' but Zehmer said, 'No, this is liquor talking. I don't want to sell the farm, I have told you that I want my son to have it. This is all a joke. ' Lucy then said at least twice, 'Zehmer, you have sold your farm,' wheeled around and started for the door. He paused at the door and said, 'I will bring you $50,000.00 tomorrow. * * * No, tomorrow is Sunday. I will bring it to you Monday.' She said you could tell definitely that he was drinking and she said to her husband, 'You should have taken him home,' but he said, 'Well, I am just about as bad off as he is.'

The waitress referred to by Mrs. Zehmer testified that when Lucy first came in 'he was mouthy.' When Zehmer came in they were laughing and joking and she thought they took a drink or two. She was sweeping and cleaning up for next day. She said she heard Lucy tell Zehmer, 'I will give you so much for the farm,' and Zehmer said, 'You haven't got that much.' Lucy answered, 'Oh, yes, I will give you that much.' Then 'they jotted down something on paper * * * and Mr. Lucy reached over and took it, said let me see it.' He looked at it, put it in his pocket and in about a minute he left. She was asked whether she saw Lucy offer Zehmer any money and replied, 'He had five dollars laying up there, they didn't take it.' She said Zehmer told Lucy he didn't want his money 'because he didn't have enough money to pay for his property, and wasn't going to sell his farm.' Both of them appeared to be drinking right much, she said.

She repeated on cross-examination that she was busy and paying no attention to what was going on. She was some distance away and did not see either of them sign the paper. She was asked whether she saw Zehmer put the agreement down on the table in front of Lucy, and her answer was this: 'Time he got through writing whatever it was on the paper, Mr. Lucy reached over and said, 'Let's see it.' He took it and put it in his pocket,' before showing it to Mrs. *500 Zehmer. Her version was that Lucy kept raising his offer until it got to $50,000.

The defendants insist that the evidence was ample to support their contention that the writing sought to be enforced was prepared as a bluff or dare to force Lucy to admit that he did not have $50,000; that the whole matter was a joke; that the writing was not delivered to Lucy and no binding contract was ever made between the parties.

[1] It is an unusual, if not bizarre, defense. When made to the writing admittedly prepared by one of the defendants and signed by both, clear evidence is required to sustain it.

[2] In his testimony Zehmer claimed that he 'was high as a Georgia pine, ' and that the transaction 'was just a bunch of two doggoned drunks bluffing to see who could talk the biggest and say the most.' That claim is inconsistent with his attempt to testify in great detail as to what was said and what was done. It is contradicted by other evidence as to the condition of both parties, and rendered of no weight by the testimony of his wife that when Lucy left the restaurant she suggested that Zehmer drive him home. The record is convincing that Zehmer was not intoxicated to the extent of being unable to comprehend the nature and consequences of the instrument he executed, and hence that instrument is not to be invalidated on that ground. 17 C.J.S., Contracts, § 133 b., p. 483; *Taliaferro v. Emery,* 124 Va. 674, 98 S.E. 627. It was in fact conceded by defendants' counsel in oral argument that under the evidence Zehmer was not too drunk

to make a valid contract.

[3] The evidence is convincing also that Zehmer wrote two agreements, the first one beginning 'I hereby agree to sell.' Zehmer first said he could not remember about that, **521 then that 'I don't think I wrote but one out. ' Mrs. Zehmer said that what he wrote was 'I hereby agree,' but that the 'I' was changed to 'We' after that night. The agreement that was written and signed is in the record and indicates no such change. Neither are the mistakes in spelling that Zehmer sought to point out readily apparent.

*501 The appearance of the contract, the fact that it was under discussion for forty minutes or more before it was signed; Lucy's objection to the first draft because it was written in the singular, and he wanted Mrs. Zehmer to sign it also; the rewriting to meet that objection and the signing by Mrs. Zehmer; the discussion of what was to be included in the sale, the provision for the examination of the title, the completeness of the instrument that was executed, the taking possession of it by Lucy with no request or suggestion by either of the defendants that he give it back, are facts which furnish persuasive evidence that the execution of the contract was a serious business transaction rather than a casual, jesting matter as defendants now contend.

On Sunday, the day after the instrument was signed on Saturday night, there was a social gathering in a home in the town of McKenney at which there were general comments that the sale had been made. Mrs. Zehmer testified that on that occasion as she passed by a group of people, including Lucy, who were talking about the transaction, $50,000 was mentioned, whereupon she stepped up and said, 'Well, with the high-price whiskey you were drinking last night you should have paid more. That was cheap.' Lucy testified that at that time Zehmer told him that he did not want to 'stick' him or hold him to the agreement because he, Lucy, was too tight and didn't know what he was doing, to which Lucy replied that he was not too tight; that he had been stuck before and was going through with it. Zehmer's version was that he said to Lucy: 'I am not trying to claim it wasn't a deal on account of the fact the price was too low. If I had wanted to sell $50,000.00 would be a good price, in fact I think you would get stuck at $50,000.00.' A disinterested witness testified that what Zehmer said to Lucy was that 'he was going to let him up off the deal, because he thought he was too tight, didn't know what he was doing. Lucy said something to the effect that 'I have been stuck before and I will go through with it.''

If it be assumed, contrary to what we think the evidence *502 shows, that Zehmer was jesting about selling his farm to Lucy and that the transaction was intended by him to be a joke, nevertheless the evidence shows that Lucy did not so understand it but considered it to be a serious business transaction and the contract to be binding on the Zehmers as well as on himself. The very next day he arranged with his brother to put up half the money and take a half interest in the land. The day after that he employed an attorney to examine the title. The next night, Tuesday, he was back at Zehmer's place and there Zehmer told him for the first time, Lucy said, that he wasn't going to sell and he told Zehmer, 'You know you sold that place fair and square.' After receiving the report from his attorney that the title was good he wrote to Zehmer that he was ready to close the deal.

Not only did Lucy actually believe, but the evidence shows he was warranted in believing, that the contract represented a serious business transaction and a good faith sale and purchase of the farm.

In the field of contracts, as generally elsewhere, 'We must look to the outward expression of a person as manifesting his intention rather than to his secret and unexpressed intention. 'The law imputes to a person an intention corresponding to the reasonable meaning of his words and acts.' *First Nat. Bank v. Roanoke Oil Co.*, 169 Va. 99, 114, 192 S.E. 764, 770.

At no time prior to the execution of the contract had Zehmer indicated to Lucy by word or act that he was not in earnest about selling the farm. They had argued about it and discussed its terms, as Zehmer admitted, for a long time. Lucy testified that if there was any jesting it was about **522 paying $50,000 that night. The contract and the evidence show that he was not expected to pay the money that night. Zehmer said that after the writing was signed he laid it down on the counter in front of Lucy. Lucy said Zehmer handed it to him. In any event there had been what appeared to be a good faith offer and a good faith acceptance, *503 followed by the execution and apparent delivery of a written contract. Both said that Lucy put the writing in his pocket and then offered Zehmer $5 to seal the bargain. Not until then, even under the defendants' evidence, was anything said or done to indicate that the matter was a joke. Both of the Zehmers testified that when Zehmer asked his wife to sign he whispered that it was a joke so Lucy wouldn't hear and that it was not intended that he should hear.

[4] The mental assent of the parties is not requisite for the formation of a

contract. If the words or other acts of one of the parties have but one reasonable meaning, his undisclosed intention is immaterial except when an unreasonable meaning which he attaches to his manifestations is known to the other party. Restatement of the Law of Contracts, Vol. I, § 71, p. 74.

'* * * The law, therefore, judges of an agreement between two persons exclusively from those expressions of their intentions which are communicated between them. * * *.' Clark on Contracts, 4 ed., § 3, p. 4.

[5] An agreement or mutual assent is of course essential to a valid contract but the law imputes to a person an intention corresponding to the reasonable meaning of his words and acts. If his words and acts, judged by a reasonable standard, manifest an intention to agree, it is immaterial what may be the real but unexpressed state of his mind. 17 C.J.S., Contracts, § 32, p. 361; 12 Am. Jur., Contracts, § 19, p. 515.

So a person cannot set up that he was merely jesting when his conduct and words would warrant a reasonable person in believing that he intended a real agreement, 17 C.J.S., Contracts, § 47, p. 390; Clark on Contracts, 4 ed., § 27, at p. 54.

[6] Whether the writing signed by the defendants and now sought to be enforced by the complainants was the result of a serious offer by Lucy and a serious acceptance by the defendants, or was a serious offer by Lucy and an acceptance in secret jest by the defendants, in either event it constituted a binding contract of sale between the parties.

*504 [7] Defendants contend further, however, that even though a contract was made, equity should decline to enforce it under the circumstances. These circumstances have been set forth in detail above. They disclose some drinking by the two parties but not to an extent that they were unable to understand fully what they were doing. There was no fraud, no misrepresentation, no sharp practice and no dealing between unequal parties. The farm had been bought for $11,000 and was assessed for taxation at $6,300. The purchase price was $50,000. Zehmer admitted that it was a good price. There is in fact present in this case none of the grounds usually urged against specific performance.

[8] Specific performance, it is true, is not a matter of absolute or arbitrary right, but is addressed to the reasonable and sound discretion of the court. *First Nat. Bank v. Roanoke Oil Co., supra,* 169 Va. at p. 116, 192 S.E. at p. 771. But it is likewise true that the discretion which may be exercised is not an arbitrary or capricious one, but one

which is controlled by the established doctrines and settled principles of equity; and, generally, where a contract is in its nature and circumstances unobjectionable, it is as much a matter of course for courts of equity to decree a specific performance of it as it is for a court of law to give damages for a breach of it. *Bond v. Crawford,* 193 Va. 437, 444, 69 S.E.(2d) 470, 475.

The complainants are entitled to have specific performance of the contracts sued on. The decree appealed from is therefore reversed and the cause is remanded for the ****523** entry of a proper decree requiring the defendants to perform the contract in accordance with the prayer of the bill.

Reversed and remanded.

All Citations

196 Va. 493, 84 S.E.2d 516

APPENDIX I

STARNES V. COMMONWEALTH

597 S.W.2d 614
Supreme Court of Kentucky.

Gardell STARNES, Appellant,
v.
COMMONWEALTH of
Kentucky, Appellee.

April 1, 1980.

Defendant was convicted in the Christian Circuit Court, Stephen F. White, Jr., J., of two counts of burglary in the first degree, and defendant appealed. The Supreme Court, Stephenson, J., held that fact that persons whose house was burglarized were in process of moving and did not stay in house on night of burglary did not affect status of house as "being usually occupied by person lodged therein" within meaning of statute defining dwelling and did not prevent entry of house by defendant from being a burglary in the first degree.

Affirmed.

[1] Burglary
↞Occupancy of Building

Fact that persons whose house was burglarized were in process of moving and did not stay in house night of burglary did not affect status of house as "being usually occupied by person lodged therein" and thus a "dwelling" within

statutory definition, and, thus, did not prevent entry of house by defendant from being a burglary in the first degree. KRS 511.010(2), 511.020.

Attorneys and Law Firms

*615 Jack Emory Farley, Public Advocate, M. Gail Robinson, Erwin W. Lewis, Asst. Public Advocates, Frankfort, for appellant.

Robert F. Stephens, Atty. Gen., C. David Clauss, Asst. Atty. Gen., Frankfort, for appellee.

Opinion

STEPHENSON, Justice.

Gardell Starnes was tried and convicted on two counts of burglary in the first degree, KRS 511.020. He was sentenced to consecutive ten-year prison terms. Starnes appeals his conviction. We affirm.

Starnes was charged with burglary of the dwelling of Floyd Carter, Jr., and Count 2, the burglary of the dwelling of Walter Smith.

The principal argument made by Starnes is directed to Count 2 of the indictment, charging burglary of the Smith dwelling.

The evidence developed at the trial was that the Smiths were in the process of moving all their belongings from the house and were staying at a new house the night of the burglary. The next day the Smiths discovered the burglary and that various articles of personal property were missing. At least some of the personal property was traced to Starnes, which resulted in his indictment and conviction of first degree burglary. The sufficiency of the evidence of the intrusion is not argued on this appeal.

Starnes asserts that the burglarized house was not a "dwelling" within the meaning of KRS 511.020 and the definition section of KRS 511.010(2), and thus his conviction of first degree burglary on Count 2 must be reversed.

KRS 511.010(2) reads, " 'Dwelling' means a building which is usually occupied by a person lodging therein."

The pertinent portion of KRS 511.020 reads as follows:

"(1) A person is guilty of burglary in the first degree when, with the intent to commit a crime, he knowingly enters or remains unlawfully;

(a) In a dwelling."

The aggravating factor elevating this incident to first degree burglary is that the intrusion occurred at night.

Starnes asserts that on the night of the burglary the Smiths were staying at the new address and that no one "lodged therein" at the burglarized address within the meaning of the statute.

This is a case of first impression. We have thus far not had occasion to construe KRS 511.010(2). We are of the opinion that the assertion by Starnes is too restrictive and does not reflect legislative intent.

We conclude that the operative word in this definition is "usually."

"Usually" is defined in Webster's New International Dictionary, second edition, as "Such as in common use; such as occurs in ordinary practice, or the ordinary course of events; customary; ordinary; habitual. . . ."

The question to be answered in this case is, had this residential property ceased to be a dwelling as defined by KRS 511.010(2)?

By the terms of the definition there cannot be a precise answer to this problem which must arise as it has here. Before the Smiths began to move to their new house there can be no question that the house was a "dwelling." It follows that at some time after they moved out the house would cease to be "usually occupied." We are of the opinion the definition must be read as a whole, and the fact the Smiths were in the process of moving and did not stay in the house the night of the burglary did not *616 affect the status of the house as being "usually occupied by a person lodging therein." While we can say on these facts that the burglarized home had not ceased to be a "dwelling," we do not express an opinion at what point in or after the moving process the house would cease to be "usually occupied."

The other assertions of error are either not preserved for appellate review or are without merit.

The judgment is affirmed.

PALMORE, C. J., and AKER, CLAYTON, LUKOWSKY, STEPHENSON and STERNBERG, JJ., sitting; all concur.

All Citations

597 S.W.2d 614

APPENDIX J

GUZMAN V. CALIFANO

480 F.Supp. 735
United States District Court, S.
D. New York.

Vitalina GUZMAN, Plaintiff,
v.
Joseph CALIFANO, as
Secretary of Health, Education
and Welfare, Defendant.

No. 79 Civ. 0606.

|

Nov. 19, 1979.

|

As Amended Jan. 18, 1980.

After disability benefits' claimant was denied benefits by the Social Security Administration, she appealed. The District Court, Sofaer, J., held that: (1) applicant had adequate notice of the right to counsel at disability hearing; (2) administrative law judge was not required to have called as a witness claimant's daughter, who would have corroborated claimant's testimony, nor would he be required to secure additional medical evidence; and (3) evidence supported administrative law judge's finding that claimant's condition was not as serious as she claimed.

Complaint dismissed.

[1] **Social Security**
⇐Counsel or other
representation

Administrative law judge's colloquy with disability benefit applicant wherein he told her that she had a right to be represented by an attorney but was not required to be so represented and that due to the fact that she appeared on her own behalf he assumed that she was ready to proceed with hearing, to which she replied that she was ready to proceed without counsel, was adequate notice to right to counsel at disability hearing.

[2] **Social Security**
⇐Disability Benefits

Substantial prejudice must be shown to justify a remand by court to the Social Security Administration for rehearing of application for disability insurance benefits.

[3] **Social Security**
⇐Disability Benefits
Social Security
⇐Medical and other expert
evidence in general

In disability hearing before the Social Security Administration, administrative law judge was not required to have called as a witness claimant's daughter, who would have corroborated claimant's testimony, nor was judge required to secure additional medical evidence.

[4] **Social Security**
⟶Nature and Severity of Condition or Impairment

In claimant's application for disability benefits before the Social Security Administration, evidence supported administrative law judge's finding that claimant's condition was not as serious as she claimed and that she was not entitled to benefits, notwithstanding claimant's testimony and alleged contents of letter from claimant's employer that allegedly supported her claim of disability.

Attorneys and Law Firms

*735 Lloyd B. Silverman, Bronx Legal Services Corp., New York City, for plaintiff by Howard Sherman, New York City, of counsel.

Robert B. Fiske, Jr., U. S. Atty., S. D. N. Y., New York City, for defendant by Jane E. Bloom, Asst. U. S. Atty., New York City, of counsel.

MEMORANDUM OPINION

SOFAER, District Judge:

This is yet another disability appeal where a Legal Aid or Legal Services attorney seeks a remand so that the applicant will have an opportunity to present his or her case in the Social Security Administration with benefit of counsel. However well the legal profession has come to recognize that administrative law cases, particularly for social benefits, are usually won or lost in the agency process, the legal services bar seems regularly to appear in disability cases only at the District Court level, after the applicant has been denied relief by a hearing officer and by the Appeals Council. This practice whatever may be the reasons for it is detrimental to benefit applicants, and wasteful of judicial and administrative *736 resources. Ms. Guzman's predicament is illustrative.

After unsuccessfully applying for disability insurance benefits, Ms. Guzman requested a hearing. This request was granted, and she was notified to appear on June 14, 1978.

Plaintiff received adequate notice of her right to counsel. In a notice of hearing dated May 15, 1978, plaintiff was notified that her hearing would be held on June 14, 1978. The notice indicated in bold face capitals that she should "READ THE BACK OF THIS NOTICE VERY

CAREFULLY." Tr. 14. The back of the notice indicated that

"While it is not required, you may be represented at the hearing by an attorney or other qualified person of your choice. If you wish to be represented by an Attorney and cannot afford it, your local social security office will provide a list of offices where you may be able to obtain such representation." (Tr. 15).

The applicant, who is forty-seven years old, appeared at the hearing with her daughter, but without counsel. The Administrative Law Judge (ALJ) said to Ms. Guzman: "You were advised in the notice of hearing . . . of your right to be represented by an attorney or other qualified person of your choice. You're not required to be so represented and due to the fact your (sic) appearing today in your own behalf, I assume you're ready to proceed with your hearing . . . is that correct?" This, plaintiff's counsel now contends, "seemingly dissuaded plaintiff from obtaining counsel." Brief 4. Because plaintiff was speaking through a translator, had limited education, and was unskilled in law, the ALJ's statement "was not adequate notice," her attorney argues.

[1] Disability applicants are notified of their right to counsel in the written notice of hearing, not only at the hearing. In this case, the ALJ's colloquy with Ms. Guzman made clear that she knew of her right to counsel, and she specifically confirmed to the hearing officer that she was ready to proceed without counsel. Tr. 21. This is adequate notice of the right to counsel at a disability hearing. Ramirez v. Secretary of HEW, 528 F.2d 902 (1st Cir. 1976); Cross v. Finch, 427 F.2d 406 (5th Cir. 1970).

[2] [3] Plaintiff's attorney argues, nevertheless, that a remand is proper here because the ALJ failed adequately to protect Ms. Guzman's rights. Substantial prejudice must be shown to justify a remand, however. Cutler v. Weinberger, 516 F.2d 1282 (2d Cir. 1975). Plaintiff now claims the ALJ should have called as a witness Ms. Guzman's daughter, who would have corroborated Ms. Guzman's testimony. The ALJ told Ms. Guzman, however, that she could introduce evidence. How much further must (or should) the hearing officer go? As it is, the ALJ questioned petitioner on a number of relevant issues, and found her testimony lacking in credibility. Tr. 26-38. What if the daughter (or any other witness called by a hearing officer) were even less credible? Would it be proper for the denial of relief to rest on the testimony of a relative or other witness called by an administrative judge? Would this be a proper practice also in cases where

an applicant has been found believable? Other arguments for why the ALJ caused substantial prejudice in the absence of counsel are even less persuasive. For example, an ALJ surely cannot be required to "secure additional medical evidence" because a petitioner claims to take Traxine and APC's for a nervous condition. Tr. 29, 30. What if further inquiry established that petitioner's condition was far less serious than she contended? Would the ALJ then have been deemed to have acted as a prosecutor rather than as a neutral judge?

[4] The petitioner also contends that a remand is necessary to inquire into a letter from petitioner's employer that supports her contention that, as a diabetic, she has no control over the frequency with which she urinates. The ALJ reviewed considerable medical evidence of petitioner's condition. Records from the Hunt's Point Multi-Service Center revealed that petitioner had failed to follow the prescribed course of *737 medication for her condition, and that when she did her condition was controllable. Tr. 84-95. An examination by Dr. David Moritz in May 1978 indicated that applicant's condition was far less serious than she contended. Tr. 10, 97-100. A conclusory statement from Metropolitan Medical Services that plaintiff is a diabetic and in the doctor's opinion "is not able to work

At the present " is worth very little if any weight. Tr. 96. The ALJ had a sufficient basis in objective data to support the conclusion that petitioner's condition was not as serious as she claimed. Under the circumstances, it was entirely proper for the ALJ to rely also on the finding that petitioner's testimony that she could not walk more than one block, and that she urinated every five minutes, was not credible.

In retrospect, an able attorney, such as petitioner's counsel in this court, could well envision several ways in which petitioner's claim could have been more forcefully presented. These deficiencies in the record including petitioner's apparently exaggerated testimony cannot be blamed on the ALJ, however. Under our system of adjudication, no hearing officer (or judge) will ever be an equivalent substitute for a lawyer devoted exclusively to a party's interests. Cases such as the present one will repeatedly arise until the legal services bar translates into action the now commonplace observation that agency cases are usually won or lost at the agency level.[1] It is in general too late here to do the applicant any good. Even assuming a court were to order a remand in this, or some other, particular case, the institutional defect remains until sufficient resources and ingenuity are applied to its solution.

[1] How this should be done is a matter which will require constructive thought. Perhaps a partial solution would be to ask agencies such as S.S.A. to give applicants who are granted hearings a telephone number and address to call for legal assistance. Perhaps the time has come to have legal services assistants (even paraprofessionals would help) assigned daily to the agency to help unrepresented applicants.

The complaint is dismissed for failure to state a claim upon which relief may be granted. F.R.Civ.P. 12(c).

SO ORDERED.

All Citations

480 F.Supp. 735

APPENDIX K

PEOPLE V. BARNEY

742 N.Y.S.2d 451
294 A.D.2d 811
Supreme Court, Appellate
Division, Fourth Department,
New York.

PEOPLE of the State of New
York, Plaintiff-Respondent,
v.
Earl BARNEY, Defendant-
Appellant.

May 3, 2002.

Defendant was convicted after jury trial in the Supreme Court, Monroe County, Fisher, J., of burglary in second degree and attempted petit larceny. Defendant appealed. The Supreme Court, Appellate Division, held that building which defendant broke into did not lose its character as dwelling upon death of sole occupant.

Affirmed.

Green, J., and Hulburt, J., filed separate opinion dissenting in part.

[1] **Burglary**
⬅Occupancy of building

Building which defendant broke into did not lose its character as dwelling upon death of sole occupant, so as to support defendant's conviction of burglary in second degree; occupant lived in building until his death, two days prior to burglary, and house remained furnished, utilities were connected, there was food in refrigerator and occupant's possessions remained in house. McKinney's Penal Law §§ 140.00, subd. 3, 140.25, subd. 2.

[2] **Burglary**
⬅Occupancy of building

For burglary purposes, a dwelling does not lose its character as a dwelling based on the temporary absence of its occupant.

[3] **Burglary**
⬅Occupancy of building

A building retains its character as a dwelling despite the death of the occupant, for purposes of burglary, when it has been used as a residence in the immediate past and has not been abandoned.

[4] **Burglary**
⬅Occupancy of building

For burglary purposes, in cases where an occupant is temporarily absent, a dwelling retains its character as such if the building was adapted for occupancy at the time of the wrongful entry, the occupant intended to return, and, on the date of the entry, a person could have occupied the building overnight.

Attorneys and Law Firms

**452 Edward J. Nowak, Public Defender, Rochester (Shirley A. Gorman Of Counsel), For Defendant-Appellant.

Howard R. Relin, District Attorney, Rochester (Kelly Christine Wolford Of Counsel), For Plaintiff-Respondent.

*817 PRESENT: PIGOTT, Jr., P. J., GREEN, HURLBUTT, KEHOE, and LAWTON, JJ.

Opinion

*811 MEMORANDUM:

Defendant appeals from a judgment convicting him following a jury trial of burglary in the second degree (Penal Law § 140.25 [2]) and attempted petit larceny (§§ 110.00, 155.25). Defendant contends that the People failed to establish that the building he entered unlawfully was a dwelling (*see* ***812** § 140.00 [3]) and that his conviction of burglary in the second degree therefore is not supported by legally sufficient evidence. Defendant contends in the alternative that Supreme Court erred in denying his request to charge

burglary in the third degree (§ 140.20) as a lesser included offense of burglary in the second degree.

The building at issue is a single-family house in the Town of Greece. The sole occupant (decedent) was killed in a motor vehicle accident on August 21, 1999. Prior to his death, decedent had been renting the house from his mother. On August 23, 1999, during a conversation with friends, defendant learned that decedent had died two days earlier and that he had kept marijuana at his house. In the early morning hours of August 24, defendant entered the house intending to steal the marijuana. A neighbor, aware that decedent had died and that his house was unoccupied, observed defendant creeping along the bushes outside decedent's house, and then observed what appeared to be a light in an upstairs bedroom. The neighbor called the police, who apprehended defendant inside the house. At the time of the burglary, the house remained furnished, the utilities were connected, there was food in the refrigerator and decedent's possessions remained in the house.

[1] [2] [3] [4] Defendant contends that the building at issue lost its character as a dwelling upon the death of the sole occupant. We disagree. Although prior to 1967, burglary in the second degree required proof of another person's actual presence in the

building wrongfully entered (*see* Penal Law former § 403), the Penal Law as revised requires only that the building be a dwelling (*see* § 140.25 [2]). A dwelling is defined as "a building which is usually occupied by a person lodging therein at night" (§ 140.00 [3]). A dwelling does not ****453** lose its character as a dwelling based on the temporary absence of its occupant (*see People v. Quattlebaum*, 91 N.Y.2d 744, 748, 675 N.Y.S.2d 585, 698 N.E.2d 421). In cases where an occupant is temporarily absent, a dwelling retains its character as such if the building was adapted for occupancy at the time of the wrongful entry, the occupant intended to return, and, on the date of the entry, a person could have occupied the building overnight (*see id.*, citing *People v. Sheirod*, 124 A.D.2d 14, 17, 510 N.Y.S.2d 945, *lv. denied* 70 N.Y.2d 656, 518 N.Y.S.2d 1050, 512 N.E.2d 576). In this case, the building at issue was adapted for occupancy and a person could have occupied it overnight. We disagree with the dissent that the fact that the occupant had died and could no longer harbor an intent to return to the house compels the conclusion that it lost its character as a dwelling. Rather, we conclude, as did the Court of Appeals of Minnesota in a recent case involving similar facts, ***813** that a building retains its character as a dwelling despite the death of the occupant when it has been used as a residence in the "immediate past"

and has not been abandoned (*State v. Edwards*, 589 N.W.2d 807, 811; *cf. People v. Ramos*, 52 Cal.App.4th 300, 302, 60 Cal.Rptr.2d 523; *People v. Hider*, 135 Mich.App. 147, 151–153, 351 N.W.2d 905, 907–908). Here, a consideration of all the relevant factors supports the conclusion that the dwelling retained its character as such based upon its immediate past residential use.

The holding of the Court of Appeals in *Quattlebaum*, 91 N.Y.2d at 748–749, 675 N.Y.S.2d 585, 698 N.E.2d 421 does not compel the result advanced by the dissent. That case involved the issue whether a school building, concededly not a dwelling, could be perceived as such for purposes of convicting defendant of burglary in the second degree. The Court held that it could not, although a fifth floor office contained a bed and it was theoretically possible for someone to have stayed overnight. That holding does not impact the present case, where the building was a dwelling and had been occupied until three days before the burglary. Nor does our decision in *People v. Murray*, 278 A.D.2d 898, 718 N.Y.S.2d 554, *lv. denied and dismissed* 96 N.Y.2d 804, 726 N.Y.S.2d 382, 750 N.E.2d 84 compel a different result. In that case, the upstairs apartment of the two-apartment residential unit at issue had been vacant for several months, and the downstairs apartment was vacant and had been boarded up by the landlord several weeks earlier. Thus, in *Murray* the building had not been used as a residence in the "immediate past" (*Edwards*, 589 N.W.2d at 811).

Contrary to defendant's alternative contention, this is not a case in which the issue whether the building was a dwelling is for the jury. Here, there is no reasonable view of the evidence to support a finding that the dwelling had lost its residential character, and thus there is no reasonable view of the evidence that defendant committed the lesser offense of burglary in the third degree but not the greater offense (*see People v. Glover*, 57 N.Y.2d 61, 63, 453 N.Y.S.2d 660, 439 N.E.2d 376). We therefore conclude that the court did not err in denying defendant's request for a charge down to burglary in the third degree.

It is hereby ORDERED that the judgment so appealed from be and the same hereby is affirmed.

All concur except GREEN and HURLBUTT, JJ., who dissent in part and vote to modify in accordance with the following Memorandum:

We respectfully dissent in part. We conclude that, upon the death of its sole occupant, the building at issue lost its character as a dwelling within the meaning of ***454** Penal Law §

140.00 (3) and that the evidence is therefore legally insufficient to support defendant's ***814** conviction of burglary in the second degree (§ 140.25 [2]). No reported decision in this State addresses the issue whether, for purposes of Penal Law article 140, a building loses its character as a dwelling upon the death of its sole occupant. Under the common law, burglary was defined as breaking and entering into the dwelling house of another in the nighttime with intent to commit a felony therein (*see* 4 Blackstone, Commentaries on the Laws of England, at 222-228 [1857]). There were no degrees of burglary (*see Quinn v. People*, 71 N.Y. 561, 569), and burglary could be committed only in a dwelling (*see* 3 Torcia, Wharton's Criminal Law § 325, at 251 [15th ed.]). The requirement that the structure unlawfully entered be a dwelling was crucial "because common-law burglary found its theoretical basis in the protection of man's right of habitation" (LaFave, Criminal Law § 8.13, at 887 [3d ed.]; *see* Marks & Paperno, Criminal Law in New York Under the Revised Penal Law § 280, at 332 [1984]). Thus, if a structure was used for habitation, it qualified as a dwelling for purposes of the common-law crime of burglary even when its occupants were absent (*see* Note, *Statutory Burglary—The Magic of Four Walls and a Roof*, 100 U. Pa.L.Rev. 411, 419 [1951]). The structure, however, had to be regularly occupied overnight, and not merely be suitable for habitation (*see* 12A CJS, Burglary § 29).

In New York, the common-law definition of burglary has undergone statutory expansion and refinement, but the crime of burglary has never lost its theoretical underpinnings as an offense against habitation. In their original statutory formulations, the most serious burglary crimes, burglary in the first and second degrees, could be committed only in "the dwelling-house of another," and only if a human being was present in the dwelling house at the time of the unlawful entry (Penal Code of 1881 §§ 496, 497; *see* former Penal Law §§ 402, 403). The term "dwelling-house" was defined, consistent with the common law, as "[a] building, any part of which is usually occupied by a person lodging therein at night" (former Penal Law § 400).

As the majority points out, the revised Penal Law, enacted in 1967, eliminated the requirement of the actual presence of a human being as an essential element of burglary in the first and second degrees (*see* *People v. Quattlebaum*, 91 N.Y.2d 744, 747, 675 N.Y.S.2d 585, 698 N.E.2d 421; *People v. Sheirod*, 124 A.D.2d 14, 17, 510 N.Y.S.2d 945, *lv. denied* 70 N.Y.2d 656, 518 N.Y.S.2d 1050, 512 N.E.2d 576; Marks & Paperno, at 335). At the same time,

however, the revised statute retained the most severe penalties for the burglary of a dwelling. Like its common-law and statutory ancestors, burglary in the first degree under the current statute can ***815** be committed only in a dwelling (*see* § 140.30). Burglary in the second degree can be committed in a dwelling (*see* § 140.25 [2]) or in a building that is not a dwelling if certain aggravating circumstances are present (*see* § 140.25 [1]). The common law and prior statutory formulations are preserved virtually intact in the current definition of "dwelling" as "a building which is usually occupied by a person lodging therein at night" (§ 140.00 [3]).

The definition of "dwelling" under the revised Penal Law encompasses structures that are vacant at the time of the burglary, even for an extended period, as long as the vacancy is temporary (*see Sheirod*, 124 A.D.2d at 17, 510 N.Y.S.2d 945). Indeed, it is now firmly established that "a dwelling does not lose its character as such merely because its occupant is *temporarily* absent" ****455** (*Quattlebaum*, 91 N.Y.2d at 748, 675 N.Y.S.2d 585, 698 N.E.2d 421 [emphasis added]; *see People v. Ferguson*, 285 A.D.2d 838, 839, 727 N.Y.S.2d 790; *People v. Melendez*, 148 A.D.2d 964, 965, 539 N.Y.S.2d 201; *Sheirod*, 124 A.D.2d at 17, 510 N.Y.S.2d 945; *People v. Lewoc*, 101 A.D.2d 927, 928, 475 N.Y.S.2d

933). In this case, however, the absence of the former occupant cannot be characterized as temporary. At issue in this case is whether, in view of the death of its sole occupant, the building that defendant entered unlawfully was "usually occupied" within the meaning of the statute. In determining whether a building satisfies the statutory definition of "dwelling," three factors are relevant: "(1) whether the nature of the structure was such that it was adapted for occupancy at the time of the wrongful entry; (2) the intent of the owner to return; and (3) whether, on the date of the entry, a person could have occupied the structure overnight" (*Quattlebaum*, 91 N.Y.2d at 748, 675 N.Y.S.2d 585, 698 N.E.2d 421, citing *Sheirod*, 124 A.D.2d at 17, 510 N.Y.S.2d 945). At the time of the burglary, decedent's house was furnished, the utilities were functioning and there was food in the refrigerator. Thus, the house was adapted for occupancy and a person could have occupied it overnight. At the time of the burglary, however, the house had no present or prospective occupant (*see People v. Murray*, 278 A.D.2d 898, 899, 718 N.Y.S.2d 554, *lv. denied and dismissed* 96 N.Y.2d 804, 726 N.Y.S.2d 382, 750 N.E.2d 84), i.e., "no one regarded it as his or her place of residence, either permanent or temporary" (*People v. Lowe*, 284 A.D.2d 413, 415, 728 N.Y.S.2d 167,

lv. denied 96 N.Y.2d 921, 732 N.Y.S.2d 638, 758 N.E.2d 664). The sole occupant of the house had died three days earlier, and the owner lived elsewhere and did not intend to use the house as her residence. Absent an identifiable person who intended to use the house for overnight lodging, it was not "usually occupied" and thus did not constitute a "dwelling" (*see id.*; *Murray*, 278 A.D.2d at 900, 718 N.Y.S.2d 554; *cf. Sheirod*, 124 A.D.2d at 18, 510 N.Y.S.2d 945).

Contrary to the conclusion of the majority, we conclude that *816 our recent decision in *Murray* compels the conclusion that the building at issue was not a dwelling. The building in *Murray*, consisting of two apartments, was neither leased to tenants nor occupied by the owner or any other identifiable person, but both apartments could have been occupied overnight. The buildings in *Murray* and in this case were each designed for and capable of occupancy, but neither was occupied, in *Murray* because of the lack of a tenant and here because of death. The length of time in which the apartments in *Murray* were unoccupied had no bearing on our conclusion that the building was not a dwelling at the time of the burglary. Rather, we concluded simply that the building was not a dwelling because "there was no occupant, the owner lived elsewhere and neither apartment was rented at the time of the burglary" (*Murray*, 278 A.D.2d at 900, 718 N.Y.S.2d 554). Similarly, in this case there was no occupant, the owner lived elsewhere and there was no identifiable person who intended to use the building for overnight lodging.

It is important to note, moreover, that our decision in *Murray* rests squarely upon the historical foundation of burglary as an offense against habitation. From at least the time of Blackstone, burglary of a dwelling has been considered among the most serious crimes because of "the midnight terror excited, and the liability created by it of danger to human life, growing out of the attempt to defend property from depredation" (*Quinn*, 71 N.Y. at 567; *see Murray*, 278 A.D.2d at 900, 718 N.Y.S.2d 554; 4 Blackstone, at 222; LaFave, at 887). Under the current Penal Law, the burglar **456 of a building that is not a dwelling is punished as severely as the burglar of a dwelling only if certain aggravating circumstances, creating an equally serious danger to human life, are present. Specifically, burglary of a building is equivalent to burglary of a dwelling only if the burglar or another participant is armed with explosives or a deadly weapon; causes physical injury to a non-participant; uses or threatens the immediate use of a dangerous instrument; or displays a pistol, revolver, rifle, shotgun, machine gun or other firearm (*see* Penal Law § 140.25 [2], *supra*). The death of the sole occupant of the house and the absence of any identifiable person intending to take his place eliminated the danger to human life that the higher degrees of burglary protect against.

Our analysis of case law from other jurisdictions further supports our conclusion that the building defendant entered unlawfully was not a dwelling. Courts in other jurisdictions generally adhere to the view that a structure is a dwelling for purposes of the crime of burglary if there is an identifiable owner or occupant who intends to use the structure as a dwelling *817 (*see e.g. People v. Pearson*, 183 Ill.App.3d 72, 74–75, 131 Ill.Dec. 646, 538 N.E.2d 1202, 1203, *appeal denied* 127 Ill.2d 633, 136 Ill.Dec. 600, 545 N.E.2d 124; *see generally* Annotation, *Occupant's Absence from Residential Structure as Affecting Nature of Offense as Burglary or Breaking and Entering*, 20 A.L.R.4th 349). In cases in which the structure is vacant at the time of the burglary, the intent of the owner or occupant to return is generally the controlling factor in determining whether the structure is a dwelling (*see State v. Smith*, 121 N.C.App. 41, 45, 464 S.E.2d 471, 474, *appeal dismissed and lv. denied* 342 N.C. 663, 467 S.E.2d 732; *State v. Kowski*,

423 N.W.2d 706, 710 [Minn.]; *People v. Hider*, 135 Mich.App. 147, 151-153, 351 N.W.2d 905, 907–908). Thus, a structure is not a dwelling if the occupants leave with the intent to abandon it (*see State v. Scarberry*, 187 W.Va. 251, 254, 418 S.E.2d 361, 364; *State v. Teasley*, 719 S.W.2d 148, 150 [Tenn.]; *Wallace v. State*, 63 Md.App. 399, 407, 492 A.2d 970, 975, *cert. denied* 304 Md. 301, 498 A.2d 1186). Conversely, a structure remains a dwelling, regardless of the length of time that it is vacant, as long as the occupant does not intend to abandon it (*see Kowski*, 423 N.W.2d at 710; *Hider*, 135 Mich.App. at 151, 351 N.W.2d at 907). It follows, therefore, that a structure loses its character as a dwelling when it is vacant as the result of the death of its sole occupant (*see People v. Ramos*, 52 Cal.App.4th 300, 302, 60 Cal.Rptr.2d 523; *Hider*, 135 Mich.App. at 153, 351 N.W.2d at 908; *but see State v. Edwards*, 589 N.W.2d 807, 811 [Minn.]). "To put it plainly, a dead [person] is not using a house for a 'dwelling' and there is no way to say that a dead man is going to return or that he has an 'intent' of any kind" (*Ramos*, 52 Cal.App.4th at 302, 60 Cal.Rptr.2d 523).

Thus, based upon our analysis of the history and purpose of Penal Law article 140 and our review of authorities from this State and other jurisdictions, we conclude that the building once occupied by decedent lost its character as a dwelling upon his death. We therefore would modify the judgment by reducing the conviction of burglary in the second degree to burglary in the third degree (Penal Law § 140.20) and vacating the sentence imposed thereon, and we would remit the matter to Supreme Court, Monroe County, for sentencing on that conviction.

All Citations

294 A.D.2d 811, 742 N.Y.S.2d 451, 2002 N.Y. Slip Op. 03503

APPENDIX L

SHACKELFORD V. COMMONWEALTH

757 S.W.2d 193
Court of Appeals of Kentucky.

Robert SHACKELFORD,
Appellant,
v.
COMMONWEALTH of
Kentucky, Appellee.

No. 86–CA–2101–MR.
|
Jan. 8, 1988.
|
Rehearing Denied June 17, 1988.
|
Discretionary Review Denied by
Supreme Court Sept. 28, 1988.

Defendant was convicted in the Campbell Circuit Court, Leonard L. Kopowski, C.J., of second-degree burglary, and he appealed. The Court of Appeals, Howerton, C.J., held that there was insufficient evidence that house in which defendant entered was "dwelling" to support conviction, where house had been irreparably damaged by tornado, was uninhabitable, and was scheduled for demolition.

Reversed and remanded.

West Headnotes (1)

[1] **Burglary**
 Character and Ownership of Premises

 There was insufficient evidence that house defendant entered was "dwelling" to support defendant's second-degree burglary conviction, where house had been irreparably damaged by tornado, was uninhabitable, and was scheduled for demolition. KRS 511.010(2), 511.030.

Attorneys and Law Firms

*193 Kathleen Chambers, Ellen Longshore, Newport, for appellant.

David L. Armstrong, Atty. Gen., Mary James Young, Asst. Atty. Gen., Frankfort, for appellee.

Before HOWERTON, C.J., and COMBS and WEST, JJ.

Opinion

HOWERTON, Chief Judge.

Robert Shackelford appeals from a judgment of the Campbell Circuit Court based on a jury verdict finding him guilty of second-degree burglary. On appeal, Shackelford claims that the evidence at trial fails to support the jury finding that he entered a dwelling house. We agree and therefore reverse and remand.

On March 28, 1986, at approximately 7:30 p.m., Shackelford and two others entered a house owned by Virginia Gross which had been recently damaged by a tornado. The house had previously been Mrs. Gross's residence, but a tornado had blown off the third floor of the house and had left a two-and-one-half foot crack on its south side. Mrs. Gross had originally intended to repair the house but determined the cost prohibitive and had received a permit to have the house demolished. The city condemned the structure and allowed entry only by permit, which allowed entrance to condemned structures only between the hours of 6:00 a.m. and 6:00 p.m. Shackelford and his companions took a dresser out of the house and were apprehended by the police in the front yard. At trial, the jury returned a verdict of second-degree burglary against Shackelford.

On appeal, Shackelford contends that the evidence does not support a finding of second-degree burglary. Under KRS 511.030 "[a] person is guilty of burglary in the second degree when, with the intent to commit a crime, he knowingly enters or remains unlawfully in a dwelling." "Dwelling" is defined by KRS 511.010 as meaning "a building which is usually occupied by a person lodging therein." Shackelford argues that Mrs. Gross's house was no longer a dwelling within the statute's meaning at the time he entered it. We agree.

There can be no question that before the tornado struck, Mrs. Gross's house was a dwelling. However, the house must have continued to be a dwelling at the time Shackelford and the others entered it. As previously stated, KRS 511.010(2) requires usual occupation by a person lodging therein for a structure to constitute a dwelling. As stated in *194 *Starnes v. Commonwealth,* Ky., 597 S.W.2d 614, 615 (1980), "usually" means "[s]uch as in common use; such as occurs in ordinary practice, or the ordinary course of events...." In *Starnes,* a family was moving out of a home when someone broke in and stole some of their personal property. The family had spent the night in their new home. The court found their old home still constituted a dwelling. The court found that the home was usually occupied at the time of the break-in. We have a different situation in the case before us. Mrs. Gross's home had been irreparably damaged by a tornado. The house was uninhabitable and scheduled for demolition. The house simply was not fit for usual occupation by a person lodging therein. The court in *Litton v. Commonwealth,* Ky., 597 S.W.2d 616, 617 (1980), noted that according to the 1971 commentary to the penal code the legislature intended burglary to be "designed to encompass all unlawful intrusions which are accompanied by alarm and danger to occupants." Here, there could be no such alarm or danger. No one, not even the owner, was permitted in the house beyond 6:00 p.m. Shackelford did not enter the house until 7:30 p.m. We do not say that Shackelford is not guilty of a lesser or other theft offense; all we now hold is that the house he entered was not a dwelling within the meaning of KRS 511.030. Therefore, Shackelford cannot be guilty of second-degree burglary.

The judgment of the Campbell Circuit Court is reversed and remanded for further proceedings consistent with this opinion.

All concur.

All Citations

757 S.W.2d 193

APPENDIX M

IN RE BOOKHARD

516 N.Y.S.2d 363
131 A.D.2d 912
Supreme Court, Appellate
Division, Third Department, New
York.

In the Matter of the Claim of
Irene BOOKHARD, Respondent.
New York City Law Department,
Appellant.
Lillian Roberts, as Commissioner
of Labor, Respondent.

June 4, 1987.

Employer appealed from decision of
the Unemployment Insurance Appeal
Board, which had ruled that former
employee was entitled to receive
benefits. The Supreme Court,
Appellate Division, Main, J.P., held
that employee did not provoke her
discharge when she took leave of
absence from law school, which had
been condition of her employment.

Affirmed.

[1]   **Unemployment
        Compensation**
        ⟊Good Cause in General

   Substantial   evidence
   supported   finding   that
   employee, who was hired as
   student legal specialist on
   condition that she attend law
   school, did not provoke her
   discharge such that she was not
   entitled   to   unemployment
benefits when she took leave
of absence from law school;
employee was required to
curtail her law school
attendance when she was
unable to make satisfactory
arrangements for proper care
of her two infant children,
resulting in considerable drop
in her grades, and leave of
absence was necessary to
avoid risk of being expelled
from law school.

Attorneys and Law Firms

**363 Frederick A.O. Schwarz, Jr.
(Ronnie Dane, New York City of
counsel), for appellant.

Bowes & Chestara (John D.
Chestara, Troy, of counsel), for Irene
Bookhard, respondent.

Before MAIN, J.P., and CASEY,
MIKOLL,   YESAWICH   and
LEVINE, JJ.

Opinion

MAIN, Justice Presiding.

Appeal from a decision of the
Unemployment Insurance Appeal
Board, filed February 6, 1986, which
ruled that claimant was entitled to
receive benefits.

Claimant, the mother of infant twins
and a night student at law school, was
hired as a student legal specialist by

the employer on July 2, 1984. A condition of her employment was that she be attending law school. During a previous semester, claimant had encountered difficulty in securing babysitters and had been forced to curtail her law school attendance. As a result and after commencing her employment, she discovered that her grades dropped substantially; she was placed on probation and was in danger of expulsion. Still unable to make satisfactory arrangements for the proper care of her children, claimant discussed her situation with her professors. She was advised to take a leave of absence until satisfactory child care arrangements could **364 be made so as to avoid the risk of expulsion. Claimant advised the employer of her predicament and although the employer attempted to locate a job for her not requiring law school attendance, such a position was not available, and claimant was terminated. On these facts, the Administrative Law Judge found that claimant's absence from school was due to circumstances beyond her control and that the employer failed to demonstrate that it had no alternative to terminating claimant. The Unemployment Insurance Appeal Board affirmed the finding that claimant was entitled to benefits.

The employer contends on this appeal that claimant provoked her discharge and thus is not entitled to unemployment benefits. We disagree. The doctrine of provoked discharge, in reality a special type of voluntary separation without good cause under Labor Law § 593(1), "is a narrowly drawn legal fiction designed to apply where an employee voluntarily engages *913 in conduct which transgresses a legitimate known obligation and leaves the employer no choice but to discharge him" (*Matter of De Grego [Levine]*, 39 N.Y.2d 180, 183, 383 N.Y.S.2d 250, 347 N.E.2d 611). The question of whether a claimant voluntarily left her employment without good cause is a factual question for the Board and, if supported by substantial evidence, its determination will not be disturbed (*see, Matter of Wacksman [County of Nassau—Roberts]*, 129 A.D.2d 848, 513 N.Y.S.2d 876).

Such substantial evidence is present here. As noted above, claimant, in order to have provoked her discharge, must *voluntarily* have engaged in the conduct which precipitated her termination (*see, Matter of Michael [Long Is. Coll. Hosp.—Ross]*, 60 A.D.2d 438, 440, 401 N.Y.S.2d 591, *lv. denied* 45 N.Y.2d 708, 409 N.Y.S.2d 1026, 381 N.E.2d 614). While it ultimately was claimant's decision to take a leave of absence from school, she really had little choice in the matter; if she did not take the leave of absence, she would risk being expelled from school and would jeopardize the attainment of her ultimate career objective. The provoked discharge doctrine is of very limited application (*see, Matter of De Grego [Levine], supra,* 39 N.Y.2d pp. 183–185, 383 N.Y.S.2d 250, 347 N.E.2d 611), and claimant's conduct in this case is not the type of voluntary conduct appropriate for application of the doctrine (*see, e.g., Matter of Malaspina [Corsi],* 309 N.Y. 413, 131 N.E.2d 709). Accordingly, although the employer terminated claimant for valid reasons, there is substantial evidence that claimant did not voluntarily leave her position without good cause, and the decision of the Board awarding her benefits should be affirmed.

Decision affirmed, without costs.

CASEY, MIKOLL, YESAWICH and LEVINE, JJ., concur.

All Citations

131 A.D.2d 912, 516 N.Y.S.2d 363

Appendix N

In re Ambrose

595 N.Y.S.2d 126
191 A.D.2d 845
Supreme Court, Appellate
Division, Third Department, New
York.

In the Matter of the Claim of
Robin C. AMBROSE,
Respondent.
Board of Education of the
Malverne Union Free School
District, Appellant.
John F. Hudacs, as
Commissioner of Labor,
Respondent.
March 11, 1993.

Board of Education appealed from decision of Unemployment Insurance Appeal Board which ruled that former probationary teacher was entitled to receive unemployment insurance benefits. The Supreme Court, Appellate Division, held that teacher, who was required as condition of continued employment to take and pass national teacher's examination, was disqualified from receiving unemployment insurance benefits in light of her failure to register for entire test on two occasions.

Reversed and remitted.

[1] **Unemployment
    Compensation**
    ⟜Inability to obtain licensure
    or certification

Former probationary teacher required as condition of continued employment to take and pass national teacher's examination was disqualified from receiving unemployment insurance benefits in light of her failure to register for entire test on two occasions; while teacher claimed that she was confused by instructions, she neglected to ask for guidance to make sure she was registering properly even though she knew that her employment was contingent on her taking and passing entire te

Attorneys and Law Firms

**126 Ehrlich, Frazer & Feldman (Florence T. Frazer, of counsel), Garden City, for appellant.

Edward L. Skolnick, White Plains, for Robin C. Ambrose, respondent.

Before LEVINE, J.P., and MERCURE, MAHONEY, CASEY and HARVEY, JJ.

Opinion

MEMORANDUM DECISION.

*845 Appeal from a decision of the Unemployment Insurance Appeal Board, filed June 6, 1991, which ruled that claimant was entitled to receive unemployment insurance benefits.

We find that the decision of the Unemployment Insurance Appeal Board is not supported by substantial evidence and must, therefore, be reversed. Claimant was employed by the Board of Education of the Malverne Union Free School District (hereinafter District) to teach business education for a three-year probationary term commencing September 1, 1989. *846 In October 1989, claimant was informed in a memorandum from the District Supervisor of Curriculum and Instruction that her continued employment with the District was contingent upon her taking and passing the National Teacher's Examination (hereinafter NTE), which was given every March, June and October, and obtaining certification. Claimant admitted at the hearing that, during a subsequent meeting with the District Supervisor, she was specifically told to take the March 1990 NTE and, if she did not pass, her job would be in jeopardy. Although the NTE consists of three separate parts and despite the District Supervisor's conversation with her, claimant admitted that she deliberately chose to take only one part in March 1990, which she **127 failed. Claimant was again specifically informed in writing that she had to take and pass the June 1990 NTE to continue working in the District. Claimant, however, only registered for two of the three parts.

Claimant contends that she was confused by the instructions but neglected to ask for guidance to make sure she was registering properly even though she knew that her employment was contingent on her taking and passing this entire test. In this respect, claimant voluntarily engaged in conduct which eliminated any possibility that she could keep her employment with the District beyond the 1989–1990 school year (*compare Matter of Hannah* [*New York City Bd. of Educ.—Hartnett*], 144 A.D.2d 765, 534 N.Y.S.2d 752, *with Matter of Michael* [*Long Is. Coll. Hosp.—Ross*], 60 A.D.2d 438, 401 N.Y.S.2d 591, *lv. denied* 45 N.Y.2d 708, 409 N.Y.S.2d 1026, 381 N.E.2d 614; *see also, De Grego v. Levine*, 39 N.Y.2d 180, 383 N.Y.S.2d 250, 347 N.E.2d 611). Under the circumstances, we find that claimant is disqualified from receiving unemployment insurance benefits. Furthermore, the overpayment in benefits is recoverable under Labor Law § 597(4).

ORDERED that the decision is reversed, without costs, and matter remitted to the Unemployment Insurance Appeal Board for further proceedings not inconsistent with this court's decision.

All Citations

191 A.D.2d 845, 595 N.Y.S.2d 126, 82 Ed. Law Rep. 153

APPENDIX O

STATE V. WILLE

728 N.W.2d 343
299 Wis.2d 531
Court of Appeals of Wisconsin.
STATE of Wisconsin, Plaintiff-
Respondent,
v.
Ronald L. WILLE, Jr.,
Defendant-Appellant.[†]

[†] Petition for Review denied
April 17, 2007.

No. 2005AP2839-CR.
|
Submitted on Briefs June 14,
2006.
|
Opinion Filed Jan. 31, 2007.

Synopsis
Background: Following a jury trial,
defendant was convicted in the
Circuit Court, Portage County, John
V. Finn, J., of causing death by
procuring alcohol for a minor.
Defendant appealed.

Holdings: The Court of Appeals,
Deininger, J., held that:

[1] reference to a single minor or
underage person in statute governing
criminal offense of causing death by
procuring alcohol for a minor does
not preclude statute's application to a
defendant who procures alcoholic
beverages for a group of persons that
the defendant knew or should have
known were underage persons;

[2] sufficient evidence existed to
satisfy knowledge element;

[3] sufficient evidence existed that
victim consumed beer that defendant
provided at party;

[4] state had to show that victim's
consumption of alcohol provided by
defendant was "a" substantial factor
in causing death, not "the"
substantial factor;

[5] trial court was not required to
instruct jury that state had to show
that victim's death was natural and
probable consequence of defendant's
conduct;

[6] trial court's error, if any, in
admitting coroner's testimony as to
victim's alcohol and drug test results
was harmless; and

[7] state did not intend to call
investigator as witness, and thus
discovery statute did not require state
to disclose investigator.

Affirmed.

[1] **Criminal Law**
←Review De Novo

Court of Appeals would
review de novo what state was
required to prove to convict
defendant of causing death by
procuring alcohol for a minor;
issue was question of statutory
interpretation.   W.S.A.
125.075(1).

[2] **Criminal Law**
←Defenses in General

Affirmative defenses to criminal liability permit defendants to avoid liability if they can show that their conduct falls within a particular subset of circumstances encompassed by a broader set of circumstances that describe the crime.

[3] **Assault and Battery**
⟜Self-Defense

Defendant who batters another may avoid a conviction for battery if he or she can prove that the battery in question was within the subset of batteries committed in self-defense.

[4] **Homicide**
⟜Injuring or Endangering Child

Reference to a single minor or underage person in statute governing criminal offense of causing death by procuring alcohol for a minor does not preclude statute's application to a defendant who procures alcoholic beverages for a group of persons that the defendant knew or should have known were underage persons. W.S.A. 125.075(1), 990.001(1).

[5] **Homicide**
⟜Injuring or Endangering Child

Violation of statute governing criminal offense of causing death by procuring alcohol for a minor is proven when a defendant is shown to have procured alcoholic beverages for one or more persons who are under 18 years of age, if the defendant knew or should have known that the underage persons were under the legal drinking age and an underage person who was under 18 when provided the beverages dies as a result. Wis. Stat. § 125.075(1).

[6] **Criminal Law**
⟜Reasonable Doubt

Test regarding sufficiency of the evidence to support conviction is not whether Court of Appeals or any of the members of the Court of Appeals are convinced of the defendant's guilt beyond reasonable doubt, but whether the Court of Appeals can conclude the trier of fact could, acting reasonably, be so convinced.

[7] **Criminal Law**
⟜Construction in Favor of Government, State, or Prosecution

Criminal Law
⟵Reasonable Doubt

Court of Appeals will not reverse a conviction for insufficient evidence unless the evidence, viewed most favorably to the state and the conviction, is so insufficient in probative value and force that it can be said as a matter of law that no trier of fact, acting reasonably, could have found guilt beyond a reasonable doubt.

[8]   **Homicide**
⟵Intent or Mens Rea

Sufficient evidence existed to satisfy knowledge element of offense of causing death by procuring alcohol for a minor; evidence indicated that defendant purchased and arranged for delivery of barrels of beer to party site where underage drinking party was to occur, defendant knew that party attendees would include people under legal drinking age, and defendant expected high-school students would hear about party and show up. W.S.A. 125.075(1)(a).

[9]   **Homicide**
⟵Predicate Offenses or Conduct

Sufficient evidence existed that victim consumed beer that defendant provided at party to support conviction for causing death by procuring alcohol for a minor, although cups were laying around at party, and although victim brought several cans of beer to party; evidence indicated that defendant sold red cups to party attendees, who could then obtain beer from barrels, attendee saw victim drink beer from red cup and did not see victim fill cup from any source other than barrel, second attendee saw victim drinking from barrel, and third attendee saw victim fill victim's cup from barrel. Wis. Stat. § 125.075(1)(a).

[10]   **Criminal Law**
⟵Instructions

Court of Appeals' review of a trial court's jury instructions is deferential; Court of Appeals inquires only whether the trial court misused its broad discretion in instructing the jury.

[11]   **Criminal Law**
⟵Construction and Effect of Charge as a Whole
Criminal Law
⟵Instructions in General

When reviewing jury instructions, the Court of Appeals will reverse and order a new trial only if the jury instructions, taken as a whole, misled the jury or communicated an incorrect statement of the law.

[12] **Criminal Law**
⟵Review De Novo

Whether jury instructions are a correct statement of the law is a question of law that the Court of Appeals reviews de novo.

[13] **Criminal Law**
⟵Instructions Already Given

Choice among requested jury instructions which correctly state the law is a matter for the exercise of trial court discretion, based upon the facts adduced at trial.

[14] **Homicide**
⟵Injuring or Endangering Child

To convict defendant of causing death by procuring alcohol for a minor, state had to show that victim's consumption of alcohol provided by defendant was "a" substantial factor in causing death, not "the" substantial

factor. W.S.A. 125.075(1).

[15] **Criminal Law**
⟵Elements of Offense and Defenses

Defendant preserved for appellate review his claim that trial court erred in instructing jury that state had to show that victim's consumption of alcohol provided by defendant was "a" substantial factor in causing death, not "the" substantial factor, in prosecution for causing death by procuring alcohol for a minor, although defendant did not object to pattern jury instruction, did not request any additional language at instruction conference, and did not object when instruction was read by court; defendant objected to supplemental instruction that court gave in response to jurors' questions during deliberations. W.S.A. 125.075.

[16] **Homicide**
⟵Injuring or Endangering Child

Court of Appeals could consider Criminal Jury Instructions Committee's rationale and conclusion as persuasive authority on issue of whether prior version of pattern jury instruction for criminal offense of causing death by procuring alcohol for a minor was supposed to be read as requiring that victim's consumption of alcohol provided by defendant was "a" substantial factor in causing death rather than "the" substantial factor. W.S.A. 125.075(1).

[17] **Criminal Law**
⟝Elements and Incidents of Offense

Trial court was not required to instruct jury in prosecution for causing death by procuring alcohol for a minor that state had to show that victim's death was natural and probable consequence of defendant's conduct; jury instruction already required state to prove that victim's consumption of alcohol provided by defendant was a substantial factor, and proposed addition to jury instruction communicated same concept as other language already included in instruction. W.S.A. 125.075(1).

[18] **Criminal Law**
⟝Reception of Evidence
Criminal Law
⟝Documentary and Demonstrative Evidence

Trial court's error, if any, in admitting coroner's testimony as to victim's alcohol and drug tests results, which allegedly violated constitutional right to confront and cross-examine witnesses and statute governing chemical tests for intoxication, was harmless in prosecution for causing death by procuring alcohol for a minor; state did not need to prove level of alcohol in victim's blood, absence of other drugs in victim's system was not element of state's case, and jury did not need to hear that coroner relied, in part, on victim's blood and urine test results to conclude that victim's consumption of beer at party was substantial factor in fatal automobile accident. U.S.C.A. Const.Amend. 6; W.S.A. 125.075(1), 901.03(1).

[19] **Criminal Law**
⟝Reception and Admissibility of Evidence

Trial court's decision to admit evidence is discretionary and will not be disturbed on appeal unless the trial court has erroneously exercised its discretion.

[20]   **Criminal Law**
        ⟵Prejudice to Defendant in
        General

When determining whether to
reverse a criminal conviction
and order a new trial, a court
may   conclude   that   a
constitutional or other error is
harmless if it is clear beyond a
reasonable doubt that a
rational jury would have found
the defendant guilty absent the
error.

[21]   **Criminal Law**
        ⟵List or Disclosure of
        Prosecution Witnesses

State did not intend to call as
witness investigator to whom
victim's bag of mints was
given to determine whether
drugs were present, and thus
discovery statute did not
require state to disclose
investigator   before
investigator testified in
prosecution for causing death
by procuring alcohol for a
minor; there had been no
indication in any police
reports, witness statements, or
victim's medical records that
victim had used controlled
substances prior to fatal
accident, and issue of victim's
use of controlled substances
arose when defense counsel,
during cross-examination of
deputy, insinuated that mints
might have been illicit drugs.
W.S.A. 125.075(1), 971.23(1).

Attorneys and Law Firms

**346 On behalf of the defendant-
appellant, the cause was submitted
on the briefs of Jerome A. Maeder
and Benjamin C. Welch of Jerome A.
Maeder, S.C., Wausau.

On behalf of the plaintiff-respondent,
the cause was submitted on the brief
of Marguerite M. Moeller, assistant
attorney general, and Peggy A.
Lautenschlager, attorney general.

Before   LUNDSTEN,   P.J.,
DEININGER   and
HIGGINBOTHAM, JJ.

Opinion

¶ 1 DEININGER, J.

*537 Ronald Wille appeals a
judgment convicting him of causing
death by procuring alcohol for a
minor, a violation of WIS. STAT. §
125.075 (1) (2003-04).[1] He contends
the evidence at trial was insufficient
to convict him of violating the cited
statute. Wille also claims the circuit
court erred in the following ways: (1)
by improperly instructing jurors
regarding the required causal link
between his actions and the ensuing
death; (2) by admitting evidence of
the victim's blood alcohol content
and the results of drug testing; and

(3) by permitting testimony from an investigator who the State had not named as a potential witness prior to trial. We conclude that (1) to show a violation of § 125.075(1), the State needed to establish only that Wille knew or should have known that the alcohol beverages he procured for a party would be consumed by persons under the age of twenty-one, and (2) the evidence at trial was sufficient to establish such knowledge. We also reject Wille's other claims of error and, accordingly, we affirm the judgment of conviction.

[1]   All references to the Wisconsin Statutes are to the 2003-04 version unless otherwise noted.

BACKGROUND

¶ 2 Seventeen-year-old Kristopher Meshak died from traumatic brain injuries he sustained in a car accident after attending a New Year's Eve party at *538 which he had consumed beer. Evidence at trial established that Ronald Wille, who was nineteen at the time, had purchased two half-barrels of beer with his credit card and arranged for their delivery to the party. Witnesses testified that Wille sold red plastic cups for $5.00 each to party attendees, who could then use the cups to obtain as much beer from the barrels as they wanted. Witnesses also testified that Meshak drank beer from the barrels Wille had procured, and that Meshak was highly intoxicated when he left the party.

¶ 3 The State charged Wille under WIS. STAT. § 125.075(1) with procuring alcohol beverages for a person under the age of eighteen, the consumption of which resulted **347 in the person's death. A jury found Wille guilty and the court placed him on five years' probation with numerous conditions. He appeals.

ANALYSIS

Sufficiency of the Evidence

[1] ¶ 4 We first address Wille's claim that the State produced insufficient evidence at trial to convict him of violating WIS. STAT. § 125.075(1). If Wille were to prevail on this claim, his claims of trial court error would be moot. See State v. Schutte, 2006 WI App 135, ¶ 13, 295 Wis.2d 256, 720 N.W.2d 469, review denied (WI Oct. 10, 2006) (No. 2005AP0658-CR). As is often the case with claims of insufficient evidence, the dispute in this case is not so much over the probative value of the State's evidence as it is over the nature of the conduct the legislature intended to criminalize. See id., ¶ 15. We therefore address first the question of what the State was required to prove in order to convict Wille of *539 violating § 125.075(1), which is a question of statutory interpretation

and thus one of law that we decide de novo. *See State v. Setagord*, 211 Wis.2d 397, 405-06, 565 N.W.2d 506 (1997).

¶ 5 WISCONSIN STAT. § 125.075(1) provides as follows:

Any person who procures alcohol beverages for or sells, dispenses or gives away alcohol beverages to a person under 18 years of age ... may be penalized as provided in sub. (2) if:

(a) The person knew or should have known that the underage person was under the legal drinking age; and

(b) The underage person dies or suffers great bodily harm ... as a result of consuming the alcohol beverages provided....

Subsection (2) of the statute renders the violation a Class G felony if the underage person dies. Section 125.075(2)(b).

¶ 6 The Criminal Jury Instructions Committee describes the elements of the offense this way:

1. The defendant provided alcohol beverages to [the victim].

"Provided," as used here, means selling, dispensing, or giving away alcohol beverages.

"Alcohol beverages" means fermented malt beverages and intoxicating liquor.

2. The defendant provided alcohol beverages to [the victim] at a time when [the victim] was under 18 years of age and was not accompanied by a parent.

*540 3. The third element requires that the defendant knew or should have known that [the victim] was under the legal drinking age ["21 years of age"].

....

4. [The victim] died ... as a result of consuming alcohol beverages provided by the defendant.

This requires that the consumption of such alcohol beverages was a substantial factor in causing death ... to [the victim].

WIS JI-CRIMINAL 5050 (footnotes omitted).[2]

2   The version of WIS JI-CRIMINAL 5050 in effect at the time of the trial in this case inadvertently omitted the article "a" before "substantial factor" in the last quoted sentence of the instruction. According to the trial transcript, when reading the instruction to the jury, the circuit court said "a substantial factor." Later, when jurors noted the omission in the

written instruction and questioned whether the sentence should be read as requiring the alcohol consumption to be "a substantial factor" or "the substantial factor," the court informed jurors that the correct reading was "a substantial factor." The court's supplemental instruction in response to the jurors' question is the subject of Wille's second claim of error.

**348 ¶ 7 Wille admits that he purchased two half-barrels of beer for the party and that, "for a brief time," he sold "red cups at the party." He claims, however, that the State produced no evidence that he sold a cup or dispensed beer to the victim, or that he even knew Meshak was at the party. Wille contends that, because the statute requires that he "knew or should have known that *the* underage person was under the legal drinking age," WIS. STAT. § 125.075(1)(a) (emphasis added), he cannot be convicted of violating the statute unless the State proved that Wille dispensed beer directly to Meshak, or at a minimum, that he knew *541 Meshak was or would be at the party consuming beer that Wille had purchased. He also asserts that, because there was evidence at trial that Meshak possessed some cans of beer at the party and may have simply poured his own beer into a red cup he picked up from the ground, the State failed to prove that Wille played any role whatsoever in providing the beer that Meshak consumed prior to the fatal accident.

¶ 8 In support of his position that WIS. STAT. § 125.075(1)(a) requires a defendant to know that a specific victim will consume the alcohol beverages provided, Wille points to the affirmative defense described in § 125.075(1m). The introductory language of subsection (1m) states that "[i]n determining ... whether a person knew or should have known that the underage person was under the legal drinking age, all relevant circumstances surrounding the procuring, selling, dispensing or giving away of the alcohol beverages may be considered." The statute then describes the following potentially exculpatory circumstances and provides that if all four of them occur, they constitute "a defense to criminal liability" under the statute:

(a) The underage person falsely represents that he or she has attained the legal drinking age.

(b) The underage person supports the representation under par. (a) with documentation that he or she has attained the legal drinking age.

(c) The alcohol beverages are provided in good faith reliance on the underage person's representation that he or she has attained the legal drinking age.

(d) The appearance of the underage person is such that an ordinary and prudent person would believe that he or she had attained the legal drinking age.

*542 Section 125.075(1m). In Wille's view, because the affirmative defense clearly contemplates "some form of interaction" between the defendant and the victim, criminal liability under the statute requires that a defendant have knowledge that a specific victim will consume the provided beverages.

[2] [3] ¶ 9 We first address Wille's contention that the elements of the statutory affirmative defense establish that the legislature intended to impose liability under WIS. STAT. § 125.075(1) only when a defendant has had direct contact with a particular victim or otherwise knows of the specific victim for whom alcohol beverages are procured. The contention suffers from a logical flaw. Affirmative defenses to criminal liability permit defendants to avoid liability if they can show that their conduct falls within a particular subset of circumstances encompassed by a broader set of circumstances that describe the crime. For example, a defendant who batters another may avoid a conviction for battery if he or

she can prove that the battery in question was within the subset of batteries committed in self-defense. Here, the legislature could well have intended to criminalize **349 the providing of alcohol to minors when a death results regardless of whether a "personal interaction" occurred between defendant and victim, while at the same time providing for an affirmative defense when the prohibited conduct falls within the subset of occasions where a personal interaction occurred that included certain features.

¶ 10 Accordingly, we conclude that the existence and elements of the affirmative defense in WIS. STAT. § 125.075(1m) tells us nothing about the scope of the conduct the legislature intended to criminalize under § 125.075(1). We thus turn to the general rules of *543 statutory construction. When we construe a statute, we begin with the language of the statute and give it its common, ordinary, and accepted meaning, except that technical or specially defined words are given their technical or special definitions. *State ex rel. Kalal v. Circuit Court for Dane County,* 2004 WI 58, ¶ 45, 271 Wis.2d 633, 681 N.W.2d 110. We interpret statutory language in the context in which it is used, not in isolation, but as part of a whole, in relation to the language of surrounding or closely related statutes, and reasonably to avoid absurd or unreasonable results. *Id.*, ¶ 46. We also consider the scope, context, and purpose of the statute insofar as they are ascertainable from the text and structure of the statute itself. *Id.*, ¶ 48.

[4] ¶ 11 Wille makes much of the fact that WIS. STAT. § 125.075(1) refers several times to the victim in the singular: "to a person under 18 years of age"; "the underage person was"; "[t]he underage person dies." *Id.* We conclude, however, that the reference to a single minor or underage person in the statute does not preclude its application to a defendant who procures alcohol beverages for a group of persons that the defendant knew or should have known were underage persons.

¶ 12 We first note that WIS. STAT. § 990.001(1) provides that, when interpreting Wisconsin statutes, "unless [it] ... would produce a result inconsistent with the manifest intent of the legislature ... [t]he singular includes the plural, and the plural includes the singular." We find no expression of "manifest [legislative] intent" that, under WIS. STAT. § 125.075(1)(a), a defendant must know that a particular individual for whom he or she procured alcohol was an underage person. Applying the directive of § 990.001(1) to § 125.075(1), *544 the statute may be interpreted as criminalizing the procuring of alcohol beverages for "person[s] under 18 years of age" if

the defendant "knew or should have known that the underage person[s were] under the legal drinking age" and one of the underage persons (who is under eighteen) dies "as a result of consuming the alcohol beverages."[3]

3   Notably, although the victim of the crime must be under eighteen, it is not necessary that the defendant knew or should have known that the persons for whom alcohol beverages were procured were "under 18 years of age"; the required knowledge is that the persons were "under the legal drinking age," i.e., under the age of twenty-one. *See* WIS. STAT. § 125.075(1)(a). Wille does not dispute that the victim, Meshak, was seventeen at the time he consumed beer at the party, and Wille acknowledged at trial that he knew that persons "under the legal drinking age" would be in attendance and consume the beer Wille procured for the party.

¶ 13 We next observe that many criminal statutes refer to the victim of the described crime in the singular. Interpreting those statutes as requiring that a defendant must knowingly direct his or her prohibited conduct toward a particular individual would produce results that are arguably "absurd or unreasonable." *See* **350 *Kalal,* 271 Wis.2d 633, ¶ 46, 681 N.W.2d 110. For example, WIS. STAT. § 941.327(2)(a) makes it a crime to "[t]amper [ ] with any household product" if the tampering is done "with intent to kill, injure or otherwise endanger the health or safety of any person." Although the statute defines the requisite intent as directed to "any person" in the singular, it would be absurd to conclude the legislature intended that a defendant could escape criminal liability because he or she intended to kill or injure many, unidentified persons by tampering with a product but had no "face-to-face" interaction with a specific victim who used the product and died as a result.

*545 ¶ 14 We conclude it would be equally absurd or unreasonable to interpret WIS. STAT. § 125.075(1) as requiring a personal interaction between the defendant and the victim, or as requiring that the defendant have knowledge that a particular underage person would consume the alcohol procured by the defendant. If we were to adopt Wille's proffered interpretation, a defendant who procures alcohol beverages and provides them to a single minor in a face-to-face transaction could be prosecuted under the statute, but a defendant who arguably engages in more blameworthy conduct by procuring alcohol beverages for dozens of minors could not be prosecuted, even though the risk of a tragic result is far greater in the second scenario. Not only would such a construction be absurd or unreasonable, we conclude that it would also be contrary to the "scope, context, and purpose" of the statute, *Kalal,* 271 Wis.2d 633, ¶ 48, 681 N.W.2d 110, given that one of the textually manifest purposes of WIS. STAT. ch. 125 is to keep alcohol beverages out of the hands of minors and other underage persons by, in part, imposing civil and criminal penalties on those who provide it to them. *See, e.g.,* WIS. STAT. §§ 125.035(4)(b); 125.07(1), (3), and (4).

[5] ¶ 15 We thus conclude that a violation of WIS. STAT. § 125.075(1) is proven when a defendant is shown to have "procure[d] alcohol beverages for ... [one or more persons who are] under 18 years of age," if the defendant "knew or should have known that the underage person[s were] under the legal drinking age" and an "underage person [who was under eighteen when provided the beverages] dies ... as a result."

[6] [7] ¶ 16 We next consider whether the State produced sufficient evidence at trial to permit jurors, *546 acting reasonably, to be convinced beyond a reasonable

doubt, by evidence they had a right to believe and accept as true, that Wille engaged in such conduct. *See State v. Poellinger,* 153 Wis.2d 493, 503-04, 451 N.W.2d 752 (1990). " 'The test is not whether this court or any of the members thereof are convinced [of the defendant's guilt] beyond reasonable doubt, but whether this court can conclude the trier of facts could, acting reasonably, be so convinced....' " *Id.* (citation omitted). We will not reverse a conviction for insufficient evidence " 'unless the evidence, viewed most favorably to the state and the conviction, is so insufficient in probative value and force that it can be said as a matter of law that no trier of fact, acting reasonably, could have found guilt beyond a reasonable doubt.' " *State v. Johannes,* 229 Wis.2d 215, 221, 598 N.W.2d 299 (Ct.App.1999) (citing *Poellinger,* 153 Wis.2d at 501, 451 N.W.2d 752). We are not so convinced.

[8] ¶ 17 Wille admitted on cross-examination that he knew when he purchased and arranged for the delivery of the barrels of beer to the party site that "an underage drinking party" was to occur and that party attendees would include "people ... under the legal drinking age." He also testified that he expected high school students would hear about the party and **351 "show up." Thus, there is plainly sufficient evidence for reasonable jurors to conclude beyond a reasonable doubt that Wille procured alcohol beverages for persons he knew were under the legal drinking age, which, as we have discussed, satisfies the knowledge element under WIS. STAT. § 125.075(1)(a). Wille does not dispute that the victim, Meshak, was under eighteen when he attended the party, or that Meshak was not accompanied by a parent. *547 [4] Although he challenges the instruction on causation and the admission of certain evidence of Meshak's level of intoxication, Wille does not dispute, for purposes of his insufficient evidence claim, that the State produced evidence at trial that would permit reasonable jurors to conclude beyond a reasonable doubt that Meshak's consumption of alcohol beverages was "a substantial factor" in causing the fatal car accident.

[4]   WISCONSIN STAT. § 125.075(1) includes a cross-reference to WIS. STAT. § 125.07(1)(a), which prohibits procuring alcohol beverages for an underage person only if the underage person is "not accompanied by his or her parent, guardian or spouse who has attained the legal drinking age."

[9] ¶ 18 What Wille does dispute is whether the State produced sufficient evidence to allow jurors to conclude

that Meshak consumed any of the beer that Wille provided to the party. Wille asserts that "no evidence was submitted to show that Wille sold a cup to Meshak or to show that Wille provided the alcohol that Meshak was drinking from the red cup." Because there was testimony that cups could be found laying around at the party and that Meshak had brought several cans of beer to the party, Wille suggests that jurors could only speculate as to the true source of the alcohol beverages that Meshak ingested prior to his car accident. We disagree and conclude instead that the State produced sufficient evidence to permit jurors to reasonably infer that Meshak consumed some of the beer that Wille admittedly procured for the underage persons at the party.

¶ 19 An attendee of the party testified that he saw Meshak drink beer from a red cup and that he saw Meshak fill the cup once from one of the kegs at the party. This witness estimated that Meshak had consumed *548 "about eight" cups of beer at the party, stating further that he had not seen Meshak fill his cup from any source of beer other than the keg and had not seen him with either a beer bottle or can in his hands. Another witness said that he was "pretty sure" that the beer he and Meshak were "slamming" near the end of the party was from one of the barrels at the party.[5] This same witness had earlier told a detective that he had seen Meshak "drinking fast and from the barrel of beer." Finally, a third witness testified that he had seen Meshak fill "his cup from the half-barrel" "more than once, I believe," although this witness later said, "I don't remember seeing him just fill it up, but I know he was drinking out of a red cup."

[5] This witness later said that he didn't "recall [Meshak] ever actually going to the half barrel and getting his beer himself. I mean, when someone goes to a half barrel and they come back with a cup of beer, I mean, you only know how much you got in your cup." Wille characterizes this testimony as a repudiation of the witness's earlier testimony that he was "pretty sure" that Meshak had consumed beer from one of the barrels at the party. We reject the characterization-jurors could reasonably interpret the witness's testimony to mean that, although the witness never watched Meshak draw a beer from the barrel, the fact that Meshak went to the barrel and came back with beer in his cup allowed the witness to be "pretty sure" Meshak's beer came from the barrel.

¶ 20 In sum, we are satisfied that the State presented sufficient evidence at **352 Wille's trial to permit jurors, acting reasonably, to be convinced beyond a reasonable doubt by evidence they had a right to believe, *see Poellinger*, 153 Wis.2d at 503-04, 451 N.W.2d 752, that Wille procured alcohol beverages for Meshak, who was a minor, knowing that the beer being provided would be consumed by underage persons, and that Meshak's consumption of the beer Wille provided was a substantial *549 factor in causing Meshak's death. Before moving on to Wille's claims of trial court error, we briefly address arguments Wille advances in his opening brief to the effect that our interpretation of WIS. STAT. § 125.075(1) contravenes legislative intent and good public policy.

¶ 21 Wille asserts that the legislature's "motive ... in drafting WIS. STAT. § 125.075 was not to have young men and women who are recent high school graduates prosecuted because they brought beer to ad hoc parties," and that the legislature "intended this statute to be used only in the circumstance[s] where a person knowingly provides a specific minor or minors with an alcoholic beverage." As we have discussed, however, nothing in the plain language of the statute or its context suggests the legislative intent that Wille proffers. Wille provides

nothing beyond his own rhetoric as proof that the legislature intended to limit the reach of WIS. STAT. § 125.075(1) as he argues.

¶ 22 For example, Wille posits that, under our interpretation of WIS. STAT. § 125.075(1), anyone who brings a bottle of wine to a family gathering, knowing "that minors could be present," risks being convicted of a felony. He then asks, "Did the legislature intend to make a felon out of any person who brings an intoxicant to a party that the victim may have shared?" Our response is straightforward: based on the language it enacted, the legislature has indeed criminalized the bringing of intoxicants to a party, *if* the alcohol beverages are provided to a person under eighteen who dies or suffers great bodily harm as a result of its consumption, *and* the provider knew or should have known that one or more underage persons would consume the provided beverages. Thus, in Wille's hypothetical, the provider of wine to a family gathering need not fear a felony prosecution if he or she knows only that "minors *550 could be present." If, however, the wine provider knows or should know, as Wille admits to having known, that the alcohol beverage is being provided for consumption by persons under the legal drinking age, a prosecution and conviction under § 125.075 could indeed follow if a minor (who is not accompanied by a parent or guardian, *see* footnote 4) consumes the provided wine and dies as a result of its consumption. In sum, Wille has not persuaded us that our interpretation will result in prosecutions that contravene public policy.

Instruction on Causation

[10] [11] [12] [13] ¶ 23 Our review of the trial court's jury instructions is deferential; we inquire only whether the trial court misused its broad discretion in instructing the jury. *See Young v. Professionals Ins. Co.*, 154 Wis.2d 742, 746, 454 N.W.2d 24 (Ct.App.1990). We will reverse and order a new trial only if the jury instructions, taken as a whole, misled the jury or communicated an incorrect statement of the law. *See Miller v. Kim,* 191 Wis.2d 187, 194, 528 N.W.2d 72 (Ct.App.1995). Whether jury instructions are a correct statement of the law is a question of law that we review de novo. *State v. Neumann,* 179 Wis.2d 687, 699, 508 N.W.2d 54 (Ct.App.1993). The choice among requested instructions which correctly state the law, however, is a matter for the exercise of trial court discretion, based upon the facts adduced at **353 trial. *See State v. Lenarchick,* 74 Wis.2d 425, 455, 247 N.W.2d 80 (1976).

[14] [15] ¶ 24 Wille claims the trial court erred in instructing jurors that,

to find Wille guilty of the charged crime, Meshak's consumption of alcohol provided by Wille was *551 required to be "a" substantial factor in causing Meshak's death, instead of "the" substantial factor, as Wille requested. Alternatively, he contends the court should have also instructed jurors that, to be "a substantial factor," the death had to be "a natural and probable consequence" of Wille's conduct.[6] We are not persuaded that the trial court erred in instructing jurors that Wille could be found guilty if Meshak's consumption of alcohol provided by Wille was "a substantial factor" in causing Meshak's death, or that it erroneously exercised its discretion by refusing to insert the additional language Wille requested.

---

6   We note that Wille neither objected to WIS JI-CRIMINAL 5050 nor requested any additional language at the instruction conference. As we have noted, however, the printed pattern instruction the parties reviewed at that time had neither "a" nor "the" immediately before "substantial factor." (*See* footnote 2.) The transcript reflects that the trial court said "a substantial factor" when instructing the jury and Wille made no objection to the instruction as read by the court.

When the jury inquired as to whether the written instruction should read "a" or "the" substantial factor, however, Wille argued for "the" and, alternatively, for the additional "natural and probable consequence" language. The court denied both requests. We are satisfied that, by objecting to the supplemental instruction given in response to the jurors' question, Wille sufficiently preserved the issue for appeal.

¶ 25 As we have noted (see footnote 2), the current version of WIS JI-CRIMINAL 5050 places the indefinite article "a" before "substantial factor," and the omission of any article in the prior version appears to have been an oversight. The Jury Instructions Committee explains as follows in a footnote to the current instruction:

The Committee has treated this offense as one involving the traditional "substantial factor" causal *552 relationship employed for criminal offenses. However, it should be noted that [WIS. STAT.] § 125.075 does not directly refer to the defendant's conduct causing the harm. Rather, the statute refers to the harm occurring "as a result of consuming the alcohol beverages provided" in violation of the statute § 125.075(1)(b). Since it is not clear whether this approach was intended to indicate a different causal requirement, the Committee concluded that the regular "substantial factor" test should be used.

This conclusion is supported by *State v. Bartlett*, 149 Wis.2d 557, 439 N.W.2d 595 (Ct.App.1989), where the court construed "results in" as used in [WIS. STAT.] § 346.17(3). The court held that the statute was not unconstitutionally vague because "results in" means "cause" and therefore defines the offense with reasonable certainty. The court further held that the evidence was sufficient to support the conviction because it showed that the defendant's conduct was a substantial factor in causing the death. The court noted that more than but-for cause is required: "The state must further establish that 'the harmful result in question be the natural and probable consequence of the accused's conduct,' *i.e.,* a substantial factor." 149 Wis.2d 557, 566, 439 N.W.2d 595, citing *State v. Serebin*, 119 Wis.2d 837, 350 N.W.2d 65 (1984).

[16] ¶ 26 We may consider the Criminal Jury Instructions Committee's rationale and conclusion as "persuasive" authority on the issue. *See* **354 *State v. Ellington*, 2005 WI App 243, ¶ 8, 288 Wis.2d 264, 707 N.W.2d 907. Moreover, our own review of the

cases the Committee relies on, *State v. Serebin*, 119 Wis.2d 837, 350 N.W.2d 65 (1984), and *State v. Bartlett*, 149 Wis.2d 557, 439 N.W.2d 595 (Ct.App.1989), convince us that the trial court correctly instructed jurors that WIS. STAT. § 125.075(1) requires a showing that Meshak's consumption ***553** of the provided alcohol needed to be "a substantial factor in causing [Meshak's] death."

[17] ¶ 27 We further conclude that the court did not err in refusing to add to the instruction that Meshak's death must be shown to have been "the natural and probable consequence of the accused's conduct," which is the language Wille requested the trial court to insert. As the supreme court explained in *Serebin*, the phrase "a substantial factor" is the equivalent of "the natural and probable consequence of the accused's conduct." *Serebin*, 119 Wis.2d at 849, 350 N.W.2d 65 (citation omitted). We agree with the State that it is not an erroneous exercise of discretion for a trial court to decline to provide jurors with alternative language that communicates the same concept as other language already included in the instruction.

¶ 28 Before taking up Wille's claims of evidentiary error, we note that he also argues in his opening brief that the jury, in attempting "to render a just verdict was clearly torn between convicting Wille of a crime that he did not do because the jury's interpretation of 'a' cause made them find him guilty," and that the jury "was hoping that the court would instruct them that it had to be 'the' cause and they would have found him not guilty." Wille provides no record citations for these assertions, nor could he. *See, e.g.*, WIS. STAT. § 906.06(2) ("[A] juror may not testify as to any matter or statement occurring during the course of the jury's deliberations or to the effect of anything upon the juror's or any other juror's mind or emotions as influencing the juror to assent to or dissent from the verdict ... or concerning the juror's mental processes in connection therewith...."). Thus, Wille's assertions regarding what prompted jurors to find him guilty are ***554** pure speculation. Moreover, even if the jury's verdict did in fact turn on whether Meshak's consumption of the provided alcohol was "a" or "the" substantial factor in causing Meshak's death, as we have explained, jurors were correctly instructed, and they could thus properly find Wille guilty if they concluded that Meshak's consumption of beer provided by Wille was a substantial factor in causing Meshak's death.

Evidentiary Issues

[18] [19] [20] ¶ 29 Wille next claims error in the admission of testimony

regarding certain test results showing (1) the victim's blood alcohol content, and (2) the absence of certain drugs in his system at the time of the fatal accident. A trial court's decision to admit evidence is discretionary and will not be disturbed unless the court has erroneously exercised its discretion. *See Schutte*, 295 Wis.2d 256, 720 N.W.2d 469, ¶ 45. In addition, "[e]rror may not be predicated upon a ruling which admits or excludes evidence unless a substantial right of the party is affected." WIS. STAT. § 901.03(1). Finally, when determining whether to reverse a criminal conviction and order a new trial, a court may conclude that a "constitutional or other error is harmless if it is 'clear beyond a reasonable doubt that a rational jury would have found the defendant guilty absent the error.' " *State v. Harvey*, 2002 WI 93, ¶ 49, 254 Wis.2d 442, 647 N.W.2d 189 (citing *Neder v. United States*, 527 U.S. 1, 18, 119 S.Ct. 1827, 144 L.Ed.2d 35 (1999)).

**355 ¶ 30 The county coroner was permitted to testify that, as part of his investigation into Meshak's death, he reviewed medical records from the hospital and clinic where Meshak was treated after the accident, and in *555 particular, a clinic record that reported Meshak's "blood alcohol level was 138 milligrams per deciliter of blood." The coroner was also permitted to testify that he reviewed a "urine toxicology screen" that tested negative for "PCP ... Benzocaine ... Cocaine ... Amphetamine groupings ... Cannabis ... Opiates ... barbiturates ... and tricyclics." The blood and urine samples were taken when Meshak was admitted to the hospital following his car accident. Wille contends that admission of the blood alcohol test results violated WIS. STAT. § 885.235, and, further, that admission of both sets of results was improper because neither was supported by chain-of-custody evidence, thereby violating Wille's right to confront and cross-examine those who drew, handled and tested the blood and urine samples.

¶ 31 We conclude that even if the trial court erred in allowing the coroner to testify as to the victim's alcohol and drug test results, no "substantial right" of Wille's was affected by the admission of the testimony in question, *see* WIS. STAT. § 901.03(1), and further, that "it is 'clear beyond a reasonable doubt that a rational jury would have found [Wille] guilty' " without hearing the challenged testimony. *See Harvey*, 254 Wis.2d 442, ¶ 49, 647 N.W.2d 189 (citation omitted). The State was under no obligation to establish the level of alcohol in Meshak's blood at the time of the accident, or even to prove that he was intoxicated to the degree required for a conviction under WIS. STAT. § 346.63 ("Operating under influence of intoxicant or other drug"). The absence of other drugs in Meshak's system also was not an element of the State's case. As we have discussed, the State needed to prove only that Meshak's consumption of alcohol beverages procured by Wille was "a substantial factor" in causing Meshak's death. We conclude there was more than sufficient evidence presented at trial to show that *556 Meshak drove away from the party in a highly intoxicated state. We therefore harbor no reasonable doubt that jurors would have found that the State established the necessary causal link between Meshak's consumption of alcohol and his death even if they had not heard the test result evidence.

¶ 32 Witnesses at the trial who had attended the party testified to all of the following. At 3:00 a.m., Meshak "had so much to drink that he shouldn't have been driving." A witness had declined to ride home with Meshak "because he was drunk." Another witness estimated Meshak had consumed "about eight" cups of beer during the party. Finally, a different witness testified that, "[t]owards the end of the party, we were slamming them [cups of beer] pretty fast." Thus, jurors did not need to hear that the coroner had relied, in part, on the victim's blood and urine test results in order for them to

conclude beyond a reasonable doubt that Meshak's consumption of beer at the party was a substantial factor in Meshak's fatal accident. The testimony of witnesses who attended the party and testified to Meshak's alcohol consumption and his condition prior to leaving the party was more than sufficient to convince reasonable jurors beyond a reasonable doubt of Wille's guilt.

¶ 33 As for the impact of the victim's negative drug screen results, Wille asserts in his opening brief that a " 'baggie' containing drugs was found on Meshak at the scene of the crash by Deputy Wanta." The record citation Wille provides for this assertion, however, is to the testimony of a **356 deputy who testified at trial to finding "some mints in a baggie on Mr. Meshak." Wille's counsel attempted without success to get the deputy to testify that the bag may have contained the drug ecstasy, not mints. The deputy acknowledged only that, *557 in his police report, he had stated that the baggie "contained what appeared to be multi-colored mints" which were turned over to another investigator for possible testing for drugs. We agree with the State that the alleged "drug evidence" never rose above the level of an insinuation by defense counsel that the mints may have been ecstasy. The testimony regarding the victim's drug screen results was thus even less probative of what caused

Meshak's fatal accident than that of the blood alcohol testing. Accordingly, we are also satisfied beyond a reasonable doubt that jurors would have found Wille guilty had they not heard the coroner testify to the results of the drug screen.

Testimony of Investigator Griesbach

[21] ¶ 34 Wille's final claim of trial court error also involves his trial counsel's insinuation while cross-examining Deputy Wanta that the mints found in Meshak's pocket at the time of the accident might have been the illicit drug ecstasy. On the morning of the second day of trial, the State called Investigator Nicholas Griesbach as a witness. Griesbach was the investigator to whom the bag of mints was given for a determination whether drugs might be present. His testimony, in short, was that, based on his experience and training in drug investigations, he determined by visual examination that the items in the baggie were not ecstasy pills nor any other type of controlled substance. Griesbach concluded that the bag contained what "looked like breath mints you'd get at a restaurant." Accordingly, the investigator did not forward the baggie of mints for further testing, and it was apparently subsequently turned over to Meshak's family with his other personal effects.

*558 ¶ 35 Wille objected to the State calling Griesbach to testify because

he had not been included in the State's pre-trial list of intended witnesses. Although Wille did not cite WIS. STAT. § 971.23(1)(d) in his argument to the trial court, he argues on appeal that the State violated the requirement under the discovery statute that the State must, "[u]pon demand," provide the defendant before trial a "list of all witnesses and their addresses whom the district attorney intends to call at the trial." *Id.* In Wille's view, the alleged violation of the discovery statute should have prompted the trial court to preclude Griesbach from testifying at trial, which the court declined to do.

¶ 36 The State advances several rationales for upholding the trial court's ruling permitting Investigator Griesbach to testify regarding his examination of the mints. We agree with its first contention-that it is clear from the record that the State had *not* intended to call Griesbach as a witness, nor should it reasonably have been expected to anticipate the need to call him. The prosecutor told the trial court during argument on Wille's objection that Griesbach had not been named in any reports he had reviewed and that he first learned of Griesbach's involvement with the mints during Deputy Wanta's testimony on the first day of trial.

¶ 37 Because there appears to have been no indication in any police reports, witness statements or Meshak's medical records that Meshak had used controlled substances prior to the fatal accident, we agree with the State that there is no basis in the present record to conclude that "a reasonable prosecutor should have known" that Investigator Griesbach's testimony **357 would be necessary or even helpful to the State's case. *See* *559 *State v. DeLao,* 2002 WI 49, ¶ 30, 252 Wis.2d 289, 643 N.W.2d 480 (explaining that WIS. STAT. § 971.23(1) embodies "an objective standard: what a reasonable prosecutor should have known and would have done under the circumstances of the case"). The prosecutor in this case could not reasonably have anticipated the defense would attempt to exploit a brief reference to possible drug testing in Deputy Wanta's report to insinuate that Meshak had used ecstasy prior to his fatal accident, thereby requiring testimony from the investigator who had examined the baggie of mints to refute the insinuation.

¶ 38 Accordingly, because the present record provides no basis for concluding that the State "intend[ed] to call" Investigator Griesbach as a witness at trial, or that a reasonable prosecutor should have anticipated the need for his testimony in the State's case-in-chief, we conclude the State did not violate WIS. STAT.

§ 971.23(1). The trial court therefore had no basis for excluding Griesbach's testimony. Given this conclusion, we need not address whether the prosecutor had "good cause" for not disclosing Griesbach as a witness prior to trial. *See* § 971.23(7m); *DeLao,* 252 Wis.2d 289, ¶ 51, 643 N.W.2d 480.

¶ 39 Likewise, because the State did not violate the discovery statute, we have no need to consider whether Wille suffered prejudice on account of the State's failure to identify Griesbach as a witness prior to trial. *See id.,* ¶ 60. We note in this regard, however, that Wille contends he was "surprised" by Griesbach's testimony and he was therefore deprived of the opportunity "to obtain expert testimony to test and to testify concerning the drugs found on Meshak." We reject this contention. The only "surprise" at trial was Wille's insinuation that the illicit drug ecstasy was somehow *560 involved in Meshak's fatal accident, and any prejudice to Wille stemming from Griesbach's testimony was thus of Wille's own making.

¶ 40 Finally, we again note that Wille repeatedly states in his brief that "drugs ... were found on Meshak" and, further, that those "drugs had ... 'vanished' " prior to trial. These statements blatantly mischaracterize the record. The only assertion in the record that "drugs ... were found on

Meshak" came from the lips of Wille's defense counsel. The State contends that what "Wille attempted to do was to create the impression that the mints were actually drugs and then to prevent the State from disabusing the jury of that notion." We agree and conclude that counsel's ploy is as unavailing in this court as it was in the trial court.

CONCLUSION

¶ 41 For the reasons discussed above, we affirm the appealed judgment.

Judgment affirmed.

All Citations

299 Wis.2d 531, 728 N.W.2d 343, 2007 WI App 27

APPENDIX P

SUGGESTED ANSWERS TO PRACTICE EXERCISES

Answers are provided for some of the exercises in this book. After completing the exercises, use the answers to check your understanding of the critical reading strategies.

Chapter 1

Before Reading: The Purpose for Reading Cases

Practice Exercise 1.2: Purpose for Reading Affects How We Read

1.2–1   Dates might be important to remember for an historical article.

1.2–2   A 1939 article might be useful to trace the historical development of the law.

1.2–3   Each stage in the development of the law would be important to examine.

1.2–4   It would be useful to understand the current rules as the last stage in the historical development of the law.

1.2–5   No, dates would not be important to remember.

1.2–6   No, because the article probably would not have current rules.

1.2–7   No, unless the historical development affects policy considerations underlying the current rules.

1.2–8   Yes, the rules are key to solving a client's problem.

Practice Exercise 1.3: Why Is This Case Difficult to Read?

1.3–1   Some students do not understand terms such as plaintiff, defendants, rendered judgment for the defendants notwithstanding the verdict, affirmed, actionable battery, malicious, and exemplary damages.

1.3–2   The last two sentences are long and difficult to understand.

1.3–3   The passage may be difficult to read because of the unfamiliar words and long sentences.

Practice Exercise 1.4: Self-Assessment

1.4–1   It is not necessary to memorize most case names unless required by your professor.

1.4–2   While it is not necessary to memorize dates, the date of the discharge would be important to note when reading the facts of the case.

1.4–3   It is important to understand the rules relating to eligibility for unemployment benefits so that these principles can be applied to Evelyn Michel's problem.

Chapter 2

Before Reading: Reading as an Advocate and Reading with Focus

Reflection Exercise 2.1: What Is Advocacy?

2.1–1   Advocacy means that someone speaks out on behalf of someone or represents their interests.

2.1–4   Reading an article to advocate on behalf of someone might influence how it was read because the reader would look for information that would support a topic or argument.

Practice Exercise 2.2: Thinking Like a Lawyer: Advocacy

2.2–1   Rules and Facts

A. Chore Requirements (Rules)	B. Chores Completed (Facts)

Element 1: Clean the room
  Sub Element 1: Put away train set.
  Sub Element 2: Pick up dirty clothes and bring to laundry room.
  Sub Element 3: Pick up coin collection.
	1. Joshua put away the train set.
	2. Joshua picked up his dirty clothes but did not bring them to the laundry room.
	3. Joshua did not put away his coin collection.

Element 2: Feed the dog.	Joshua gave the dog fresh water.
Element 3: Brush the dog.	Joshua brushed the dog.
Element 4: Read for 30 minutes.	Joshua read for 20 minutes.

2.2–2   Joshua's Arguments

A. Chore Requirements (Rules)	B. Arguments

Element 1: Clean the room
  Sub Element 1: Put away train set.
 	
  Sub Element 2: Pick up dirty clothes and bring them to the laundry room.
	1. Joshua did all of sub element 1(1) because he put away the train set.
	2. Joshua did half of sub element 1(2) because he picked up his dirty clothes but

Sub Element 3: Pick up coin collection.	did not bring them to the laundry room. 3. The facts indicate he did not put away the coin collection but are silent regarding whether he picked them up.
Element 2: Feed the dog.	While Joshua gave the dog fresh water, the facts do not indicate whether he fed the dog.
Element 3: Brush the dog.	Joshua brushed the dog.
Element 4: Read for 30 minutes.	Joshua read for 20 minutes.

2.2–3   Best Overall Argument for Joshua

> There are several possible answers. One argument is that since Joshua did over half of the work, he should be allowed to get fireworks. Specifically, he
>
> - did half of sub element 1(1), half of sub element 1(2), and may have done sub element 1(3) (facts are silent),
>
> - did half of the requirements for elements 2 and 3 as he gave the dog water and brushed the dog, and
>
> - did the majority of the requirements for element 4 as he read for 20 minutes.

2.2–4 Parents' Arguments

A. Chore Requirements (Rules)	B. Arguments
Element 1: Clean the room Sub Element 1: Put away train set. Sub Element 2: Pick up dirty clothes and bring to laundry room. Sub Element 3: Pick up coin collection.	1. Joshua completed this chore. 2. Joshua did not bring his clothes to the laundry room. 3. Joshua did not put away his coin collection.
Element 2: Feed the dog.	Joshua only gave the dog fresh water.
Element 3: Brush the dog.	Joshua brushed the dog.

Element 4: Read for 30 minutes.	Joshua did not read for 30 minutes.

2.2–5 Best Overall Argument for Parents

Parents could argue that the rules were required to be completed in full. The only element he completed was element 3. Otherwise, he did not complete his chores.

2.2–6 Judge's Decision

One possible decision follows:

There are strong arguments that can be made for both sides. Joshua did not meet all of the elements that were required by 6 PM. However, the facts are silent on two points, i.e., whether Joshua picked up the coins and fed the dog. If both of these chores had been done, Joshua would have met almost all of the requirements. The Judge's decision is that Joshua is to be given 30 minutes to complete any remaining chores. If he can do that, he is permitted to buy fireworks with his parents.

Practice Exercise 2.6: Self-Assessment

2.6–1   When De Grego wore a button that said "Impeachment with Honor," the company President told him to remove the button. When De Grego refused to do so, he was fired.

2.6–2   De Grego was initially denied benefits because it was found that he "quit his job without good cause by refusing to comply with a reasonable directive from his employer." *De Grego*, 347 N.E.2d at 612.

2.6–3   The employer argued that De Grego provoked his own discharge.

Chapter 3

Before Reading: Case Structure and Procedure

Practice Exercise 3.2: Case Structure Exercise

3.2–1	584 N.W. 2d 859 (N.D. Ct. App. 1998)	Yes
3.2–2	Martin Wishnatsky (Plaintiff) David Huey (Defendant)	Yes
3.2–3	North Dakota Court of Appeals	Yes
3.2–4	1998	Yes
3.2–5	Yes	No
3.2–6	2	No
3.2–7	Per curiam means that the entire panel of judges joined in the decision.	Yes

3.2–8	Yes	Yes
3.2–9	Yes, the court discusses cases on the subjects of summary judgment, battery, and immunity.	Yes
3.2–10	Yes, the court affirms the judgment of the trial court.	Yes

Practice Exercise 3.3: Differences Between Reported Decisions and Cases in Textbooks

3.3–1	7	19
3.3–2	Yes	Yes
3.3–3	No	Yes
3.3–4	No	Yes

Practice Exercise 3.4: Civil Procedure

3.4–1   Appealed: after the court entered judgment, the plaintiff asked a higher court to reverse the decision.

3.4–2   Summary judgment dismissing: Summary judgment is an application to the court for judgment claiming that there are no issues of fact and one party should win based upon the law. Dismissing means that the court granted the defendant's motion and dismissed or rejected plaintiff's complaint.

3.4–3   Order denying motion to alter judgment: After judgment was entered by the court, the plaintiff asked the court to change the judgment. The court entered an order denying this motion.

3.4–4   We affirm the judgment and the order: Affirm means that the appellate court agreed with the lower court. Judgment is the decision of the court. Order is the court's ruling on a motion.

Practice Exercise 3.5: Criminal Procedure

3.5–1   657 S.W.2d 948 (Ky. 1983)

3.5–2   Haynes and the Commonwealth of Kentucky

3.5–3   Kentucky Supreme Court

3.5–4   No

3.5–5   Counts are charges that may be found in a charging document such as an indictment or complaint.

Practice Exercise 3.6: Self-Assessment

3.6–1   Yes, the court starts the opinion by explaining that the appeal involves the concept of provoked discharge and eligibility for unemployment compensation benefits.

3.6–2   Yes, the facts are found in the second and third paragraphs of the opinion.

3.6–3   Yes, the court analyzes previous decisions from New York courts on this subject.

3.6–4   After the Unemployment Insurance Appeal Board found that De Grego had provoked his discharge, the intermediate appellate court in New York, the Appellate Division, reversed and found that De Grego was exercising his First Amendment freedom of speech. The highest court in New York, the Court of Appeals, reviewed the decision of the Appellate Division and affirmed the order of the Appellate Division but provided different reasoning.

Chapter 4

Before Reading: Context and Overview

Practice Exercise 4.2: Case Context and Overview Civil Case

4.2–1   Assault and battery, labor and employment. Assault and battery relates to battery.

4.2–2   Morgan et al. and Loyacomo are referred to in the caption. Morgan brought the appeal with some other unidentified parties.

4.2–3   The Mississippi Supreme Court decided the case.

4.2–4   1941

4.2–5   The words in banc are found at the beginning of the opinion. This means that the entire panel of judges heard the appeal. However, Justice Griffith wrote the decision.

4.2–6   The reported decision is two pages long.

4.2–7   The second paragraph indicates that the case involves an assault and battery.

4.2–8   There are no headings but the paragraphs address different topics. The second paragraph relates to assault and battery, the third paragraph deals whether the actions of the manager were within the scope of his responsibilities as manager, and the last paragraph addresses the reasonableness of the damage award.

4.2–9   The plaintiff customers won.

Practice Exercise 4.3: Case Context and Overview Criminal Case

4.3–1   Yes, topic listed under (5) relates to burglary.

4.3–2   The headnote topics are criminal law and burglary.

4.3–3   The parties are Terry Haynes and the Commonwealth of Kentucky. The parties are listed twice because Haynes appealed his conviction and the Commonwealth appealed an order suppressing evidence.

4.3–4 Kentucky Supreme Court

4.3–5 1983

4.3–6 Justice Aker

4.3–7 Six pages in the regional reporter, ten pages in the online opinion.

4.3–8 The first paragraph provides a general overview of the two appeals in the case. It does not provide specific information about the burglary issue.

4.3–9 The case does not have headings but the court indicates that there are four assignments of error and the opinion addresses each issue separately. The first topic relates to the defendant's motion for a written report made by a witness. The second topic relates to the trial court's refusal to suppress the defendant's oral statements. The third topic relates to the meaning of the word dwelling in the burglary statutes. The final topic involves comments made by the prosecutor during closing arguments.

4.3–10 The Commonwealth won as the trial court decision was affirmed. The court did not address the Commonwealth's appeal as it did not need to reach that question.

Practice Exercise 4.4: Self-Assessment

4.4–1 Read the case summary and the headnotes.

4.4–2 Skim the case for an overview to determine its length, organization, and who won. It is seven pages long (regional reporter) and has a majority and dissenting opinion. There are no headings but the first sentence of the opinion sets forth the general subject of the case. It is organized as most opinions are structured with the facts followed by procedural facts, precedents, holding, and reasoning. It ends with the disposition followed by a dissenting opinion. The claimant won.

Chapter 5

During Reading: Facts

Practice Exercise 5.2: Are the Facts Important?

5.2–1 There are different ways to answer this question. However, it is important to read the facts in a case to determine if the case can be used to solve a new legal problem.

5.2–2 It is not possible to do analogical reasoning, which involves the comparison of problem facts with case facts, without reading the case facts.

Practice Exercise 5.3: Organizing Facts

5.3–1   While the case summary does not use the term battery, it explains the facts and indicates that the case was remanded to determine if the boy knew with "substantial certainty" that the plaintiff would try to sit down when the chair was moved.

5.3–2   Infants, assault and battery, appeal and error, trial, and new trial.

5.3–3   The parties are Ruth Garratt, the appellant, and Brian Dailey, by his guardian George Dailey, the respondent.

5.3–4   Supreme Court of Washington

5.3–5   1955

5.3–6   Justice Hill

5.3–7   There are nine pages in the online version of the case. The regional reporter starts on page 1091 and ends on page1095.

5.3–8   The first sentence explains that the "liability of an infant for an alleged battery is presented to this court for the first time." This means that the Supreme Court of Washington has never addressed this topic before. The paragraph also sets forth the facts.

5.3–9   There are no headings but the case examines the separate issues of battery, the plaintiff's right to cross-examine Brian, and the plaintiff's right to take Brian's deposition.

5.3–10 The case was remanded to the trial court for clarification.

5.3–11 The plaintiff, Ruth Garratt, is an individual who allegedly was subjected to battery and the defendant, Brian Dailey, was a visitor allegedly responsible for battery.

5.3–12 The substantive facts could be organized with a diagram that outlines where Ruth Garratt and Brian were in the backyard. The facts could also be organized with a short chronology of events.

5.13–13 Substantive Facts:

1. 7/16/51 Brian visits sisters Naomi & Ruth Garratt at Ruth's home.

2. Brian goes to the backyard with Naomi.

3. Ruth comes out of her house into the backyard.

4. Brian picks up a lawn chair and moves it sideways a few feet and sits down.

5. Ruth was about to sit down where the lawn chair had been before Brian moved it.

6. Brian tries to move the chair back so Ruth could sit in it.

7. Ruth falls and breaks a hip.

5.3–14 The trial court dismissed the case.

5.3–15 The Supreme Court of Washington remanded the case back to the trial court for clarification regarding whether Brian knew with substantial certainty that the plaintiff would sit down.

5.3–16 Chronology

5.3–17 1. Complaint filed alleging battery.

2. Trial court dismisses action, makes finding that P's damages would be $11,000, & denies motion for new trial.

3. Supreme Court remands case to trial court to make findings on whether Brian knew "with substantial certainty" that the plaintiff would try to sit down where the chair had been before he moved it.

Practice Exercise 5.4: Self-Assessment

5.4–1 The caption indicates that the Industrial Commissioner, Levine, was the appellant. Usually, the name of the appellant comes first in the caption.

5.4–2 De Grego initiated the case when his application for unemployment benefits was denied, and he filed an appeal before a referee. De Grego sued the Industrial Commissioner.

5.4–3 Chronological order

5.4–4 The substantive facts:

1. D was employed as plumber's helper for 2 years—satisfactory performance, wore uniform, other employees sometimes wore buttons.

2. 9/18/73 D wore button "Impeachment with Honor." Pres. told him he could not wear button though no complaints from customers. D refused to remove button and was fired.

5.4–5 The procedural facts:

1. Application for u.e. benefits denied by Labor Depart. because D quit job without good cause by refusing to comply with reasonable directive from employer.

2. Hearing before referee & referee sustained decision.

3. Appeal to Unemployment Insurance Appeal Bd. Bd. sustained decision & found D "provoked his discharge which was the equivalent of voluntary leaving employment without good cause."

4. App. Div. reversed & found benefits could not be denied where employee exercised freedom of speech.

5. Ct. Appeals affirmed on other grounds.

Chapter 6

During Reading: Strategies to Understand Text

Practice Exercise 6.2: Strategies for Understanding Language in Cases

6.2–1   The first sentence in the opinion indicates that Morgan and the other parties were the "owners and operators of forty-eight retail stores." *Morgan v. Loyacomo*, 1 So. 2d 510 (Miss. 1941). Loyacomo is not identified in the opinion but must have been a customer who sued Morgan and the other owners.

6.2–2   Chronologically and/or with a diagram of the incident.

6.2–3   Rereading can be helpful.

6.2–4   Individual answers will vary regarding whether words are unfamiliar.

6.2–5   Conjunctions are helpful to notice in understanding the chronology.

6.2–6   There are pronouns that refer to White (he), appellee (she), and the package (it). It is important to keep these pronoun references sorted out.

6.2–7   It would be helpful to break this long sentence into five parts:

1. Without making any inquiry either of the clerk or of appellee before appellee left the store, which if done would have readily revealed that the manager's suspicions were without any ground,

2. White permitted appellee to leave the store, but followed her,

3. and when about a block away and in the presence of several persons, he called to appellee, stated that he was obliged to investigate whether she had taken two articles while paying for only one,

4. forcibly seized the package from under her arm, opened it, examined and exhibited the contents in the presence of the third persons, and found that he was in error,

5. which, as already mentioned, he could easily have ascertained by a proper inquiry conducted in a proper manner before appellee left the store." *Id.* at 511.

6.2–8   It might be helpful to read this sentence aloud.

6.2–9   Substantive facts:

1. P. bought underwear at a store, paid for it, and left.

2. The manager White saw P make the purchase but suspected that P had taken 2 garments and paid for one. Without checking with anyone, White followed P and grabbed the package from under her arm only to discover she only had one item.

6.2–10 It might be helpful to reread.

6.2–11 Individual answers will vary regarding the vocabulary.

6.2–12 Conjunctions are important to notice. The references to "or" in the last sentence are significant in understanding the rule for battery. The sentence can be outlined as follows:

"to constitute an assault and battery,

it is not necessary to touch the plaintiff's body

or

even his clothing;

knocking

or

snatching anything from plaintiff's hand

or

touching anything connected with his person,

when done in a rude

or

insolent manner,

is sufficient.

6.2–13 There are repeated references to assault and battery and touch.

6.2–14 The last sentence could be divided into several parts.

1. The authorities are agreed that, to constitute an assault and battery,

2. it is not necessary to touch the plaintiff's body or even his clothing;

3. knocking or snatching anything from plaintiff's hand or touching anything connected with his person, when done in a rude or insolent manner, is sufficient.

6.2–15 Individual answers will vary.

Practice Exercise 6.3: Self-Assessment

6.3–1   Individual answers will vary.

6.3–2   Individual answers will vary.

6.3–3   There is one important conjunction. The employee must voluntarily engage in conduct **and** leave the employer no choice but to discharge him.

6.3–4   The sentence could be broken into several parts:

1.   Provoked discharge, a gloss over the statutory disqualification for voluntary separation without good cause,

2.   is designed to apply where an employee voluntarily engages in conduct which transgresses a legitimate known obligation and,

3.   leaves the employer no choice but to discharge him.

6.3–5   Individual answers will vary.

Chapter 7

During Reading: Strategies to Understand Main Ideas (Issue, Holding, and Reasoning)

Practice Exercise 7.2: Strategies to Find Main Ideas in Law Review Article

7.2–1   Answers will vary.

7.2–2   The main idea is that critical reading is difficult for first year law students and that critical reading instruction may improve legal writing.

Practice Exercise 7.3: Finding Main Ideas in *Lucy*

7.3–1   The case summary indicates that the plaintiff claimed there was a contract for the purchase of land and that the defendant alleged that there was no contract because he entered into the contract as a joke. The summary states that the court found that the contract was a "serious business transaction" and plaintiff prevailed.

7.3–2   There are headnotes on the topics of specific performance, contracts, and vendor and purchaser.

7.3–3   The parties are W.O. Lucy and J.C. Lucy and A.H. Zehmer and Ida S. Zehmer. The caption does not indicate who brought the lawsuit.

7.3–4   The court was the Supreme Court of Appeals of Virginia.

7.3–5   1954

7.3–6   Judge Buchanan

7.3–7   8 pages

7.3–8 The first paragraph indicates that the case is about the specific performance of a contract for the purchase of land.

7.3–9 There are no headings.

7.3–10 The last page of Appendix H indicates that the complainants or plaintiffs won and got specific performance of the contract.

7.3–11 Mr. and Mrs. Lucy sued Mr. and Mrs. Zehmer.

7.3–12 One way to organize the decision is chronologically.

7.3–13 Substantive facts:

1. 12/20/52 Lucy and Z were drinking and Lucy asked Z if he would sell the Ferguson farm for $50,000.

2. Lucy told Zehmer to write up an agreement.

3. Zehmer wrote on the back of a restaurant check that "I do hereby agree to sell to W.O. Lucy the Ferguson Farm for $50,000 complete."

4. Lucy told him to change it to "we" because Mrs. Zehmer would have to sign it.

5. Zehmer tore up the memo, rewrote the agreement, and had Mrs. Zehmer sign it.

6. Lucy offered to give $5 to Z & Z said "you don't need to give me money, you have the agreement there signed by both of us."

7. 1/2/53 Lucy told Z he was ready to pay in cash.

8. Z said he never agreed to sell because he was "as high as a Georgia pine." Z claimed his comments were intended to be a joke.

7.3–14 Procedural facts

1. Complaint for specific performance of contact.

2. Answer states offer was made "in jest" and he had no intention of selling farm.

3. Case dismissed. Appeal.

4. Court reverses & remands for entry of decree requiring Z to perform contract.

7.3–15 It would be helpful to notice conjunctions and divide the sentence into the following shorter sections.

If the words

or

other acts of one of the parties have but one reasonable meaning, his undisclosed intention is immaterial

except when an unreasonable meaning which he attaches to his manifestations is known to the other party.

Other strategies may work as well.

7.3–16 The issue is whether the mental assent of the parties is necessary for the formation of a contract when it is reasonable to believe that the parties have agreed but one party has an undisclosed intention not to agree.

7.3–17 When the actions of the parties would indicate to a reasonable person that the parties agreed to a contract, a contract was formed even though one party did not intend to form a contract and believed that the agreement was a joke.

7.3–18 The court's reasoning was based upon an examination of the Restatement of Contracts and encyclopedias relating to contracts. The court reasoned that in the field of contracts, it is necessary to consider the "outward expression of a person as manifesting his intention" and it is not appropriate to rely upon the person's "secret and unexpressed intention." *Id.* at 521.

Practice Exercise 7.4

7.4–1   Did De Grego provoke his discharge when he refused to remove a button from his work uniform?

7.4–2   When De Grego refused to remove his button, he did not provoke his discharge because the employer was not compelled to fire him and there was no evidence of misconduct.

7.4–3   De Grego voluntarily left his employment rather than abide by a reasonable rule.

Chapter 8

During Reading: Finding Rules

Reflection Exercise 8.1: Inferences from a Photo

Note: The photo was taken in a law professor's office when her dog, Darby, came to visit students.

Practice Exercise 8.2: Making Inferences in Texts and Cases

8.2–1   Possible answers: understand the purpose for reading cases, read as an advocate, focus, use context, and understand case structure.

8.2–2   Understand the purpose for reading.

8.2–3   Prior knowledge.

8.2–4   Possible answers: insulted, humiliated.

8.2–5 Jurisdictions or states

8.2–6 Battery

Practice Exercise 8.3: Finding Rules in Cases

8.3–1 1.   Defendants were hunting wolves.

2.   Plaintiff's dog looked like a wolf.

3.   Defendants killed the dog.

8.3–2 Court affirmed the jury verdict that awarded $50 to plaintiff. Even though the defendants acted in good faith, they were liable for their mistake.

8.3–3 While the defendants intended to shoot the animal, they thought the dog was a wolf. In this claim to recover the value of the dog, good faith mistake was not a defense.

8.3–4

Facts	Court's Decision	Rule
1. Defendants were hunting wolves. 2. Plaintiff's dog looked like a wolf. 3. Defendants killed the dog.	Court affirmed the jury verdict that awarded $50 to plaintiff for the value of a dog. Defendants were liable for their mistake when they intended to shoot the animal and thought the dog was a wolf.	For some intentional torts involving personal property, if the defendant intends to do an act, there is no defense for a good faith mistake.

Practice Exercise 8.4: Finding Rules in Cases

8.4–1 Answers will vary but should include reading for a purpose and as an advocate, noticing case context by reviewing the case summary and headnotes, and doing an overview of the case before reading more carefully.

8.4–2 Answers will vary.

8.4–3 Facts

1.   The Smiths were in the process of moving to a new house and were staying at the new house the night of the burglary.

2.   Starnes entered the home and took personal property that had not yet been moved to the new home.

8.4–4 Answers will vary.

8.4–5   Court decided that a house that was burglarized while residents were in the process of moving out should be considered a dwelling because it was "usually" occupied during this time.

8.4–6   Court relies on the definition of "usually" in the dictionary as well as the definition of "dwelling" in Ky. Rev. Stat. Ann. § 511.010(2).

8.4–7   One explanation may be that houses can be considered to be "usually occupied" if individuals have some possessions in a house and plan to go back to get them. The court mentions the definition of "usually," which means ordinary practice. Perhaps the court thought it was ordinary practice for people to gradually move. In this situation, the house would be considered "usually occupied" until the move was completed.

8.4–8   A house is considered to be "usually occupied" when residents use it as it has customarily been used even if it is not occupied at the time of the burglary.

8.4–9   *Starnes* would be helpful. Analogical reasoning could be used to compare the facts in *Starnes* with the facts in Craft's case. While someone does not need to be present in a house for it to be considered "usually occupied," it must be used as it customarily has been used. Arguments could be made that Caskey's house was not usually occupied on 6/1/16 because no one was living there and the utilities were not working. It appears that Caskey's possessions had been removed. These facts are different from *Starnes* where the family had left possessions in the house and planned to return to the house to get them.

Practice Exercise 8.5: Self-Assessment

8.5–1   *In re Malaspina* (Collective bargaining agreement mandated discharge of those who refused to join union). Provoked discharge takes place when an employee voluntarily engages in conduct which violates a rule and the employer has no choice but to fire the employee.

   In re James For unemployment insurance purposes, provoked discharge only occurs where employer has no discretion and is compelled to fire an employee. If employee engages in misconduct, he is not eligible for benefits.

8.5–2   Rule: Employee is entitled to unemployment benefits if he does not provoke his own discharge or engage in misconduct. Where there is no evidence of misconduct, employee cannot be fired for provoked discharge unless employer has no discretion and is compelled to fire the employee.

Chapter 9

After Reading: Case Evaluation

Practice Exercise 9.1: Levels of Analysis

9.1–1   Read for the purpose of solving a client's Social Security case, read as an advocate for a client, review the case summary and headnotes to understand the general subject of the decision, and read for an overview paying attention to the parties, date, court, and judge.

9.1–2   Substantive facts:

1.   Guzman (G) was denied disability benefits and requested a hearing.

2.   While G received written notice that she could be provided with an attorney, she appeared at the hearing without a lawyer.

3.   The ALJ stated that he assumed G was ready to proceed without a lawyer and G indicated she was ready to proceed without a lawyer.

4.   G's lawyer claims that the ALJ failed to protect her rights and should have called her daughter to testify.

Procedural facts:

1.   Complaint filed appealing denial of disability benefits.

2.   Complaint dismissed.

9.1–3   The court held that Guzman received adequate notice of her right to counsel when she received written notice of her right and was questioned by the ALJ to confirm that she knew of her right and was ready to proceed without counsel. The court also held that the ALJ adequately protected G's rights and no substantial prejudice was demonstrated by the ALJ's conduct of the hearing.

9.1–4   Guzman received written and oral notice of her right to counsel.

9.1–5   Court decided this was adequate notice.

9.1–6   Answers will vary.

Practice Exercise 9.2: What Is Appropriate to Evaluate?

9.2–1   No, this is a factual question and the court found that G knew her rights and was ready to proceed without counsel.

9.2–2   No, this is a factual question.

9.2–3   Yes, this is a legal question that would be relevant to an evaluation of an appeal of the case.

Practice Exercise 9.3: Evaluate a Case to Solve a Client's Problem

9.3–1   Read for the purpose of solving Gregory Jones' case, read as an advocate for Jones, review the case summary and headnotes to understand the general subject of the decision, and read for an overview paying attention to the parties, date, court, and judge.

9.3–2   Substantive facts:

1.   8/21/99 decedent was killed in accident. He had been renting house from mother.

2.   8/24/99 Barney entered house to steal marijuana. House furnished, utilities connected, food in refrigerator, decedent's possessions in house.

Procedural facts:

1.   D convicted burglary second degree. Affirmed by Appellate Division.

9.3–3   Court held that the house should be considered a dwelling because it was "adapted for occupancy and a person could have occupied it overnight." 742 N.Y.S.2d at 453. Court held that house was a dwelling because it "had been used as a residence in the 'immediate past' and has not been abandoned." *Id.* Court rejected D's argument that house was not a dwelling because the occupant had died.

9.3–4

Element of Rule	Case Facts *Barney*	Problem Facts	Similar/Different
Home is dwelling if it is "usually occupied by a person lodging therein at night." N.Y. Penal Law §140.00(3).	Decedent had occupied home until death. At time of entry, home was furnished, utilities connected, food in refrigerator, and decedent's possessions were in home.	Cabin used during the summer for two weeks. No utilities during winter but water and electricity connected in the summer. No clothes, no heat, but had bed, couch and chairs.	Similarities: cabin capable of being used in the summer when electricity and water were connected. Differences: cabin not capable of being occupied in the winter, no clothes, limited furniture.

9.3–5   It could be argued that the case facts and problem facts are different enough that a court would not find that Newman's cabin was a dwelling. While the home in *Barney* could have been occupied overnight, was furnished, had utilities that were connected, and had food in the refrigerator, Newman's cabin could not be occupied in the winter. There was no heat, electricity, or water. There was also limited furniture.

9.3–6   New York could interpret *Barney* to apply to Jones' situation. The argument could be made that the case facts and problem facts are similar because both the cabin and the home could be occupied. The cabin had a fireplace for heat and some furniture and the electricity and water could be turned on.

Practice Exercise 9.4: What Do You Think?

9.4–1   Majority: The home should be considered a dwelling because it was "adapted for occupancy and a person could have occupied it overnight." *Id.* at 453. It retained its character as a dwelling even though the occupant died two days before the burglary. The Penal Law eliminated the requirement that a person be present at the time of the burglary.

9.4–2   Dissent: While the home was capable of occupancy, the fact that the occupant had died meant that no one intended to use the home "for overnight lodging." *Id.* at 455. The death of the occupant eliminated the "danger to human life that the higher degrees of burglary protect against." *Id.* at 456.

Practice Exercise 9.5: Evaluation: Prepare for Exams

9.5–1   Owner died two days before the burglary but relatives stayed at the home in preparation for the funeral. Burglary occurred while relatives were staying at the house.

9.5–2   Owner died two days before the burglary. Owner had been in a nursing home for 2 months before his death. Relatives had turned off all utilities, stopped the mail, moved most of the furniture out of the house, and closed up the house. No one stayed there during the 2 months.

Practice Exercise 9.6: Self-Assessment

9.6–1   Ms. Michel's attorney could argue that the facts in *De Grego* are similar to her situation and that she did not provoke her discharge. While she failed her exam, her employer could have given her the opportunity to retake the exam and her employer was not required to fire her. The State Unemployment Commission could argue that the facts in *De Grego* are different, and she did provoke her discharge. They could argue that nurses are required to pass this exam to work and an employer had no alternative but to fire her if she failed.

9.6–2   Opinions will vary.

Chapter 10

During and After Reading: Case Brief

Practice Exercise 10.2: Writing Summaries

10.2–1   Plaintiff (P) brought her mother's car to Barry Pontiac-Buick, Inc. (BP) to fix a broken signal light.

10.2–2   After BP fixed a broken signal light and did an annual inspection, BP advised P that the brakes needed to be replaced. P then brought the car to Kent's Alignment (K) where it was found that the brakes were fine.

10.2–3   During an annual inspection, BP advised P that the brakes needed to be replaced. After K's told P the brakes were fine, P contacted a TV station to report her experiences. After K inspected, BP asked K to re-inspect.

10.2–4   After K inspected, K called BP and the BP service manager arrived with the defendant (D) employee of BP because BP wanted to inspect the brakes.

10.2–5   P took a picture of D which showed D pointing his index finger at P.

10.2–6   During an annual inspection, BP advised P that the brakes needed to be replaced. After K's told P the brakes were fine, P contacted a TV station to report her experiences. After K inspected, K called BP and the BP service manager arrived with the D to inspect the brakes. P took a picture of D and D then pointed his index finger at P, lunged at P and grabbed her around the shoulders. P and D spun around wrestling, and D released P after someone said, "let her go." P then left the garage.

Practice Exercise 10.3: Case Brief

10.3–1   *Shackelford v. Commonwealth*, 757 S.W.2d 193 (Ky. Ct. App. 1988).

10.3–2   Facts:

   1.   S entered house damaged by tornado and removed dresser.

   2.   House was uninhabitable, condemned, and only people with permits were allowed in between 6 am and 6 pm.

10.3–3   Procedural Facts:

   1.   S found guilty of second-degree burglary, Ky. Rev. Stat. Ann. § 511.030 (West 2017).

   2.   Ky. Ct. Appeals reversed and found evidence did not support finding that S entered a dwelling.

10.3–4 S argued house was not a dwelling according to Ky. Rev. Stat. Ann. § 511.010 (West 2017).

   Commonwealth argued it was a dwelling.

10.3–5 Is a house that is condemned and scheduled for demolition a dwelling, which is a building that is "usually occupied by a person lodging therein?" *Id.*

10.3–6 A home that has been condemned and is uninhabitable is not a dwelling because it is not fit for occupation "by a person lodging therein." *Id.*

10.3–7 A house is not considered to be "usually occupied" and a dwelling if it cannot be occupied.

10.3–8 Burglary is designed to protect the public from the "alarm or danger" of unlawful intrusions. This concern is not present when a home is not capable of being occupied.

10.3–9 Judgment was reversed and remanded for further proceedings.

10.3–10 Since occupancy was permitted between 6 am and 6 pm, would the result have been different if S had entered during this time period?

Practice Exercise 10.4: Self-Assessment

10.4–1 *DeGrego v. Levine*, 347 N.E.2d 611 (N.Y. 1976).

10.4–2 Facts:

   1.   De Grego (G) was employed as plumber's helper for 2 years, his work was satisfactory, he wore a uniform, & other employees sometimes wore buttons.

   2.   9/18/73 G wore button "Impeachment with Honor." Pres. of Co. told him he could not wear button though there were no complaints from customers. G refused to remove button and was fired.

10.4–3 Procedural facts:

   1.   Application for u.e. benefits denied by Labor Dept.

   2.   Hearing before referee who sustained decision.

   3.   Appeal to Unemployment Insurance Appeal Bd. that sustained decision & found G "provoked his discharge which was the equivalent of voluntary leaving employment without good cause." *DeGrego*, 347 N.E.2d at 612.

4.   App. Div. reversed & found benefits could not be denied where employee exercised freedom of speech.

5.   Ct Appeals affirmed on other grounds.

10.4–4 G argued he had a First Amendment right to wear the button. Labor Dept. argued he provoked his own discharge.

10.4–5 Did G provoke his own discharge when he refused to remove a political button from his work uniform?

10.4–6 When G refused to remove his button, he did not provoke his discharge because the employer was not compelled to fire him and there was no evidence of misconduct.

10.4–7 Provoked discharge is limited to a situation where an employer has no choice but to discharge an employee.

10.4–8 Provoked discharge must be narrowly interpreted and only applies when the employee violates an obligation that leaves the employer with no alternative but to discharge the employee.

10.4–9 Order of Appellate Division was affirmed.

10.4–10 How would Court of Appeals have decided the constitutional issue? What if employer had a rule that prohibited political buttons? Would the result be different?

Chapter 11

After Reading: Case Synthesis

Practice Exercise 11.1: Finding and Synthesizing Rules

11.1–1 Synthesis is necessary because there are conflicting results.

11.1–2

Date	Facts	Rule	Result
2012	Dog: No walks, fed 2 days. Read: 1 book. Room: None.	Not allowed to buy fireworks if completed less than half of chores.	Not allowed to buy fireworks.
2013	Dog: None. Read: None. Room: None.	Allowed to buy fireworks even if chores were not completed if helped someone else who needed assistance.	Allowed to buy fireworks.
2014	Dog: Fed and walked most days.	Allowed to buy fireworks if completed more than half of chores.	Allowed to buy fireworks.

	Read: 4 short & half of long book. Room: Picked up clothes every day.		
2015	Dog: Friends fed and walked. Read: 7 short and part of a long book. Room: Friends cleaned.	Not allowed to buy fireworks if someone else did chores.	Not allowed to buy fireworks.
2016	Dog: None. Read: None. Room: Cleaned every day.	Allowed to buy fireworks even if less than half of chores were completed if offered to share fireworks with someone else.	Allowed to buy fireworks.

11.1–3 Allowed to buy fireworks when he completed more than half of chores, helped someone else, or offered to share his fireworks with someone else. Not allowed to buy fireworks when he completed less than half of his chores or if someone else did his chores.

11.1–4 Themes: amount of chores completed, person who did the work, assistance to others.

Date	Work Completed	Help someone else	Who does the work
2012	Less than half done.		Did work.
2013	None.	Assisted someone else.	Did not do any chores.
2014	More than half done.		Did work.
2015	More than half done.		Friends did work.
2016	Less than half done.	Shared fireworks with friend.	Did work.

11.1–5

General rules:

1. Must complete more than half of chores to buy fireworks.

2.   Must do work yourself.

More specific aspects of rules:

1.   Can get fireworks if help someone else.

2.   Can get fireworks if offer to share them with someone else.

11.1–6 Joshua was allowed to get fireworks if he completed more than half of the chores by himself. If he did not complete half of his chores, he was allowed to get fireworks if he helped someone or offered to share his fireworks with someone else.

Practice Exercise 11.2: Synthesizing Rules

11.2–1 The assignment topic relates to whether a home is a dwelling or building under Ky. Rev. Stat. Ann. § 511.010.

Case	Facts	Holding	Rule	Result
11.2–2 *Starnes*	• Starnes entered home of Walter Smith. • Smith was in the process of moving to new home when Starnes entered.	The house was considered a dwelling when residents were in the process of moving.	A house is considered to be "usually occupied" when residents intend to return to the house for a short period of time. .	House was dwelling.
11.2–3 *Haynes*	• 3/15/80, Haynes entered home of the heirs of Elswicks. • After the Elswick deaths, John Elswick occupied house for day or two when he visited.	The house was considered a dwelling because the heirs stayed at the house sporadically.	A house is considered to be "usually occupied" when it is occasionally occupied.	House was dwelling.
11.2–4 *Shackelford*	• 3/28/86 at 7:30 pm, Shackelford entered house which had been damaged by tornado. • House was "uninhabitable and scheduled for demolition."	The house was not considered a dwelling because it was uninhabitable, had been condemned, and no one was permitted to be at the house without a permit during the day.	A house is not considered to be "usually occupied" if it is not fit for occupation.	House was not dwelling.

	• House was condemned and only people with permits were allowed to enter between 6 am and 6 pm.			

11.2–5 Synthesis is necessary because while the rules are similar, two cases found that the house was considered to be a dwelling and one case decided that the house was not considered to be a dwelling.

11.2–6 All three cases address the same rule. However, *Shackelford* also addresses the rule for houses that have been determined to be uninhabitable.

11.2–7 Cases on a spectrum.

Starnes	*Shackelford*
Haynes	
←	→
Dwelling	Building, not dwelling

11.2–8 After placing the cases on the spectrum, the following factors were considered.

Case	Capacity for use	Danger to occupants
Starnes	House could be used.	Not mentioned.
Haynes	House was being used.	Not mentioned.
Shackelford	House could not be used.	Court comments that there was no danger as no one was permitted in house after 6 PM.

11.2–9 The rules should be ordered with the more general rules followed by the more specific rules. The general rule is that a house is considered to be "usually occupied" even if it is not occupied at the time of the burglary if the house has been customarily used as a home. The more specific rule is that if a house is uninhabitable, it is not considered to be "usually occupied."

11.2–10 The synthesized rule is: A house is considered to be a dwelling under Ky. Rev. Stat. Ann. § 511.020 when it is capable of being occupied as a home even if it is only occupied sporadically and is not occupied at the time of the burglary.

Practice Exercise 11.3: Self-Assessment

Case	Facts	Holding	Rule	Result
In re Bookhard	Claimant, the mother of twins and a night law student, was hired as legal specialist on the condition that she attend law school. She was terminated when she had to take a leave from school because of child care issues.	Claimant did not provoke her discharge as she did not have a choice in taking a leave of absence from school. Without the leave she would have been expelled.	Provoked discharge does not apply when claimant involuntarily fails to fulfill an employment condition.	Benefits.
In re Ambrose	Teacher's employment was contingent on taking and passing national teacher exam. Teacher took only one part of exam and failed.	Claimant voluntarily engaged in conduct that made it impossible for her to be employed when she did not take the required exam.	Provoked discharge applies when claimant voluntarily engages in conduct that makes it impossible for claimant to keep a job.	No benefits.

The answers for *De Grego* are found in Practice Exercises 5.4 (facts), 7.4 (holding), and 8.5 (rule).

Synthesized Rule: Employee is entitled to unemployment benefits if he does not provoke his own discharge or engage in misconduct. While a claimant can provoke a discharge by voluntarily refusing to comply with a condition of employment, provoked discharge is not found when the employee is unable to satisfy the employment condition and the employer is not required to terminate the employee.

Chapter 12
Reading Statutes

Practice Exercise 12.1: Analyzing a Statute

Wis. Stat. § 125.075 can be outlined as follows:

(1) Any person who <u>procures</u> alcohol beverages for

> **or**
>
> <u>sells,</u>
>
> <u>dispenses</u>
>
> **or**
>
> <u>gives away</u> alcohol beverages to a person under 18 years of age in violation of s. 125.07(1)(a)1. or 2.
>
> **may be penalized** as provided in sub. (2)
>
> **if:**

(a) The person knew

> **or**
>
> should have known
>
> that the underage person was under the legal drinking age;
>
> **and**

(b) The underage person dies

> **or**
>
> suffers great bodily harm, as defined in s. 939.22(14), as a result of consuming the alcohol beverages provided in violation of s. 125.07(1)(a)1. or 2.

Practice Exercise 12.2: Statutory Interpretation

12.2–1 Note the purpose for the assignment, read the case as an advocate for one of the parties, and note the context by reading the case summary and the headnotes.

12.2–2 The heading titled sufficiency of the evidence relates to the assignment.

12.2–3 Substantive facts:

1. 17 year old Meshak died from injuries in a car accident after he drank beer.

2. Wille purchased 2 half-barrels of beer and arranged for delivery to party.

3. Wille sold red cups to attendees to drink the beer.

4.   There was testimony that Meshak consumed 8 cups of beer and an attendee saw him drink beer from a red cup.

Procedural facts:

1.   State charged Wille under Wis. Stat. § 125.075(1) with procuring alcohol beverages for person under 18, the consumption of which resulted in person's death.

2.   Jury found Wille guilty and he was placed on probation.

3.   Court affirmed the jury verdict.

12.2–4   The court held that Wis. Stat. § 125.075(1) is violated when a defendant procures alcohol beverages for a group of persons who the defendant knew or should have known were under 18 years of age. The court also found that there was sufficient evidence that Wille violated the statute.

12.2–5   Defendant claimed that the defendant should only be convicted if he knew that a specific victim drank the alcohol.

12.2–6   The court begins by analyzing the language of the statute. The court states that "we begin with the language of the statute and give it its common, ordinary, and accepted meaning, except that technical or specially defined words are given their technical or special definitions." *Wille*, 728 N.W.2d at 349. The court also noted that language should be interpreted "in the context in which it is used, not in isolation, but as part of a whole, in relation to the language of surrounding or closely related statutes, and reasonably to avoid absurd or unreasonable results." *Id.* The court also considered the "scope, context, and purpose of the statute." *Id.*

12.2–7   The court refers to Wis. Stat. § 990.001(1) which indicates that the singular includes the plural unless it "would produce a result inconsistent with the manifest intent of the legislature." *Id.*

12.2–8   The court examined other criminal statutes and concluded that it would be absurd to conclude that a defendant could "escape criminal liability because he or she intended to kill or injure many, unidentified persons by tampering with a product but had no 'face-to-face' interaction with a specific victim who used the product and died as a result." *Id.*

12.2–9   The court rejected defendant's argument and stated that there was "nothing beyond his own rhetoric as proof that the legislature intended to limit the reach" of the statute as he suggested. *Id.* at 352.

Practice Exercise 12.3: Self-Assessment

12.3–1   Terms from definitions are in bold.

590. Rights to benefits

1.   Entitlement to **benefits**. A **claimant** shall be entitled to accumulate **effective days** for the purpose of **benefit** rights only if he has complied with the provisions of this article regarding the filing of his claim, including the filing of a **valid original claim**, registered as **totally unemployed**, reported his subsequent employment and unemployment, and reported for work or otherwise given notice of the continuance of his unemployment.

12.3–2

A claimant shall be entitled to accumulate effective days for the purpose of benefit rights

only if

he has complied with the provisions of this article regarding the filing of his claim, **including**

- o   the filing of a valid original claim,
- o   registered as totally unemployed,
- o   reported his subsequent employment

    and

- o   unemployment,

and

- o   reported for work

    or

- o   otherwise given notice of the continuance of his unemployment.

APPENDIX Q

GLOSSARY

A

Act: Law (12)

Action: Lawsuit. (3)

Advocate: Spokesperson for someone. (2)

Affirm: Appellate court upholds a lower court's decision. (3)

Analogical Reasoning: The process of comparing the facts between two scenarios to determine if they are similar or different. (5)

Answer: Response to claims made in the complaint. (3)

Appeal: Application to higher court for different decision. (3)

Appellant: Party who lost in the lower court and seeks review in a higher court. (3)

Appellee: Party who won in the lower court. (3)

Arraignment: Court appearance of person accused of crime to hear charges and enter plea of guilty or not guilty. (3)

B

Brief: Document filed by parties setting forth legal basis for the appeal. (3)

C

Caption: Heading for legal document that contains names of the parties, court, case number, and date. (3)

Case Summary: The first paragraph following the caption that summarizes a case and is written by editors, not the court. (3)

Casebook: Legal textbook. (3)

Case Brief: Short outline and summary of the court's opinion. (1)

Cause of Action: Facts that permit a legal recovery. (3)

Citation: The volume, book, first page of the opinion, court, and date. (3)

Civil Case: Dispute between two parties that is not a criminal case. (3)

Claim: Assertion or demand. (3)

Common Law: Judge made law. (5)

Common Law System: Court system where lower courts must follow decisions of higher courts. (5)

Complaint (civil): Document filed by the plaintiff that sets forth the facts underlying the dispute, legal claims, the injury suffered and relief requested. (3)

Complaint (criminal): Statement charging individual with criminal violation. (3)

Concurring Opinion: Opinion that agrees with the majority's conclusion, but contains different or additional reasoning. (6)

Criminal Case: Case where someone is charged with a crime. (3)

D

Defendant: Party who is sued or accused of a crime. (3)

Demurrer: Objection to pleading. Similar to motion to dismiss. Term found in older cases. (3)

Deposition: Out of court testimony taken during discovery. (3)

Determinative Facts: Facts that can change a legal result. (5)

Dictum: Superfluous statements in the court's opinion that are not necessary for the holding. (7)

Discovery: Parties gather facts and evidence, request documents, and question witnesses. (3)

Disposition: Resolution of a case. (3)

Dissenting Opinion: Opinion that disagrees with majority opinion. (7)

E

En banc: Court hears case with all judges present. (3)

F

Facts: Summary of facts that formed the basis for the dispute. (3)

G

Grand Jury: Jury that has the power to bring formal criminal charges against person when there is probable cause to believe a crime has been committed. (3)

H

Headnotes: Summaries of specific points of law addressed in decision. Written by editors, not the court. (3)

Holding: Court's decision and application of rules to the facts in a dispute. (3)

I

Indictment: Grand jury's written accusation charging person with a crime. (3)

Interrogatories: Written questions asked during discovery by parties which another party must answer. (3)

Issue: Precise problem or question addressed by the court. (7)

J

Judgment: Court's resolution of the dispute. (3)

Judgment Notwithstanding Verdict: (JNOV) Request for court to grant judgment to one side despite a contrary ruling by the jury. (3)

Jurisdiction: Power of court to hear case. (3)

Jury Instructions: Instructions given at the end of the trial that provide the jury with the law for their decision. (3)

K

K: Abbreviation often used for contract in a case brief. (10)

L

Liable: Legally responsible.

M

Mandatory Authority: Cases that courts must follow because they were decided by the highest court in their jurisdiction. (11)

Memorandum: Written document submitted by a party in support of a motion. (3)

Metacognition: Reader's awareness of what is known and not known. (1)

Mindfulness: Paying attention to the present. (2)

Motion: Request that the court take action. (3)

Motion for Directed Verdict: Request to dismiss case because there is no legally sufficient evidentiary basis for a reasonable jury to reach a different conclusion. (3)

Motion for Summary Judgment: Request to end lawsuit without a trial because there are no factual disputes and one side is entitled to win based upon the law. (3)

Motion to Dismiss: Request to end the case because the complaint does not state a legal claim. (3)

Motion to Suppress: Request that the court refuse to allow certain evidence to be admitted at trial. (3)

O

Opinion: Written document that explains the court's decision. (3)

P

Parties: Individuals, corporations, or governments involved in a lawsuit. (4)

Per Curiam: Decision written by entire panel of judges. (3)

Persuasive Authority: Cases that courts may consider that were decided in other jurisdictions. (11)

Petition: Document that initiates a lawsuit. Similar to a complaint. (3)

Petitioner: Party who starts a civil case or party who appeals. (3)

Plaintiff: Party who starts a civil case. (3)

Pleadings: Documents filed to initiate a lawsuit and respond to the suit such as the complaint and answer. (3)

Precedent: Rules in older court decisions. (3)

Preliminary Hearing: Court hearing to determine whether there is probable cause to try the defendant. (3)

Procedural Facts: Facts that relate to how the lawsuit progresses through the court system. (3)

Procedural History: The disposition of a case in trial and appellate courts.

R

Rationale: Explanation for court's decision. (7)

Relevant Facts: Facts that would change a legal result. (5)

Remand: Appellate court sends the case back to the trial court for further action. (3)

Reporter: Book that contains judicial decisions. (3)

Respondent: Party who is sued or party against whom the appeal is brought. (3)

Reverse: Appellate court decides that the lower court's legal or factual

interpretations were incorrect. (3)

Rule: General principle that regulates conduct. (8)

S

Stare Decisis: Latin term meaning to stand by a decision. (5)

Statutes: Laws enacted by the legislative branch. (12)

Substantive Facts: Facts that form the basis for the dispute. (5)

Summons: Notice telling sheriff or other officer to notify a person named in a lawsuit that an action has been commenced against him in court and that he is required to respond to the complaint.(3)

T

Tort: A civil wrong for which damages may be recovered. (1)

Trial: Court or jury considers testimony of witnesses and other types of evidence. (3)

V

Verdict: The jury's ruling. (3)

W

Warrant: A statement charging an individual with a criminal violation. (3)

INDEX

References are to Pages